Beyond Forever

Evolutionism's End Game

Signature Edition

Warren LeRoi Johns

Author of *Ride to Glory* and
Dateline Sunday, U.S.A.

Beyond Forever

Signature Edition
January, 2009

A Publication of
www.CreationDigest.com
wjedit@DTCcom.net

ISBN 978-0-9790958-0-1
Library of Congress Control Number 2006904794
Printed in the United States of America

In Honor of

Henry M. Morris, PhD & Phillip E. Johnson, JD

Champions of Life by Design

Contents

Introduction

"Spontaneous generation is quaint myth.
First life did not form independent of an intelligent act.
Humans did not descend from fish via millions of accruing mutations.
Evolutionism is flawed fiction, founded on a fabric of speculative assumptions."
Warren L. Johns

Creationists and evolutionists share a belief that life on earth had a beginning. Evolutionists credit random chance, an accidental event arranged through the collaboration of Mother Earth and Father Time. Creationists point to an ancient written record that identifies God as the Creator of all things in the course of a literal seven-day week.

Evolutionism, usurping the science banner, claims, straight-faced, humans descended from a fish with a conjectured genealogy that includes an unidentified "hermaphrodite," a critter with pointed ears and a tail, and eventually an ape-like ancestor that swung through the trees.

Favorite, knee-jerk "proofs" cite changes in the sizes and shapes of finch beaks; bacteria that display immunity to wonder drugs; or pepper tree moths that modify color from white-to-gray. But these examples only demonstrate each genome's ability to diversify relying on the information inherent in its own DNA.

From beginning to end, bacteria continue, ad infinitum, to produce bacteria; finches remain finches; and moth descendants flutter on as moths.

Citing the real to substantiate the never-was, is evolutionism's dark secret! Inherent genetic versatility doesn't prove Darwinian conjecture. Repetitious extrapolation doesn't cut it!

So where's the molecule-to-man conjectured by neo-Darwinism?

It can't be found in the fossil record nor in molecular biology's microscopic vision! Dumb luck, coincidence, and mutations can't substitute for genetic information vested originally by the Intelligent Designer in each life.

Diversity within a life kind thanks to change resulting from the life form's own Intra-Genomic Adaptability? Absolutely! As to Darwin's quaint notion that humans likely descended from fish ancestry? Never!

There's nothing evident in the last 4,000 years of living history that demonstrates one life form mutating into a new and entirely different kind of life---either gradually or by giant leaps! Its arguable that Darwin's idea might have been trashed ab initio if exposed to technology and data commonplace in 21st century culture.

Evolutionist G. A. Kerkut identified seven assumptions anchoring evo theory. Opinion built on assumption requires faith and evo is faith based, out-of-context with testable science.

Beyond Forever could, and perhaps should be two books: the first exposing the flaws in neo-Darwinian conjecture and the second featuring rationale for faith in the Creator in the context of a "Big Picture."

The text examines evidence that a lawyer might present to persuade a jury searching for truth. Neither lawyer nor scientist can claim ultimate knowledge or infallible wisdom. A doctorate in jurisprudence does not equate a degree in microbiology. But lawyers are trained to assemble, evaluate and present evidence. That's why, in an attempt to present the "whole truth, *Beyond Forever* combines both books, and presents the aggregate evidence including the truth about God and the miracle of His creation.

The weight of evidence offers little comfort to the extravagant, unsubstantiated assertions of neo-Darwinism. Abstract theory concocted from unproven assumptions coupled with extrapolations from the real to prove the never was proves nothing.

In a free society, the public serves as the ultimate jury.

I believe the *overwhelming weight of evidence* points to the miracle of life having been intelligently designed by the Creator of the universe and placed on earth in the course of a literal, seven-day creation week. I like to think that a significant number of readers composing the public jury reviewing *Beyond Forever* will agree.

WLJ

1

Evo's Dark Secret
Extrapolated Mythology

*"...The 'General Theory of Evolution' and the evidence that supports it
is not sufficiently strong to allow us to consider it
as anything more than a working hypothesis."*
G. A. Kerkut[1]

Are you an evolutionist? Whether you think you are or not, try this test on yourself. You just might change your perception.

Do any of these statements represent scientific fact? Answer with a "yes" or "no."

The size and shape of finch beaks may adapt over time?
Descendant bacteria can display immunity to antibiotics?
Mutations can alter the number of fruit fly wings and legs?

Chances are you answered "yes" to all three questions! So you consider yourself an evolutionist? Think again! Believers in a literal seven-day creation week also say "yes."

So what's the big deal?

Each life is vested with built-in survivability using the adaptation potential powered by its own genetic code! While the three examples are sometimes cited as evo proof, they are nothing of the kind---finches remain finches forever; bacteria change but never mutate into any other life form than bacteria; and after thousands of generations, pesky fruit fly descendants remain stuck with the less than auspicious fruit fly pedigree.

Now, one final clincher!

Do you believe a fish is the ancestor of your own family?

A "yes" to that one puts you in the inner sanctum of evolution's pantheon of the make-believe! So does this mean that gourmet quality Cajun style salmon steak will come off your menu?

Evolutionism Darwin Style
Darwin made no attempt to explain the origin of first life.

So what ground-breaking thought did he propose that so po-larized minds and crowned him "king" of science?

His idea came into play after the first living cell managed to miraculously début in some warm little pond. He imagined that from this dubious beginning, millions of gradual transitions led from the simple to the increasingly complex life kinds, over eons of time.

He postulated simple-to-complex intermediate forms climb-ing up an imagined taxonomic tree. He envisioned transmutants resulting from millions of miniscule increments accrued over eons of time riding into reality on the backs of unknown in-termediates. He believed in the chronic shifting of an unstable genome, in constant flux, en route to an unpredictable "biologic transit stop."

Allegedly, natural selection powered this evolutionary, mol-ecule-to-man scenario.

During his high-seas odyssey, Darwin spotted Galapagos finches sporting beaks of different lengths, shapes and sizes. He seized upon the phenomena as evidence supporting his evolving theory.

The variable shaped finch beaks that caught Darwin's eye contributed to his speculation that he could "...see no difficulty in a race of bears being rendered, by natural selection, more and more aquatic in their habits, with larger and larger mouths, till a creature was produced as monstrous as a whale."[2]

So Charles Darwin was right? A "whale" from a "bear?"

While this "bear" postulation never made it past 1859's first edition of *The Origin of Species*, he nevertheless frosted his vision with a rather unpalatable molecule-to-man scenario. "...Early progenitors of man were no doubt once covered with hair, both sexes having beards; their ears were pointed and capable of movement; and their bodies were provided with a tail..."[3]

While Galapagos finches displayed versatility inherent in the finch genome, they remained and continue to remain finches, albeit with a variety of beaks. Finches continue as finches for-ever---never eagles, hummingbirds or robins, much less flying squirrels! The same with pigeons. Different traits could be developed by breeding but no eagles took to the skies from Darwin's coop---only pigeons.

Evolutionism can't be proven because it never happened!

Intra-genomic Adaptability Using "Genetic Reserves"

No question about it, species possess the power to adapt, enhancing survivability. Change relying on information already present in the genome demonstrates genetic versatility that may shift descendants laterally or downward, exhibiting diversity at the species and sub-species levels.

Adaptive change within a genome does not validate Darwin's dream! Intra-Genomic Adaptability (IGA) supporting survival of a genome doesn't authenticate evolutionism's microbe-to-man idea!

IGA offers no refuge for Darwinian theory. There is no there, there!

This capacity for genetic adaptability doesn't transit to another kind of life confirming evolutionism's fantasies. The natural selection process, relied on by neo-Darwinism as the engine driving evolutionary change, acts to eliminate the less fit but does nothing to create an entirely new and different kind of the more fit.

Intra-genomic expression kicks-in to accommodate the survivability of each genome. Versatility, relying on genetic reserves inherent in every life kind, serves to preserve that life form, rather than to promote something radically different. The genetic card deck has simply been shuffled to bolster the genome's survivability and to preserve its identity.

Natural selection works for survivability of the genome, overriding or avoiding hazards rather than launching a life kind on the road to some entirely new creature. Built-in genetic flexibility, protective of survival, is 180° the opposite from evolutionism's theoretical, transitional step toward offspring destined to ultimately supercede the parent generation.

Genetic information may be lost or scrambled, but without new information, finches, fruit flies and bacteria continue as finches, fruit flies and bacteria---ad infinitum!

This is not evolutionism.

Joseph Mastropaolo sees genomic versatility attributable to what he identifies as "genetic reserves." Noting the entire life span of the Monarch butterfly "can be observed," he traces the transition from egg that hatches in three days to a sixteen-legged caterpillar and ultimately to a six-legged butterfly capable of flight, eating and mating---all in an elaborate, 60-day sequence directed by the expression of genetic reserves.[4]

Dr. Mastropaolo's analysis emphasizes that genetic reserves "...may be aroused in a matter of hours, not millions of years. They cannot be incorporated by evolution because the organism cannot experience what is needed until the event, and it will not survive unless the need is immediately satisfied."

Genetic reserves "...provide each life form with remarkable arrays of morphological, functional, and behavioral mechanisms to meet punctually and precisely the variabilities of any environment and to survive the extremes. And they do it right the first time...Calling any of these evolution misleads us because the immediate response is an attribute of the current physiological configuration from the DNA."[5]

The Jamaican click beetle shifts color from "yellow-green to orange in the ventral light organs, and green to yellow-green in the dorsal organs."[6] While the color shift demonstrates dynamic versatility, the Jamaican beetle remains a beetle.

Goldfinches shift cyclically from brilliant yellow-gold in the summer to winter's dull green. Burnished crimson canopies envelope fall landscapes like clockwork, painting forests in a riot of blazing hues. Come spring, the cycle repeats, swallowing the woods with a shower of blossoms and the bright green shoots shouting life renewed. Our senses devour nature's theater presented for our pleasure. We revel in the predictable cycle, science on parade.

Cyclical adaptation is not evolutionism!

Downstream Not Upriver

Streams flow downhill, feeding rivers that merge with oceans. No voice argues that flowing water defies gravity, reverses its natural course, and flows uphill. Change in the natural world is obvious---water moves, the earth rotates shifting its position, tides rise and fall and radically different sizes and shapes of dog breeds descend from a common gene pool.

Genomic versatility assures diversified breeds, sub-species and species. The change moves descendants either laterally or downstream from a given ancestor kind---never upstream against the genetic current to an entirely different order, class or phylum as envisioned by Darwin's "tree of life."

The canine genome never reverses course producing cats.

"Fido," the friendly family dog that licks your hand and barks in wild ecstasy when you return from wherever, is living proof of the versatility potential within a genome. Whether a "Heinz 57" or an AKC registered blue ribbon winner at next year's Westminster show, man's best friend descended from a common canine ancestor with every other dog breed champion or otherwise. The dog genome, deciphered in 2005, demonstrates that all dog breeds originate from the same gene pool with slight DNA differences.

"All dogs from the smallest Chihuahua to the biggest Great Dane emerge from the same basic set of genes. At the DNA level, two randomly chosen dogs differ by only about as much as two randomly chosen people do, yet the variation in appearance, size and behavior in dogs is 'just mind-boggling'..."[7]

Not only do all dog breeds claim common ancestry but also coyotes and wolves likely have been cut from the same bolt of genetic cloth. The fact that a German Shepherd and an English Bulldog were selectively bred from the same gene pool demonstrates eye-popping change! This genetic flexibility has nothing to do with evolutionism!

According to the Westminster Kennel Club, an estimated four-hundred species of dogs claim descent from a single canine ancestry. Courtesy of select gene mixing, collies and poodles look different, but are still dogs. The marvelously diverse dog breeds lack the genetic wherewithal to parent cats. All descendant dog species answer to the same family heritage---never producing a feline! And never authenticating evolutionism!

Without introducing new genetic information to an ancestor gene pool, an entirely new and different kind of life form doesn't happen in a laboratory supervised by human intelligence much less accidentally in nature.

Mutations, or genetic mistakes, don't move the genetic stream uphill toward a radically different genome! This reality anchors one of the most misunderstood and misconstrued issues in the creation/evolution debate.

The law of gravity dictates that water changes position and moves only downstream, toward an ocean, never retreating backwards to higher terrain in defiance of the law of gravity. So also, the laws of genetic descent dictate that offspring from a common gene pool only move downstream, never reversing course and jumping to an entirely new and different body plan without adding new information.

Pantheon of the Make-Believe

Century twenty-one media hypes evolutionism, shilling obsolete myths buried in blizzards of clichés. Facts have a way of disappearing in the hands of spinmeisters adept at whitewashing redundancies, affixing labels and wrapping unproven conjecture in mantles of authenticity. Evolutionism theory pleads for reassurance in the pantheon of scientific respectability.

Science magazine touted "Evolution in Action" as 2005's "Breakthrough of the Year." Saluting the dogma as "the foundation of all biology," the assessment opined "...every discovery in biology and medicine rests on it, in much the same way that all terrestrial vertebrates can trace their ancestry back to the first bold fishes to explore land."[8] Attempting to fortify the case, the authors referenced the ability of the marine stickleback fish "...to adapt rapidly to a new environment." Warblers, corn borers, butterflies, crickets, cichlids, and, of course, the ever favorite fruit fly, were also cited as prime "breakthrough" examples.

Big problem here! Each change referenced represents a genome's adaptability, not evidence of evolutionism. The "breakthrough" creatures remained fish, warblers, corn borers, butterflies, crickets, cichlids, and fruit flies respectively! None emerged as some new and entirely different life kind.

Dazzling diversity, for sure! Up-the-down staircase to entirely new and different families, orders, and classes topped with a giant leap to a different phylum?

Never!

Beware of the semantics game. Playing the semantics game doesn't alter reality. Adaptation using the information already present within any genome from its beginning, never move it beyond the its genetic limits. Intra-genomic change doesn't reverse direction leading up the taxonomic tree of life toward a new and different phylum. Intra-Genomic Adaptation is real, assuring diversity and survival. One of evolutionism's dark secrets is insistence that IGA reality corroborates Darwinian projections.

The demonstrated diversity potential within a single genome proves its inherent *adaptability* not *evolutionism*. Prolific varieties of finches, orchids, and dog breeds derive from genetic information built into the DNA of their respective genomes. IGA assures dazzling diversity in every basic plant and animal form but has nothing to do with radical transitions to new and different life forms envisioned by neo-Darwinism.

IGA relies on genes already present in the organism to show off its dynamic versatility within its own body plan. Evolutionism conjecture builds on multitudes of mutations, genetic abnormalities that theoretically lead to an entirely new and different genome given enough time. Debilitating mutations downgrade the genome. No mega-million-year time chunk is required. Nothing here illustrates the leap to an entirely new and different life kind. Yawning, genetic chasms separating distinct kinds of organic lives have never been bridged by the much sought-after mutation/natural selection combo.

No one alleges that the human ability to build immunity to disease certifies evolutionism. "...Bacterial antibiotic resistance, insect pesticide resistance, industrial melanism [peppered moth], sickle-cell anemia, and increased fitness in irradiated populations of *Drosophila*..."[9] are favorite touts, extrapolated then recycled by neo-Darwinists as proofs of evolution. In reality, this recycled litany builds a pantheon of the make-believe.

Bacteria can mutate and multiply to their heart's content but are stuck in their bacteria mode. The ability of bacteria to adapt to changed circumstances and to shuffle genes to build descendants immune to antibiotics falls far short of Darwin's grand scheme imagining a "race of bears" transforming itself to something "as monstrous as a whale."

When a news journal described evolution as a "fundamental fact of biology," it extrapolated from laboratory induced *E. coli* modifications to support the claim. It relied on laboratory findings of variations in twelve populations of *E. coli* bacteria that reproduced "every 3.5 hours or so." After thousands of generations, the once genetically identical population had "adapted in its own way to the conditions in its test-tube home."[10]

End of story? Hardly!

E. coli populations remain *E. coli* because of built-in genetic information enabling heroic feats of adjustment. *E coli* parents produced nothing but *E coli* offspring.

Genetic cards may be reshuffled; genes may be lost or damaged; and a genome may adapt to its environment and switch its genes on or off to survive. Survival of the modified *E. coli* represents the opposite of transition to some radically new and different life kind.

Biologist Jonathan Wells writes that "…Mutations and natural selection are significant factors at the molecular level, especially in rendering bacteria resistant to antibiotics, or insects and other pests resistant to pesticides…Like antibiotic resistance, most insecticide resistance is due to inactivating enzymes," or "spontaneous mutations…Raw materials for large-scale evolution must be able to contribute to fundamental changes in an organism's shape or structure." Biochemical mutations don't affect the shape or structure alleged in evolution.[11] When the insecticide is no longer used, the population could conceivably revert back to the non-immune brand of the same bug. Whatever the modifications, the insect pest population remains insect.

For decades, the public has endured repetitious media pronouncements and waded through biology textbooks citing population swings of gray and white peppered moths as evidence that evolutionism is real. The textbook favored peppered moth still comes in multi-hued gray and white colors, but continue as peppered moths---never parenting a completely different brand of descendant. Change within a genome is real. But this kind of adaptive change within a genome's genetic limits is not the fish-to-man evolutionism contemplated by Charles Darwin.

While studying the rainforest fruit fly's ability to adapt, a team of Australian scholars from Victoria's La Trobe University encountered the stark reality of the limits to change imposed by the *Drosophila birchii's* genetic material.

Ary A. Hoffmann's scientists tested the limits of the fruit fly's ability to adapt to an increasingly dry environment. Starting with the most "desiccation resistant...they subjected the insects to very dry conditions until 90 percent had died, and then they bred the survivors."

The remaining more hardy ten percent, were bred further for fifty more generations. The researchers expected to produce "even more dryness-tolerant flies. But what they got were flies basically no different from the ones straight out of the rainforest."[12]

Hundreds of generations of those ubiquitous fruit flies, subjected to laboratory induced mutations, may add or subtract wings and legs but continue relentlessly producing fruit flies, ad infinitum---never butterflies or dragonflies!

Ecologists at Auburn University Alabama, studied two populations of house finches that had recently moved into new habitats. One group of birds moved from New York to Alabama, the other from California to Montana. Each group rapidly adapted to its new climate and after thirty years the two populations were quite different in appearance and behavior.

In Alabama males grew faster than females and display wider bills and longer tails. In Montana females grew faster and were larger. The differences occurred because mother birds can control the order in which they lay eggs containing male and females.

The result in both places was an increased survival rate for the offspring overall. According to David Resnick, evolutionary biologist from the University of California, Riverside, the study indicates "A Time scale of decades (not centuries) is really enough for animals to evolve."[13]

No matter how its sliced, diced, and hyped, the pantheon of the make-believe demonstrates Intra-Genomic Adaptation (IGA) in action, not the evolutionism envisioned in Darwin's dream.

Hybrids

So what about those hybrids? Does a mule, the offspring of a horse and a donkey, pass muster as evolutionism in action?

The canny Clarence Darrow laced the 1925 *Scopes* trial record with the clever ruse that hybrids confirm evolutionism.

The written testimony of one scientist cited a plant breeder's skill at modifying vegetables or flowers as "evolution...occurring today...under man's control."[14] Maynard M. Metcalf, an early twentieth century zoologist with a Johns Hopkins University Ph.D., rode the coattails of hybridization as proof of evolution's change over time.

"Not only has evolution occurred; it is occurring today and occurring even under man's control. If one wishes a new vegetable or a new flower it is within limits, true that he can order it from the plant breeder and in a few years he will produce it...This is evolution of just the sort that has always occurred..." Winterton C. Curtis, another zoologist with a Johns Hopkins doctorate shared this misinterpretation view.[15]

Given the research of Gregor Mendel and Luther Burbank, extrapolation of the reality of hybridization represents science in action but does nothing to prove Darwinian theory.

Hybrids happen when intelligent minds manipulate genetic information. The hybrid Honey Bell tangelo is seedless, a hybrid cross from the Dancy tangerine and the Duncan grapefruit, shaped like a bell, fiery-gold in color, sweeter than an orange. The hybrid Honey Bell remains a citrus fruit!

Pre-existing genes produced a hybrid weed in nature---a result comparable to the hybrid garden peas Gregor Mendel produced in his garden experiments and the multi-hued poinsettia hybrids developed by a California nursery. *The London Times* announced its début but erroneously tagged it with evolutionism's label.

Richard Abbott, St Andrews University, Scotland-based plant evolutionary biologist, checked the DNA of a weed found in York, and identified the plant as a natural hybrid between the common Groundsel and the Oxford Ragwort. Since it breeds true, produces fertile offspring, and does not breed with parent species *The Times* reported the process as "evolution in action." The daily gleefully crowed that, "Charles Darwin was right and the creationists are wrong...the first new species to have evolved naturally in Britain the past 50 years."[16]

According to evolutionary biologist Alan Feduccia, "The corn in Mexico, originally the size of the head of a wheat plant, has no resemblance to modern-day corn. If that's not evolution in action, I don't know what is."[17] But the corn is still corn, not the mega leap to entirely different kind of plant as envisioned by Darwin.

Remarkable change, of course. Evolution in action? Hardly!

The English hybrid weed continues as a weed just as California's dazzling hybrid poinsettias reproduce only descendant poinsettias and modified Mexican corn reproduces as just another corn variety. Despite the headlines, extravagant extrapolation from hybrid reality doesn't bolster the otherwise impossible.

Extrapolation

Extrapolating from a genome's inherent genetic ability to adapt utilizing "genetic reserves" as evidence of the radical, across-the-board type of changes essential to confirm neo-Darwinism represents evo's deep, dark secret.

IGA has yet to be demonstrated sending a descendant's body plan upwards toward a radically new and entirely different Phylum. Neo-Darwinism is dead wrong in extrapolating reality as proof that a fish or an ape-like animal could evolve eventually into a *Homo sapiens*!

The public is persistently fed a diet touting a genome's ability to adjust to survive as proof of evo. Extrapolating the obviously real to prove the never-was and never will be proves nothing!

Street shops in India sell "Earnest Hemmingway" novels for a pittance. But when the swindled purchaser looks inside, the text can be anything but a Hemingway best-seller.

In retailing, bait-and-switch deceives. In science, the technique dances to the semantics game. Confronted with evidentiary shortfall, evo apologists hijack intra-genomic changes in dog breeds, orchids and finches in attempts to demonstrate evolutionism in action.[18]

Evolutionist G. A. Kerkut recognized and addressed the extrapolation issue point blank with a rhetorical question and answer. "...Why can't one extrapolate and say this has in effect led to the changes we have seen right from the Viruses to the Mammals? Of course one can say that the small observable changes in modern species may be the sort of thing that lead to all the major changes, but what right have we to make such an extrapolation?"[19]

Extrapolation pushes conjecture's envelope over the brink to wallow in the realm of philosophical make-believe. It corrupts science, proving nothing more than shoddy conjecture covering for evidentiary gaps. "Darwinian theory, which explains complex life as the product of small genetic mutations and 'survival of the fittest,' is known to be valid only for variations within the biological species."[20]

Artful exploitation of semantics can't conceal bait-and-switch. Or in the quaint vernacular of down-home Texans, "You can bake your boots in the oven but that doesn't make them biscuits."

There is no evidence that metamorphic transition to an entirely new and different life-form by mutation and natural selection has occurred in the last 4,000 years. If not in four thousand years, how then in four million? Does deep time render the impossible, possible?

Despite a century of public misperception, the natural limits to biological change continue to stymie Darwin's dream. "... evolution is not a formulation of the true scientific method...(it is) the initial formation of unknown organisms from unknown chemicals produced in an unknown atmosphere...of unknown composition under unknown conditions, which organisms have then climbed an unknown evolutionary ladder by an unknown process leaving unknown evidence."[21]

"Nowhere was Darwin able to point to one bona fide case of natural selection having actually generated evolutionary change in nature."[22] Or as emphasized by a team of four science scholars, "Biological change occurs within basic 'kinds' and not between them."[23]

Confined to a whiff of time and a sliver of space, humans reach for evidence correlating our genesis with today and an infinity of tomorrows. Even granted the best scenario, evidence supporting neo-Darwinism seems miniscule, hiding in some as yet undiscovered never-never land. It isn't happening now as a current, newsworthy event; it hasn't happened in the recent past; it just never happened---even in a bazillion years.

Forget the knee-jerk mantra asserting life's emergence from primordial soup with a mindless march from the sea. Beginning with an unexplained, primitive single-cell and continuing with a sequence leading to multi-celled, invertebrates, vertebrates, fish, amphibians, reptiles, birds, mammals and eventually to *Homo sapiens*---it never happened!!!

Giuseppe Sermonti, retired Professor of Genetics at the University of Perugia, makes the point artfully. "...All the currently envisioned physical causes of evolution are either degenerative or conservative; therefore not one of them guarantees passage from the simple to the complex, from the inferior to the better."[24]

Change within a prototype life kind? Yes, of course!!!

But molecule-to-man? That dog won't hunt---even in a bazillion!!!

2

Treadmill to Oblivion
Darwin's Obsolete Assumptions

"There is something fascinating about science.
One gets such wholesale returns of conjecture
out of such a trifling investment of fact."
Mark Twain[1]

With a whiff of prescience, Charles Robert Darwin (1809-1882) confessed doubts about his idea. He worried that he may "...have devoted my life to a phantasy."[2] He fretted that his grandiose "phantasy" seemed "...a mere rag of an hypothesis with as many flaw[s] & holes as sound parts."[3]

He had reason to worry. Time would prove his fretting justified! Enough "flaws" and "holes" to fill pages of erudite books have surfaced. Evolutionism's darkest secrets lurk in the murky mists of misunderstanding.

Darwin made no attempt to explain the origin of the cosmos. Nor did he delve into the mystery as to how, when or where the original spark of life managed to first appear from inorganic matter, thanks to random chance. The canny philosopher simply swept this mystery under the intellectual rug, sagely admitting "...Science as yet throws no light on the far higher problem of the essence or origin of life."[4] His theory addressed the origin of diversity of life forms rather than the origin of first ever life.

The lack of this cornerstone clue didn't deter Darwin's pursuit of his scheme. Perceiving that first living cell to be nothing more than a blob of protoplasm, and conceding ignorance as to its origin, he built a castle of dreams on a foundation of make-believe. The philosopher envisioned human intelligence emerging by random chance from prebiotic soup with all species mere blips on the biologic screen, eventually melting to nothingness.

The 1859 publication of *The Origin of Species* marketed his idea. Awash in the boundless potential of wishful thinking, Darwin perceived life as a freak of nature. Starting with his primitive perception of the cell, his tortured trail of genealogy leads from fish, to amphibians, to reptiles, to birds, to mammals, and ultimately to *Homo sapiens*. Laced with prolific equivocations such as "probably," "apparently," and "it would appear," Darwin touted "natural selection" working "solely by and for the good of each being" assuring that "all corporeal and mental endowments will tend to progress towards perfection."[5]

He believed that small, incremental changes, over mega chunks of deep time, would produce descendants with a radically different body plan eventually exterminating the ancestor species. Unaware of genes, he imagined that acquired physical traits (eg. bulging muscles from weight lifting) could be transferred genetically to offspring. Recognizing that myriads of transitional life forms must have existed if his theory were true, the missing intermediates in the fossil record, troubled him mightily.

Choice words highlighted unproven assertion. Never mind the suggestion of exaggerated leaps over vast chasms of biological diversity---the elixir of unlimited chunks of time made anything possible. But when his raw verbiage is scrutinized, Darwinspeak's paucity of scientific substance jumps out like a photo emerging in a tray of developer.

The essence of his conjecture relied on a series of unproven assumptions. To his credit, Darwin harbored reservations about his conjectures. "...I am quite conscious that my speculations run beyond the bounds of true science..."[6]   His speculations took on a jaundiced view of life, outlining a tortuous treadmill to oblivion!

Assumptions

The formula for first life baffles the most devout evolutionist. Evo advocates cannot replicate the simplest cell and are at a loss to explain the source of genetic information packed into that first cell's DNA. Assertions built on assumptions don't necessarily resemble fact. Superstitious nonsense results when the assumption virus invades reasoning. Science, like religion, can be compromised by assumption.

The media in a free society champions free speech in its relentless pursuit of truth. Subtle enticements beckoning from evolutionism's "working hypothesis" can overwhelm fact. The Editors of USA Today fell prey to the trap in the August 9, 2005 edition, exalting evolution while taking a swipe at "Intelligent Design," a nemesis of the doctrine. "It is the cornerstone of modern biology. Though there are various 'missing links' in the evolutionary chain, it has never been refuted on a scientific basis."[7]

Is something out of kilter here?

Its strange irony that a team of intelligent minds composed phrases, designed a layout, printed and distributed millions of copies while insisting human brains originated accidentally, by random chance, from some undetermined, unintelligent source---without design or designer.

Redundant propaganda catering to assumptions and masquerading as fact tends to camouflage the congenital defects plaguing evolutionism's dearest dogma. Without corroborating proof, the entire scheme teeters like a tower of tipsy cards.

What exactly did Darwin "postulate" that "scientists have confirmed?" After reviewing ponderous words, objective analysis might conclude that if Darwin's postulates were a publicly traded stock, it might be prudent to anticipate a market collapse.

G. A. Kerkut, British scientist and credentialed evolutionist, acknowledged evolutionism is riddled with assumptions including the "assumption...that non-living things gave rise to living material, i.e. spontaneous generation occurred."

His unresolved roster of assumptions, lurk menacingly, nagging at the fringes of Darwinian thought, as relentlessly "assuming" as when initially identified in 1960. According to Dr. Kerkut, Darwinian thought was built on seven, unproven, non-provable assumptions that "...by their nature are not capable of experimental verification."[8]

Top billing on the list belongs to the assumption "...that non-living things gave rise to living material, i.e. spontaneous generation occurred."[9] Sir Fred Hoyle, another British evolutionist, also scoffed at the concept of a genetic code emerging from some primordial organic soup by chance, branding the idea "nonsense of a high order."[10]

Kerkut's six other eye-opening assumptions do nothing to fortify evolutionism's credibility.

"The second assumption is that spontaneous generation occurred only once...The third assumption is that viruses, bacteria, plants and animals are all interrelated. The fourth assumption is that the Protozoa gave rise to the Metazoa. The fifth assumption is that the various invertebrate phyla are interrelated. The sixth assumption is that the invertebrates gave rise to the vertebrates. The seventh assumption is that within the vertebrates the fish gave rise to the amphibia, the amphibia to the reptiles, and the reptiles to the birds and mammals..."[11]

Referencing the "General Theory of Evolution," Kerkut concluded "...the evidence that supports it is not sufficiently strong to allow us to consider it as anything more than a working hypothesis."[12] A menu of assumptions falls short of verifiable science and provides a shaky foundation for any "working hypothesis."

Just a minute, here!

What's that "assumption" word have to do with the evo "working hypothesis" propagandized as "fact?" Isn't that the knock aimed at scholars daring to think outside the box who consider a Supreme Creator at work in the universe?

Lively imaginations grease the wheels of assumption's fond dreams. But imagination is a mediocre counterfeit for evidence. Assumptions provide cosmetic cover to unproven conjecture. Unless validated, assumptions melt like wax touched by the rays of the noontime sun. At best, assumption is an exercise in faith! And faith resonates "religion!"

Nothing has changed since Kerkut's reality checks. Speculation that some primordial soup mixed with doses of heat, cold, water, and lightning somehow delivered genetic information creating a living cell proves nothing other than unverifiable imaginings. Post-1859 breakthroughs have not rescued Darwin's ideas to warrant christening evolutionism a "fundamental fact of biology."

Dr. Colin Patterson, lifelong evolutionist researcher and author, shocked colleagues by expressing serious doubts about evo theory in a 1981 lecture. To the dismay of those committed to Darwinian thought, Patterson publicly questioned whether evolution should be taught in high schools. His insight jolted a distinguished audience of scientists assembled at New York's American Museum of Natural History.

He described "evolution as faith...evolution does not convey any knowledge, or if so, I haven't yet heard it...One morning I woke up, and something had happened in the night, and it struck me that I had been working on this stuff for twenty years, and there was not one thing I knew about it."

"It does seem that the level of knowledge about evolution is remarkably shallow...Most of us think that we are working in evolutionary research. But is its explanatory power any more than verbal?...Evolution not only conveys no knowledge, but seems somehow to convey anti-knowledge, apparent knowledge which is actually harmful to systematics...During the last few years, if you had thought about it at all, you've experienced a shift from evolution as knowledge to evolution as faith. I know that's true of me, and I think it's true of a good many of you in here."[13]

The disclosure stunned listeners!

Neo-Darwinist Dr. Stanley Salthe, an author of evolutionary textbooks, followed Patterson's example, expressing eye-catching doubts. "Darwinian evolutionary theory was my field of specializing in biology. Among other things, I wrote a textbook on the subject thirty years ago. Meanwhile, however I have become an apostate from Darwinian theory and have described it as part of modernism's origination myth."[14]

Microbiologist Michael Denton also recognized evo's shortfall. Darwin's "...general theory, that all life on earth had originated and evolved by a gradual successive accumulation of fortuitous mutations, is still, as it was in Darwin's time, a highly speculative hypothesis entirely without direct factual support and very far from that self-evident axiom some of its more aggressive advocates would have us believe."[15]

Who Was Charles Robert Darwin?

Thunder clapped and rolled across angry skies. Black clouds shed empathetic tears for an unfolding tragedy. Inside the candle-lit house, a ten-year-old girl breathed in short gasps. Nothing her anguished father could do. All the wealth he possessed could not buy her life.

Within moments, Annie breathed her last and passed into the mists of the unknown. Medical science in 1851 could only stand by, wringing collective hands helplessly. It happened to children, every day, in every part of the world---victims of bewildering maladies that wrested away young lives with brutal abandon. Even in Victorian England.

The difference on this occasion: Annie was the beloved daughter of Charles Darwin. Already drifting far from ties to a religious faith, Annie's death helped push him over the edge. "...Annie died at the age of 10---probably from tuberculosis---an instance of suffering that only led him down darker paths of despair."[16]

Bereaved of his daughter's life, and bereft of rational explanation of eternal life beyond the grave, Charles Darwin had reason to mourn, above and beyond the agony of the loss of a child!

Annie Darwin! Bleak City! No wonder he despaired!!!

One human being! Just one of billions...but only one! Nothing more than a blob of protoplasm, a freak of nature without a past traceable to a rational beginning? And a future leading to abstract nothingness?

Darwin despaired trying to explain just how the first spark of biologic life happened to appear from inorganic matter. Nor did he begin to comprehend death, the other side of the origins coin. Bedeviled by the mysteries of life and death, he believed his own, home-spun fables. The innovative naturalist died bereft of any explanation as to the when, where, what. how or why the first cell of human life came to exist or just what his daughter could expect after death.

He only felt the vice-like grip of anguish on his heart as Annie slipped from his arms! This draining, emotional trauma, combined with his jaundiced view of God, imprinted young Charles Darwin's psyche.

Born to Wealth and Privilege

Just who was Charles Darwin, this Victorian era merchant of myth? Certainly not an academically credentialed scientist.

He lacked formal academic training in any science discipline. His resume encompassed a fruitless pursuit of a physician's career. A three-year stint at Cambridge, studying religion, convinced him he wasn't cut out for the clergy. Armed with pitifully little science education, a five-year tour of the world provided a platform for philosophical adventure. Thanks to seasoning aboard the H.M.S. Beagle, Darwin emerged a well-traveled Englishman, inspired to launch his career as naturalist exploring science mysteries, philosopher and prolific author.

The aggregate 1477 pages of *The Origin of Species* and *The Descent of Man* were released to a Victorian culture with a built-in caste system of wealth and privilege. The sun never set on Queen Victoria's "Union Jack." Darwin thrived amidst this robust "Rule Britannia" mind-set. He felt sheltered within the exotic echelons of a dominant power class that ruled 19th century England.

After sweeping the mystery of the first cell's origin under the rug, evolutionism traced a molecule-to-man sequence beginning in mysterious circumstances and extending to aristocracy's lofty pinnacle. Charles didn't shy away from implicitly awarding regal lineage to a dynasty of the intellectual and cultural elite in evolution's time odyssey. He scripted a biological Horatio Alger happy ending starring Charles Robert Darwin and his elitist peers.

Whether due to his "progress towards perfection" mantra or to subliminal coincidence, Charles and friends, emerge at the apex of the postulated pyramid, symbolic self-crowned sovereigns of a "survival of the fittest" monarchy. Lofty aspirations for a privileged citizen who typically spent four-hour days pursuing his hobby and who may never have punched a time clock or broken a sweat toiling at manual labor.

He married a cousin and settled in as an English country squire. Emma, wealthy in her own right, was heir to a Wedgwood fortune. Living the good life southeast of London, ensconced in their beloved Downe estate, the couple basked in the sunshine of inherited wealth and successful investment strategies.

By 1851, "Besides the Beesby farm in Lincolnshire...Charles had acquired assets worth about £40,000 on his father's death..." Emma's property included Wedgwood trust assets of at least £25,000. "In all, she and Charles had more than £80,000 in investments."[17] Thanks to astute management, their joint income eventually exceeded the equivalent of $40,000 per month in 1996 dollars.[18]

The family employed a staff of eight to manage the household. But despite lavish endowments, Charles didn't squander the family's larder on a lab assistant.

From this pinnacle of privilege he shilled the trickle-down benefits to society. Darwin's vision of evolution's impact reached out to embrace and then endorse the class divisions that plagued English society. He ranked the wealthy aristocracy as superior to labor. "The presence of...well-instructed men, who have not to labour for their daily bread, is important to a degree which cannot be overestimated; as all high intellectual work is carried on by them, and on such work material progress of all kinds mainly depends."[19]

Jaundiced View of Religion

In one of the great ironies, Darwin rejected a counterfeit picture of God in which the Creator was portrayed to the masses as a fearful tyrant, unjust, unfair, inflicting brutal punishment on dissidents---the precise opposite of the God of love portrayed in New Testament Scripture. The warped picture of a vengeful God, who allegedly tortured souls in a forever fire for failing to acknowledge His existence, laid a foundation for religious disillusionment.

During the millennium immediately prior to Darwin's day, religious history comes through bleak and tawdry, laced as it was with notorious examples of superstition, corruption, cruelty, and arrogance. Innocents such as Joan of Arc were burned at the stake; generations suffered death needlessly during the Crusades---all in the name of God.

The religion of Darwin's time and place didn't match his mind set. Disenchantment with religion simmered. It is unclear whether his three-year stint studying theology included serious study of the Bible. Exposure to hell-fire dogma contributed to his jaundiced view of what he perceived to be the establishment creed of his day.

At one time he ascribed to the Church of England's Thirty-nine Articles of Faith. Ultimately, he turned his back on a sterile, state-sponsored religion encumbered with repetitive ritual. "The Anglican Church, fat, complacent, and corrupt, lived luxuriously on its tithes and endowments, as it had for a century. Desirable parishes were routinely auctioned to the highest bidder."[20]

Darwin lived immersed in a culture propagating a twisted caricature of the Creator, parading in a robe of superficial righteousness.

Eight-years before the release of *The Origin of Species*, his world came crashing down, confronting death with the agonizing loss of his ten-year-old daughter, Annie. This crushing loss shook the already wavering faith of the naturalist. Heartbroken, the distraught philosopher eventually railed against any disjointed religion that pictured God as a vengeful tyrant, intent on condemning the wayward to a eternity of torture in a raging inferno. He strenuously objected to a teaching that "seems to show that the men who do not believe, and this would include my Father, Brother and almost all my best friends, will be everlastingly punished. And this is a damnable doctrine." [21]

Is the Creator a vengeful tyrant or a forgiving God? Is it consistent to portray a just God of love presiding over forever-torture of unbelievers? Or was the "damnable doctrine" an inappropriate dogma masquerading as Christian theology, a scare tactic intended to coerce "faith?" Was the Revelator's vivid depiction of an eternal "ascending" smoke symbolic language such as the description of "the sword that came out of the mouth of the rider?"[22] Or is "hell" simply the vivid symbol of eternal death, the irrevocable penalty for rebellion against God?

The "damnable doctrine" could have been the clincher that confirmed Darwin as an acknowledged "agnostic," who did not "believe in the Bible as a divine revelation, & therefore not in Jesus Christ as the Son of God."[23]

He devoted a lifetime attempting to explain the origin of life on Planet Earth without an Intelligent Designer. He challenged anyone "...who is not content to look, like a savage, at the phenomena of nature as disconnected, cannot any longer believe that man is the work of a separate act of creation."[24] He boasted, "I have, at least as I hope, done good service in aiding the overthrow of the dogma of separate creations."[25]

Darwinspeak

Darwin's primitive laboratory tools handicapped perspective. He lacked access to electricity and the electron microscope; he lived oblivious to the mysteries of the atom; and although a contemporary of Gregor Mendel, he was either uninformed or intentionally ignorant of the Austrian monk's landmark genetic discoveries. Darwin didn't understand a cell had a nucleus much less a stash of DNA. A century passed before computer science reached drawing board conception.

James Burnett touted "descent of man from ape" late in the 18th century. Grandfather Erasmus Darwin, composer of erotic poetry, authored *Zoonomia*, planting seeds of evolutionary thought in the fertile mind of grandson Charles.   Influential contemporary, Herbert Spencer, coined the catch phrase, "survival of the fittest" in 1864, which Charles borrowed in later editions of *Origin*.

Darwin's published words speak eloquently for themselves.

Genders

Unabashed chauvinist, his conjectures wandered to gender bashing. Rooted in "survival of the fittest" thinking, he bluntly opined "...man has ultimately become superior to woman,"[26] and "...the average standard of mental power in man must be above that of woman."[27]

Casting caution aside, he praised man's "superiority" in detail.

"The chief distinction in the intellectual power of the two sexes is shown by man attaining to a higher eminence, in whatever he takes up, than woman can attain---whether requiring deep thought, reason, or imagination, or merely the use of the sense and hands. If two lists were made of the most eminent men and women in poetry, painting, sculpture, music---comprising composition and performance, history, science, and philosophy, with half-a-dozen names under each subject, the two lists would not bear comparison. We may also infer...the average standard of mental power in man must be above that of a woman." [28]

Vaccination

Evolutionism's guru pushed the envelope of private bias to decry vaccination's impact on society. He fretted that vaccination spared the lives of small-pox victims. "...Vaccination has preserved thousands, who from a weak constitution would formerly have succumbed to small-pox. Thus the weak members of civilized societies propagate their kind... this must be highly injurious to the race of man. It is surprising how soon a want of care, or care wrongly directed, leads to the degeneration of a domestic race...we must bear without complaining the undoubtedly bad effects of the weak surviving and propagating their kind..." [29]

Modern medicine stands diametrically opposed to his callous outburst reflecting deep-seated cultural bias endemic to his views.

"The introduction of vaccines during the early part of the last century...contributed to the decline of diseases that had been responsible for much of the morbidity and mortality of humans during recorded history. Indeed, vaccination is considered the most effective medical intervention..." [30]

Natural Selection & Gradualism Paired

"...Natural selection acts through the competition of the inhabitants and consequently leads to success in the battle for life." [31] "...Natural selection acts by life and death,---by the survival of the fittest and by the destruction of the less well-fitted individuals..." [32] "...Natural selection works solely by and for the good of each being, all corporeal and mental endowments will tend to progress towards perfection." [33]

"...Natural selection will pick out with unerring skill each improvement. Let this process go on for millions of years..."[34] "...Natural selection acts only by taking advantage of slight successive variations; she can never take a great and sudden leap, but must advance by short and sure, though slow, steps."[35] "If it could be demonstrated that any complex organ existed, which could not possibly have been formed by numerous successive, slight modifications, my theory would absolutely break down."[36]

"Irreducible complexity" wreaks havoc, breaking down that "theory."

Acquired Physical Traits

"...Use in our domestic animals has strengthened and enlarged certain parts and disuse diminished them; and that such modifications are inherited."[38] "...Some intelligent actions---as when birds on oceanic islands first learn to avoid man---after being performed during many generations, became converted into instincts and are inherited."[39]

"The nascent giraffe...had some part or several parts of their bodies rather more elongated than usual, would generally have survived...One kind of animal will almost certainly be able to browse higher than the others; and it is almost equally certain that this one kind alone could have its neck elongated for this purpose, through natural selection and the effects of increased use."[40]

"...Every highly developed organism has passed through many changes...each modified structure tends to be inherited...each modification will not readily be quite lost, but may be again, and again further altered...structure of each part is the sum of many inherited changes...during its successive adaptations to changed habits and conditions of life."[41]

"...I can see no difficulty...in the continued preservation of individuals with fuller and fuller flank-membranes, each modification being useful, each being propagated, until, by the accumulated effects of this process of natural selection, a perfect so-called flying squirrel was produced."[42]

"The Most Obvious and Serious Objection"

"Numberless intermediate varieties…must assuredly have existed…"[43] "…The number of intermediate and transitional links between all living and extinct species must have been inconceivably great…"[44]

"…Geological research…does not yield the infinitely many fine gradations between past and present species required on the theory…Why do we not find beneath this system great piles of strata stored with the remains of the progenitors of the Cambrian fossils…?"[45] "Geology assuredly does not reveal any such finely-graduated organic chain; and this, perhaps, is the most obvious and serious objection which can be urged against my theory."[46]

"…Why, if species have descended from other species by fine gradations, do we not everywhere see innumerable transitional forms? Why is not all nature in confusion, instead of the species being, as we see them, well defined?"[47]

Why indeed?

Human Ancestry

"…All the organic beings which have ever lived on this earth may be descended from some one primordial form."[48] "…Animals are descended from at most only four or five progenitors and plants from an equal or lesser number."[49]

"…All the members of the vertebrate kingdom are derived from some fish-like animal, less highly organized than any as yet found in the lowest known formations…Five great vertebrate classes, namely, mammals, birds, reptiles, amphibians, and fishes, are all descended from some one prototype…"[50]

"…Some extremely remote progenitor of the whole vertebrate kingdom appears to have been hermaphrodite or androgynous."[51] "…The early progenitor of all the Vertebrata must have been an aquatic animal, provided with branchiae, with the two sexes united in the same individual, and with the most important organs of the body (such as the brain and heart) imperfectly developed."[52]

"…All the higher mammals are probably derived from an ancient marsupial, and this through a long line of diversified forms, either from some reptile-like or some amphibian-like creature, and this again from some fish-like animal."[53]

"...Man is descended from some less highly organized form...man is the co-descendant with other mammals of a common progenitor."[54] "...Man is descended from a hairy quadruped, furnished with a tail and pointed ears, probably arboreal in its habits..."[55] "...Man appears to have diverged from the Catarhine or Old World division of the Simiadae, after these had diverged from the New World division."[56]

Blind faith in this series of conjectures seems more challenging than believing the art of herding cats can be readily mastered.

The aspiring naturalist attempted to construct the semblance of a family tree, gamely grafting lifeless sticks of non-existent links to an imaginary trunk rooted in prebiotic soup's mysterious quagmire. Darwin posited that beginning from the first cell base of this chain of life, miniscule changes moved upward gradually, leaping giant chasms to produce radically new and different life forms---all by random chance.

Such scientifically perverse postulates saturate evolutionism's legacy.

Taxonomy identifies plant and animal kingdoms as two of five general classifications of distinct life forms. Within each kingdom, categories move downward from phyla to the increasingly specific realms of class, order, family, genus and species.

Observed biologic change typically reaches down, a genomic shift in the direction of species and sub-species, Evolutionism , as per Darwin, argues for travel up nature's down staircase.

Galapagos finch beak observations represented downward or, at best, lateral changes, never upward above the taxonomic "family." Darwin succumbed to extrapolating from the very real Intra-Genomic Adaptability inherent in the DNA of every life form to predict upward transition in the chain of life---without input of entirely new information being added to the genetic code.

It never happened!

Reality Check

Already burdened by assumption baggage, an avalanche of scientific shortfall threatens neo-Darwinism.

The objective investigator will inquire as to the odds against the spontaneous generation of a cell occurring by random chance; the source of DNA information present in first life; the inability of mutations to create new information or to upgrade a genome; and the sober reality of irreducible complexity resisting the gradual transition of an organism to an entirely new life kind.

Darwin loyalists strive to patch acknowledged "holes" and "flaws" in evolutionism's fragile fabric. But despite relentless tinkering, Darwin's conjectures still fall short of the starting gate. Many scholars remain unimpressed. "Evolutionism is a fairy tale for grown-ups. This theory has helped nothing in the progress of science. It is useless."[57] Mere "superstitious nonsense" in the eyes of Dr. Joseph Mastropaolo.

Michelangelo produced works of art, Mozart melodies, and Mark Twain literary masterpieces. A team of fifty-five visionaries the likes of Thomas Jefferson and James Madison, crafted a constitution that placed mankind on a legal pedestal. Charles Darwin harnessed his intelligence to conjure up his hypothesis that diminished human kind, suggesting *Homo sapiens* descended from a fish.

Michael Denton, a physician and molecular biologist, ranks Darwin's "gradual accumulation of random change" as both a "nonsensical claim" and a "flagrant denial of common sense." Spotlighting evo's abysmal performance, he challenged that "... Nowhere was Darwin able to point to one bona fide case of natural selection having actually generated evolutionary change in nature."[58]

"My fundamental problem with the theory is that there are so many highly complicated organs, systems and structures, from the nature of the lung of a bird, to the eye of the rock lobster, for which I cannot conceive of how these things have come about in terms of a gradual accumulation of random changes.

"It strikes me as being a flagrant denial of common sense to swallow that all these things were built up by accumulative small random changes. This is simply a nonsensical claim...a huge number of highly complex systems in nature cannot be plausibly accounted for in terms of a gradual build-up of small random mutations..."

"...Everybody knows the lung of the bird is unique in being a circulatory lung rather than a bellows lung. I think it doesn't require a great deal of profound knowledge of biology to see that an organ, which is so central to the physiology of any higher organism, its drastic modification in that way by a series of small events is almost inconceivable. This is something we can't throw under the carpet again because, basically, as Darwin said, if any organ can be shown to be incapable of being achieved gradually in little steps, his theory would be totally overthrown."[59]

Devoid of solid science or sound logic, evolutionism echoes Wizard of Oz sophistry. Its dismal legacy offers blank supposition for the origin of human history and lacks the slimmest shred of purpose for the future. To cling to primitive conjecture, blind to competing possibilities, condemns minds to an intellectual cocoon.

The longer an idea thrives in the thoughts, the deeper its roots. Cherished error, left untended and unchallenged, solidifies. Once ego kicks in, pride feeds calcification. Knee-jerk collective bias, whether religious, political or scientific, builds intellectual barriers, hostile to truth.

Evolutionism misleads!

"The idea that humans evolved from unicellular organisms belongs to an overflowing crate of flat worlds, gods living on mountain tops, and superstitions."[60] Its reminiscent of the swaggering city-slicker, feigning familiarity with horses and cattle, who comes across as all hat and no ranch.

Despite pages of fancy phrased rhetoric, science still "...throws no light on the far higher problem of the essence or origin of life."

What then is evolutionism if the explanation of the "essence or origin of life" continues to elude the minds of ardent evolutionists? How can science build a hypothesis on the foundation of an unknown abstraction riddled with assumptions and pronounce it "fact?" Twisted "truth" distorts facts, sows seeds of confusion and misleads vulnerable minds to dead-end darkness. Unimpeachable truth blazes with North Star intensity, setting minds free from intellectual bondage.

Swedish biologist, Søren Løvtrup unleashed a scorching analysis that awarded Darwin's quaint imaginings unique status perched on history's hot seat. "...One day the Darwinian myth will be ranked the greatest deceit in the history of science."[61]

3

Formula One
"...the far higher problem..."

'The chances that life just occurred are about as unlikely
as a typhoon blowing through a junkyard
and constructing a [Boeing] 747."
Chandra Wickramasinghe[1]

A good news/bad news scenario has been laid at the unsuspecting feet of the twenty-first century public. Its enough to make a person want to laugh or cry or both!

The "good" news: There is an unconfirmed report that the mystery of the origin of first life on Planet Earth may have been solved!

The bad news: Allegedly our ultimate ancestor may well have been a "biochemical moron!"

Hello? Is this a serious blast from the past? Or is this some mistake from a text newly deciphered from a cuneiform tablet?

Take a look for yourself. The report starts simply enough, announcing that "...many scientists believe that viruses evolved very early on, possibly even earlier than everything else. If so, they are not merely some ornamentation on the tree of life but rather may compose its very roots."[2]

Our ancestor was a virus parasite? But wait! There's more!

"We humans...are nobody's great idea; we are the fortunate mistakes of countless biochemical morons. That's evolution. It is humbling but somehow comforting."[3]

Comforting? To see a depiction of some great-great-grandfather virus front-and-center in the family's ancestry album?

The premise flounders in a cul de sac of logic: since parasites require a "more advanced living host" in which to function, just how could parasites provide the roots of organic life if a host life had not yet evolved? To paraphrase the words of comedian Laurel, addressed to his pal, Hardy, "Now that's a fine kettle of fish you've gotten us into!"

Taking a swipe at "Intelligent Design" theory, the report asserts "...the viruses appear to present a creation story of their own: a stirring, topsy-turvy, and decidedly unintelligent design where life arose more by reckless accident than original intent, through an accumulation of genetic accounting errors committed by hordes of mindless microscopic replication machines."[4]

"Unintelligent" may be the understatement of the century! The misfit of an idea approximates the classic "elevator that doesn't quite make it to the top" or the epitome of shortfall---"three bricks shy of a full load."

Throw in "reckless accident...mindless...genetic accounting errors...mistakes..." and of course, "countless biochemical morons" and the idea begins to resemble a journey to la-la land.

While the verbiage may inspire a field day of punditry, the idea carries a serious side. Where's the substantiating evidence? Recognition that viruses were older and more complex than once believed and may compose the "very roots" of the "tree of life" contributes little luster to human genealogy!

Also missing from the "enlightening" report is any attempt to explain the source of the DNA information in the virus! Hardly energizing for a theory that rejects design originating from an intelligent source! Spontaneous generation of a living cell from inorganic matter overwhelms imaginations. Just how would an accidental cell, without ancestry, arrive from nowhere, pre-loaded with genetic information?

Richard Hutton, Executive Producer of the controversial PBS TV series, "Evolution," was asked, "What are some of the larger questions still unanswered by evolutionary theory?" He replied: "The origin of life. There is no consensus at all here---lots of theories, *little science*. That's one of the reasons we didn't cover it in the series. The evidence wasn't very good."[5]

Another understatement!

First Life

Biological evolution theory requires some first life substance from which to evolve. Evolutionists, aware of the limitations inherent in the Oparin-Haldane hypothesis, look for an alternative explanation for the origin of life other than acknowledging the creative power of God.

Apart from the Genesis account, three evolutionary approaches compete for attention including Darwin's own awkward attempt to pose a nod to a "Creator." Evo's guru admitted "... science as yet throws no light on the far higher problem of the essence or origin of life"[6] while imagining life's Formula One may have emerged from some "warm little pond" or an undersea hydrothermal vent.

While side-stepping any attempt to account otherwise for "the essence or origin of life," the naturalist tossed a canny curve to critics, conceding "life" had been "...originally breathed by the Creator into a few forms or into one..."[7] Hardly an endorsement of the Biblical creation week, this allusion from the last paragraph of *Origin* may have appeased some Christians while giving root to his conjectured "one" or a "few" simple life forms supposedly growing a "tree of life."

Panspermia offers a faint hint of intellectual refuge for some. The fancy term conjectures that first life perhaps arrived on Earth from outer-space. But it doesn't explain how life originated somewhere else in the cosmos. Like the squeezed air bubble in a balloon, the dilemma doesn't go away, but only begs the question.

Avid evolutionists searching for signs of extra-terrestrial life look for information signals activated by intelligent life. Inexplicably, these same advocates cling to an assumption that life on earth arrived by accident without benefit of intelligent design or designer.

Panspermia comes laced with conceptual problems. Just how did that first life fragment from "outer-space" originate? What transport delivered life safely through space? How did such life survive mind-boggling ages of travel time through an environment notoriously hostile to life?

The lofty label Panspermia conceals thin scientific substance! Conjecture that first life reached Planet Earth from outer space explains nothing---it conveniently begs the question!

Creating Life in a Lab

Some Panspermia doubters, embrace spontaneous generation as an alternative despite its discredited credentials. Inorganic
chemical recipes generate predictable reactions. But no amount
of mixing in a laboratory or in nature has been able to create the
information or the technology essential to originate a cell that
throbs with the force of life.

It's not that it hasn't been tried!

Celebrating the end of World War II, science explored a broad
range of new frontiers---with smashing success! TV brought movies to the living room; the Jonas Salk vaccine conquered polio;
and rocket science propelled explorers into space so that men
could walk the moon.

So why not confront the ultimate challenge to human intelligence and create life in a lab? Stanley Miller and Harold Urey
stepped to the plate, gung ho to give it the old college try!

They shaped their experiment following a trail marked by
Russian Alexander I. Oparin's and British chemist J.H.S. Haldane's
attempt to rescue spontaneous generation theory from history's
dust bin of discarded ideas. A reducing atmosphere keyed their
speculations.

The Oparin-Haldane "abiogenesis" conjecture proposes that
the early earth atmosphere consisted of a mix of carbon dioxide,
carbon monoxide, ammonia, methane, hydrogen and water vapor, without oxygen. These inorganic "...chemicals combined
to form organic compounds, such as amino acids, which in turn
combined to form large, complex molecules, such as proteins,
which aggregated to form an interconnecting network and a cell
wall."[8]

The team envisioned a twisting trail of happenstance with
each step unaccountably surviving the prebiotic soup's "warm little pond." They counted on energy from lightning, earthquakes,
volcanoes, and the sun's rays to trigger chemical reactions with
atmospheric gases such as methane, ammonia, hydrogen, eth-
ane and water vapors, thereby converting them to amino acids,
fatty acids and sugars in the oceans. These compounds were
supposed to link up to form larger protein and DNA molecules,

ultimately becoming "the first true cell" capable of "metabolism, genetic coding, and the ability to reproduce" when wrapped with a membrane.[9]

One public school text has advised that "...primitive earth may have had an atmosphere largely of hydrogen which was later lost to space. A secondary atmosphere may have included ammonia, methane, water, and hydrogen sulfide...Ultraviolet light from the sun, electrical storms, and decay of radioactive elements may have provided the energy to combine these molecules as sugars and amino acids. Amino acids could have combined to form proteins..."[10]

"May have" and "could have" don't disguise blatant speculation. Could lightning, heat from volcanoes and the sun's ultraviolet rays have actually "...affected gases in the primitive earth's atmosphere and changed them into more complicated organic compounds..." such as fatty acids, amino acids, sugars, and nucleotides? Which in turn allegedly "accumulated in the ocean and then linked up with each other to form very complex molecules..." such as lipids, peptides, carbohydrates, polynucleotides and eventually combined to form "amazingly complex proteins?"[11]

You'd think that confronting the mystery of Formula One, human minds equipped with state-of-the-art laboratory tools, could theoretically design and create a living cell if nature could do it accidentally in some "warm little pond."

No such luck!

Amino acids, the building blocks of cell proteins, have been synthesized in laboratory environments created by humans. But building a full range of complex proteins from amino acids is an unfulfilled dream---to say nothing of the daunting hurdle confronting the creation of enzymes, DNA, and RNA. Laboratory replication of a single cell from scratch, life from non-life, more complex than any mechanism humans have yet devised, complete with a full code of genes, continues to elude. No human intelligence at work has yet duplicated what spontaneous generation allegedly accomplished in a speculative prebiotic soup mix or some ocean-floor hydrothermal vent spouting a recipe of organic building blocks.

Stanley Miller and Harold Urey introduced human intelligence to the equation in their 1953 venture hoping to verify the Oparin-Haldane hypothesis. Inadvertently, intrusion of human intelligence sabotaged the experiment's credibility before the first test tube was brought to the table. Adding intelligence to the process struck at the heart of an equation structured to prove random chance, unintelligent accident!

But even the presence of bright human minds proved inadequate for the unprecedented task! Life from non-life remained as great a mystery as in the days when men of science believed they saw life generating spontaneously in the warmth of wet rags.

The team attempted to replicate a reducing atmosphere by circulating a high energy spark through methane, ammonia, and hydrogen gases and a circulating hot water vapor. The effort produced "a small mass of black tar" along with "a condensed red liquid" containing some amino acids. The experiment "... only works as long as oxygen is absent and certain critical ratios of hydrogen and carbon dioxide are maintained..." Subsequent experiments using ultraviolet radiation produced "nineteen of the twenty biological amino acids and five nucleic acid bases of DNA and RNA."[12]

"Urey and Miller assumed that methane was plentiful in the early earth's conditions. If this is true, the sun's ultraviolet light would have caused hydrocarbons to form and absorb in the clay at the bottom of the ocean. The deposits from Precambrian periods should then contain significant hydrocarbons or remains of carbons, as well as some nitrogen containing compounds. None of these are present in these deposits."[13]

Evidence confirming plentiful methane in the early earth environment remains elusive.

Overeager celebrants initially interpreted the experiment's result as a break-through in creating virtual life from non-life in a test tube. Realists recognized much less. Miller and Urey did not create life. Nor did they demonstrate that life could have originated spontaneously from inorganic matter.

Certainly, amino acids are essential building blocks for cell proteins. But the enigma of a complex cell persistently challenges. No scientist has yet successfully synthesized life from inert non-life, nor explained the how, when and where Formula One originated by accident. "...The chemical reactions required to form proteins and DNA do not occur readily. In fact, these products haven't appeared in any simulation experiment to date."[14]

In 1995, Kirk R. Johnson and Richard K. Stucky reported that "DNA (deoxyribonucleic acid) and RNA (ribonucleic acid) molecules, which are composed of complex arrays of amino acids and are the templates for all living organisms, have yet to be artificially created."[15]

The Miller-Urey experiment faced "...withering criticism from chemists for ignoring the role of competing and destructive cross-reactions with chemical ions that would be expected in any hypothetical ocean or pond. These reactions would have tied up or terminated any growing polymer-chain."[16]

Spontaneous Generation

Innovative brilliance didn't do the trick for 1953's fizzled experiment. More than half a century after the fact, and counting, human intelligence continues unable to create life from inorganic matter. Regardless, evo clings tenaciously to Formula One having appeared fortuitously, by random chance, from a surreptitious flight from outer space; or by spontaneously generating itself in a "warm little pond"; or maybe from a hydrothermic vent concealed in some ocean's dark recesses, spewing a recipe for first life.

Mark Twain's tongue-in-cheek humor seems apropos. "There is something fascinating about science. One gets such wholesale returns of conjecture out of such a trifling investment of fact."[17]

The spontaneous generation scenario is reminiscent of Wile E. Coyote's futile chase of the crafty Road Runner in epic cartoons starring a reckless Wile E. racing past the cliff's edge, legs churning wildly, momentarily suspended in space, before gravity kicks in, sending him crashing to earth. Life creating itself without intelligent input, is less likely that Tiger Woods scoring a hole-in-one in the British Open by teeing off from the roof of New York's Empire State Building.

Hope springs eternal in the minds of coyotes---and children!

Depression era kids built their own toys, chasing impossible dreams. One seven-year-old let his imagination run wild, assuming that with a bit of luck, he could fashion a do-it-yourself radio by gluing a radio dial on a cardboard box and lacing the insides with string. Older siblings laughed while wise parents smiled knowingly. Undaunted, the youngster waited endless days for his dream machine to sputter with static.

Nature didn't oblige!

The sun beat down, the wind blew, and rain pelted the forlorn carton. Despite the naive wish of a child, the disintegrating contraption never delivered the announcer's mellow, pre-WWII sounds: "You are listening to KFI Los Angeles, Earl C. Anthony Incorporated, California distributor of Packard motor cars." Products composed of inorganic materials require more than blind chance to function. The seven-year-old exploited his full reservoir of intelligence to design the contraption but a failing effort fell far short of enough, shattering fondest hopes!

Comedians tease about Texas tool kits consisting of WD-40 and duct tape. If it doesn't move and you want it to move, apply the all-purpose lubricant; if it moves and you want it to stay put, duct tape is the answer. Far from the primitive, one-size-fits-all array of such handy gadgets, the most sophisticated laboratory devices manned by brilliant scientific minds can't come close to mastering, duplicating then creating the recipe for the simplest living cell.

Evolutionism's recipe for Formula One evades hot pursuit. By default, it is left to Mother Nature's whims and Father Time's antiquity to parent first life.

Evolutionism requires heavy doses of deep time for that first, "simple" cell to form itself---accidentally. The unlikely event demands a confluence of gratuitous coincidences---a split second in a billions-of-years time span; a lucky location no more than a micro-mini speck in the cross-hairs of space; and a congregation of life-essential elements assembling at that intricate juncture of time and place. Add millions of years of bonus time to enable random natural forces to chaperon the alleged transit of life towards something more "complex."

A class-five hurricane scrambles and devours telephone lines marking its fickle path of raging fury. No one has seen this fearsome force shape the jumble of metal strewn in its twisted wake to create a radio or a personal computer—much less manufacture self-replicating models!

Accidental creation of an operational radio by a hurricane's havoc seems less than farfetched compared to the chance of a living cell spawning itself spontaneously from fickle chaos! "In nature, we have not documented a single case of spontaneous generation/chemical evolution."[18]

Kerkut's seven assumptions "…not capable of experimental verification" haunt evo's academic ramparts. Heading the "we can't explain" list is the assumption "…that non-living things gave rise to living material, i.e. spontaneous generation occurred."[19]

British evolutionist, Sir Fred Hoyle rejected "…the notion of life---with its incredibly intricate genetic code---originating by chance in some sort of primordial organic soup, was…'nonsense of a high order.'"[20] Nobel laureate Sir Francis Crick observed, "An honest man, armed with all the knowledge available to us now, could only state that in some sense, the origin of life appears at the moment to be almost a miracle, so many are the conditions which would have had to have been satisfied to get it going."[21]

Louis Pasteur (1822-1895), the French chemist who fathered microbiology and introduced vaccines for anthrax and rabies, overpowered the myth. He discarded superstition by demonstrating the vacuity of the belief that inorganic matter spontaneously generates life. His experiments staked out findings that pruned out the heart of naturalism's tap root. Confirming the fact that life begets life and like begets like, he demonstrated "the impossibility of the appearance of life from non-living matter…To bring about spontaneous generation would be to create a germ.

It would be creating life...God as author of life would then no longer be needed. Matter would replace Him."[22]

Evo stalwarts stood firm, taking comfort in supposition.

Nobel Prize winner George Wald conceded the impossibility of spontaneous generation creating "a living thing." Still, he stubbornly ignored the obvious, steadfastly affirming his commitment to a conjectured miracle of the abstract. "...Here we are---as a result, I believe, of spontaneous generation."[23]

Ernst Haeckel, Darwin devotee and poster boy for manufacturing fake evidence, saluted spontaneous generation as a "...necessary event in the process of the development of the earth. We admit that this process, as long as it is not directly observed or repeated by experiment, remains pure hypothesis." Undeterred, Haeckel confessed "this hypothesis is indispensable for the consistent, non-miraculous history of creation."[24]

Molecular biologist Michael Denton dismisses spontaneous generation as "freakish." "The complexity of the simplest known type of cell is so great that it is impossible to accept that such an object could have been thrown together suddenly by some kind of freakish, vastly improbable event. Such an occurrence would be indistinguishable from a miracle."[25]

Phillip E. Johnson, Berkeley law professor and a point man for Intelligent Design theory, dismisses the idea of spontaneous generation with a lawyer's logic. "...Scientists employing the full power of their intelligence cannot manufacture living organisms from amino acids, sugars and the like. How then was the trick done before scientific intelligence was in existence?"[26]

Whether evolutionist or creationist, faith dominates the origin of life scene. "...Either life was created on the earth by the will of a being outside the grasp of scientific understanding, or it evolved on the planet spontaneously, through chemical reactions occurring in nonliving matter lying on the surface of the earth. The first theory...is a statement of faith in the power of a Supreme Being...The second theory is also an act of faith...assuming that the scientific view of the origin of life is correct, without having concrete evidence to support the belief."[27]

Let's get this straight!

Does this mean spontaneous generation of first life is admittedly unscientific? If belief in spontaneous generation is not faith, then where's the science? Is it consistent to acknowledge the core anchor of a belief-system as faith-based assumption and then to characterize a theory anchored to that assumption as "science?"

Regardless of the label, marketing a poison pill as a vitamin does nothing to enhance public health!

The Warm Little Pond

"Urschleim," an imaginary slime-like material existing at ocean depths, supposedly functioned as the nursery for first life. This warm little pond scenario posits the action of energy sources forming organic compounds in the atmosphere "...which were washed down by rain and accumulated in the primitive oceans until they reached the consistency of a hot dilute soup. According to this model, life appeared from the chemical reactions and transformations that took place in this prebiotic soup."[28]

The alleged soup must have contained a remarkable mix. Big problem here: evidence confirming existence of the imaginary hot green pond has not been found! "...Prebiotic chemical soup, presumably a worldwide phenomenon, left no known trace in the geological record."[29]

Darwin's biological evolution hypothesis still can't fly without clearance for take-off.

"Dawn rocks" from Western Greenland, conventionally dated at 3.9 billion years before the present and reputedly the oldest known dated rocks on the planet, show nothing resembling prebiotic soup. "...Rocks of great antiquity have been examined... and in none of them has any trace of abiotically produced organic compounds been found...

"...Considering the way the prebiotic soup is referred to in so many discussions of the origin of life as an already established reality, it comes as something of a shock to realize that there is absolutely no positive evidence for its existence."[30]

Chalk up another shattered myth!

Hubert Yockey dismisses "primeval soup" as a non-event.

"The origin of life by chance in a primeval soup is impossible in probability in the same way that a perpetual motion machine is impossible in probability."[31]

Abiogenesis should be viewed skeptically as "...just a relic of the cosmology of the time it was invented...There is no evidence that a 'hot dilute soup' ever existed. In spite of this fact, adherents of this paradigm think it *ought* to have existed for philosophical or ideological reasons...Scientists are divided into segregated schools that do not even agree on the standards of scientific inquiry..." With respect to the "prebiotic soup theory of the origin of life...objective scientific principle of a search for the truth is replaced by the subjective aesthetic principle of a well-constructed story."[32]

The never-happened spontaneous generation blossoms in the fiction of the never-was Urschleim. "...In science one must follow the results of experiments and mathematics and not one's faith, religion, philosophy or ideology. The primeval soup is unobservable since, by the paradigm it was destroyed by the organisms from which it presumably emerged."[33]

The Cell

Darwin's "far higher problem" stretched out-of-reach of anything he could have imagined. Primitive wisdom envisioned the cell as merely infinitesimal scraps of living matter. The two-hundred power microscopes of the era, portrayed a cell as little more than cytoplasm, with a nucleus, wrapped in a membrane, "a relatively disappointing spectacle appearing only as an ever-changing and apparently disordered pattern of blobs and particles." In contrast, when scrutinized using tools available to molecular biology's arsenal, the cell displays a format of "supreme technology and bewildering complexity" built from "about ten million atoms."[34]

Human bodies contain as many as 75 trillion cells with "...200 million variations, ranging from microscopic red blood cells to long, skinny nerve cells that stretch from the base of the spine to the foot...Every cell contains an estimated one billion compounds...and among these compounds are five million different kinds of proteins...These compounds are highly variable in shape, size, electrical charge, and configuration; many can complete a function in a millionth of a second."[35]

Once the electron microscope debuted with its million times magnification capability, researchers devoured an unfolding panorama of knowledge. What observers had once discounted as blobs of protoplasm jumped out as data treasure troves. By 1929, barely four years after *Scopes*, H. G. Wells and Julian S. Huxley described "snakelike threads" writhing "slowly through the cell" which they called "mitochondria" while noting they could see nothing "inside the nucleus but a clear fluid."[36]

This imperfect glimpse of a cell's inner workings presaged an avalanche of knowledge to come!

A living cell consists of nitrogen, hydrogen, carbon and oxygen; it stores an encyclopedia of information; it performs highly technical tasks; and it reproduces a copy of itself. "Life is far more than chemicals, and building life immensely more complex than pasting carbon, hydrogen, oxygen, and nitrogen together in clever ways. Every coffin in the cemetery is filled with those same chemicals, but no one walks out in the morning."[37]

Today's molecular biologists have pulled open the curtain to the previously unseen to stare in wonder at a pulsating package of coordinated microscopic motors and machines driving life's core. Michael Denton's research reveals the simplest cell throbs with life far more complex in structure and function than any mechanism yet conceived by humans.

"...The tiniest bacteria cells are incredibly small, weighing less than 10^{-12} gms   each is in effect a veritable microminiaturized factory containing thousands of exquisitely designed pieces of intricate molecular machinery, made up altogether of one hundred thousand million atoms, far more complicated than any machine built in the non-living world...nor is there the slightest empirical hint of an evolutionary sequence among all the incredibly diverse cells on earth."[38]

"To grasp the reality of life as it has been revealed by molecular biology, we must magnify a cell a thousand million times until it is 20 kilometers in diameter and resembles a giant airship large enough to cover a great city like London or New York.

"What we would then see would be an object of unparalleled complexity and adaptive design. On the surface of the cell we would see millions of openings, like the portholes of a vast spaceship, opening and closing to allow a continual stream of materials to flow in and out. If we were to enter one of these openings we would find ourselves in a world of supreme technology and bewildering complexity...

"The simplest of the functional components of the cell, the protein molecules, were astonishingly, complex pieces of molecular machinery, each one consisting of about 3,000 atoms...What we would be witnessing would be an object resembling an immense automated factory...larger than any city and carrying out almost as many unique functions as all the manufacturing activities of man on earth...a factory which would have one capacity not equaled in any of our own most advanced machines, for it would be capable of replicating its entire structure within a matter of a few hours." [39]

Biochemist Michael Behe, working with an assistant in the NIH lab "...analyzed the supposed miracle of the first living cell coming into being by historical accident. 'What would you need?' they asked each other. 'You need a membrane, a power supply, and you need some genetic information. You need a replication system. And we kind of stopped and looked at each other. We said, 'Nah.'"[40]

Francis Crick and James Dewey Watson earned their figurative spurs in the science hall of fame by uncovering DNA's delicate, double helix design in 1953. Throughout the first century post-Darwin, fossil bones powered pre-history investigations, providing grist for Darwinian endorsement. Today, the investigative focus has shifted from assessing bits and pieces of bone displayed in museums to the microscopic---the "Language of Life."

Identification of DNA's double helix design hexed evo's grand imaginings. The "simple" cell dogma faded, existing now only in the outmoded lexicon of primitive science.   Molecular biology pushed cell design and maintenance front and center.

The intricacy of the cell carries the mother lode of life's information code, overriding the primacy of fossil bone fragments as key to origin's quest. By the year 2,000, the human genome, with its staggering 3 billion+ base pairs, had been deciphered.

Beyond a pulsating pack of cytoplasm with a nucleus wrapped in a membrane, the cell contains a package of machinery performing a multitude of actions every split second. Mitochondria, located within the cytoplasm, generate and store energy. Ribosomes craft chains of proteins from a smorgasbord of twenty amino acids. At a minimum, a living cell requires a system of regulatory mechanisms, a constant supply of energy, an abundance of four nitrogenous bases, ribotide phosphates, twenty aminoacyl nucleotidates, deoxyribonucleic acid (DNA), DNA polymerase, and RNA polymerase.[41]

A cell must absorb food, discard wastes, repair, replace, grow, possess regulatory mechanisms and reproduce---all functioning pursuant to a built-in information code.[42] Even the simplest known cell's genome carries nearly 500 genes (while a viral parasite may have as few as ten). All this is wrapped in a functional membrane, a far-fetched candidate to be explained by fortuitous coincidence.

Tissues, organs, and systems, all functioning in synchronized concert, are composed of living cells. "...Organisms consist of a number of subsystems which are all coadapted to react together in a coherent manner; molecules are assembled into multimolecular systems" which combine "into cells, cells into organs" and organs into a "complete organism."[43]

The same genetic information is available in each cell but the gene chosen for expression enables selective coding for the heart, skin, and brain. What prevents a cell from crossing over and performing the wrong service for the wrong organ? The cell's awesome complexity logically brings assumption of its accidental origin to its knees but for evo's entrenched bias.

Impossible Dice Roll

Regardless of how many times a pair of standard dice is rolled, the dot total never aggregates more than twelve. The chance appearance of life from non-life shares such impossible odds.

Even if all conditions mandatory to sustain life existed in perfect calibration, its never been shown that original life could appear by random accident. Inorganic nature, by itself, lacked the information recipe to deliver "Formula One." Evolutionism's thesis relies on a "miracle" at its base! "To get a cell by chance would require at least one hundred functional proteins to appear simultaneously in one place. That is one hundred simultaneous events each of an independent probability which could hardly be more than 10^{-20} giving a maximum combined probability of 10^{-2000}." [44]

Listen to the voices of science!

"No matter how large the environment one considers, life cannot have had a random beginning...there are about two thousand enzymes, and the chance of obtaining them all in a random trial is only one part in $(10^{30})^{2000} = 10^{40,000}$, an outrageously small probability that could not be faced even if the whole universe consisted of organic soup. If one is not prejudiced either by social beliefs or by a scientific training into the conviction that life originated on the Earth, this simple calculation wipes the idea entirely out of court..." [45]

Carl Sagan considered the possibility of other life in the universe. Still, he "...estimated that the chance of life evolving on any given single planet, like the Earth, is one chance in $1 \times 10^{2,000,000,000}$. This figure is so large that it would take 6,000 books of 300 pages each just to write the number. A number this large is so infinitely beyond one followed by 50 zeroes (Borel's upper limit for such an event to occur) that it is simply mind-boggling. There is, then according to Borel's law of probability, absolutely no chance that life could have 'evolved spontaneously' on the Earth." [46]

The blind chance of spontaneous generation producing the complete formula of molecules, amino acids, and proteins essential for a cell one-tenth the size of *Mycoplasm hominis H. 39* "...is less than one in $10^{340,000,000}$ or 10 with 340 million zeros after it...such odds for the chance formation of a cell, even the smallest and simplest one, are zero." [47]

Harold J. Morowitz "...calculated the increase in chemical

bonding energy required in forming an *E. coli* bacterium and the probability of such a bacterium forming spontaneously anywhere in the entire universe over a period of five billion years under equilibrium conditions" computing the "odds to be one in $10^{10(110)}$...The difficulties in producing a protein from the mythical prebiotic soup are very large, but more difficult still is the probability of random processes producing the simplest living cell..."[48]

"The concept that all the parts of the first living thing preexisted, and its formation was simply a matter of spontaneous generation therefrom is mathematical absurdity, not probability. All present approaches to the problem of the origin of life are either irrelevant or lead to a blind alley."[49]

Bradley and Thaxton concluded "...that even assuming that all the carbon on earth existed in the form of amino acids and react at the greatest possible rate of 10^{12}/s for one billion years...; the mathematically impossible probability for the formation of one functional protein would be ~10^{-65}." [50]

Sir Fred Hoyle, atheist and evolutionist, calculated that "...the likelihood of even one very simple *enzyme* arising at the right time in the right place was only one chance in 10^{20} or 1 in 100,000,00 0,000,000,000,000...that about 2,000 enzymes were needed with each one performing a specific task to form a single bacterium like *E.coli*. Computing the probability of all of these different enzymes forming in one place at one time to produce a single bacterium, Hoyle and his colleague, Chandra Wickersham, calculated the odds at 1 in $10^{40,000}$. This number is so vast...that it amounts to total impossibility."[51]

And we think the chances of a dice throw coming up with a number higher than twelve sounds outrageous!

Molecular Discontinuity

The overwhelming discontinuity at the molecular level is summarized graphically in Michael Denton's *Evolution: A Theory in Crises*. "We now know not only of the existence of a break between the living and non-living world, but also that it represents the most dramatic and fundamental of all the discontinuities of nature...."[52]

"It is well established that the pattern of diversity at a molecular level conforms to a highly ordered hierarchic system. Each class at a molecular level is unique, isolated and unlinked by intermediates. Thus molecules, like fossils have failed to provide the elusive intermediates so long sought by evolutionary biology."[53]

Molecular biology surfaced decades after *Origin of Species* raised eyebrows and temperatures. Investigation of life forms smaller than a dot at the end of a sentence turned the study of origins on its end.

From focus on fossils, microscopic life previously unseen and unknown took center stage. "There is little doubt that if this molecular evidence had been available one century ago it would have been seized upon with devastating effect by the opponents of evolution theory...and the idea of organic evolution might never have been accepted."[54]

Spontaneous generation relies on unproven conjecture yet to be achieved either by chance in nature or in a laboratory when designed by human intelligence. Several billion years is not enough time to override impossible odds.

It *never* happened—ever!

4

The Gene Machine
Information

*"I believe that one day the Darwinian myth will be ranked
the greatest deceit in the history of science."*
Søren Løvtrup[1]

Molecular biology turned naturalistic interpretations of life's origin upside down. Scrutinized under the probing eye of the electron microscope, the living cell, once perceived to be a simple blob of protoplasm, emerged as a vibrant speck of organic life, more complex than any machinery yet designed by human intelligence.

Evo's strike-prone theory has moved into the last of the ninth inning of the ball game, desperately in need of a run. Its greatest strength has been a vociferous cheering section, oblivious to the score.

"Neither of the two fundamental axioms" of neo-Darwinism, "...continuity of nature...linking all species together and ultimately leading back to a primeval cell" and "adaptive design... from a blind random process have been validated by one single empirical discovery or scientific advance since 1859."[2]

So let's get this straight!

Strike One: Spontaneous generation never happened as per G. A. Kerkut. The origin of the first living cell confounds.

Strike Two: The chains of fossil transitionals Darwin described as essential to corroborate his hypothesis, don't exist!

Strike Three: The molecular world displays discontinuity!

So, three strikes and your out: end of batter; end of inning; end of academic ball game. With whiff after whiff in the batter's box, resulting in a big, fat zero of a score, its past time for team evolutionism to hang it up!

Right?

Sounds rational, but not so fast. Evo wants extra innings!

With a giant zip on the science scoreboard and with the top of the lineup having gone down swinging, how does evolutionism survive? What keeps a bankrupt franchise in business?

Darwin's *Origin of Species* required intelligent cause. No evolutionist suggests his hypothesis evolved without thought---an idea stitched together accidentally by an obscure natural process.

Paradoxically, the very publication that's raised such a ruckus disputing intelligent cause in the origin of earth's plethora of life forms, is itself the product of intelligent cause---albeit misdirected. Like the machine existing with the sole function of turning itself off, intelligence has been exploited to propose the impossible---the creation of information from a non-intelligent source.

Naturalism's devalued life concept exists on paper, as "fact-free science." Add to its abysmal showing at the plate along with its failure to explain the source of a cell's original information, little of consequence remains for the shreds of Darwin's dream but an overdue eulogy.

The Language of Life

Matter exists in the form of 100+ known elements. The number of protons contained in the nucleus of an atom gives each element its distinguishing number.

Ten years after Darwin floated his ideas, Russian chemist, Dmitri Mendeleev arranged the 63 then-known inorganic elements in a chart of rows and columns dubbed a *Periodic Table of the Chemical Elements*. English ecologist Philip Stewart has recently introduced a colorful galaxy design of the known chemical elements that swirl out from the center in a system of related spokes. Both the original and the updated innovation of the chart confirm the intrinsic organization and consistency of matter.

Carefully crafted molecular mixes assure predictable results when formulas are followed precisely. Corporate wheels ride the cavalcade of chemical recipes created by imaginative scientists that produce the innovative products underwriting industrial might.

The simplest cell imaginable is incredibly complex, loaded with a information code that directs its life---a pattern of designed data, every bit as precise as the *Periodic Table of the Elements*. One physical chemist claims the 482 genes of *Mycoplasma* qualifies it as possibly the "simplest known self-reproducing life form."[3]

Even the lowly parasitic virus carries coded instructions. A typical virus may have as few as 10 genes while the "giant" *Mimivirus* (so-called because it appears to mimic bacteria) has more than 1000.[4]

The simplest cell is overwhelmingly complex and loaded with genetic data that directs its life. Each cell's function is shaped by its own, genetic information. Each life kind possesses a unique assembly of DNA derived from an intelligent source.

First graders, up to their ears in ABC's, recognize 26 letters in the English language alphabet. They learn to spell "cat" and "dog" with aplomb. Chances are good that by the time these kids reach high school, they will have discovered that English boasts a plethora of mind-bending combos of those 26---a vocabulary of 200,000+ words with a capacity to communicate information on an encyclopedic scale.

This doesn't come close to matching the DNA combos displayed in the "Language of Life."

Imagine trying to play a card game by shuffling a deck of blank cuts of white cardboard, each card lacking information imprints. No winners, no losers, no game---just a meaningless shuffle of nothingness. Cells contain imprints, a different, definitive genetic format for each of the estimated more than six million plant and animal species living today. The genes built into the cell determines prototype---not the inherited experiences of mind and muscle.

Without original, information built-in from the get-go, a cell would lack the resources to direct its life or to reproduce. Not only did theorists of Darwin's era lack perception of the cell's complexity, the very existence of a cell's genetic composition had yet to be deciphered.

Molecular biology changed the equation forever. Living cells boggle objective thought!

Michael Denton's, *Evolution: A Theory in Crises*, opened the door to an avalanche of insight. "...The tiniest bacterial cells are... made up altogether of one hundred thousand million atoms, far more complicated than any machine built by man and absolutely without parallel in the non-living world."[5]

"What has been revealed as a result of the sequential comparisons of homologous proteins is an order as emphatic as that of the periodic table. Yet in the face of this extraordinary discovery the biological community seems content to offer explanations which are no more than apologetic tautologies."[6]

Its axiomatic that intelligence is an imperative to life's language, the source for the information stored in a living cell. The quaint notion that a cell, bereft of an intelligent source, emerged from some ancient warm little pond provides comic fodder.

Does anyone seriously believe inorganic matter possesses the slightest fragment of intelligence? Where do biochemical instructions, embedded in DNA information, originate if not from prior intelligence? When, where and how was that original information deposited in the cell?

The Information Enigma

The genome's intricate complexity defies random chance explanation. Amino acids don't organize themselves without an array of the appropriate genes orchestrating the process.

Dean Kenyon sees no "biochemical predestination" in molecular genetics. "The enormous information content of even the simplest living systems...cannot in our view be generated by what are often called 'natural' processes...For life to have originated on the Earth it would be necessary that quite explicit instruction should have been provided for its assembly...There is no way in which we can expect to avoid the need for information, no way in which we can simply get by with a bigger and better organic soup..."[7]

Genetic information given to every cell of every living organism displays a distinctive watermark. A dragonfly sees through two eyes, each with 30,000 lenses. The bee gets by with 6,300. Genes dictate the difference. The hexagonal honeycomb design in a bee hive utilizes a minimal amount of wax to hold a maximum amount of honey. Where did the honeybee obtain the built-in design information that increases storage capacity? Answering mega years of trial and error doesn't cut it!

Its one thing to speculate that spontaneous generation triggered first life. Its quite another to pony-up far-fetched imaginings for the source of its information.

Stephen C. Meyer and William Dembski, nationally known scientists riding point for Intelligent Design, recognize a "design inference" as the result of intelligence producing information that shapes design. Dembski's "Explanatory Filter" is built on the idea that neither law nor chance explain an event. Natural selection doesn't create information nor does it explain its source.[8] The magnitude of a cell's dependence on information overwhelms any theory of its origin that fails to explain its source.

The first living cell's DNA base pair could not exist without design instructions from non-material "bits" of information. Its been estimated the DNA of a single cell comes packed with information sufficient to fill 3,000 encyclopedia sets. Physicist Lee Spetner suggests that the "genome of a mammal has from two to four billion" symbols. This data "...would fill two thousand volumes---enough to take up a library shelf the length of a football field! All this is in the tiny chromosomes of each cell."[9]

The human body consists of an estimated fifty trillion cells composed of ten million atoms each. The 23 human chromosome pairs residing in the cell's nucleus, contain DNA with an estimated 30,000 or more genes packed into three million plus nucleotide links composed of G, C, A, and T bases., instructing each cell how to live and to reproduce in cohesive synchronization. The magnitude of complexity overwhelms the senses when this elaborate mechanism is multiplied 50,000,000,000,000 times.

Did the DNA housing these genes arrive compliments of the tooth fairy? How did it get here? Certainly not through millions of years of chaotic heating, cooling, and thawing spurred on with torrents of rain, flashes of lightning and gusts of wind.

As long as the "design inference" is ignored, logic eludes. The quest for answers starts with the cell. The question of the cell's information source nags at the heels of objective research: just where did original DNA information for the first living cell come from?

A Left-Handed Mystique

Typically there are 500 amino acid chains in a protein. There are more than 30,000 distinct proteins. The sequence and arrangement of amino acids keys a cell's proteins folding into three-dimensional shapes. Protein functions are based on these 3-D shapes.[10]

Proteins can't order themselves. Twenty different kinds of amino acid chains provide the raw material from which proteins are built. "...A protein may have many of each kind. A typical protein will have a few hundred amino acids...To make a protein that will do something useful, the cell has to get the right amino acids in the right order."[11]

Protein molecules constitute "...the simplest of the functional components of the cell..." Each of these molecular machines consists of "about three thousand atoms arranged in highly organized 3-D spatial conformation...The life of the cell depends on the integrated activities of thousands, certainly tens, and probably hundreds of thousands of different protein molecules...It would be a factory which would have one capacity not equaled in any of our own most advanced machines, for it would be capable of replicating its entire structure within a matter of a few hours."[12]

After assembly in correct sequence, a protein's "...long amino acid chain automatically folds into a specific stable 3D configuration...Particular protein functions depend on highly specific 3D shapes...Significant functional modification of a protein would require several simultaneous amino acid replacements of a relatively improbable nature."[13] Failure to fold correctly would likely lead to a non-functional result.

Amino acids exist in both left-handed and right-handed formats. "Amino acid, when found in nonliving material...comes in two chemically equivalent forms. Half are right-handed and half are left-handed—mirror images of each other.[14]

Amino acids are not ambidextrous. Living cells build only from left-handed amino acids---never right-handed!

"...Amino acids in life, including plants, animals, bacteria, molds, and even viruses, are essentially all left-handed. No known natural process can isolate either the left-handed or the right-handed variety. The mathematical probability that chance processes could produce merely one tiny protein molecule with only left-handed amino acids is virtually zero."[15]

Equally mysterious, amino acids revert to inorganic matter's separation of left-handed/right-handed status at death.

Enzymes, protein forms within the cytoplasm, stand guard as catalysts, expediting the life processes of the cell. "The protein's most widespread role is as a catalyst in biochemical reactions, and in this role it is called an *enzyme*...Each reaction has its own enzyme..." which can "speed up a reaction rate by at least a million...An increase in rate by factors of ten billion to a hundred trillion are not uncommon...A factor of a hundred million means that what takes a thousandth of a second with the enzyme, would take about 3,000 years without it."[16]

Without the lightning-like speeds introduced by enzymes, biochemical reactions would take so long, they could fail to function.

DNA

Tucked into the cell's nucleus are the strands of deoxyribonucleic acid containing the code of life for an organism---DNA for short. This vast compendium of living data is so miniscule, it can't be seen by the naked human eye! "...Each gene is a sequence of DNA about one thousand nucleotides long."[17]

Cells store information in "long chain-like DNA...The capacity of DNA to store information vastly exceeds that of any other known system; it is so efficient that all the information needed to specify an organism as complex as man weighs less than a few thousand millionths of a gram."[18]

These ladder-like spirals are built on side rails with alternating molecules of phosphate and deoxyribose "held together by 'rungs' called nucleotides (or bases) consisting of four specific chemical molecules: thymine (T), adenine (A), cytosine (C) and guanine (G)...Millions upon millions of nucleotides are known to exist in the nuclear DNA structure of living cells..."[19]

Nucleotides A and T bond together to form an AT or a TA base while G and C bond as GC or CG. Neither an A nor a T bonds with a C or a G. Each life kind carries its unique sequence of bases.

"Nucleotides cannot be added at will; even if they did, they could not align themselves in a meaningful sequence....any physical change of any size, shape, or form, is strictly the result of purposeful alignment of billions of nucleotides..."[20]

Ribonucleic acid (RNA) acts as DNA's transfer agent taking the code from the nucleus to the cytoplasm. With a single rail composed of phosphate and ribose molecules and rungs with uracil (U) instead of thymine (T), messenger RNA enters the nucleus at a moment when the DNA unwinds, reads and copies the information then delivers the code to a ribosome protein-producing factory.

"The order of dRNT-s of DNA determines its information content, provided that the rest of the cell's machinery is present." This refers to the "complex apparatus which duplicates DNA, transcribes it to a readable message and then reads the message and produces a functioning protein...Where the information for the appropriate order of dNT-s comes from is usually not discussed, because what is there to say?"[21]

The complexity of a cell's information is compounded by the fact that not all genetic data resides in the cell's nucleus. "...Mitochondria have their own DNA/RNA structure...a semi-independent order-giver in its own right, a computer sub-station so to speak...Human mitochondrial DNA has slightly more than 16 thousand nucleotides."[22]

If this infinitesimal information resource were placed in a teaspoon, together with the DNA "necessary to specify the design" for all the estimated one thousand million species of organisms ever to have lived on the planet, "there would still be room left for all the information in every book ever written."[23]

Bill Gates, pioneer internet entrepreneur, recognizes the limits of cyberspace language compared to the cell's ability to store and utilize living data. "DNA is like a computer program but far more advanced than any software we've ever created."[24]

Multiple protein families provide an array of potential building blocks for specific life kinds. Assembly of living organisms requires the instruction from symbolic blue prints. No protein exists without the DNA molecule that provides and stores that instructional information. Proteins can't exist without DNA and DNA can't live without proteins. They exist simultaneously as a composite whole, mutually interdependent with each other.

Unlike the quandary as to "which came first," the chicken or the egg, the living cell débuted on the scene, hitting the ground running, with all its proteins and DNA information in place and fully functional. There's no room for a multi-million-year time gap for either one to catch up to join with the other! It's an "irreducibly complex" package deal---something like "love and marriage!"

Since "DNA and RNA molecules do not form spontaneously or abiotically in any 'primordial earth' type experiment..."[25] just what could have been the first cell's original information source?

Certainly it didn't drift in from a spontaneous generation fog playing roulette with nature's chemistry set in some warm little pond! Not only did that primitive supposition offer no scientific explanation as to the origin of first life, but also the myth lacked the faintest hint as to the simultaneous appearance of its DNA and RNA!

Leave it to the theater of the absurd to answer with abstract rhetoric. A recent entry in the sweepstakes of the make-believe credits "11 small carbon molecules...that could have played a role in other chemical reactions that led to the development of such biomolecules as amino acids, lipids, sugars, and eventually some kind of genetic molecule such as RNA."[26]

Breathtaking! Shades of medieval alchemy!

Little did those "small carbon molecules" realize the magnitude of the creative authority theoretically vested in their inorganic, atomic composition. Lee Spetner calculates if "...all the copies of the DNA in all the cells of your body were straightened and laid end-to-end they would be about 50 billion kilometers long" and would stretch from the earth to beyond the Solar System.[27]

No serious scholar clings to the obsolete notion that acquired physical characteristics can be transferred genetically. It's universally recognized that "...physical growth is the result of a very specific sequence of hundreds of thousands of nucleotides in its own DNA..." which dictates the order giving sequence that "seeps down to the growth mechanisms. It never acts in the reverse direction..."[28]

"...The DNA molecule may be the one and only perfect solution to the twin problems of information storage and duplication for self-replicating automata...It is astonishing...that this remarkable piece of machinery which possesses the ultimate capacity to construct every living thing that ever existed on Earth, from a giant redwood to the human brain, can construct all its own components in a matter of minutes and weigh less than 10^{-16} grams." This "...is of the order of several thousand million-million times smaller than the smallest piece of functional machinery ever constructed by man."[29]

Molecular Discontinuity

Frank Sinatra once belted out lyrics reassuring romantics that "love and marriage go together like a horse and carriage." The elegant "tension," that fires the mutuality of attraction comes compliments of the human gene machine assigning chromosomes "X" and "Y" to prospective humans. Those electrifying gender differences that inspire poetry and underwrite the entertainment media rest in the intricate workings of DNA codes.

Homo sapiens would disappear abruptly if the gender determining "X-Y" chromosome pair reigned exclusively in a single gender. "It takes two to tango" and for humans to reproduce. "For sexual reproduction a separate male and female set of genes are required. In a standard evolutionary model both male and female genomes would need to evolve side-by-side in order to continue to reproduce."[30]

Imagine the sorry dilemma if only a single gender survived evo's tortuous trek, jumping through millions of hoops and ending up being saddled with multiple genetic mistakes, only to be greeted by a "warm little pond" at the end of the trail rather than finding joyful union with a human mate! As per Sinatra, a carriage without a horse wouldn't offer much of a drive!

Every prototype organic life existing on Planet Earth carries a staggering stash of genetic information, in place from the get-go, guaranteeing a kaleidoscope of diversity in descendant generations. "The difference in DNA between species resides almost strictly in the sequential positioning of the nucleotide...No two individual plants or animals have DNA spirals that are identical..."[31]

Every cell of every living organism carries its distinctive DNA watermark. "Bacterial genomes are very different from eukaryotic genomes in that they usually do not possess 'exons' and 'introns' and do not have extensive scaffolding. Bacteria even lack membrane-bound nuclei, so that their genes can be expressed much more quickly than those of the eukaryotes..."[32]

No way should the genome of a Chimpanzee, or any other life form, be confused with the human genome. Nor is there a whit of molecular evidence, in the unique DNA of any life kind, that an elephant, a monarch butterfly, or a hummingbird could have descended from some common ancestor.

The string of precisely sequenced nucleotides code distinct patterns for the format of each distinctive life. Comparing genomes of different species show vast gaps that defy bridging by reshuffling the card deck and redealing the hand. Without adding new cards with entirely new information---numbers, colors, and suites other than diamonds, hearts, spades, and clubs---combos dealt will be confined to the mix potential of the original cards in the deck.

Take a peak at the human variety potential thanks to DNA loaded with an estimated 3-billion+ nucleotide base pairs. A staggering number of potential genetic results are possible by sharing and shuffling the genes of two *Homo sapiens* parents.

The reservoir of genetic information inherent in each genome explains how the Galapagos finches observed by Darwin produced offspring endowed with different shaped beaks! But this genetic adaptability does not extrapolate to confirm evo fantasies. *No new genetic information has been introduced to the genome;* only the genetic card deck has been shuffled.

Built-in genetic adaptability prevents reptile parents being shocked with a nest-full of finch offspring endowed with the capability of growing feathers and flying away to the refuge of trees!

Genetic mistakes solve nothing. Not only are mutations incapable of introducing new information, typically they impair what's already there! "The genome is fragile, subject to environmental insults (radiation, oxidation etc.) Extensive repair systems are guarding the integrity of the genome second-by-second. Without their work, life would become extinct."[33]

Just as fingerprints disclose patterns unique to an individual, every body cell portrays the DNA sequence of a genome, unlikely to be shared with another human. The master DNA that dictates eye color, sex, and the shape of the face, is usually distinct and one of a kind.

DNA not only revolutionized investigation of life's origin but also emerged as a tool of the court system, shining light on crime detection. When DNA doesn't match crime scene evidence, convictions have been overturned, sometimes years-after-the-fact. DNAPrint Genomics of Sarasota, Florida, pushes the envelope farther, claiming that "...by examining tiny genetic markers on the DNA that tend to be similar in people of certain population groups, it can tell whether a suspect's heritage is European, Sub-Saharan African, Southeast Asian, Native American or a mix of those..."[34]

A Billion Chances to Nowhere

With 20 kinds of amino acids and 500 amino acids in a protein, it's a tall order to deliver 100,000 different proteins to the human body by random chance methodology. Michael Denton dismisses chance in the cell formation process. "It is the sheer universality of perfection, the fact that everywhere we look, to whatever depth we look, we find an elegance and ingenuity of an absolutely transcending quality, which so mitigates against the idea of chance."[35]

"To get a cell by chance would require at least one hundred functional proteins to appear simultaneously in one place. That is one hundred simultaneous events each of an independent probability which could hardly be more than 10^{-20} giving a maximum combined probability of 10^{-2000}." [36]

Based on mathematical probability factors alone, "...any viable DNA strand having over 84 nucleotides cannot be the result of haphazard mutations. At that stage, the probabilities are 1 in 4.80×10^{50}...Mathematicians agree that any requisite number beyond 10^{50} has, statistically, a zero probability of occurrence...Any species known to us, including the smallest single-cell bacteria, have enormously larger numbers of nucleotides than 100 or 1000...This means, that there is no mathematical probability whatever for any known species to have been the product of a random occurrence---random mutations..."[37]

"Zero odds" is not difficult to understand! Freely translated from the jargon of math science, it sounds something like, "never!"

The odds against the 2,000 enzymes essential to the simplest life form appearing spontaneously from inorganic matter, at one time and in one place, reputedly runs at something in the range of $10^{40,000}$ to one.[38] Unlikelihood of such an event is astronomically beyond the 10^{50} mathematically impossible range. Another sizeable, fat zero!

Has "one single functional protein molecule" ever been discovered resulting from random chance processes? Can evolutionism explain the origin of information contained in the cells of first life? Did the microscopic strands of human DNA actually result from mega-trillions of haphazard mutations?

"...Pure unguided random events cannot achieve any sort of interesting, or complex end...The fact remains that nature has not been reduced to the continuum that the Darwinian model demands, nor has the credibility of chance as the creative agent of life been secured."[39]

Embracing evo's seven assumptions defined by Dr. G. A. Kerkut requires a deep dose of faith. A dogma built on ambiguous abstraction lacks logic. Beyond the first assumption that "non-living things gave rise to living material," Kerkut dismantles Darwin's grand scheme of an organic chain, link-by-link, discounting assumptions that "viruses, bacteria, plants and animals are all interrelated...that the Protozoa gave rise to the Metazoa...that various invertebrate phyla are interrelated...that the invertebrates gave rise to the vertebrates...fish gave rise to the amphibia, the amphibia to the reptiles, and the reptiles to the birds and mammals."[40]

"At a molecular level...there is no trace of the evolutionary transition from fish to amphibian to reptile to mammal. So amphibia, always traditionally considered intermediate between fish and the other terrestrial vertebrates, are in molecular terms as far from fish as any group of reptiles or mammals."[41]

More than a mechanical organic machine, the composite human brims with spiritual capacity. Above and beyond the information vested in the cell's DNA, life's experiences are stored in the brain contributing raw data for compilation and review by reason. A cloak of emotional reactions triggering laughter, love, loyalty, and compassion grace the physical package.

While the physical system functions internally in orchestrated synchronization, a human's cohesive whole coordinates powers of reason, communication and creative design. The likes of Leonardo DaVinci, Amadeus Mozart and Albert Einstein were endowed with genetic information that spawned creative genius. A single cell's DNA, stretching far into the heavens if laid end-to-end, had to originate from somewhere other than Darwin's "warm little pond!"

Primitive minds investigating life sciences, studied what they could see—embryos and bones. Striking similarities were erroneously interpreted as relatedness. Embryonic transformation from misunderstood "simple" cells to a fully developed animal encouraged conjecture that comparable transformations of any simple cell could lead eventually to most any complex creature—given spin-the-bottle luck and mega years of evolutionary gestation.

Superstition-tainted perceptions powered the same medieval hot air that floated spontaneous generation fallacy. Darwinists looked in the wrong direction—toward fully developed life forms and their fossils. The world might have been spared specious speculations had molecular biology emerged as a nineteenth-century science.

Evo's assumptions persist as just that. Nothing more. Giant leaps from molecule-to-man never happened!

Make no mistake!

The origin of first life or the source of the living cell's information forever baffles evo theory! However lofty the credentials, the nothingness answer doesn't cut it!

Technical tools enable science to look to the infinite in either direction.

The electron microscope delivers a glimpse of infinitesimal threads of DNA, exposing the data driving a cell's machinery, more complex than any human designed mechanism while the Hubble telescope scans the heavens unrolling a glimpse of the "Pillars of Creation," set in a panoply of endless space.

Michael Denton confirms the inability of chance to produce change necessary to close the massive gaps existing at the molecular level. "No evolutionary biologist has ever produced any quantitative proof that the designs of nature are in fact within the reach of chance...It is surely a little premature to claim that random processes could have assembled mosquitoes and elephants when we still have to determine the actual probability of the discovery by chance of one single functional protein molecule."[42]

The nagging question continues: *just where did the information, pre-loaded into the cell's DNA, come from and how did it get there?*

The inquiry itself humbles. Unless afflicted with myopic blinders, objectivity directs the intellect to a "design inference." Early this century, more than 500 scientists signed-on to a declaration questioning the viability of evo's conventional dogma. "We are skeptical of claims for the ability of random mutation and natural selection to account for the complexity of life. Careful examination of the evidence for Darwinian theory should be encouraged."[43]

Intelligent, finite minds, capable of creating computers, have never successfully designed and built a living cell from inorganic matter, much less shaped a strand of its information-packed DNA. Just where, then, does that leave a postulate that inanimate atoms might have conjured up information from nothingness to accomplish what is beyond the competence of human thought?

5

Synthetic "Science"
Genetic Mistakes

"Whoever thinks macroevolution can be made by mutations
that lose information is like the merchant who lost a little money on every sale
but thought he could make it up on volume."
Lee Spetner[1]

Prior to sophisticated technology, research could be vulnerable to superstition, tradition and personal bias. Not only did the 1859 era scientists lack access to electron microscopes, laboratories did not bask under the warm glow of electric light bulbs. Language filtered through the stentorian tones of an elegant English accent helped bridge yawning gaps between supposition and fact.

Primitive investigative naturalists lacked the first clue about complex life codes vested in a cell's DNA. They studied what they could see—embryos and bones. Striking similarities were erroneously interpreted as relatedness. Embryonic transformation from misunderstood simple cells to a fully developed animal encouraged conjecture that comparable transformations of any simple cell could lead eventually to most any complex creature with mathematically impossible luck and heavy doses of deep time.

Theories of origin came burdened with the same medieval hot air that floated spontaneous generation fallacy. Darwinists looked in the wrong direction—toward fully developed life forms and their fossils. Conceivably the world could have been spared specious speculations had molecular biology been a nineteenth-century science.

When Darwin opted for life by random chance accident rather than by design, his primitive perception of the living cell smacked of the mystical. He lacked the faintest perception of the cell's complexity much less its DNA language of life. In his quest to validate the evolutionary process he sought a mechanism that would pass along acquired physical traits to descendant generations.

In trying to explain the unexplainable, he latched on to what he described as "gemmules," a make-believe magical potion he credited with the task of carrying acquired physical traits from somatic cells to germ cells. Bit-by-bit, these accumulating changes underwrote evolution, or so the theory supposed. Forget for a moment that gemmules didn't exist except in imagination.

The hopeful guru seized upon the towering neck of the giraffe, a top ten attraction at zoos, as prime evidence of the pangenesis process. Fairy tale logic manufactured uncorroborated fiction. When persistent droughts dried the fields of grass grazed by the giraffe's less elongated ancestor, survival hinged on stretching its neck to nibble tree leaves. The animal's bone and muscle structure managed to preserve each stretch of the neck and forward each miniscule change to the next generation, thanks to gemmules. These incremental adaptations supposedly resulted in the long-necked giraffe that populates animal parks---a hopelessly bogus idea.

Pangenesis' naive suggestion that acquired physical traits could be passed to another generation, eventually bit the proverbial dust. Scenarios of giraffe's neck-stretching exercises, perpetuating elongated necks to the next generation via gemmules, proved untenable. The myth suffered from at least two major-league flaws. Why didn't other animals that grazed the same African landscape, like the zebra, evolve similar long necks? And of course, the fact that gemmules don't exist demolished the idea.

If the idea were valid, a muscle builder like Arnold Swartznegger could pass along a set of magnificent muscles to his children.

Gregor Mendel's Garden

The legacies of two European contemporaries of the mid-nineteenth century launched ripples impacting origin science that resonate today. Gregor Mendel (1822-1884), an obscure Czech monk and Darwin contemporary, discovered genetic principles in the quietude of a monastery garden while Englishman Charles Robert Darwin postulated relentless change in life forms driven by natural selection picking from a smorgasbord of modified traits acquired by random chance.

Mendel's experiment revolutionized knowledge of the mechanism of inheritance. He bred several generations of peas focusing on seven of its basic characteristics. What he discovered about hybrids clashed head-on with Darwinian theory.

Mendel published his findings in the *Journal of the Brünn Society for the Study of Natural Science* in 1865---six years after Darwin published *Origin*. This *Journal* edition was distributed to 120 libraries including some in England and eleven in the United States. His work, either ignored or overlooked, was referenced in the *Encyclopedia Britannica's* 1892 edition.[2]

When the twentieth century dawned, the stage was set for a direct assault on a core component of the Darwinian notion that had fascinated late nineteenth century academia.

The landmark findings of Gregor Mendel, dormant and virtually unnoticed since his 1866 presentation to the Natural History Society of Brunn, Austria, were translated and published in English in 1900. Driving force pushing the release was an admirer of Mendel's scholarship: 39-year-old British biologist, William Bateson (1861-1926), founder of the science of genetics, and eventual president of the British Association for the Advancement of Science.

The publication of these simple garden experiments rocked intellectual circles with the fury of a bombshell blast. There is speculation as to whether Darwin's theory of evolution would have "evolved" and seen the light of day had he studied Mendel's findings. Bateson, a biologist, expressed doubts. "...Darwin would never have written the *Origin of Species* if he had known Mendel's work."[3]

Maybe "yes," maybe "no," but we'll never know!

What we do know is that contemporary knowledge about the cell and its DNA correlates with Mendel's law of heredity and does little to corroborate Darwin's theory. Darwin's collaborator and co-evolutionist, Alfred Russel Wallace, viewed Mendel's findings as a threat to evolutionism. "On the general relation of Mendelism to evolution, I have come to a very definite conclusion. That is, that it is really antagonistic to evolution."[4]

Eventually Mendel's pioneer research anchored the science of genetics confirming life forms function through precisely expressed genetic information with predictable results. Mendel's law of genetic inheritance blows the cover off empty rhetoric embellishing make-believe and opened doors to discoveries of genes, chromosomes, and DNA—the master genetic templates that determine and distinguish life prototypes. "Cell biologists identified chromosomes as the carriers of Mendel's heredity factors, and in 1909 Wilhelm Johanssen named them 'genes.'"[5]

Since Darwin lacked knowledge of genes, he went looking for corroboration of his theory in all the wrong places. He relied on the visible for support! His belief that acquired physical traits could be passed on to offspring proved to be gross error. His hope that evidence from fossil fields would reveal a chain of organic life, continuous from simple to complex, fell apart, shattered on the rocks.

Knowledge as to ancestry and origins lay obscured in data invisible to the naked eye. In time, investigation of molecular biology opened doors to evidence beyond the reach of nineteenth century science.

Genetic "Abnormalities"

What Mendel did with garden peas, Hugo deVries tried with the primrose. He reported flowers rising "...suddenly, spontaneously, by steps, by jumps. They jumped out among the offspring." He observed the Intra-Genomic Adaptability of the primrose. He described variables as "new species" which he designated "mutations." Eventually, "mutations" joined evolutionism's lexicon attempting to explain changes in nature.[6]

In 1908, Alfred Russel Wallace not only dismissed Mendel's discovery but also discounted mutations as minimally significant. "As playing any essential part in the scheme of organic development, the phenomena seem to me to be of the very slightest importance. They arise out of what are essentially abnormalities, whether called varieties, 'mutations,' or sports.''

Wallace saw "...their extinction under natural conditions more certain and more rapid, thus preventing the injurious effects that might result from their competing with the normal form while undergoing slow adaptive modification...Any species which gave birth to a large number of such abnormal and unchange-able individuals would be so hampered by them whenever adaptive modification became necessary that the whole species might be in danger of extinction." He scorned these "abnormalities" as "refuse material of nature's workshop, as proved by the fact that none of them ever maintain themselves in a state of nature."[7]

His analysis of these genetic "abnormalities" as "refuse material" rings true a century after the fact! Inadvertently, and apparently unforeseen by Wallace, his negative appraisals of mutations run counter to subsequently postulated neo-Darwinism: the *Modern Synthetic Theory of Evolution*!

Wallace was not the only man of influence reluctant to jump for joy when confronted with Mendel's law of genetic inheritance. The news shook the faith of other evolutionists candid enough to express doubt.

Princeton's Prof. Scott complained the findings "...rendered but little assistance in making the evolution process more intelligent, but instead of removing difficulties have rather increased them."[8]

The Chair of Evolution for the University of Paris, aired his concerns to a 1916 Harvard audience. "It comes to pass that some biologists of the greatest authority in the study of Mendelian principles of heredity are led to the expression of ideas which would almost take us back to creationism...The data of Mendelism embarrasses us quite considerably."[9]

The year of the 1925 Scopes Trial, an English Zoology Professor, E.W. McBride, reminisced for the *Science Progress* of January, 1925. His words betrayed a touch of nostalgia laced with keen disappointment. He recognized Mendel's law as something of a wet blanket cast over evolution theory after first being greeted with "enthusiasm." His frustration echoes. "We thought at last the key to evolution had been discovered. But as our knowledge of the facts grew, the difficulty of using Mendelian phenomena to explain evolution became apparent, and this early hope sickened and died. The way that Mendel pointed seemed to lead into a cul-de-sac."[10]

Pangenesis, burdened with the flawed idea that acquired physical traits could be passed to another generation, ultimately qualified as pure poppycock. The dismal surmise broke down completely under the scrutiny of Gregor Mendel's irrefutable findings. Natural selection was left stranded high and dry, without anything viable to select.

Given the shaken faith of the devout, the stage beckoned for solid evidence reconfirming evolutionism.

By the mid-1930s, serious evolutionists recognized the Pangenesis myth as anything but the magic elixir that could team-up with natural selection to propel transitions of one life kind to a new and different body plan. Confronted with the absurdity of entrapment by a primitive superstition, the time arrived to review, retrench and revise. And not a moment too soon---a crescendo of doubting voices could be heard reacting negatively to evo's eroding credibility.

Albert Fleischman delivered a blunt assessment in 1933.

"[T]he theory suffers from grave defects, which are becoming more and more apparent as time advances. It can no longer square with practical scientific knowledge, nor does it suffice for our theoretical grasp of the facts...No one can demonstrate that the limits of a species have ever been passed. These are the Rubicons which evolutionists cannot cross. Darwin ransacked other spheres of practical research work for ideas...but his whole resulting scheme remains, to this day, foreign to scientifically established zoology, since actual changes of species by such means are still unknown."[11]

Theodosius Dobzhansky floated a theoretical life preserver in 1937 postulating that "mutations and chromosomal changes... constantly and unremittingly supply the raw materials for evolution."[12] Dobzhansky's idea attracted attention despite its direct contradiction of Wallace's 1908 dismissal of mutations as "abnormalities" composed of the "refuse material of nature's workshop."

Synthetic "Science"

In 1941, evolutionists such as Julian Huxley and George Gaylord Simpson, put their heads together in an effort to salvage Darwinian thought without dumping the baby with the bathwater. Evolutionism's movers and shakers grasped Dobzhansky's straw in the wind, discarding the gemmule embarrassment and replacing the void with mutations, a new patch on a threadbare cape.

Looking to mutations as the "raw materials for evolution" seems as fanciful as envisioning the equivalent of a thundering Niagara Falls spraying its mist in a Mojave Desert mirage. But any port in a storm! Overlooking the information shortfall while fleeing the discredited gemmule pathway to nowhere, evolutionists seized upon the notion of gene mutations providing the "raw material" for natural selection to do its thing.

Embracing mutations, neo-Darwinism tried reinventing itself by blazing a trail through the shifting sands of genetic mistakes. Those dedicated to life's origin without input from intelligence, massaged Darwin's dogma by awarding it a grand title: *Modern Synthetic Theory of Evolution*, or neo-Darwinism for short. Hugo deVries didn't live long enough to realize his aptly-named "mutations" surfaced in time to temporarily resuscitate a theory struggling to extricate itself from the choking limitations of prebiotic slime!

Darwinists, symbolically walking in "tall cotton," met in Chicago in 1959 to celebrate the centennial anniversary of the publication of *The Origin of Species*.

Sir Julian Huxley, grandson of the 19th century Huxley that ran interference for Darwin, waxed eloquent. According to Sir Julian, "Darwin's theory...is no longer a theory but a fact...We are no longer having to bother about establishing the fact of evolution..." He ruled out "either need or room for the supernatural..."[13]

Huxley's whistling-in-the dark mentality might better have been an obituary for a fragile, obsolete idea confronting its death throes. Despite Huxley's chest thumping, evolutionism's delicate threads had begun to unravel, reminiscent of Darwin's own words signaling unease. The envisioned partnership linking mutations to natural selection could not salvage a bankrupt theory. Yawning, genetic chasms separating distinct kinds of organic formats have never been bridged by the combo---even in a bazillion years.

Neo-Darwinism designates natural selection as a critical component of its theory. But natural selection can't do its thing without an existing life form presenting something from which to select. The synthetic theory offers no help! It fails to explain both the origin of first ever life as well as the source of its stash of DNA information that controls its functions.

Even after neo-Darwinism attempted to patch up glaring "holes" and "flaws" in the theory, vigorous dissent rumbled. "The Darwinian theory of descent has not a single fact to confirm it in the realm of nature. It is not the result of scientific research, but purely the product of imagination."[14] "...Let it be stated in no uncertain terms that there is no evidence that evolution ever has occurred or ever can occur across the kinds."[15] "No matter how numerous they may be, mutations do not produce any kind of evolution....There is no law against day dreaming, but science must not indulge in it."[16]

Despite redundant clichés citing changes in finch beaks, fruit flies, and bacteria as proof of evolutionism, the variations confirm only the adaptation potential within preexisting genetic information.

Intra-genomic adaptability (IGA) does not equate neo-Darwinism! There is not a scintilla of evidence that any mutation or series of mutations have joined with natural selection to activate random chance mandates. Insurmountable hurdles block the route.

Bacteria replicate prodigiously as bacteria...ad infinitum. No change blazes an upward genetic trail to some other new and entire different life-kind or "class." Mutations never provide the new information to a genetic code enabling a "bear" to "evolve into something as monstrous as a whale."

Mutations are overwhelmingly deleterious, typically handicapping the genome by inducing a corruption or a loss of genetic information that weakens the organism. Fruit flies remain fruit-flies after thousands of mutated generations (albeit possibly crippled and deformed). Accumulated mutations typically degrade overall fitness leading to possible extinction, reminiscent of Russel Wallace's 1908 analysis. Even in the rare case of an arguably "good" mutation, new information is not added to the genetic code.

Mutations themselves are subject to an organism's self-correcting mechanism, thanks to repair enzymes. If the repair system itself mutates, the organism's survival could be jeopardized. Mutations are much too slow to accomplish their evo conjectured mission.

A diminished gene pool assures decline in diversity—never a leap linking one life form to an entirely new and different prototype. Changes wrought by mutations paired with natural selection may shift a descendant organism down or laterally within the basic genome but never a vertical change up the down staircase to a different *class* or *order* with a distinctly new kind of body plan.

The late Dr. Henry M. Morris, visionary scientist investigating origins from the creationist perspective, tackled the issue head-on. "Mutations take place, but they are either reversible, deteriorative, or neutral...Natural selection takes place, but this is a conservative phenomenon, which weeds out defective mutants and keeps the population stable. Adaptations take place, but these are horizontal changes which conserve the species against extinction, but do not produce new species."[17]

"...If one must depend on mutation and natural selection to produce new species---let alone, new families, orders and phyla as evolutionists assume, then not even billions of years would suffice."[18]

The mutation silver bullet, intended to salvage evolutionism, more aptly resembles an executioner's shot aimed at its heart.

Natural Selection

Natural selection is real!   But don't hold your breath expecting evolutionary change if the "selection" relies on mutations. Natural selection works counter to the other half of evo's equation by normally screening out harmful mutations.

"Natural selection can serve only to 'weed out' those mutations that are harmful, at best preserving the 'status quo.'"[19] It "...can act only on those biologic properties that already exist..."[20] "No one has ever produced a species by mechanisms of natural selection."[21] "...The Darwinian theory of natural selection, whether or not coupled with Mendelism, is false."[22]

The law of gravity stands secure as an irrefutable landmark in the science of physics. No less a fact of biology, is Mendel's law of genetic inheritance. No debate here.

But evolutionism is as far from absolute fact as the fabled Wizard of Oz. Evolutionists Wallace, Scott and McBride recognized Mendel's law not only didn't track with the theory of evolution but also threw a monkey-wrench into its mechanism.

Genetic Wrong Numbers

Punching a single digit error on a telephone keypad misdirects the connection. If you want New York area code 212 and mistakenly touch 213 you will reach California. A 202 connects nowhere to nothingness. As with any cell phone, the gene machine demands precision. Mutations are genetic mistakes that access wrong numbers!

Genetic information appears vulnerable to assault from radiation and chemical reactions. Some point to virus parasites as ultimate villains that invade cells and wreak havoc on nuclei.

"When a virus penetrates a cell, it disappears inside the nucleus for four to eight hours, giving the outward appearance of complete normalcy. Then the viral particles that the cell has been coerced into making suddenly burst forth, shattering the host."[23]

While some argue "...that viruses were involved very early on in the evolutionary emergence of life,"[24] the contrary view questions just how such insidious, disease-causing critters could contribute anything other than genetic flaws. DNA mistakes degrade the genome. They bring no helpful new information to the party, only a corruption or reshuffling of the old. Genetic errors, duplications, translocations, and deletions in the genetic machinery can trigger debilitation and susceptibility to disease.

This reality deserves billboard attention: if mutations provide the "raw materials" from which natural selection is to "select," neo-Darwinism faces bleak times! "Major functional disorders in humans, animals and plants are caused by the loss or displacement of a single DNA molecule, or even a single nucleotide within that molecule..."[25]

Crippling mutations respect no person!

A once monster of a man, now twisted and bent almost in half, totters feebly, aided by a walker. Parkinson's disease, the insidious scourge, laid low the robust physique of the former football star. A mutated gene stands accused as the culprit![26]

Mutations unload a bleak litany of physical flaws and debilitating diseases on the genome! Mutations have plagued humans with a list of 4,500 already identified bad results (other estimates range to 13,500)—and still counting. Harmful gene mutations discovered in 1996 alone, cast a pall.

The roster disconcerts!

Progressive myoclonus epilepsy is caused by a gene mutation on chromosome 21. Treacher Callins Syndrome, hemochromatosis, is linked to a defective gene on chromosome 6. A gene mutation on chromosome 5 generates deformities of the face, ears, down-slanting eyes, and deafness. Progressive blindness described as retinitis pigmentosa is a disorder linked to a gene from the X chromosome. A chromosome 9 gene mutation causes skin cancer. A mutated gene on chromosome 16 is tied to fanconi anemia, affecting children who rarely live past their sixteenth birthday. A gene missing from chromosome 7 causes Williams Syndrome. Anhidrotic ectodermal dysplasia, resulting from a mutation on the X chromosome, can afflict victims with baldness, loss of teeth, or deprive them of ability to sweat.[27]

"...Not one mutation that increased the efficiency of a genetically coded human protein has been found. Instead of a 'blind watchmaker,' the mutations behave like a 'blind gunman,' a destroyer who shoots his deadly 'bullets' randomly into beautifully designed models of living molecular machinery. Sometimes the 'bullets' only cause minor damage; sometimes they maim and cripple; sometimes they kill."[28]

There are "genetic flaws that make people fat..."[29] Werner's syndrome results from a mutated site on human chromosome 8 that causes victims to "age prematurely fast and usually die before they reach 50."[30] "Best's macular dystrophy...destroys the part of the retina responsible for the sharpest vision 'has been linked to mutations' in the gene now called bestrophin."[31] Since 1990, "discoveries of heart-handicapping mutations have been pouring out of numerous labs at an ever-increasing rate, yielding more than 100 mutations in more than a dozen genes."[32]

Another genetic mutation "...causes children to die of old age...Children with Hutchinson-Gilford progeria syndrome age at a rate five to 10 times faster than normal. They lose their hair, their skin wrinkles, and they die of arteriosclerosis, or hardening of the arteries, by their early teens." The defect is in "...a gene that controls the structure of the nucleus..."[33]

"A genetic polymorphism called 11307K in either of...two APC genes doubles the risk of colon cancer."[34] Spontaneous blood clots can form with the power to cause sudden death where a "patient with the disorder has inherited at least one defective gene encoding protein C."[35] A mutated gene on chromosome 11 contributes to inherited hearing impairment.[36]

Then there's the unappetizing smorgasbord of birth defects caused by mutated genes: muscular dystrophy, spinabifida, cystic fibrosis, Huntington's Disease, hermachromatosis, and Down's Syndrome. Leukemia may result when a piece of chromosome translocates to another chromosome in the midst of cell division.

Regarding humans, researchers "calculated an unusually high rate of 4.2 mutations per generation, of which 1.6 diminish the fitness of the species...the species must survive in part because people who have accumulated dangerous mutations are least likely to successfully have children...the human reproductive strategy helps purge harmful mutations in batches...they mix their genes with another's, and presumably some of the worst defects aren't passed along. That wouldn't happen if humans reproduced asexually."[37]

Fat Chance Odds

"Genetic variation depends on the process of mutation, and mutations are rare events. Any particular new DNA mutation will occur only once in about 100 million gametes. Moreover, when a single mutation occurs in a single newborn, even if it is a favorable mutation, there is a fair probability that it will not be presented in the next generation because its single carrier may not, by chance, pass it on to its few offspring."[38]

Change in a single nucleotide would be the smallest possible modification of a genome. One of neo-Darwinism's architects guesstimated that as few as 500 mutations could evolve a new species. Mathematical odds challenge the possibility.

"...It's a matter of chance that a mutant survives. It might spread through the population and take it over, but more likely it will just vanish...even good mutations are likely to disappear from the population" if it occurs just once. "The chance of 500 of these steps succeeding is 1/300,000 multiplied by itself 500 times. The odds against that happening are about $3.6 \times 10^{2,738}$ to one, or the chance of it happening is about $2.7 \times 10^{-2,739}$...It's more than 2,000 orders of magnitude smaller than...*impossible*."[39]

Impossible trumps improbable---and wishful thinking.

Computations of the likelihood for any single event beyond 10^{50} chances qualifies as impossible unless absolutism is willing to concede the intrusion of a miracle. No matter how many billions of chances and multi-millions of years allocated, the chance of those 500 "beneficial" mutation steps succeeding continues *impossible* ad infinitum. Even an artfully loaded pair of standard dice will never roll a number higher than 12 no matter how many tosses.

Neo-Darwinism's reliance on beneficial mutations conjured up by blind chance as natural selection's raw material doesn't compute. Mathematic impossibility renders an already implausible theory extinct. Nothing remains but a Kerkut style assumption, lacking legs, heart or brains much less rational intellectual life.

As to the tired cliché that mutations benefit bacteria by building immunity to antibiotics such as streptomycin, reality indicates "the mutation reduces the specificity of the ribosome protein, and that means losing genetic information" with "a loss of sensitivity." Despite some "selective value," this mutation "decreases rather than increases genetic information."[40]

"...Antibiotic resistance is the result of loss of a protein, loss of the binding capacity of a protein, or the loss of a transporting system...It's a loss of something...If you're removing a transport protein to eliminate the bacteria's sensitivity to antibiotics, then how is that explaining common descent by modification...?"[41]

"There aren't any known, clear, examples of a mutation that has added information." Instead, mutations lead "to a loss of sensitivity to the drug...the effect is heritable, and a whole strain of resistant bacteria can arise from the mutation...A change in one of its proteins is then likely to degrade the organism...Information cannot be built up by mutations that lose it."[42]

"For information to build up in living organisms, it must be created somewhere...Although in some special cases a loss of information can lead to an advantage for the organism, the large-scale evolution for which the NDT [neo-Darwinian Theory] is supposed to account cannot be based on such mutations."[43]

As to the neck of an 18-foot-tall giraffe with a heart 2 ½ feet long, mutations contribute nothing more to the explanation of its origin than do fictitious gemmules. The heart powerful enough to pump blood up the extended neck to the brain is also powerful enough "to burst the blood vessels of its brain" when it reaches down for a drink of water. But when the giraffe bends down, "a protective mechanism" kicks in causing "valves in the arteries in its neck" to begin to close.[44]

"...Most mutations which cause changes in the amino acid sequence of proteins tend to damage function to a greater or lesser degree…most of the amino acids in the centre of the protein cannot be changed without having drastic deleterious effects on the stability and function of the molecule."[45]

"There's no mutation that gives them [evolutionists] what is necessary for common descent with modifications. There are all kinds of mutations that eliminate proteins. They may eliminate transport protein, an enzyme, the action of an enzyme, or regulatory systems." Mutations are "…not making new transport proteins! They're not making new regulatory systems! Antibiotic resistance is an example…Every time you read about antibiotic resistance…they're going to talk about this as…an absolute example of evolution." One of Darwin's false assumptions "…was that natural selection had a building or creating capacity, and it doesn't…" It removes information.[46]

"…Every molecular example of a mutation we currently have fails to provide a mechanism that can account for the origin of any genetic activity or function."[47] Dr. David Berlinski, innovative thinker and critically dismissive of Darwinian hypothesis, tells it as it is: "The idea that mutations are considered the engine of evolution has only one problem, there's no evidence to support it…absolutely no evidence."[48]

As to natural selection, it functions but it doesn't power evolution.

Marcel Schutzenberger sees odds of 10^{-1000} "against improving meaningful information by random changes…Astronomers Fred Hoyle and Chandra Wickramasinghe placed the probability that life would originate from non-life as $10^{-40,000}$ and the probability of added complexity arising by mutations and natural selection very near this figure."[49]

Limits to Change

Mutations simply can't breach genomic barriers to change.

Microbiologist Michael Denton says it loud and clear. "… The degree of change that can be experimentally induced in a wide variety of organisms, from bacteria to mammals, even under the most intensive selection pressures, is always limited by a distinct barrier beyond which further change is impossible."[50]

Wheat, corn, chickens, strawberries, and dogs can be bred to size, shape, and color by shuffling the gene cards. But genetic information defines limits to change unless something like gene splicing (guided by intelligence) introduces new information into the genome. Even then, modified products continue as selected strains of wheat, corn, chickens, strawberries, and dogs.

Luther Burbank made the case for limitations alluding to what he defined as *Reversion to the Average*. "...I can develop a plum half an inch long or one 2½ inches long, with every possible length in between, but I am willing to admit that it is hopeless to try to get a plum the size of a small pea, or one as big as a grapefruit...there are limits to the development possible, and these limits follow a law."[51]

Plant breeders have been able to increase sugar content in sugar beets from 6% to 17%.[52] Apple growers managed to convert the Hawkeye, "a round, blushed yellow apple of surpassing sweetness," discovered in 1880 in a Madison County, Iowa orchard, into Washington's once immensely popular Red Delicious, with unique points at its base. "Breeders and nurseries patented and propagated the most rubied mutations" altering the color, shape, flavor, skin and juiciness.[53] The Iowa "Hawkeye" apple bred to become the Washington "Red Delicious" still occupies apple counter space in the local grocery store.

Crowds of thousands, seated on the grass just west of the U.S.A.'s Capitol steps, respond with goose bumps and cheers to the National Symphony's rendition of John Phillip Sousa's *Stars and Stripes Forever*. "The Three Irish Tenors" inspire standing ovations at the nearby MCI Center while rhythmic beats created on the Kennedy Center stage cover the waterfront of melody. All these tunes and arrangements share the identical octave of musical notes! The piano keyboard's five black keys offer intermediate sounds inviting creative innovation.

Different sequences of half-notes, quarter notes, or wholes laced with syncopated beats; the pace of the rhythm generating a march or the swing of a waltz; and arrangements featuring an artsy mix of instruments---thousands of melodies all built within the limits of music's octave scale.

A living genome provides analogous potential for variety!

Sharing similar genes does not equate genetic links nor prove common ancestry any more than different songs, derived from the same octave of sounds, establish musical relationship. The genetic mix, sequences, and formulas vary radically, just as songs fashioned from the same sound options, produce radically different musical compositions!

Then there is the atom, invisible to the naked eye, with its positively charged nucleus encircled by an array of electrons---the smallest unit of any element charted in the classic periodic table displayed in High School classrooms. Inorganic matter is so reliably constant in its identifiable properties that elements can be combined pursuant to chemical recipes producing results readily replicated.

From the microscopic minutiae to the cosmic; from the inorganic to the living; natural world science exemplifies precision!!!! The glaring exception to this universal commonality of science order and the mathematically real is evolutionism's mutant "science" where the logic of the measurable equation is thrown to the winds in favor of assumptive myth.

Evolutionism ignores the real and postulates the unreal. Empty rhetoric poses as substance once all hype, bells, and whistles are removed. Slick diagrams, catchy slogans and colorful imagination can't substitute for scientific respectability. Against impossible odds, evolutionism attracts minds to the obscenity that some ancient, ancestor fish accidentally spawned all humanity.

Truth stands tall in three dimensions; it needs no defense. Falsehood collapses on its own petard, melting to abstract nothingness under the scrutiny of the sunlight of day. "Evolutionism is a fairy tale for grown-ups. This theory has helped nothing in the progress of science. It is useless." [54]

The late Stephen J. Gould, a devout evolutionist, undercut the core essence of neo-Darwinism with cold-eyed logic. "You don't make new species by mutating the species...A mutation is not the cause of evolutionary change." [55]

So where does that leave neo-Darwinism's iconic lynchpin?

6

Evo Skips a Beat...or Two
Fossils AWOL

*"All species are separated from each other by bridgeless gaps;
intermediates between species are not observed."*
Ernst Mayr[1]

Charles Darwin fretted, "Why do we not find beneath this system great piles of strata stored with the remains of the progenitors of the Cambrian fossils?"

One likely answer: "They don't exist!"

While outlining the core of his theory, Darwin predicted, "...not one living species will transmit its unaltered likeness to a distant futurity."[2] He envisioned a protracted process in which "...natural selection acts only by taking advantage of slight successive variations" never taking "a great and sudden leap, but ...by short and sure, though slow, steps."[3]

The naturalist devised a "finely graduated organic chain," leading from the first ever living cell to humans while carefully skirting "...the far higher problem of the essence or origin of life..."[4]

Side-stepping this "far higher problem," he envisioned a trail of alleged continuity, suggesting "...all the higher mammals are probably derived from an ancient marsupial, and this through a long line of diversified forms, either from some reptile-like or some amphibian-like creature, and this again from some fish-like animal."[5]

He crafted a sequence of theoretical links spawning the molecule-to-man chain in a series of generalized words and phrases. "Progenitor...hermaphrodite;" "Fish-like...animal;" "Aquatic animal;" "Amphibian-like creature;" "Reptile-like;" "Covered with hair both sexes having beards...ears pointed...tail;" "Higher mammals;" "Old World division of the Simiadæ;" and "Man."

Loaded with a dreamer's optimism, Darwin put the credibility of his tree of life conjecture on the line imposing a contingency test. "...If my theory be true, numberless intermediate varieties, linking closely together all the species of the same group, must assuredly have existed..."[6]

Astutely he sensed the ingredients that could shatter his dream. "If it could be demonstrated that any complex organ existed which could not possibly have been formed by numerous, successive, slight modification, my theory would absolutely break down."[7]

Aware of lurking threats to his idea, the naturalist bemoaned the glaring gap between theory and evidence. "...Geological research...does not yield the infinitely many fine gradations between past and present species required on the theory..."[8] Noting the lack of "...any such finely-graduated organic chain..." he admitted "...this, perhaps, is the most obvious and serious objection which can be urged against the theory." [9]

Resigned to this Achilles heel, and ever the theorist, he brushed off the "serious objection," ascribing the missing branches in his fossil tree of life to the "...extreme imperfection of the geological record..."[10] He sought time as his ally, counting future discoveries to turn up evidence confirming his dream.

But more than a century of discoveries have proved stingy!

Bones of extinct species proliferate! Even arguably intermediate fossils prove scarce.   Never mind that similarly shaped bone fragments exist. But dead bones don't necessarily confirm genetic relationship. Look-alike fossil bone shards from extinct life forms, don't, by themselves, demonstrate transition linkage. Quite the contrary, the fossil record overflows with a fascinating mix of ancient life forms displaying remarkable resemblance to hardy descendants living today!

Not only do fossils fail to exonerate evolutionism's working hypothesis but molecular biology, a relative new player in the pantheon of science technology, has emerged preeminent in the study of life's origin. Rather than uncovering evidence ratifying neo-Darwinism, revelations of the "simple" cell's undreamed of complexity further unravel the texture of its threadbare mantle.

Evo's believability base continues shrinking, trapped in a scientific no-man's land between the dual pressures of virtually no support from fossil transitionals on the one side and molecular biology's revelatory discoveries on the other. Far from confirming "...virtually all of Darwin's postulates..." subsequent discoveries often intensify doubts.

Most every link in Darwin's elaborate, "finely graduated" fossil chain continues missing in action. An organic chain of intermediates linking single celled life-to-complex non-vertebrates; to fish; to amphibians; to reptiles; to birds; with major mammals after dinosaurs until ultimately, mammals-to-man, exists only in the fog of poetic fantasy.

"Break Down" Time

The theory confronted the "break down" Darwin feared! Recent discoveries exacerbate the evidentiary shortfall!

Conventional tradition postulates that some shrew-like critter was the only mammal that coexisted with dinosaurs before dinos went extinct 65 million years before the present (BP). "Now the discovery of a furry aquatic creature with seal-like teeth and a flat tail like a beaver has demolished that image. Some 164 million years ago [conventional time measurement], the newly discovered mammal was swimming in lakes in what is now northern China, eating fish and living with dinosaurs."[11]

What's a fully-functional beaver-like mammal, complete with fur, doing sharing space with dinos for 100 million-years? The appearance of this pesky critter seems to toss another dose of sand in the gears of Darwin's simulated sequential transitions!

Evolutionism's expectations are also impaired by the presence of fully-formed fossils conjectured to be dated more than 500 million years BP. Strata reveal a wide range of complex life forms that appear abruptly without evidence of prior ancestry. Multi-celled animal embryos, no bigger than a grain of sand, have been discovered in China, preserved in calcium phosphate and dated at the edge of the Cambrian/Precambrian time frame—marking the prolific explosion of organic life during which "virtually all the major animal body plans seen on Earth today blossomed in a sudden riotous evolutionary springtime."[12]

Cambrian life seemed to jump out in a "sudden leap," worldwide and fully-formed! At least 7,640 complex animal species saturate the known fossil record of the Cambrian without a trace of prior ancestors.[13] It should come as no surprise that the "almost abrupt appearance of the major animal groups," representing as many as 50 phyla, ranks as "...one of the most difficult problems in evolutionary paleontology..."[14] It does nothing to enhance the "gradualism" hypothesis.

Could Cambrian species themselves have been intermediate varieties leading to radically different future prototypes? Far from supporting any thought of descending from a chain of organic intermediates, the Pre-Cambrian fossil record offers a "paleontological desert," virtually barren of identifiable fossil ancestors. Only bits and pieces of animal-like Ediacaran fauna have been discovered.

Multi-celled organisms of Cambrian times cover the waterfront as to invertebrate animal phyla, both living and extinct. Arthropods, mollusks, and echinoderms—there they are, without a fossil clue as to prior "numerous, successive, slight modifications."

"Most orders, classes, and phyla appear abruptly, and commonly have already acquired all the characters that distinguish them."[15] "For all of the animal phyla to appear in one single, short burst of diversification is not an obviously predicable outcome of evolution."[16]

Fully-formed, complex life proliferates from the beginning. A virtual blank screen! Intermediates continue AWOL, with no reliable evidence confirming an organic chain of ancestral links!

Using Darwin's own yardstick, his theory collapses when measured at the moment of complex life's earliest recognized threshold. The missing evidence, vital to Darwinian expectations, spells theory "break down."

Stasis

Since Pre-Cambrian and Cambrian Period strata don't support Darwinian expectations, is the post-Cambrian landscape saturated with endorsing evidence?

Not really! Instead, think more blank screen!

The fossil record bulges with evidence of "stasis" while fossil chains demonstrating organic continuity bridging across-the-board, molecule-to-man transitions remain virtually invisible.

The naturalist conjectured chunks of deep time made anything possible---even exaggerated leaps over vast chasms of biological diversity. Darwin predicted that given enough time, every parent species would be wiped out by superior descendants. "...We may safely infer that not one living species will transmit its unaltered likeness to a distant futurity...The production of new forms has caused the extinction of about the same number of old forms."[17] Choice words highlighted unproven assertion.

Those optimistic predictions have not fared well exposed to the shovels and microscopes investigating post-Cambrian evidence. In a game of paleontological hide-and-seek, intensive quests for the as yet undiscovered fossil intermediates fail to expose the hiding places of organic lives that never existed!

Since the publication of *Origin*, millions of fossils have been rescued from layers of rock. But the still missing chains of intermediates recognized by Darwin as "...the most obvious and serious objection..." to his theory, continue missing in action, falsifying his predictions!

Instead of a reliable geologic column brimming with obvious transitionals, stasis intrudes. Close matches to descendant life forms emerge from ancient strata. "...All fossil roundworms found to date are indistinguishable from modern forms..." Fossils conventionally dated "...more than 3 billion years old are virtually identical to organisms, called cyanobacteria, living today"[18] although, like fossil roundworms, they may lack sufficient detail for conclusive comparison with living species.

Ancestral alligators, oysters, sea urchins, horseshoe crabs, bowfins, Australian lung fish, sturgeons, crinoids, bats, arrow worms, opossums, star-fish, corals, and the platypus weave a pattern of resemblance with descendants. After 425 million years of conventional time, the Ostracode, remains unchanged.[19] "Clams have always been clams; brachiopods have always been brachiopods; fish have always been fish."[20]   Even the lowly cockroach survives unscathed from the ravages of mega-time.

Fossil insect species identified in ancient Scandinavian amber bear a striking resemblance to today's descendants. "Lungfish almost identical to those of modern Africa are found as fossils in the rocks of the Devonian era…alongside fossils of the earliest amphibians and the very fish groups from which the amphibia supposedly arose."[21]

The Western Pacific's nautilus is a dead ringer for its long-fossilized ancestor. "In every way they are virtually identical to the living chambered nautilus. The creature that swims in our oceans today is the same one that was swimming 100 million years ago."[22]

Stasis caught evolutionist Henry Gee's attention. While the gifted editor believes "Over millions of years, tree-living reptiles evolved into birds," he acknowledges "…it is impossible to know for certain whether one species is the ancestor of another."[23]

He shares a laundry list of species that dodged extinction's bullet, unscathed and relatively unchanged. The horseshoe crab is "…An animal that has not changed its basic form for hundreds of millions of years."[24] "All fossil roundworms found to date are indistinguishable from modern forms."[25]

Gee recognizes chasms of discontinuity. A realist, he recognizes "…that adaptive scenarios are simply justifications for particular arrangements of fossils made after the fact, and which rely for their justification on authority rather than on testable hypotheses."[26] Insightfully, he discounts evolutionism's supposed organic chain of ancestry as "…a completely human invention created after the fact, shaped to accord with human prejudices…Each fossil represents an isolated point, with no knowable connection to any other given fossil, and all float around in an overwhelming sea of gaps."[27]

R.L. Wysong sang a similar tune. "Surprising as it may seem, the only real evidence for the geological succession of life, as represented by the timetable, is found in the mind of the geologist and on the paper upon which the chart is drawn. Nowhere in the earth is the complete succession of fossils found as they are portrayed in the chart."[28]

As with non-existent "organic chains" in the animal kingdom, the plant kingdom shows comparable discontinuity. Descendants of fossil Wollemi pine trees, alleged to be 150 million years old, live in Australia, far from extinct.[29] Hickory, walnut, magnolia, and gingko trees, along with grape vines, and water lilies boast fossil ancestries essentially matching 21st century's distinctive counterparts.

Living descendants of fossil trees embedded in coal beds thrive. This roster of persistent survivability features the familiar sassafras, laurel, poplar, willow, maple, beech, birch and elm. Late in the 20th century, a Cambridge University Botany scientist ventured, "...to the unprejudiced, the fossil record of plants favours [favors] special creation."[30]

Disconcerting discontinuity attracted Darwin's eye. "Nothing is more extraordinary in the history of the Vegetable Kingdom...than the apparently very sudden or abrupt development of the higher plants."[31] "The rapid development, as far as we can judge, of all the higher plants within recent geological times is an abominable mystery."[32]

Non-existent plant kingdom intermediates contribute nothing to the solution of the "mystery" that baffled evolutionism's spokesman!

Believable chains have yet to be forged from unrelated fragments of fossil bones. "With few exceptions, radically new kinds of organisms appear for the first time in the fossil record already fully evolved, with most of their characteristic features present."[33]

Recorded History

If simple to complex linkage is virtually missing from the rocks, what about living nature? If Darwin's thought was on the money, nature should abound with examples of life kinds in transit. But where are they?

Why can't observers point to organic chains of intermediates unfolding in the living world for all to see? If "...not one living species will transmit its unaltered likeness to a distant futurity..." shouldn't at least modest, incremental changes be transparent to microscopic technology?

During the most recent 4,000 years of earth's living history, verifiable transitionals don't clutter the landscape. Instead, stasis dominates!

Egyptian mummies possess the four blood types identical to the blood types pumping life through the bodies of today's *Homo sapiens*. Changes exhibiting dynamic adaptation, thanks to the information inherent in the genome of each life kind, dazzle and inspire. But genetic versatility is not evolutionism.

Where in nature's living world can Darwinian thought be authenticated? Has evolution ceased functioning and abandoned the field during the last few thousand years of recorded history? Does AWOL reality mean evolution has run its course, surrendering to a fait accompli?

As with the record in rocks, the living world seems bereft of evolutionism in action---no half-formed eye, partial ear, or appendages in transit from fin-to-limb-to-wing.

Nada!

Organic Fossil Chains

Early in the twentieth century, Princeton's W.B. Scott spotted the massive data gap essential to link modern man to an alleged, ape-like ancestor. "...What we want most is not *the* missing link, but *whole chains* which show the descent of man."[34] The Princeton scholar's jaundiced eye recognized the gaping disconnects across the board. Other academics share the assessment.

"Many fossils have been collected since 1859, tons of them, yet the impact they have had on our understanding of the relationships between living organisms is barely perceptible...In fact, I do not think it unfair to say that fossils, or at least the transitional interpretation of fossils, have clouded rather than clarified our attempts to reconstruct phylogeny"[35] "Evolution requires intermediate forms between species, and paleontology does not provide them."[36] "Most orders, classes, and phyla appear abruptly, and commonly have already acquired all the characters that distinguish them."[37]

Even Harvard's George Gaylord Simpson, an avowed evolutionist, acknowledged the organic life fossil chains absent without leave. Referencing both plants and animals, he pronounced the chains non- existent. "...Transitions between major grades of organization are seldom well recorded by fossils....It is thus possible to claim that such transitions are not recorded because they did not exist."[38]

"This regular absence of transitional forms is an almost universal phenomenon, as had long been noted by paleontologists. It is true of almost all orders of all classes of animals, both vertebrate and invertebrate. A fortiori, it is true also of the classes, themselves, and of the major animal phyla, and it is apparently also true of analogous categories of plants."[39]

While the vast chains of fossil intermediates predicted by Darwin have yet to surface, stay tuned for recent discoveries.

The Archaeopteryx Enigma

The missing organic chains of transitional life didn't discourage innovative evolutionists. Some hung their hopes on the coelacanth "fossil" fish, a "poster child" example of an extinct life form corroborating neo-Darwinism. Conventional dating credited the "extinct" coelacanth as having coexisted with dinos, 70 million years before the present. Its bony structure along with its appendages, seemed to at least arguably qualify the fish as ancestral to an amphibian.

But the intermediate nominee refused to bite the hook of an obsolete idea by continuing to swim and reproduce. In 1938, all speculative scenarios slipped away in the ocean's brine when a much alive and mirror-image of its ancestor coelacanth turned up off the coast of Madagascar. The descendant, still very much a fish and not remotely an amphibian, emerged from obscurity as a fisherman's catch. More than an anomaly, other coelacanth catches followed.

Hope, however faint, springs eternal!

The bones of a long extinct land mammal has been designated by some evolutionists as a prime example of an intermediate species en route to evolving into a whale. No matter how persuasive the argument may seem on paper, an unresolved dilemma remains! Just where are the other fossil examples of the thousands of transitional species essential to complete the evolutionary journey from land mammal to home in the sea as a whale?

A more recent candidate for fish-to-amphibian transitional status was unearthed from its hiding place in Canadian rock. *Tiktaalik roseae*, was alleged to tip the time scale at 375 million years. "Until now, the few fossils representing missing links between aquatic and terrestrial vertebrates have tended to be mostly fishlike or tetrapodlike instead of true intermediates."

Admittedly, "*Tiktaalik* is not quite midway on the path to life on land." Displaying "typical scales," the head of a fish and a title translated to mean "big freshwater fish," those looking for a tetrapod-bound intermediate believed they observed "fins better engineered for standing than swimming," with "novel joints" suggesting the fossil "could swing its fins out and forward, enabling it to push up and eventually lumber onto shore."[40]

A "not quite midway" transitional or just another extinct species?

With or without *Tiktaalik*, evo's predicted fish-to-amphibian scheme epitomizes evolutionism's dilemma. Three kinds of fish appear simultaneously in the fossil record, hardly ancestral to each other. Transition to amphibian status for any one of the three presents an unlikely scenario. For starters, transit to land would require fins to feet and gills to lungs. Drop a luckless coelacanth on land, and visions of a transiting fish would find an inglorious end in a flurry of flops, gasping for air.

Many Darwin loyalists insist birds as diverse as cardinals, eagles, and hummers, descended from dinosaurs. Bavarian limestone coughed up a chicken-sized fossil, destined to become one of as many as ten (by 2006) designated crown jewels allegedly linking birds to reptile ancestry. "...*Archaeopteryx* is said to be the paleontologist's 'Rosetta Stone' providing irrefutable evidence that evolution of the species actually occurred."[41]

Naysayers dismiss this claim arguing that *Archaeopteryx* carried fundamental bird traits; appeared suddenly, without identifiable ancestry; then faded away, without bird descendants.

Barring major cosmetic surgery, the crown was a poor fit! Radically different physical characteristics distinguish birds from dinos.

Birds are warm-blooded! A bird flies with hollow bones and feathers. Asymmetrical feathers, key to a bird's flight, sport shafts, barbs, and barbules essential for aerodynamics and insulation—unlike the symmetrical feather shafts of flightless birds. Acrobatic flight is possible thanks to the alula, the thumb-like joint at the end of the wings.

Scaly hide wraps an armor shield around the dino's ponderous package of heavy bones kept alive by circulating cold blood. Bird feathers and reptilian scales are produced from different skin layers. No one has seen reptile scales elongate when exposed to excessive solar heat. Pity the critter spending a lifetime trying to master flight by launching thousands of futile leaps from trees, relying on partially sprouted wings covered with a combo of scales and feathers, only to crash to the ground in pain.

Regardless, eager to identify a dino-to-bird link, staunch advocates of transition theory remain obsessed with the notion that the quite remarkable *Archaeopteryx* fills the linkage "bill" (pun intended). When fossils resembling modern birds, pre-dating *Archaeopteryx* were discovered, this feathered "Rosetta Stone" of presumed intermediates flew away, abandoning its fictitious perch.

Archaeopteryx could not have been an extinct transitional linking modern birds to dinosaurs. It's "not an ancestral bird, nor is it an 'ideal intermediate' between reptiles and birds. There are no derived characters uniquely shared by *Archaeopteryx* and modern birds alone."[42]

"Cold-blooded animals like crocodiles have narrow, hollow nasal cavities. Warm-blooded animals…have wide cavities housing sheets of bone or cartilage called turbinates."[43] Dinosaurs were cold-blooded beasts a la crocodiles. The fossil clue? Dinos lacked turbinates!

Paleontologist John A. Ruben examined photos of a fossilized dinosaur from China, so remarkably preserved that its guts could be identified. Heart and lungs were separated from other organs by a diaphragm—and birds don't have diaphragms! Warm-blooded birds without diaphragms coexisted with cold-blooded dinos with diaphragms. Dr. Ruben concluded that the dino's "...lung was like a crocodile's" and was "not capable of exchanging enough oxygen in the air for carbon dioxide in the blood to accommodate the needs of an active, warm-blooded animal."[44] Ruben's subsequent examination of a *Scipionyx samniticus* in Salerno, Italy, fortifies his finding that the "hepatic-piston diaphragm, in theropod dinosaurs rules out the possibility that they breathed with a sophisticated bird-like lung."[45]

Two fossil bird specimens, dubbed *Protoavis*, turned up in Texas rocks, reputedly seventy-five million years older than *Archaeopteryx* by conventional dating. The still controversial *Protoavis* shows "a keel-like breastbone, or sternum, and hollow bones" in addition to other modern bird-like features. The crow-sized *Protoavis* claims antiquity "as old as the oldest fossil dinosaur."[46]

Since when do descendants precede ancestors?

The *Archaeopteryx* candidacy for transitional status doesn't fly. No bird—hummingbird, eagle, woodpecker, or cardinal—can trace its ancestry to a dinosaur. *Archaeopteryx* doesn't bridge the chasm between the species. It's meager fossil remains offer thin clues underwriting evolutionism's quest for intermediates.

Punctuated Equilibria

"For more than a century biologists have portrayed the evolution of life as a gradual unfolding...Today the fossil record...is forcing us to revise this conventional view"[47] Understandably, "No real evolutionist, whether gradualist or punctuationist, uses the fossil record as evidence in favour [favor] of the theory of evolution as opposed to special creation."[48]

Early in the 1970's, Steven Jay Gould, articulate evolutionist, recognized Darwinian expectations of gradualism fell abysmally short of scientific adequacy. Remember Darwin's assertion that "...natural selection acts only...by short and sure, though slow, steps" never taking "a great and sudden leap?"

Gould disagreed, intellectually dismantling the flimsy tradition!

"The absence of fossil evidence for intermediary stages between major transitions in organic design...has been a persistent and nagging problem for gradualistic accounts of evolution."[49] "...The fossil record with its abrupt transitions offers no support for gradual change."[50]

Gould ridiculed the lack of fossil evidence pointing to gradualism. "The overwhelming prevalence of stasis became an embarrassing feature of the fossil record."[51] "...Most species exhibit no directional change during their tenure on earth...In any local area, a species does not arise gradually by the steady transformation of its ancestors, it appears all at once and fully formed."[52]

He hammered away at the obviously missing intermediates. "The extreme rarity of transitional forms in the fossil record persists as the trade secret of paleontology. The evolutionary trees that adorn our textbooks have data only at the tips and nodes of their branches; the rest is inference, however reasonable, not the evidence of fossils."[53]

Gould's doubts were not enough to convert him to creationism but his keen skepticism ripped giant holes in neo-Darwinian whole cloth. His reservations resonated. Not content to merely shake establishment tradition, Gould laid two corner stones on which to build his and Niles Eldredge's alternative theory of origins. "Punctuated equilibria," built on "stasis" and "sudden appearance," represents sea change from evolutionism's discredited notion of incremental accumulation of slight changes leading eventually to entirely new and different life formats.

"(1) Stasis. Most species represent no directional change during their tenure on earth. They appear in the fossil record much the same as when they disappear; morphological change is usually limited and directionless.

"(2) Sudden Appearance. In any local area, a species does not arise gradually by the steady transformation of its ancestors; it appears all at once and fully formed."[54]

Stasis lives! The debunking of a myth was underway---inside the rank and file of committed evolutionists, no less!

While Gould's punctuated equilibria explanation of origins has yet to capture the fancy of all evolutionists, his analysis struck a nerve. His collaborator, Eldredge, added fuel to the stasis/sudden appearance fire announcing, unequivocally, that Darwin's contrary predictions were just plain "wrong!"

"...It has become abundantly clear that the fossil record will not confirm this part of Darwin's predictions. Nor is the problem a miserably poor record. The fossil record simply shows that this prediction is wrong...The observation that species are amazingly conservative and static entities throughout long periods of time has all the qualities of the emperor's new clothes: everyone knew it but preferred to ignore it. Paleontologists, faced with a recalcitrant record obstinately refusing to yield Darwin's predicted pattern, simply looked the other way."[55]

Discontinuity

Distinguished evolutionist, Collin Patterson, sent shivers through academic establishments when he publicly released his range of reservations about evolutionism, including personal doubts about missing transitionals. His blunt assessment pulled no punches. "Gould and the American Museum people are hard to contradict when they say there are no transitional fossils...I will lay it on the line---there is not one such fossil for which one could make a watertight argument."[56]

Succinctly put, "Evolution requires intermediate forms between species, and paleontology does not provide them."[57]

Paleontologist David Raup spoke candidly in a letter to the editor of *Science* in 1981. "A large number of well-trained scientists outside of evolutionary biology have unfortunately gotten the idea that the fossil record is far more Darwinian than it is. This probably comes from the over-simplification inevitable in secondary sources: low-level textbooks, semi-popular articles, and so on. Also, there is probably some wishful thinking involved. In the years after Darwin, his advocates hoped to find predictable progressions. In general, these have not been found---yet the optimist dies hard, and some pure fantasy has crept into textbooks."[58]

Viewed with 20/20 hindsight, technical tools available to mid-nineteenth century labs seem pitifully primitive measured by today's standards. In those so-called "good-old-days," true science suffered. Molecular biology overwhelms primitive perceptions of life. The electron microscope opens doors to unimagined insights of cell structure and its DNA. But despite its revolutionary perspective, this tool of the science trade offers no more comfort to gradualism than the fossil chains still missing in stratified rock layers.

The vast majority of the world's paleontological discoveries have taken place since Darwin. Although most of the more than 100,000 fossil species known today were unknown to him, the phantom chains continue missing. Microbiologist Michael Denton, an acclaimed authority on cell structure and function, confirms "...The fossil record is about as discontinuous as it was when Darwin was writing *Origin*."[59] Other than providing shards and chips for decorative necklace chains, the fossils do nothing to substantiate Darwinian life linkages.

While discontinuity in the fossil record leaves the evolutionary theory up the evidentiary creek without a paddle, microbiology drains the creek dry. "Instead of revealing a multitude of transitional forms through which the evolution of a cell might have occurred, molecular biology has served only to emphasize the enormity of the gap...In terms of their basic biochemical design...no living system can be thought of as being primitive or ancestral with respect to any other system, nor is there the slightest empirical hint of an evolutionary sequence among all the incredibly diverse cells on earth...All direct evidence for evolution is emphatically absent."[60]

Denton agrees with Colin Patterson "...that much of today's explanation of nature, in terms of neo-Darwinism, or the synthetic theory, may be empty rhetoric" as well as Beverly Halstead's view that "...no species can be considered ancestral to any other...In the final analysis, nature's order is not sequential."[61]

Discontinuity reigns!

If evolutionism's "geologic column" is reliable, and simpler life forms exist on the lowest strata, higher strata should abound with sequential, intermediate life forms! But they're not to be found on a convincing scale.   Since these transitional fossil chains continue missing in action, can the geologic column itself be conclusively reliable?

Sudden appearance of fully-formed species followed by stasis and a cupboard virtually bare of transitionals undermines a critical chunk of evolutionism's dearest dogma. Not only are the predicted fossil chains absent without leave, but also, descendants of ancient species thrive, reproducing "after their kind," oblivious to Darwin's dire obituaries.

Jeremy Rifkin offers blunt assessment. "Today the millions of fossils stand as very visible, ever-present reminders of the paltriness of the arguments and the overall shabbiness of the theory that marches under the banner of evolution."[62]

Imagine sitting in a courtroom's jury box, sifting evidence assessing whether neo-Darwinism should be rated honest-to-goodness "fact" or be ranked as "superstitious nonsense" once all the smoke blows away. Consider the weight of evidence---

--- Spontaneous generation of first life, is unproven assumption;

--- The source of information in the first DNA is not identified;

--- Fully-formed life appears abruptly, not by increments;

--- Fossil evidence reveals stasis, rather than chains of transitionals; and

--- Mutations never add new genetic information.

Its incongruous to argue the feasibility of gradualistic change via incremental mutations aggregating over millions of years without clear-cut evidence confirming a chain of a multitude of transitionals saturating the fossil record or through the revelatory magic of electronic technology scrutinizing molecular life!

Think about it!

Darwin laid out a make-or-break milestone to test the validity of his explanation for the origin of species: "...*If my theory be true...!*"

Should a jury of the public take him at his word and declare his theory faces "*break-down?*"

7

The Mouse That Laughed
Irreducible Complexity

*"...Natural selection can only choose systems that are already working...
if a biological system cannot be produced gradually
it would have to arise as an integrated unit, in one fell swoop,
for natural selection to have anything to act on."*
Michael J. Behe[1]

A sleek Indy 500 racer rumbles, poised at the starting gate. A pumped-up driver grasps the wheel, waiting for the wave of the starter's flag. But when the flag drops and other engines roar, the Darwinmobile doesn't budge. It just sits there, going nowhere---at high speed no less!

The colorfully painted hulk covers rusted metal scraps, patched-together with a tattered fabric, posing an illusion of power. The jazzed-up entry in the "science of the century" sweepstakes lacks wheels. Even the engine shows up missing.

The mirage of a machine collapses at the touch---designed by fond imaginings and powered by wishful thinking. History's junkyard waits to welcome the sham of an entrant.

Darwin's no-wheel dream car already lost the race, locked-down at the starting flag. Since first ever life never happened by chance, his bankrupt theory lacked the core material essential to enter the race.

Charles Darwin assembled a wish list of predictions, preconceptions, assumptions, and uncorroborated assertions in weaving together the whole cloth of life without design or designer. He "... ransacked other spheres of practical research work for ideas...But his whole resulting scheme remains, to this day, foreign to scientifically established zoology, since actual changes of species by such means are still unknown."[2]

Imagine a sleek, NASCAR entrant, finely honed and good-to-go in every detail except for a single, glaring omission---the car lacks a gas tank. Despite hundreds of technical details properly installed, whether race car or roadster, without a whiff of fuel, the partially-built vehicle can't be driven. The absence of a single part guarantees it won't budge.

Race cars don't self-assemble. Irreducibly complex, unless fully and completely formed, the auto won't move an inch much less perform at high speed around a two-and-one-half mile oval track.

Incredibly more complex living organs cannot function unless full formed. Like the race car minus a gas tank, it's a case of all or nothing at all with the human eye. Sight is contingent upon every lens, blood vessel, and nerve being in place and fully operational. The same with human ears, hearts and lungs. All living mechanisms function irreducibly complex.

Piece-meal gradualism, an icon of neo-Darwinism, bites the dust at the starting gate! Part-way-there transitionals couldn't survive!

Evolutionism's "Flaws" and "Holes"

Let's see now!

Just how do Darwin's updated speculations stand up under the spotlight of twenty-first century evidence?

Intuitively, the philosopher dodged any serious attempt at explaining the origin of first life on earth, be it spontaneous generation or otherwise.

Primitive peeks at a living cell revealed little more than a blob of protoplasm without a hint of genetic information carried by DNA. Molecular biology's electron microscope demolished "simple" cell mentality. And contrary to simple-to-complex mantra with its theoretical gradual transitions, the fossil record discloses millions of fully-formed complex life kinds that appear abruptly, without a trace of prior ancestry.

Unlike the theory's dire prediction that ancestor species would be wiped out and replaced by descendant generations of new and different life kinds with innovative body plans, earth's strata bulges with stasis. A plethora of living species appear remarkably similar to ancient ancestors. The much touted "tree of life," with an envisioned chain of continuity demonstrating evolutionism in action, shows only a cupboard bare of transitional fossils. As recently as 1982, evolutionist Ernst Mayr conceded, "Intermediates between species are not observed" (See lead in endnote in Chapter #6).

So just where is the multiplicity of fossil intermediates theoretically linking 4,500 mammal species to a fish ancestor?

Discontinuity reigns. Gaps dominate.

The Modern Synthetic Theory of Evolution dug deep attempting to salvage Darwinian thought by coupling mutations with natural selection as the driving forces producing evolutionary chains. The one-step-forward "solution" exposed a trail of two-step-back problems: (1) mutations typically corrupt genetic information, never adding information or upgrading the quality of the organism; and (2) five-hundred-million years is not nearly enough time to accumulate the millions of beneficial mutations essential for random chance to accidentally manufacture an irreducibly complex human from a fish.

So...we are supposed to ignore the evidence, or lack thereof, and swallow the mantra that evolutionism qualifies as scientific "fact?"

Sir John William Dawson, a Darwin contemporary, condemned the concept head-on. "This evolutionist doctrine is itself one of the strangest phenomena of humanity...a system destitute of any shadow of proof, and supported merely by vague analogies and figures of speech...Now no one pretends that they rest on facts actually observed...Let the reader take up either of Darwin's great books, or Spencer's *Biology*, and merely ask himself as he reads each paragraph, 'What is assumed here and what is proved?' and he will find the whole fabric melt away like a vision....We thus see that evolution as an hypothesis has no basis in experience or in scientific fact, and that its imagined series of transmutations has breaks which cannot be filled."[3]

One hundred years after Dawson cast his vote against molecule-to-man by chance, Swedish biologist, Søren Løvtrup, focused a jaundiced eye towards evolutionism's scenario. "I believe that one day the Darwinian myth will be ranked the greatest deceit in the history of science."[4]

Given the issues, surely evolutionism must have an ace or two up its sleeve in century 21?

"Yes" and "no!"   There may be a card but its more like a joker!

So Darwin's theory is alive and well?

The scarcity of supporting evidence, erodes evolutionism's health. Still, many minds doggedly cling to its tenets, keeping the idea alive on artificial life support. With news from the evidence front consistently somber, some loyalists resort to "bait and switch" by extrapolation.

No question about it, nature bursts with dynamic change. Genomes adapt, displaying incredible versatility. But this inherent capacity to adapt, relies on information pre-existing within the genome. IGA (Intra-Genomic Adaptability) maximizes survival along with nature's smorgasbord of color, shapes and sizes.

This genetic ability to adapt does not prove Darwin's postulates. IGA is not evolutionism. Bacteria may develop immunity to drugs but consistently remain bacteria; black or white moths continue to produce moths; and finch beaks appear in multiple sizes and shapes but finches never "evolve" into red-headed woodpeckers. Mutations, neo-Darwinism's change engine of choice, lacks both the capacity to add new information or to generate entirely new body plans.

The Laughing Mouse

Irreducible complexity is the "joker" in evolutionism's card deck!

Since natural selection rejects a component part that doesn't work, any incomplete, irreducibly complex cell, organ, or system would be discarded by the natural selection process. As a practical matter, the reality of irreducible complexity prevents activation of the very natural selection demanded by neo-Darwinism's formula.

Michael Behe, originator of the "irreducible complexity" phrase, approaches the world of molecular machines by introducing the simple mousetrap with its five basic parts anchored by four staples.

The household contraption could neither design nor build itself. It requires the complete package for minimal function. A spring too weak, a trigger too short, or a missing staple and the mouse would steal the cheese, survive unscathed and chuckle with the last laugh.

A skeptic reportedly suggested the trap could do without the wooden base by stapling the metal parts to the floor. The argument fails---the wood floor itself becomes an essential part to an irreducibly complex mechanism.

A fully functioning mousetrap, like a race car, exists based on a design conceived by intelligence. A bow lacking a bowstring could never fire an arrow to the heart of a bull's eye. A forked stick, by itself, makes an impotent slingshot.

No one argues that inanimate objects like a mousetrap, a car, or even a slingshot design themselves without input from an intelligent source. All living mechanisms display designs infinitely more complex than inanimate objects.

Darwin's admission opens the door to a reality check.

"If it could be demonstrated that any complex organ existed, which could not possibly have been formed by numerous, successive, slight modifications, my theory would absolutely break down."[5] Michael Denton's analysis takes Darwin at his word and challenges make believe.

"My fundamental problem with the theory is that there are so many highly complicated organs, systems and structures, from the nature of the lung of a bird, to the eye of the rock lobster, for which I cannot conceive of how these things have come about in terms of a gradual accumulation of random changes.

"It strikes me as being a flagrant denial of common sense to swallow that all these things were built up by accumulative small random changes. This is simply a nonsensical claim...a huge number of highly complex systems in nature cannot be plausibly accounted for in terms of a gradual build-up of small random mutations..."

"...Everybody knows the lung of the bird is unique in being a circulatory lung rather than a bellows lung...It doesn't require a great deal of profound knowledge of biology to see that an organ, which is so central to the physiology of any higher organism, its drastic modification in that way by a series of small events is almost inconceivable. This is something we can't throw under the carpet again because, basically, as Darwin said, if any organ can be shown to be incapable of being achieved gradually in little steps, his theory would be totally overthrown."[6]

Pogo Stick to Automobile

If you add Michael Behe's "irreducible complexity" take to the mix, evolutionism's terminal philosophy, has little to look forward to except long-overdue last rites.

Imagine evolution of a pogo stick to an automobile. Outrageous, of course!

Even with a design conceived and put in place by an intelligent act, the construction process would require hundreds of new parts, skilled labor and more than a few minutes of time. When complete, the end-product would likely represent something far less than a sleek work of art.

Now picture a partially complete product, neither functional as a pogo stick nor a car. Any half-built monstrosity could never start an engine much less ride the highway unless every essential part functioned simultaneously and in place. Ugly in appearance, the would-be-vehicle would be worthless in its decrepit state. A "Transitionmobile" lacks identity, function, purpose or use. At zero miles per gallon, it would persist unclaimed either in a toy store or a used car lot.

Suppose this piece of mindless metal approached 90% completion, maybe all but gears, gas tank, and fuel pump! Can it now function? No longer a pogo stick; not yet an automobile; just a non-functioning eyesore without one red cent of value except for junk yard scrap!

Irreducibly complex mechanisms, whether non-living or living, are non-functional until fully-formed. Half-formed hearts and lungs are no more practical than half-built automobiles. And don't forget---the fossil record continues sparse as to partially formed, non-functional systems.

Molecular Machinery

"If anyone was chasing a phantom or retreating from empiricism it was surely Darwin, who himself freely admitted that he had absolutely no hard empirical evidence that any of the major evolutionary transformations he proposed had ever actually occurred. It was Darwin, the evolutionist, who admitted in a letter to Asa Gray, that one's 'imagination must fill up the very wide blanks.'"[7]

In the landmark words of Michael J. Behe's catchy phrase, simple life forms in molecular systems *"irreducibly complex."*

"...Canyons separating everyday life forms have their counterparts in the canyons that separate biological systems on a microscopic scale. Like a fractal pattern in mathematics...unbridgeable chasms occur even at the tiniest level of life."[8]

Prime example of a molecular machine is the bacterial flagellum with its 40 separate components, 30 of which are unique. The microscopic propeller cranks at an amazing 100,000 RPM's per minute and is capable of stopping and reversing on a quarter turn. If any one single component is missing, the entire organelle breaks down, incapable of function. Time is of the essence: its an all or nothing at all scenario; each component must be in place concurrently for the mechanism to function.[9]

Behe cites the chemical apparatus marshaled by the half-inch bombardier beetle as an irreducibly complex system in action. When threatened by an enemy it can release a scalding hot liquid as a defense mechanism.

"The components of the system are (1) hydrogen peroxide and hydroquinone, which are produced by the secretory lobes; (2) the enzyme catalysts, which are made by the ectodermal glands; (3) the collecting vesicle; (4) the sphincter muscle; (5) the explosion chamber; and (6) the outlet duct."

Dr. Behe inquires, First, "What exactly *are* the stages of beetle evolution, in all their complex glory? Second, given these stages, how does Darwinism get us from one to the next?"[10]

"As the number of required parts increases, the difficulty of gradually putting the system together skyrockets, and the likelihood of indirect scenarios plummets. Darwin looks more and more forlorn."[11]

Blood anchors animal life. Unique formulas match the need of each species. One of four blood types flows through human veins. Transfusing blood from ape to man can kill; extreme blood loss can kill; blood too thin to clot can kill; and blood that clots at the wrong time and place can kill.

Behe defines the magical qualities of clotting. "If blood congeals at the wrong time or place...the clot may block circulation as it does in heart attacks and strokes...A clot has to stop bleeding all along the length of the cut, sealing it completely. Yet blood clotting must be confined to the cut or the entire blood system of the animal might solidify, killing it."[12]

Properly functioning blood clotting in the human circulatory system that can save life involves no fewer than twenty steps. "The blood coagulation cascade" utilizes "proteins in promoting clot formation" and proteins "involved in the prevention, localization, or removal of blood clots."[13]

"...None of the cascade proteins are used for anything but controlling the formation of a blood clot. Yet in the absence of any one of the components, blood does not clot, and the system fails...Not only is the entire blood-clotting system irreducibly complex, but so is each step in the pathway."[14]

"Remember a mousetrap spring might in some way resemble a clock spring, and a crowbar might resemble a mousetrap hammer, but the similarities say nothing about how a mousetrap is produced. In order to claim that a species developed gradually by a Darwinian mechanism a person must show that the function of the system could 'have been formed by numerous successive, slight modifications.'"[15]

Mathematical odds say, "no way!" Blood clotting could not evolve "by numerous successive, slight modifications."

Tissue Plasminogen Activator binds to several substances including fibrin. TPA "has four different types of domains...the odds of getting those four domains together is 30,000 to the fourth power. Now if the Irish Sweepstakes had odds of winning of one-tenth to the eighteenth power, and if a million people played the lottery each year, it would take an average of about a thousand billion years before *anyone* (not just a particular person) won the lottery. A thousand billion years is roughly a hundred times the current estimate of the age of the universe."[16]

"We calculated the odds of getting TPA alone to be one-tenth to the eighteenth power; the odds of getting TPA and its activator together would be about one-tenth to the thirty-sixth power...Such an event would not be expected to happen even if the universe's ten-billion year life compressed into a single second and relived for every second for ten billion years...The fact is, no one on earth has the vaguest idea how the cascade coagulation came to be."[17]

Jawbone Dentition

Donald R. Moeller, a science researcher blessed with joint physician/dentist credentials, shoots down any possibility that unique dentition sizes and shapes result from mutations. Sophisticated reasoning devastates neo-Darwinism's reliance on "numerous, successive, slight modifications" as core dogma! Get ready for some "jaw-boning" with oversized words beyond everyday conversations!

Modern craniofacial/maxillafacial genetics demonstrates that pleiotropy is present in all of the approximately one hundred genetic disorders. "Thus the simplistic idea of genetic mutations being able to cause only incremental small useful changes in the occlusion and/or jaw relationships is not supported by current research There are no known mutations affecting single tooth morphology or single tooth enamel microstructure.

"Any viable theory which attempts to explain the complex interaction and precision of the maxillofacial-occlusal complex must include genetic mechanisms, developmental processes, and fossil evidences of these processes affected by mutations and natural selection.

"Current publications in orthodontics and oral and maxillofacial pathology thoroughly document that dysfunctions in all of the cranio- maxillo-occlusal systems actually do occur, and are based on known mutations and malfunctions of development. Examples include: (1) malpositions and eruption sequencing dysfunction causing teeth to either remain unerupted and cause cysts or crowding; (2) maxillo-mandibular growth discoordination causing mandibular prognathism (protruding lower jaw).

"These developmental departures should therefore be expected in the fossil record, especially since chordate-maxilloocclusal relationships are so widely varied across species boundaries. An endless parade of transitional variations of all the subsystems should be evident, as well as the problematic effects caused by lack of coordination between the subsystems.

"Multiple examples of malposed teeth, cysts in jaws, retained deciduous teeth, maxillary-mandibular growth and size discoordination, losses of entire classes of teeth, variation in eruption height of the various classes of teeth, tooth size arch-discrepancy variation, animal size, and tooth size coordination, should be in the fossil record.

"This evidence is not seen.

"The subsystem of tooth replacement presents a quandary. The reptiles have a "wave-like" replacement of every third tooth, yet all early mammals have a whole set replacement of their deciduous teeth

"There are no transitional dentitions. The earliest deciduous dentitions are fully functional.

"The same quandary appears with respect to tooth attachment. There are at least eight, well-developed methods of tooth attachment in the chordates, none of which could be called primitive or advanced or could be arranged in a sequence from simple to complex. Furthermore, failure of the attachment apparatus would be evidenced by missing teeth due to dysfunction in periodontal attachment. Transitional attachment mechanisms are not found in the fossil record.

"What the craniofacial and maxillary occlusal fossil evidences suggest is that all ten subsystems (and probably more) were fully functional in all chordates from their first appearance in the fossil record. There is absolutely no fossil evidence of either developmental processes or pathology which would suggest any evolutionary process leading to the development of the dentition. There is also no known genetic or developmental process to suggest a legitimate mechanism to support an evolutionary basis for the development of the precision exhibited by the dental apparatus."[18]

Dr. Moeller's insight corroborates Dr. Behe's irreducible complexity!

Systemic Inter-Dependence

Conceptual design of molecular mechanisms requires intelligence. Designed, irreducibly complex mechanical and living systems have been created by intelligent action. Assembling the designed systems requires sophisticated insight beyond the capacity of nature's whims.

If the source of creative design is able to mastermind a human brain, it makes no sense to mandate mega-year time spans for the implementation of such power. There is no logical reason for an Intelligent Creator to require millions of years to assemble a brain or any other life system. Recognition of Supreme power accepts the plausibility of a creation event in the blink of an eye.

Park Rangers at Tennessee's Reelfoot Lake protect wildlife and restore the injured. When recovery is complete, healthy eagles are released to circle the heavens.

A screech owl that collided with a car is alive, as well as can be expected, after losing an eye in the accident. But he will never be released to fend for himself. The Rangers say that a bird (like the red-tailed hawk, blessed with acute vision extending a mile in any direction) couldn't survive on its own with only a single full-functioning eye.

Perhaps Darwin didn't consider the owl or a hawk when he conjectured the evolution of an eye from a primitive tissue theoretically able to recognize light. Gradual eye evolution wouldn't do the trick for a raptor. Any "blind-as-a-bat owl," restricted with partially half-built talons and wing stumps incapable of flight, represents a transitional creature pathetically short of the "fitness" essential to survival in evo's "luck-of-the-draw" life plan. Like Reelfoot Lake's one-eyed screech owl, it could never make it in a future without human help.

Swallows swoop to mud puddles, scavenging nest material. Eagles build 3-foot wide nests in tree tops. Parrots, arrayed in multi-colored hues and oversize beaks, mimic human sounds. Little in the fossil record, molecular biology, or today's experience suggests these full-formed and functioning birds descended from reptiles. And virtually nothing substantiates partially or non-functioning intermediates.

The eye of an arthropod also astounds.

Trilobites, "...could see an undistorted image under water... with undistorted vision in all directions...to determine distance... while at the same time have the optimum sensor for motion detection."[19] Understandably, "The composition of the arthropod head is one of the bitterest and longest-running problems in animal evolution. Unresolved after more than a century of debate, this sorry tale is [in]famously known as the 'endless dispute.'" [20]

Whether honey bee or trilobite, arthropod eyes "...have always been complex---and there have always been arthropods... The bee's ability to convey the location of a food source to fellow workers via a sophisticated 'dance' is legendary."[21]

When the delicate balance of a complex life is disrupted by dysfunction, life terminates. Conversely, life, as well as its sophisticated systems such as the arthropod's vision, can't spring from an incomplete organism lacking critical components.

In the case of a living system, such as an eye or a wing, however long or short the time for its "evolution," it would be non-functional throughout the entire open-ended interval. Extinction would intrude, long before expiration of evo theory's postulated mega-million years.

Prolonged failure to function is a recipe for the destruction of most any living system trapped interminably in some intermediate state. A creature trying to evolve a wing from a leg, unable to walk or to fly, is destined to die. A hawk, flapping half-formed wings while trying to hunt with eyes scarcely able to detect night from day, couldn't feed or protect itself. An even less "evolved" parent, if miraculously alive, couldn't help its crippled offspring.

Fossils composing the Cambrian Explosion confirm irreducible complexity. More than 7,000 species appeared across-the-board: fully-formed, fully-functional, and without evidence of prior ancestry.

Irreducible complexity comes into play ecologically. Life systems function inter-dependently. Trees contribute to rainfall; water grows green grass; and cattle munch on grass. Living nature hangs on a multitude of systems, existing and operating simultaneously in ecological balance.

Gradualism is out the window if tested against irreducible complexity's all-or-nothing reality. Just as a race car without wheels will never get the checkered flag, any complex living machine missing a part won't be able to enter the race for survival. A significant composite of out-of-kilter, non-functioning systems would likely render ecological balance dysfunctional.

Evidence supports a compelling case that life did not require vast chunks of deep time to originate abruptly and fully-formed. The plant kingdom delivers food for animal kingdom survival. Ecological inter-dependence of multiple plant and animal kinds argues for irreducibly complex life systems appearing simultaneously and functioning in concert.

8

Smart Rocks
Intelligence from an Unintelligent Source?

"As evidence of evolution, the four-winged fruit fly is no better
Than a two-headed calf in a circus sideshow."
Jonathan Wells[1]

Metropolitan centers glow 24/7 thanks to the genius of a man who harnessed electrical energy by designing efficient incandescent lighting twenty years after Darwin's *Origin* hit the streets. Today's world is a brighter place thanks to the inventor's industrious pursuit of knowledge.

Legend has it Edison made 1,000 trial-and-error attempts to find a time-worthy filament for the vacuum tube. Unfettered in the privacy of his New Jersey lab, he methodically explored open-ended possibilities. No pre-determined boundaries imposed limits on his relentless patience nor prevented his testing with tungsten. Eventually, a forest of burning brightness, controlled by an on/off switch, crowned his efforts.

Taking any avenue of scientific research off the table because it reaches above and beyond the visibly materialistic, compromises the result. To attempt to explain life's origin by excluding consideration of the Designer of light, condemns research to groping for answers in the dimness of an intellectual twilight zone. The world---and science---would be brightened by investigating the origin of life while recognizing the pervasive evidence of intelligent design.

Paraphrasing words credited to rocket scientist Wernher von Braun, "you don't need a candle to see the sun."

Computers
Fast forward to Century Twenty-one.

Imagine this hypothetical conversation between two high school students fresh on the heels of a daunting math test.

Student #1---"Could have used a Bill Gates or at least my personal computer on that mind blower!"

Student #2---"You mean that 100 cubic inches of spatial capacity custom-designed to fit your bony cranium didn't provide enough memory bites?"

#1---"It's not my fault if nature's evolution shortchanged my memory chips!"

#2---"Do you buy into the line that given billions of years of exposure to lightning, rain, drought, hot, cold, snow, ice, and wind, your brain's ancestry evolved from some unknown, unintelligent source?"

#1---"What's to prove? Scientists declare evolution to be a fact! Even *National "G"* and the History Channel stand by Darwin."

#2---"So you understand your PC is a product of intelligent design but your brain's jungle of nerve cells with a *thousand million-million* connections exists by chance---without short-circuiting or blowing a fuse---courtesy of unintelligent sources playing gambling games with inorganic matter?"

#1---"Whoa there Charlie Brown! Who am I not to follow the lead of thinking academics?"

#2---"And lemmings follow the crowd, over the cliff to oblivion!"

Brain Power

Given genetic information composed of more than 3 billion DNA base pairs per-parent, millions of combinations are possible in the mix. Siblings share many of the same genes but each individual stands unique---a human with a virtually one-of-a-kind DNA sequence.

Individual *Homo sapiens* exist *sui generis*.

A frame designed to walk upright on two legs; a body not covered by fur with clothing needed to match the weather; and language skills sorting out more than 200,000 words, in English dialogue. The package thrives with bonus brains, loaded with creativity and capable of creatively calculating complex equations---even an imagination capable of concocting and dispensing theories of life's origin.

Still, there is infinitely more that distinguishes *Homo sapiens* from the rest of Planet Earth's animal kingdom.

Humans sing songs, with a bass soloist able to hit the bottom of a low note. Humans also write books; compose poetry and music; perform in chamber orchestras using multi-shaped instruments producing distinctive sounds; travel in space; produce movies; play golf; and invent machines as complex as a computer and as simple as a mousetrap.

No thoughtful person argues the computer designed and assembled itself by random reactions of inert matter. Regardless, some bright minds insist human brains originated without a design or a designer's intelligent input.

Where's the logic? Intelligent man from unintelligent matter? The concept sounds dumber than a box of rocks. If so, why can't man's brilliance create that first ever cell?

Darwin offered Wizard of Oz style legerdemain. Devotees pledging allegiance to the idea of brain from non-brain are destined to wander in Munchkin Land.   Evolutionism survives as intellectual scam, a heist, riding legitimate science coat tails. No reputable university has ever awarded a Ph.D. to a chimp. These cute pets display clever behavior but not at a level warranting a kindergarten graduation certificate.

Gene expression profiles in the brain's cerebral cortex differ between chimps and humans. Comparing the two, Svante Pääbo observes, "...it seems that the brain is really special in that humans have accelerated patterns of gene activity."[2] Give credit where credit is due. Chimps and dogs understand many human language words and parrots mimic spoken words and phrases they hear. But fact trumps theory: no animal brain matches the computer-like mind of *Homo sapiens*.

The human brain develops from a gene complex in place at conception, nine-months before birth. All creative thought, sensory reaction, speech, and memory are programmed by a living, "personal computer" built from the DNA inherited from two parents. Consider "a three-pound brain...composed of twelve billion neurons...with...120 trillion connections" encased in a trauma-resistant, compact cranial container.[3]

That one-of-a-kind memory bank "consists of about ten thousand million nerve cells. Each nerve cell puts out somewhere in the region of between ten thousand and one hundred thousand connecting fibres by which it makes contact with other nerve cells in the brain. Altogether, the total number of connections in the human brain approaches 10^{15} or a thousand-million-million..."[4] an unfathomable number, virtually beyond comprehension.

"Imagine an area about half the size of the USA (one million square miles) covered in a forest of trees containing ten thousand trees per square mile. If each tree contained one hundred thousand leaves the total number of leaves in the forest would be 10^{15}, equivalent to the number of connections in the human brain!"[4]

Consider the challenge confronting the world's most skilled electrician attempting to mastermind the wiring of a jungle of wires requiring a thousand million-million connections without mis-wiring, short-circuiting, or blowing a fuse!

If that doesn't deflate the ignorance of egocentric arrogance, try confining that jumble to the micro dimensions of a three-pound brain fitted snugly within the custom-designed bony cranium that offers something less than 100 cubic inches of spatial capacity!

So this feat of electrical/biological engineering supposedly designed and installed its own wiring diagram mechanism without so much as a master plan derivative of Supreme intelligence?

And humans, endowed with this real-life computer, are supposed to believe it evolved over several billion years resulting from the unpredictable whims of untold millions of good-luck mutations?

Hong Kong neurosurgeon C.P. Yu sees the human brain as "...the most complex 3 pound structure of this Universe." A Fellow of the Hong Kong College of Surgeons, Dr. Yu describes the "basic unit" consisting "of a neurone and glial cells" with at least "10 to 30 billion neurones and ten times that number of glial cells. Each neurone has 10,000 to 50,000 interconnections with other neurones.   Electron microscopy differentiates excitatory from inhibitory neurones by the presence of a micro-spine."[5]

The nucleus of each neurone contains a "DNA molecule" which if unraveled would stretch a meter in length "within a cell 1/30,000 the size of a pinhead." Eight layers of bone with a "thick irregular plate" at the base "with openings for cranial nerves, blood vessels, and the spinal cord" compose a geometrically designed skull encasing the brain.   Inside the skull, "the brain is surrounded by pressurized cerebrospinal fluid…providing nutrition and providing an active suspension system for the brain."[5]

Smooth movement of a coordinated body is taken for granted---until upset by the insidious Parkinson's disease which disrupts basal ganglia function.   "…A tiny structure called the Subthalamic Nucleus (STN) is the pacemaker of the body.   Numerous feedback loops and connections between the STN and other nuclei within the entire basal ganglia are responsible for the ultra-smoothness of movements."[5]

Dr. Yu emphasizes that the brain, this message center for human life, manages five senses: smell, taste, hearing, touch, and vision.

The brain "can distinguish more than 10,000 odors through tiny olfactory nerves at the roof of our nose." And with that delicate sense of smell operational, taste buds introduce discriminating gourmets to the joys of dining.

Humans listen to multi-directional sound courtesy of built-in stereo capability. Each ear comes equipped with "24,000 'hair cells' which convert vibrations to electrical impulses." The hearing nerve "enters the internal auditory meatus which houses 3 other nerves, 2 vestibular and 1 facial nerve, all tightly packed together and yet never pose any electrical leak or cross-over distortion." And don't forget those three miniature bones, tiniest in the body, anchoring the listening process in each ear.

The brain orders the hand to jerk away automatically from a too hot surface without conscious thought.   The skin's sense of touch equips the brain to respond appropriately to the danger of pain or the gentle caress of velvet.   Feel, taste, sound, and smell impact thought processes that activate the full range of human emotions.

Human eyes complete the cycle!

According to Dr. Yu, "Apart from having auto-focus, auto-exposure, excellent low light response, excellent depth perception that no camera comes close, the eye can perceive: 1. Velocity, 2. Direction, 3. Location, 4. Texture, 5. Identity, and 6. Color."[5]

The neurosurgeon's summation exposes the preposterous notion of evolutionism's discordant attempts to account for the human brain's genesis.

"What is the probability of life arising from atoms to molecules, amino acids to protein (don't forget all life proteins are left-handed in configuration), DNA to messenger RNA, single cell to sexual reproduction, all the way to the human body with wonders of the brain and its senses, the heart and the circulation, the clotting cascade, the immune system, the wound repair and healing mechanisms?

"Bear in mind that all these have to go against the second law of thermodynamics, [the] law of irreducible complexity, and the fact that most mutations are harmful."[5]

And don't forget, the brain functions, thanks to a circulatory system powered by a heart that pumps automatically, round-the-clock. The heart and the brain survive as mutually dependent colleagues. Without constant flow of blood to the brain, death arrives in minutes. The average human heart does its thing--- beating rhythmically 100,800 times a day (with a pulse rate of 70 beats per minute) and pumping ten tons of blood daily, the weight equivalent of 140 adult humans.[6]

The phenomenal human brain possesses capacity for prodigious memory feats!

Pliny the Elder, a Roman scholar, authored *Natural History*, a literary work suggesting Cyrus the Great, the Achaemenian King of Persia, "knew the names of all the men in his army" Allegedly, Lucius Scipio was familiar with "the names of all the people of Rome." Whether myth or hyperbole, tradition reports "Mithridates of Pontus knew the languages of all the twenty-two peoples in his domains."[7]

Thomas Cranmer, Archbishop of Canterbury, is reputed to

have memorized the entire Bible in three months. A blindfolded chess-master, George Koltanowski, played 56 matches simultaneously in a nine-hour marathon, winning fifty while tying the other six.[7]

And then there's the rare genius that astounds other high IQ elites. Think of the remarkable Wolfgang Amadeus Mozart who walked the earth for a brief 35-years, composing volumes of musical scores that continue to enchant concert aficionados.

The six-year-old Mozart made his first public musical virtuoso appearance in Linz. At ten, he performed a symphony of his own in Amsterdam. In April, 1770, Amadeus visited Rome's Sistine Chapel where he listened to Allegri's *Miserere*. The Vatican reserved the complex musical for private concerts presented to honored guests. The 14-year-old genius listened intently and later accessed his incredible memory to reproduce the entire score in flawless detail.

Our brains function in mega dimension beyond the capability of the most intricately designed computer. It defies credibility to allege seriously that a human's ability to sort out sights and sounds and to store prodigious quantities of data in a brain bereft of intelligent design or designer.

Creativity

Free will energizes creativity.

Charles Robert Darwin orchestrated his own brain's creativity, squandering a lifetime while fashioning a curious, phantom "science." His considerable brain power argued perversely that his thinking process evolved by coincidence from some less-than-intelligent source.

The brain, exercising free moral agency, mobilizes mental, spiritual and physical resources to guide rational choices. Unlike an automaton, human intelligence energizes the power to choose.

Collective choices shape character. Every person fits into a *big picture*, above and beyond the luck of the draw. The Creator of all life authored the "Big Picture."

At this point, you're pondering the theme of this book. Thanks to your brain's reasoning process, your reaction is building. Your impression results from your free moral agency in play, processing information.

Conclusions can be tainted if permeated with hard-rock bias. Anyone can be vulnerable to knee jerk, sieg heil mentality. Your ability to shake tradition and peer-pressured environments tests objectivity. Sorting out conflicting ideas in structural format confirms a creative skill that defies materialistic explanation.

The brain represents more than a computerized control center. Unlike computers, human minds integrate with a mobile physical body that moves with alacrity, stores visual and audio memories, reasons, accumulates wisdom, creates, feels love, reproduces, and communicates with human beings, each vested with the power of choice inherent in free-moral agency.

Humans don't exist as blobs of matter, automatons at the mercy of natural phenomena. The brain harnesses the senses, collects and stores data, and demonstrates free will by coordinating its spiritual, mental, and physical resources.

Emotions

The genesis of a first living cell perpetually baffles evolutionism's elaborate musings! Equally unresolved is the mystery as to just how that first ever cell managed to derive its genetic information from inert matter. And millions of years of alleged molecular modification have yet to account for the source of the torrent of human emotions unleashed every day in every life.

Emotions!!!

While the physical system functions internally in orchestrated synchronization running on auto pilot, a human's cohesive whole coordinates powers of reason, communication and creative design. Beyond the information vested in the cell's DNA, life's experiences are stored in the brain assuring the capacity to reason and react.

More than a mechanical organic machine, the brain brims with a sensitive spiritual capacity triggering every spontaneous human emotion. Laughter, surprise, a sense of danger, love, loyalty, sadness, joy, compassion, exhilaration, justice---you name it---the brain brings out the full dimension of the spirit within a living soul.

Love's ecstatic joy unleashed through the souls, minds and bodies of a honeymooning couple captures a surging sensation inspiring poetry. At the other end of the emotion spectrum, cascades of agonized tears flow spontaneously and unchecked in reaction to tragic loss.   Irrepressible smiles, fits of indignation, raucous laughter erupting at the least hint of outrageous humor; and shades of embarrassment take turns impacting the human spirit.

Above-and-beyond physical passion, love shares unselfishly, forgives, protects youngsters, honors the aged, and commits loyally forever. Love is the antonym to evolution's winner-take-all, "survival-of-the-fittest" mantra.

The physical package is graced with an instinctive recognition of God, inspiring worship of the Creator. Materialistic evolutionism lacks capacity to account for this spiritual dimension pervasive to the human experience.

Taking a cue from Michael J. Behe, it can be argued that his "mousetrap" example of *irreducible complexity* applies to human behavior as well as to the complex physical functions of the heart, lungs, and brain.

What kind of a semi-evolved, only part-human creature would it be if burdened with half-baked, uncertain emotional responses?

Were ancient, not-quite-humans merely emotionless zombies, not knowing whether to laugh or cry at the death of a family member?

Where's the evidence that *mutations* coupled with *natural selection* evolved spiritual reactions from physical matter?

Genetic Precision

Your brain has spent a lifetime soaking up bits and pieces of data. Reasoned opinion results from a brain at work, reacting to evidence.

Evaluate the evidence! It presents a lifetime choice!

Objective free will is a gift of the spiritual, the core of the human soul. The majestic beauty of a human's freedom to think and act is off the screen of inert matter. Random rearrangements of the material can't design a human soul.

Free will mobilizes intelligence that powers personal choice. Informed choices shape character, a lifelong process built on choices evaluating right and wrong. The cumulative direction of those choices determines a person's characterization as "good" or "evil."

Every discipline of natural science demands precision. From the microscopic minutiae to the cosmic; from the inorganic to the living; science symbolizes precision!!!! And precision documents intelligence---the architect of order.

The glaring exception to this universal commonality of the science of order and the mathematically real is evolutionism's mutant "science." Logic of a measurable equation is thrown to the winds in favor of assumption and myth. Unproven hypothesis, reliant only on random chance, doesn't qualify as science when it ignores the real and postulates the unreal. Slick phrases, empty verbiage, and full-color graphics don't guarantee authentic respectability. Once the bells, whistles, and fancy rhetoric melt away, mutant "science's" confetti cloak is exposed.

Evolutionism suffers from a terminal case of shoddy assertions. Evidence abounds corroborating Darwin's own admission that his ideas reach "beyond the bounds of true science."

Valid reasons exist for his symbolic hand-wringing.

9

Darwin's "Family" Tree
A Whale of a Fish Tale

"When I want to know how a fish can become a man,
I am not enlightened by being told that the organisms that leave the most offspring
are the ones that leave the most offspring."
Phillip E. Johnson[1]

"Well I'll be a monkey's uncle!"

A trite cliché, typically announcing astonished surprise without genealogical inference---unless, perhaps, you happen to be a devout evolutionist?

Genealogy fascinates---and sometimes fabricates!

Many proletariat wouldn't mind discovering a king or two in their ancestry. Its unlikely any human will claim bragging rights at prospect of a King Salmon fish or a King Simian monkey parenting roots of a family tree.

Charles Darwin lacked any such reticence. Without the first clue as to the meaning of "genome" or the DNA helix, he undertook the role of master genealogist for the human race.

Since he lacked the most basic tools of 21st century science, his fantasies could be brushed aside as wishful thinking. Still, some contemporary believers surrender to his hypothesis and buy into corrupted genealogy concepts hook, line and mutation!

Just a minute here! An ancestor fish in the family tree?

If you're counting on Darwinian scholarship to diagram your family's genealogy you'll be rowing upriver short at least one oar.

First of all, he admitted he lacked the faintest clue as to how life originated. "… Science as yet throws no light on the far higher problem of the essence or origin of life."[2]   He frankly didn't know.

Think about it!

The Origin of Species and *The Descent of Man* were built on a candid "science as yet throws no light" on the origin of first life. This "I don't know" "science" of 1859 as to the "essence or origin of life" explains nothing. Devotees of random-chance life resolutely fend off questioners asking "where's the science" that's built from metaphysical conjecture!

Darwin sought support from the fossil record. "...If my theory be true, numberless intermediate varieties, linking closely together all the species of the same group, must assuredly have existed..."[3] Unlike the skimpy fossil collections of 1859, today's museum shelves bulge with fossil finds. Still, transitionals continue incommunicado.

Billions of fossils have been found since Darwin's words broke print. Far from "numberless," the few arguably intermediates typically represent nothing more than extinct species. Attempting to link fossils in an alleged transitional sequence represents an exercise in futility. Evolutionist Dr. Henry Gee, says as much.

"To take a line of fossils and claim that they represent a lineage is not scientific hypothesis that can be tested, but an assertion that carries the same validity as a bedtime story—amusing perhaps even instructive, but not scientific."[4]

Has Darwin's own "if my theory be true" test passed with flying colors, overcoming all challenges? And still no verifiable scientific explanation as to how life originated? And so the public is expected to swallow the bait that fish must be human relatives, ancestral in our family tree???

Now about selling you that Brooklyn Bridge.........!!!

The pieced-together fabric of evo thinking has yet to find a place of honor in any family genealogy authenticated by professional genealogists. This didn't stop the 19th century guru of unverified origins from propounding what he asserted to be the roots of the Darwin family tree.

Darwin's "Family" Tree

The ancestral chain envisioned by Darwin linking man-to-molecule by luck-of-the-draw lacks corroborative evidence.

Abstract "links" arouse skepticism---particularly so when built around evolutionism's fantasy "fish story!"

After blazing an unlikely and unproven transitional trail back "through a long line of diversified forms" starting with "higher mammals," leading to "an ancient marsupial," then latching on to "some reptile-like or some amphibian-like creature," Darwin eventually identified his ancient parentage as "some fish-like animal."[5]

Remarkable linkage---and without a scintilla of proof!

But evolutionism's patron saint waxed eloquent, plunging ahead on a genealogical roll, subsequently saddling his family tree with a mysterious, androgynous creature he identified as neither male nor female. "...The early progenitor of all the Vertebrata must have been an aquatic animal, provided with branchiae, with the two sexes united in the same individual...."[6]

By grafting a hermaphrodite to the root stalk of the human family tree, he suggested a gender bender that would have erased any hint of romance in primitive dating games.

The philosopher/naturalist jump-starts the make-believe process, bridging the gap to Vertebrata by asserting "...all the members of the vertebrate kingdom are derived from some fish-like animal."[7] Remember he envisioned a path of continuity, equivocating that "...all the higher mammals are probably derived from an ancient marsupial...through a long line of diversified forms, either from some reptile-like or some amphibian-like creature..."[8]

His depiction of human ancestry reached the realm of quaint notions!

"...The progenitors of man must have been aquatic in their habits; for morphology plainly tells us that our lungs consist of a modified swim-bladder...the heart existed as a simple pulsating vessel..."[9] and "...man is the co-descendant with other mammals of a common progenitor..."[10] His rag-tag surmising stretched credibility further by suggesting "...early progenitors of man were no doubt once covered with hair, both sexes having beards; their ears were pointed and capable of movement; and their bodies were provided with a tail ..."[11] A vivid imagination conjured up man as having "...descended from a hairy quadruped...probably arboreal in its habits."[12]

This slant on human genealogy resembles more a roll call at the zoo!

The "arboreal" assertion set the stage for the human family tree descending from some ape-type critter. Without a hint of tongue-in-cheek equivocation, he pinned the tale on the monkey for the entire human family. He identified the supposed Simiadæ connection as an "Old World division...after these had diverged from the New World division!"[13]

After linking humans and monkeys to common ancestry, Darwin admonished followers to hold their heads high, suggesting, "...we may, with our present knowledge, approximately recognize our heritage; nor need we feel ashamed of it..." This unambiguous declaration of "heritage," immediately followed his uncorroborated revelation that "The Simiadae... branched off into two great stems; the New World and Old World monkeys; and from the latter, at a remote period, Man, the wonder and glory of the Universe proceeded..."[14]

There it is! Did "Man" really descend from "Old World monkeys?" Or is the wacky mish-mash "about a half bubble off plumb?"

While there may be a reluctance to display a monkey-to-man message on a family coat-of-arms, evolutionist Ernst Mayr joined Darwin's allegiance to ancestor apes by stretching out on a limb of his own making. "...Every knowing person agrees that man is descended from the apes."[15] Does Mayr contend that an objector to this unproven genealogy is not a "knowing person?"

Perhaps Darwin wasn't "ashamed" of the monkey swinging from the chandelier in his family's Downe homestead, but his pointed portrayal of this predecessor posing as some ancient great-grand-parent might have raised an eyebrow or two if peer-reviewed in a Victorian era family album. No one boasts of a hairy ape ancestor noted for arboreal stunts or an ancestral fish, a worthy candidate for a Cajun-style gourmet entrée.

Families typically share family tree curiosity. But have you heard anyone claim seriously to be a "monkey's uncle" or the multiple times great-great-great grandchild of a monkey? Or to eagerly recruit a chimp for a family reunion?

Fact is, neither monkeys nor fish have anything to do with any human family tree---including Charles Darwin's. A limb from a fake Christmas tree, even one draped in glitter and gold, can never be grafted successfully to the trunk of a rooted evergreen. Darwin's fictional "tree of life" is a weird aberration, with no connection to real life.

Identification of a family pedigree requires heavy doses of certified documentation. Four thousand year-old evidence reveals a line of human beings, just like us---even carrying identical four basic blood types.

Imagination and generous chunks of deep time, common tools in Darwin's intellectual workshop, were utilized to postulate fictitious human genealogy that never was and never could be.

Is there any grandparent who laces bedtime stories to grandkids with tales of a family tree rooted in some ancient, scaly-skinned, Pisces---hatched in the briny deep, an aquatic marvel in the 100 meter freestyle but shortchanged of the arms and legs characteristic of an Olympic athlete? Does any warm-blooded grandparent believe his or her grandchildren should be told their genealogy traces to a cold-blooded fish?

This sorry fiction doesn't make the cut.

Eleven generations back, early in the seventeenth century, John Libby, a Cornwall immigrant who happened to be an ancestor of mine, landed on the Maine coast minus fanfare. I'm pleased to share the anecdotal history of the family Libby with my grandkids. If I tried to graft the fish tale to the roots or the outer tips of the family tree, the youngsters would convulse with laughter, convinced "Papa Warren" had stumbled onto senility's slippery slope.

No kids, fish descendants still swim, as described in the lyrics of a 1940's era pop song, like "three little 'fishies' in the itty-bitty pool," never imagining, much less claiming, *Homo sapiens* as blood brothers.

Irregardless, many moguls of evolutionism turn up their noses at the creation equation and insist that kids be taught fabricated fish fiction as scientific fact!!! Perhaps Darwin should be forgiven devotion to myths since he scribbled his fantasies at a time when authors of fairy tales embellished the ranks of literary circles.

But to embrace nonsense in the 21st century?   And label it "science?"

Time for a reality check!

The same guy that saw no need to hang heads in embarrassment as to ape-like ancestry turned a blind-eye to racism, going out of his way to look down his figurative nose on what he categorized as "savage" races.

After leading readers all the way from primordial warm water to the arboreal swing set, Darwin found a place for man parading from the "barbarian" or "savage state" onward to "lower races" and ultimately allegedly upward to "men of a superior class."[16] "...Various races differ much from each other...the capacity of the lungs, the form and capacity of the skull...in their intellectual, faculties...The races differ...in constitution...their mental characteristics are likewise very distinct; chiefly as it would appear in their emotional but partly in their intellectual faculties."[17]

Lest there be any doubt, he reassured his peers of Britannia's empire, that "The western nations of Europe...immeasurably surpass their former savage progenitors and stand at the summit of civilization...,"[18] adding the zinger that given the relentless march of evolution loaded with ample measures of time, "...the civilized races of man will almost certainly exterminate and replace throughout the world the savage races."[19]

Ever since Darwin conjectured man's divergence from ape ancestry, paleontologists have scrambled, combing strata, looking for clues corroborating this pronouncement. But, evolutionism's curious quest confirming monkey-to-man required endless detours.

The Gender Dilemma

Darwin went to great pains to suggest that human descent from some ape-like ancestor not be cause for embarrassment. In a blizzard of lofty-sounding phraseology, evolutionists were encouraged to not hang heads or turn away blushing at mention of these genealogical roots.

Darwin's fictional pedigree for all mankind conjectured a hermaphrodite ancestor, "two sexes united in the same individual," that supposedly resided in water. In a murky understatement, evolutionism's guru postulated this single-sex monstrosity suffered from "...the most important organs of the body (such as the brain and heart) imperfectly developed...."[20]

The radical impossibility of the concept raises skeptics' eyebrows. It's no small stretch to suggest the human brain evolved from a fish. To postulate human genders split off from some unidentified hermaphrodite boggles credibility.

The nineteenth century philosopher appears out-of-touch and over his head in the science of gynecology (as well as genealogy). He knew nothing about human chromosomes. Any exposure he might have had to the radical differences between "X" and "Y" would have been confined to possible familiarity with algebraic formulas.

It would have been historically premature for the classic French phrase, "viva la difference," to be relevant to some "androgynous" era Darwin assigned to vertebrates. His conjecture lacked the faintest first clue as to how to get here from there without reproductive capabilities vested in a *Homo sapiens* couple.

It didn't happen by luck of the draw! It simply didn't happen!!!

The transition from Darwin's imagined single sex ancestor to the male and female genders distinguishing humans shatters at the "irreducible complexity" barrier. Any part-way-there transition suggests the likelihood of both sterility and impotency destroying reproductive capability. Complete and concurrent evolution of both genders would be an imperative. Incomplete evolution of either or both sexes would veto reproductive capacity in any single generation and would terminate a species.

Gender differences run deeper than skin. Apart from the obvious body parts, hormones accentuate distinctions. Males sport facial hair, can be taller, heavier and stronger in the shoulders and upper body. In Western culture, men serve the family as protectors and bread winners. Females are sensitive nurturers, living in a skeletal structure designed for child bearing, and displaying finer, more delicate facial features and blessed with a musical voice.

Men and women share a built-in mutual attraction that can blossom into full-blown passion and lifetime commitments when cultivated. A single sperm, once merged with a microscopic-sized egg, can produce an embryo loaded with millions of potential combinations, drawn from that joint DNA data bank. This one-of-a-kind gene combo creates a unique person and determines the color of the eyes, hair and skin; the size and shape of the body; and the gender.

Physician Howard Glicksman details the dismal prospect of male and female genders evolving gradually and jointly by intricate steps without running afoul of irreducible complexity and species dead-end.

Twenty-three chromosome pairs provide the genetic code for a human. "The mother's egg always provides an   X chromosome and the father's sperm supplies either an X or a Y chromosome to the zygote. A person is considered, chromosomally, a female if they have an XX pattern and a male if they have an XY combination."[21]

It functions as an all or nothing package deal!

"Human embryo sexual differentiation involves the development of three different...initial primordial tissues...(1) undifferentiated gonads, which develop into either testes or ovaries; (2) the genital duct systems, the Mullerian ducts (female)-which form the fallopian tubes, the uterus and the upper vagina, or the Wolffian ducts (male)-which form the epididymis, vas deferens, and seminal vesicles; (3) the (uro)genital sinus, swellings, folds and tubercle, which form either a female lower vagina, labia, and clitoris, or a male prostate, scrotum, and penis."[21]

"The default sex of every human embryo is female." The sex determining region (SRY) of the Y chromosome contains the information for a testes determining factor (TDF) which prevents the undifferentiated gonads becoming ovaries. "This TDF turns out to be the masterswitch for turning on the biochemical machinery that results in the formation of the testes." Once this master switch is turned on, unless DMRT-1 from chromosome #9 kicks in, the "gonadal tissue will form into *ovaries* and not *testes*. Therefore, every human, including women, has the genetic and biomolecular machinery within themselves to become male, it only requires that the masterswitch on the Y chromosome activate the system."[21]

Once the embryonic testes are formed, they begin to secrete testosterone, "derived from cholesterol." Enzymes "located on several different chromosomes" are needed "to convert cholesterol into testosterone…Each of the many enzymes necessary for adequate testosterone formation must be fully functional or else the male of the species will not be functionally able to reproduce." The epididymis, vas deferens and seminal vesicles are derived from the Wolffian ducts which are "totally dependent on testosterone for allowing them to continue to survive and develop into this male genital duct system."[21]

Testosterone alone is not enough.

"…An androgen receptor within the cytoplasm…is encoded on the X chromosome that allows the Wolffian duct cells to identify testosterone as the trigger for further development. Without a properly functioning androgen receptor, it doesn't matter how much testosterone one has floating around in one's bloodstream, it will be biologically useless and the Wolffian ducts will in fact degenerate and not develop into the male genital duct system. But once the Wolffian duct degenerates from the impotency of testosterone due to the absence of functioning androgen receptors, a very strange thing takes place. Since the external genitalia are destined to become female unless acted upon by androgens, lack of functioning androgen receptors results in this XY person having testes but female external genitalia. So why isn't there a uterus too?

"It turns out that the testes not only secrete testosterone, they also produce something called Anti-Mullerian Hormone (AMH) and it...is incapable of causing an effect at the cellular level unless it locks on to a specific protein...the AMH receptor" a protein "genetically encoded for on the 12th chromosome." The AMH "reaction with the AMH receptor located in the Mullerian duct cells causes them to degenerate.

"So the Wolffian duct must be stimulated by testosterone or it degenerates, but the Mullerian duct will become the female internal genital system by default unless specifically acted upon by the AMH in concert with the AMH receptor located in the Mullerian duct cells. This is precisely why the XY female who lacks properly functioning androgen receptors doesn't have a uterus. 'Her' testes also made AMH which caused the involution of the Mullerian duct system. Also, any dysfunction of either AMH production or the AMH receptor results in sterility."[21]

There is more!

Development of external male genitalia requires "the biochemical ability to convert testosterone into 5 alpha-dihydrotestosterone...a hormone that comes about by the enzymatic action of 5 alpha-reductase on testosterone." Deficiency here leads to deformed genitalia and impotency.

"...The human embryo by default is destined to become female unless it is acted upon by several biomolecules acting together through specific receptors contained in the primordial undifferentiated cells that are to become the male reproductive system."[21]

Shortfall of the essential hormones and enzymes can result "in the development of either a female phenotype, or a male that is impotent and infertile. Either way, reproduction as we know it, resulting in the continuation of any species leading up to *Homo sapiens*, would be physically impossible and the idea that only natural selection acting on random variation could explain human evolution would literally be dead."[21]

Instead of species dead end, high voltage electricity powering the attraction shared by the two genders provides the setting for romance, marriage, and parenting.

The French say it best: "Viva la difference!"

Apart from gender, the ultimate issue relates to human ancestry.

Dr. Glicksman zeros in on evolutionism's irreducible complexity dilemma, verbally indicting blind rejection of intelligent design. "...We and our children are supposed to believe this paradox spun out by evolutionary biologists. That the very intellect that each of us possesses, which gives us the capacity to detect intelligence, came about by the unguided random forces of nature; forces that all experience tells us can't produce anything that is considered intellectually significant.

"...We all are human and have philosophical and ideological models that we follow in life. Scientists who continue to expound dogmatically on the truth of macroevolution, without at least admitting to the weaknesses of their claims, while showing no appreciation for its effects on our culture, at best, are ignorant of the human heart and mind, and at worst, are being disingenuous and intellectually dishonest." [21]

10

Forty Million Mistakes
Debunking Common Ancestry

*"To take a line of fossils and claim that they represent a lineage
is not scientific hypothesis that can be tested,
but an assertion that carries the same validity as a bedtime story—
amusing, perhaps even instructive, but not scientific."*
Henry Gee[1]

Nothing in the history of remote generations of humans suggests shared descent from some monkey-like critter much less a non-descript single-sex, hermaphrodite. Family albums carry dusty portraits of craggy featured faces etched by the ravages of Father Time conspiring with Mother Nature's whims. No album portrays the slightest hint of some furry creature with pointed ears and a tail or a fish battling ocean currents.

Fossil Bones

Fossil bone scraps, even arguably ancestral to humans, have been paltry. Devotees of evolutionism have more than once pushed the bounds of "discovery" into fraudulent realms (eg. Piltdown man; Nebraska man). The missing organic chain linking *Homo sapiens* to an ancestor common to monkeys continues devoid of iron-clad links.

Richard Leakey and Roger Lewin, fossil finders and interpreters, acknowledged earlier, "...Until someone is lucky enough to come across a complete human skeleton of one of our ancestors, much of what we can say about them is pure inference, guesswork."[2]

Paleontologist David Raup echoed similar sentiments in a letter to the editor of *Science* in 1981. "A large number of well-trained scientists outside of evolutionary biology have unfortunately gotten the idea that the fossil record is far more Darwinian than it is. This probably comes from the over-simplification inevitable in secondary sources: low-level textbooks, semi-popular articles, and so on."

Raup saw "wishful thinking involved" where evo advocates sought predictable progressions. "In general, these have not been found---yet the optimist dies hard, and some pure fantasy has crept into textbooks."[3]

Evolutionist Henry Gee, *Nature* magazine Senior Editor, reports less-than bonanza finds. "...All the evidence for the hominid lineage between about 10 and 5 million years ago---several thousand generations of living creatures---can be fitted into a small box."[4]

With a zoology Ph.D. from the University of Cambridge, Dr. Gee believes that "...fossils are isolated points in Deep Time that cannot be connected with any other to form a narrative of ancestry and descent."[5]

Tattered bone chips contribute little to the calligraphy of human ancestry maps. Look-alike bits and pieces don't suffice when scrutinized under the "best evidence rule." It is pointless to argue that skeletal structural similarities between a chimp and a human suggests common ancestry any more than claiming willow trees and redwood trees sprouted from the same root stock because they both have a trunk.

Occasionally, scholars intent on finding fossil evidence in tune with Darwin's tree of life, resort to flimflam. Those burdened with bias are vulnerable to clever deceit. In a scenario reminiscent of the long ago media show, *Time to Stump the Experts*, the skull of the alleged "Piltdown Man" stumped the pros for nearly a half-century. Eager to fill fossil gaps confirming human evolution, brilliant minds swallowed the con job hook, line and jaw bone.

The British museum exulted, unabashedly promoting Mr. Piltdown as a rare piece of missing-link antiquity.

Tradition has it that the perpetrators of the hoax were fossil aficionados craving recognition. It took some time (1912 to 1953) to uncover the scandal. The much touted but quite fraudulent "proof" went "poof." The slick "discovery" of a "missing link" proved to be the jaw of an ape deviously crafted together with pieces of a not-so-ancient human skull, stained to look old. Eventually, Piltdown evolved to embarrassing meltdown!

Scientists other than Dr. Henry Gee, also view fossil evidence of human evolution murky at best. "Despite decades of patient work in pitiless places, we still know rather little about the evolution of humanity...I have told it as plainly as I can, to show you how hard it is to justify any kind of narrative based on the evidence...Lineages leading to modern humans and chimps diverged around 5 million years ago. Few hominid fossils are known from the interval between 5 and 10 million years ago, and all of these are uninformative scraps."[6]

"...In the present state of our knowledge, I do not believe it is possible to fit the known hominid fossils into a reliable pattern."[7] "The human fossil record is no exception to the general rule that the main lesson to be learned from paleontology is that evolution always takes place somewhere else."[8] "...One is forced to conclude that there is no clear-cut scientific picture of human evolution."[9] "'...Paleoanthropology has the form but not the substance of science.'"[10]

Genealogy Revisited

Tracing *Homo sapiens'* ancestry from five million years ago to the present, adds little clarity to an otherwise sketchy silhouette of the so-called tree of life. Within the context of conventional evolutionary theory, that represents the time frame junction in the road in which apes and humans went their separate ways. Bone fragment candidates proposed for linkage between then and now consist primarily of innovative postulates. The already murky evidence is muddied further if the Kanapoi elbow bone (KNM-KP 271) dating is taken at face value.

Harvard University's David Pilbeam referenced the Kanapoi bone fragment, reporting that "Multivariate statistical analysis of the humeral fragment aligns it unequivocally with man rather than with the chimpanzee, the hominoid most similar to man in this anatomical region."[11] Measurements subjected to computer analysis "...show that the Kanapoi specimen, which is 4 to 4.5 million years old, is indistinguishable from modern *Homo sapiens.*"[12]

If the original owner of the Kanapoi elbow bone was indeed human, "man was virtually the same 3.5 million years ago (on the evolutionist time scale) as he is today" suggesting "humans appeared on the scene suddenly and without evolutionary ancestors."[13]   Dr. Pilbeam concluded "There is no clear-cut and inexorable pathway from ape to human being."[14]

In the context of these conventional dates, the argument can be made that "...true humans were on the scene before the australopithecines appear in the fossil record...anatomically modern *Homo sapiens*, Neandertal, archaic *Homo sapiens* and *Homo erectus* all lived as contemporaries at one time or another...when humans appear in the fossil record, they are already human."[15]

A *Homo erectus* skull possesses a "strikingly modern feature: the delicate bony platform behind the eyes on which the brain rests, called the cranial base...inside its head they found a strongly flexed cranial base."[16]

"The fact that *sapiens*-like fossils have appeared in the fossil record before the australopithecines and lived as contemporaries with the australopithecines throughout all of their history reveals that the australopithecines had nothing to do with human origins. Australopithecine authority, Charles Oxnard...concludes, 'The genus *Homo*, may, in fact, be so ancient as to parallel entirely the genus *Australopithecus*, thus denying the latter a direct place in the human lineage.'"[17]

"Other Paleoanthropologists have expressed their belief that none of the australopithecines are legitimate human ancestors. Surveying one-hundred years of paleoanthropology, Matt Cartmill (Duke University), David Pilbeam (Harvard University), and the late Glen Isaac (Harvard University) observe, 'The australopithecines are rapidly sinking back to the status of peculiarly specialized apes.'"[18]

As to those robust Neanderthals, characterized by pronounced eyebrow ridges and cranial capacities exceeding those of modern humans, they walked upright and buried their dead with compassionate care. The disappearance of these distinctly human   contemporaries of our ancestors, might best be explained by assimilation with other *Homo sapiens*.

Ape-like Ancestors?

When "I'll be a monkey's uncle" creeps into a conversation, it exclaims surprised absurdity, not a genealogical link. Evolutionists pledge allegiance to the theoretical but when it comes to mounting the likeness of a fish or an ape atop their own family's genealogy chart, the alleged relationship is missing from the marquee. Swallowing this fiction compares to some "ancestor" fish biting a baited hook.

But when Charles Darwin spoke, he went to extremes to at least feign a modicum of pride at the concocted "family" connection.

"...I would as soon be descended from that heroic little monkey, who braved his dreaded enemy in order to save the life of his keeper; or from that old baboon, who, descending from the mountains, carried away in triumph his young comrade from a crow of astonished dogs---as from a savage who delights to torture his enemies, offers up bloody sacrifices, practices infanticide without remorse, treats his wives like slaves, knows no decency, and is haunted by the grossest superstitions.

"Man may be excused for feeling some pride at having risen...to the very summit of the organic scale; and the fact of his having thus risen...may give him hopes for a still higher destiny in the distant future."[19]

Heads nod in agreement at Darwin's assessment of man's lofty position of eminence in the organic world. But is there any serious genealogist who would boast claiming a monkey or a baboon-type ancestor swinging from a branch of their family tree?

Sharing an efficient leg bone hardly confirms genetic relationship. The fact that monkeys have arms, legs, eyes, ears, mouths, hands, hearts, lungs and blood, does not ipso facto confirm common ancestry with *Homo sapiens*. It does suggest a common Designer, just as an architect may design buildings of many sizes and shapes that display distinctive arrangements while using similar materials

Human eyes and the eyes of an octopus are "very much alike in structure and function." This similarity (homology) doesn't suggest genetic relationship or common ancestry. "...To be taken seriously, similar (homologue) organs in different creatures should also be coded with similar (homologue) DNA codes However, they are not."[20] It should be recognized that the specific genetic composition is different, as in the case of a genome's regulatory genes.

The eye similarity in radically different body styles, raised the eyebrows of evolutionist Frank Salisbury. "Even something as complex as the eye has appeared several times; for example, in the squid, the vertebrates, and the arthropods. It's bad enough accounting for the origin of such things once, but the thought of producing them several times according to the modern synthetic theory makes my head swim."[21]

Fossil bone fragments recovered from strata, contribute little linking ape-like creatures to *Homo sapiens*. The bone cupboard approaches bare as far as reliable evidence prior to 5 million years BP, the time juncture when evolutionists project divergence between ape-like creatures and humans.

Remember Henry Gee's assessment: "Few hominid fossils are known from the interval between 5 and 10 million years ago, and all of these are uninformative scraps" and that fossils suggesting hominoid lineage during that time "...can be fitted into a small box."[22]

From Gee's perspective, the "...conventional, linear view easily becomes a story in which the features of humanity are acquired in a sequence that can be discerned retrospectively---first an upright stance, then a bigger brain, then the invention of tool making, and so on..." He describes the postulated "chain of ancestry" as "...a completely human invention created after the fact, shaped to accord with human prejudices...Each fossil represents an isolated point, with no knowable connection to any other given fossil, and all float around in an overwhelming sea of gaps."[23]

So what about fossil evidence of human evolution following the alleged point of divergence? With fossil lineage prior to the conventional 5 million year BP a virtual blank, what about bones after that conjectured divergence date? There are significantly more hominid type fossils to study than the meager "small box" candidates. Fully formed *Homo sapiens* fossils have surfaced in significant numbers. And there are numerous skulls and fossils of animals clearly apes.

Joel Achenbach, writing for the September, 2005 *National Geographic*, described the study of human origins as "tricky." "The plot keeps thickening. It's a heck of a tale, still unfolding." For starters he reports that Ernst Mayr believes Peking man, Java man, and *Homo erectus* are the same.

A field, once seen as coherent, "...has again become a rather glorious mess...some key details are still unknown." Noting that the human "family tree" has "a lot of dead ends in it" he acknowledges, even with a recent fossil find, "We have essentially no fossils...of chimpanzees."

He reports Harvard paleontologist Don Lieberman thinking, in Achenbach's words, that "some of his colleagues have tried too hard to tell the story of human origins from a relatively limited set of fossils." He quotes Lieberman admitting "We're not doing a very good job of being honest about what we don't know. Sometimes I think we're trying to squeeze too much blood out of these stones."

Achenbach wrapped his report concluding sagely that evolution can't be observed like Newton's fall of an apple because "Life---despite all the efforts of modern science---is messy."[24]

Digging up "markedly ape-like" jawbone fragments, broken teeth and a thighbone, and then claiming the shards fill gaps in Darwin's "tree of life" from 3.8 to 4.2 million years BP illustrates "trying to squeeze too much blood" out of meager evidence. One imaginative "squeezer" sees the paltry pieces as allowing "...scientists to link together the most complete chain of human evolution so far."

Really?

Meave Leakey had questions. "I don't believe this. We do not have the specimens to fill the gaps." Paleoanthropologist Bernard Wood, of George Washington University, warned we "should beware coming out with a complete explanation when we don't have all the evidence." Dr. Brad Harrub pooh-poohed the linkage claim. "This discovery does not document human evolution or phases of man. It demonstrates some larger teeth that were found in the Awash region."[25]

Molecular Biology Takes a Look

An objective observer is not likely to find clear-cut ape/like-to-human ancestry linkage in the fossil record. Molecular biology provides a far more inviting data source for assessing ancestry than inorganic layers of strata. But even in the microscopic realm, linking man-to-monkey is far from a slam dunk!

Once the preliminary mapping of the human genome was completed in the summer of 2000, followed by the 2005 initial sequencing of the chimp genome, researchers zeroed in on human and chimp DNA comparisons. Differences in reported findings range from an estimated 1.5% to 5%. Measured against 3,000,000 DNA base pairs, the molecular gap yawns.

For one thing, gene expression differs in humans and apes. Ajit Varki, a University of California, San Diego glycobiologist, observed that all mammals, other than humans, carry two variants on their cell surfaces: Neu5Ac and Neu5Gc. "Whereas modern ape bones have a mixture of Nau5Ge and Neu5Ac, Neanderthal fossils---and modern human bones primarily have Neu5Ac."[26]

Unlike chimps, Neu5Gc goes AWOL in the human brain!

Critical to serious analysis, other substantial differences exist "...not generally included in calculations of percent DNA similarity." For example, "the size of the chimpanzee genome is 10% greater than the size of the human genome."[27]

Chromosome counts vary from the human 23 pairs to the chimp's 24. The genes and markers on chromosomes 4, 9, and 12 show intrinsic differences and "...are not in the same order in the human and the chimpanzee."[28] "The Y chromosome in particular is of a different size and has many markers that do not line up between the human and the chimpanzee."[29]

"At the end of each chromosome is a string of repeating DNA sequences called a telomere. Chimpanzees and other apes have about 23 kilobases (a kilobase is 1,000 base pairs of DNA) of repeats. Humans are unique among primates with much shorter telomeres only 10 kilobases long."[30]

Despite the headline "Humans, Chimps Almost a Match," and the claim that 40 million differences between human and chimp genetic codes represents "'elegant confirmation' of Darwin's theory of evolution"[31] the assertion is less front page news than junk science.

Like moths to a flame, some pundits seem intent on grafting an ape-like critter to the root stock of their family trees. Under a headline alleging "New Analyses Bolster the Theory of Evolution," two observers reported "...of all 3 billion bits of genetic code that go into making a chimpanzee...the sequence was more than 96 percent identical to the human genome."[32]

The authors assured readers that when scientists "tallied the harmful mutations in the chimp genome, the number fit perfectly into the range that evolutionary theory had predicted."

This rationale comes across as intellectual confetti. Mutations don't add new genetic information but are overwhelmingly deleterious corrupting the genetic information already in place.

Recent discoveries reveal a blizzard of birth defects in the human genome caused by mutations! Macular degeneration, a curse plaguing fifteen million elderly Americans, has been linked to a gene mutation. Birth defects, such as Downe Syndrome, typify the harvest reaped from genetic mistakes. Looking for the "good" mutations required by the Modern Synthetic Theory of Evolution compares to the daunting quest for a needle in a haystack.

"Currently, more than 13,500 human mutations have been described and reported in the medical literature...The box score is more than 13,500 medically described mutations cause debilitation, morbidity or death and zero are a biological advantage."[33]

This horrific batting average contributes nothing to Darwin's "progress towards perfection" prediction. Thousands of years of devolution of the human species offers not a trace of confirming evidence that *Homo sapiens* exists only as some intermediate transit stop evolving in the direction of a new and improved life format.

Far from the promised evolution, the only obvious change is devolutionary---down the postulated stairway.

Can anyone name a significant list of "good" mutations?

Speaking of mutations, how did monkey-style blood evolve into human blood? Diseased blood, corrupted by mutations, kills. Blood transfusions pump life through the human body, but blood from a chimp or an ape would kill a human. Just how and when could chimp blood mutate and produce human blood?

The mummified remains of Egyptian Pharaohs, from up to 4,000 years before the present, carried the identical basic blood types treasured in today's human life systems. There's not a scintilla of evidence of ape-to-man transitional blood during the most recent four millennia. There's certainly nothing remotely ape-like in the remains of ancient Egyptians!

California Institute of Technology's Roy J. Britten looked at 779,000 base pairs comparing chimp to human DNA. "He found that 1.4% of the bases had been substituted...A nucleotide substitution is a mutation where one base (A, G, C, or T) is replaced with another." When Britten checked nucleotide bases that were missing ("indels" for insertion/deletion), he discovered "an additional 3.4% of base pairs that were different."[34]

"It has long been believed that the DNA of chimps and humans is about 98.5 percent identical, making chimps our closest relative." Britten "...found more differences than previously noted..." He concluded "...that humans and chimps share only about 95 percent of the same DNA, according to a report released last week [2002] by the Proceedings of the National Academy of Sciences..."[35]

Calculated mathematically, the magnitude of the variations looms large. Forty million differences hardly promote "cousin" status. A 5% difference pushes the variables to an astounding 150 million differences. The magnitude of the genetic gap represents enough written data to fill as many as 50 encyclopedias brimming with 15 million words. Differences in nucleotide base pair sequences coupled with on-off actions and reactions within the genome, accentuate an unbridged genetic chasm.

Evolutionism theory claims apes and humans split from some

unidentified common ancestor five-million conventional years before the present. The Kanapoi human elbow joint has been dated at 3.5 to 4.5 million years BP. That leaves a maximum of 1,500,000 years to activate the genetic code differences between humans and chimps.

So all that stands between humans and their alleged chimp "cousins" are at least forty million or as many as one-hundred-fifty million mistakes? And these mistakes are supposedly "good" mutations?

Let's do the math!

The best possible odds for 40-million mutations require something like 8 "good" mutations per year in 5 million years. The ante goes up to 100 "good" mutations per year if the 150-million differences were put into the formula in 1.5 million years. When the chance probability of a single event exceeds 10^{50} it rises to mathematic impossibility. Even forty million differences overwhelm the equation.

"There has simply been insufficient time for ape-like creatures to turn into humans...Due to the cost of substitution (death of the unfit) of one gene for another in a population, it would take over 7×10^{11} of human-like generations to substitute...120 million base pairs. Or in 10 million years (twice the time since the chimp/human common ancestor is alleged to have lived), only 1667 substitutions could occur, or 0.001% of the difference.[36] Biologists call the mathematical quandary "Haldane's Dilemma" in honor of mid-twentieth century evolutionary geneticist, J.B.S. Haldane.

"Extrapolate backward from this known species [man] to a time 10 million years ago. This is three times earlier than the said occurrence of the four foot high australopithecine 'Lucy.' This is twice as old as the alleged split between gorilla, chimpanzee, and man...

"Given 10 million years, the population could selectively replace a maximum of 1,667 nucleotides. This would have the information content of less than 10 lines in this book [Walter James ReMine's, *The Biotic Message*]. It amounts to one three-hundredths of one-hundredth of one-percent of the human genome."[37]

Is evolutionism suggesting something akin to a "miracle" here? Sounds beyond mere coincidence, even when nonchalantly swallowing 5 million year deep time estimates for the transition as gospel. Before taking a blasé gulp, its prudent to pause, inhale deeply, and ask, "Is the earth really that old?"

The common ancestor divergence theme---one line down to apes and another lineage down to humans---not only strikes out in the fossil record and by the lack of molecular biological support, but also the multi-million year dates assigned are suspect. It is no public secret that the chunks of deep time attributed to bone fragments are calculated by relying on circular reasoning.

The way it works is less than convincing. Fossils derive their age from the believed age of the strata and a layer of strata derives its age from the fossils it shelters. Its round-and-round she goes, a vice-versa merry-go-round with all the accuracy of a blind-folded gamer pinning the tale on the ape.

"The rocks do date the fossils, but the fossils date the rocks more accurately. Stratigraphy cannot avoid this kind of reasoning, if it insists on using only temporal concepts, because circularity is inherent in the derivation of time scales."[38]

Despite radically different opinions, writers use their considerable talents to create and articulate ideas---right, wrong or a muddled mixed bag. Some credit brain power to complex design created by an Intelligent Designer while others salute nature's random whims, asserting human intelligence derived from an unintelligent source.

Assuming 40-million "good" mutations evolved an intelligent human defies chance probability. And how about the crippling condition imposed on some mythical ape-to-man transitional---limping along, trying to walk tall on the ground, hopelessly too clumsy to swing from trees?

The Dash Between the Dates

Humans exemplify *sui generis*---one of a kind! Borrowing the poetic phrase, "let me count the ways."

Compared to simian types, our legs are longer and arms shorter, rendering the shape of that ancient Kanapoi elbow suspiciously human. Swinging from trees with a tail is not an option while walking upright on two legs, without knuckles dragging on the ground, works fine.

The gift of speech powers articulate communication, and in several hundred different languages, no less. Winston Churchill and Ronald Reagan epitomized persuasive communication. When the likes of Mark Twain and Charles Dickens touched pen to paper, vibrant phrases sang in unison.

Apes, chimps and bonobos don't sing songs, humans do. Frank Sinatra's platinum performances illustrate such talent. People compose melodies, craft instruments and orchestrate symphonies of sound. The genius Mozart, at the age of 14, listened to a privately presented concert at the Vatican and went home to write the score from memory---including the arrangements for each instrument!

Paintings by Rembrandt, John Singer Sargant and Winslow Homer didn't appear by a monkey dipping its tail in a rainbow of oils, then swishing the make-do "brush" on a canvass.

The human skull's design is a thing of beauty, providing protective space for a three-pound brain---larger than simian brains. With that mind in command, harnessing dexterous manual skills, individual creativity builds houses, space ships, and computers.

And human minds investigate science and store mega-bits of data in living memory banks from which ideas flow---including theories as to the origin of life in the universe!

Often in the heat of verbal swordsmanship, conflicting views slash and cut with venomous strokes. An adversary articulating opposing scientific views may be depicted as close-minded; a supreme egoist; or a scholar wanna-be burdened with sub-par academic credentials.

Despite verbal fire and smoke shrouding the attack mode, most advocates who cradle rigid views as "flexible as a garden hose in winter," warrant being respected at face value, however tainted by brainwashed bias.

Human life spans are measured by two dates divided by a dash. However long or short a life, the dash between the dates symbolizes an interval of time, a person's legacy---the sum total of choices, good or bad. Nothing achieved within the dates framing that dash suggests kinship with the simian world.

Much more than a compacted blob of protoplasm, a person lives, breathes, loves and reasons. Unlike a fish or the pointed-ear creature depicted by Darwin's mythical ancestry chain, human beings possess a soul, created with love in the image of God.

Many believe that humans are just a good-luck branch of evolution's genealogy tree, shared with an ape. Seriously now, does any human family truly believe it descended from a fish or an ape-like ancestor?

So where did the monkey-to-man myth originate?

Not in the bone shards scraped from strata! In the words of Henry Gee: "...fossils are isolated points in Deep Time that cannot be connected with any other to form a narrative of ancestry and descent."[39]

And molecular biology doesn't come to evolutionism's rescue given that only 1,667 beneficial mutations are mathematically feasible in ten million years when at least 40 million are required for the conjectured transition---and in five-million years.

The source of the monkey-to-man fable? Looks like all credit goes to the minds of men willing to imagine a monkey-like ancestor hanging from their family tree!

"You are not an accident. Your parents may not have planned you but God did. He wanted you alive and created you for a purpose...You were made by God and for God, and until you understand that, life will never make sense. Only in God do we discover our origin, our identity, our meaning, our purpose, our significance, and our destiny."[40]

11

The "Perfect" Cataclysm
Hydraulic Action

*"...Evolution is the central most disorganizing, anti-intellectual anti-science
principle that biologists have ever been dictatorially forced
to learn to understand the world...
it stands as the greatest scandal in science of the last 140 years."*
Joseph Mastropaolo [1]

Two hundred miles east of Seattle, a colossal cataclysm
sculpted a 16,000 square mile gouge in the earth in the blink of
an eye. Investigating geologist J. Harlan Bretz raised eyebrows
when he suggested to professional peers in a 1927 lecture to the
Geological Society of Washington, D.C. that the Scablands scar
didn't result from an eroding river or a moving glacier.

Professional peers were scandalized by his radical hypothesis
that the massive swath gouged the earth suddenly thanks to a
mega-flood. The listening audience of geologists dismissed the
suggestion out-of-hand because it carried Biblical implications.
The Bretz idea flew in the face of conventional thought that earth
sculptures of this magnitude required millions of years of gradual
erosion by a river or a glacier.

It took time for the revolutionary thought to gain favor. But
more than a half-century after the fact, the favor finally arrived, a
bit tardy, and in a ceremony tied with symbolic ribbons. In 1980,
geologists honored Bretz with their highest award.[2]

The Scablands geology doesn't necessarily prove the reality of
the deluge of Noah's day. It does suggest the power of a surging
wall of water as high as 800 feet, released by a ruptured ice dam,
can scour jagged incisions through the face of the earth in a day.

Since gradual river erosion or glacial-paced mountains of ice
are not the exclusive tools of nature for carving canyons, could
it be also that a world-wide hydraulic cataclysm supplied the ice
age water?

Darwin v. Genesis

Planet Earth originally boasted perfection: a pervasively mild climate; a thick carpet of lush forests and verdant vegetation; a plethora of jumbo-sized organic life forms; and an atmospheric envelope conducive to ecological balance.

Perfection reigned!

But according to the Genesis account, deterioration set in the moment first parents abused their power of choice in pursuit of faux "wisdom." Since that springtime of life, precipitous ecological decline followed, engulfing the natural world.

Then came a hydraulic cataclysm that submerged the entire earth in raging torrents of water. "...All the springs of the great deep burst forth, and the floodgates of the heavens were opened." Underground fountains of water surged to the surface to mix with 960 hours of unremitting sheets of rain. "All the high mountains under the heavens were covered...to a depth of more than twenty feet." inundating the earth's highest peak covered with water twenty-feet deep."[3] Next came "a wind over the earth"[4] capable of unleashing mountainous, churning waves.

The fearful devastation shattered life and scrambled and scarred land surfaces leaving them unrecognizable. The 2005 Katrina hurricane that marred the Caribbean Gulf Coast left in its wake the merest, infinitesimal hint of what a planet-wide wind and water powered calamity could do.

Imagine the consequences if other natural destructive forces were added to the equation: land masses ripped apart by earthquakes so violent as to shift tectonic plates; new, raggedly-chiseled mountain ranges, abruptly pushing to the sky; and multiple, climate-modifying volcanoes, surpassing the magnitude of the 1815 Mt. Tambura explosion, erupting simultaneously, spewing clouds of ash while unleashing rivers of voracious lava!

As a bonus, consider adding in a volley of crushing meteorites comparable to what hit the Gulf of Mexico, just off the Yucatan Peninsula, allegedly wiping out the world's dinosaur population!

Talk about the "perfect" cataclysm!

With flood water residue crowning the extreme tips of the earth with sheets of ice and snow, its understandable the post-flood civilization would inhabit the moderate climates lining the equator.

Darwin took sharp issue with the Genesis report, rejecting it entirely! He had no choice.

If the entire surface of the earth had been devastated by flood waters, his theory would have been demolished, swept away as if it were a shred of fossilized flotsam. He, asserted, without equivocation, "...we may feel certain...that no cataclysm has desolated the whole world."[5]   This assessment flowed from a speculative pen lacking credentials as hydrologist, geologist, or paleontologist.

His understandable bias is pitted against a contrary account written at least three millennia before his birth---much closer to the event. There is at least the possibility that the Genesis author had access both to word-of-mouth traditions and some form of written inscriptions, as well as inspiration from the Creator.

While many who see no problem with a universal cataclysm that could destroy the dinosaur population planet-wide, they follow Darwin's lead, rejecting *a priori* the possibility of an inundating flood that took out 100% of the earth's surface.

What Darwin neglected to explain was just how the vast cemeteries of fossils, coal, and petroleum deposits were buried by water born sediments throughout "the whole world." Nor did he account for land animal fossil finds such as the dinos *Muttaburrasaurus* in Australia and T-Rex in Canada "found buried with marine creatures such as shellfish, turtles and fish..."[6]

Did Darwin understand that 70% of the planet is currently covered by water? Quite likely! Travel aboard the HMS Beagle provided eyewitness proof. Did he recognize that floods occurred? Of course! Or that virtually every fraction of earth's land mass had been covered by flood waters at one time or another?

With 70% presently under water, what evidence suggests the remaining 30% hasn't been inundated simultaneously in a "whole world" cataclysm?

Neo-Darwinism argues "progress towards perfection." Creationism points to a sudden, world-scale cataclysm that sabotaged primal perfection and diminished life diversity. The Epic of Gilgamesh contains a flood reference recorded on partially damaged cuneiform tablets found in the Nineveh library and dated during the reign of the Assyrian king, Ashurbanipal (669-633 BC).

While some argue the Genesis author could have borrowed the story of the deluge of Noah's day from the Gilgamesh account, the question might more appropriately be asked as to whether the Gilgamesh author borrowed the story from Genesis?

Remember, more than one-hundred cultures, worldwide, carry traditions of a flood!

Christ of the Bible endorsed the Genesis account of the flood. Darwin never met Noah nor witnessed the event. But those who embrace the Genesis flood story rely on an authoritative account recorded nearly 2,000 years before the present. Christ, the Creator, said, "For in the days before the flood, people were eating and drinking, marrying and giving in marriage, up to the day Noah entered the ark; and they knew nothing about what would happen until the flood came and took them all away."[7]

Christians attempting to reconcile the radically incompatible confront the impossible. The poles apart choices loom as either/or! Residual evidence scattered across the face of the planet testifies to a world-wide upheaval, unparalleled in science archives. Sudden ecological disaster doesn't accommodate gradual ecological change.

We are not privy to the source of Darwin's information doubting a worldwide flood, but a mountain of evidence suggests he didn't know what he was talking about. While Alfred Russell Wallace may have agreed with Darwin, Wallace did cite "denudation" and "destruction" of the earth's geology as explanation for the lack of transitionals. Inadvertently, his descriptions of observed conditions on the earth's face arguably trace markings compatible with a worldwide deluge.

"...Denudation is always going on, and the rocks that we now find at the earth's surface are only a small fragment of those which were originally laid down...the frequent uncomformability of strata with those which overlie them, tell us plainly of repeated elevations and depressions of the surface, and denudation on an enormous scale.

"Almost every mountain range, with its peaks, ridges, and valleys, is but the remnant of some vast plateau eaten away by sub-aerial agencies; every range of sea-cliffs tell us of long slopes of land destroyed by the waves; while almost all the older rocks which now form the surface of the earth have been once covered with newer deposits which have long since disappeared."

Wallace opined that "...areas of unknown extent are buried under strata which rest on them uncomfortably, and could not therefore, constitute the original capping under which the whole of these rocks must once have been deeply buried; because granite can only be formed, and metamorphism can only go on, deep down in the crust of the earth...What an overwhelming idea does this give us of the destruction of whole piles of rock, miles in thickness and covering areas comparable with those of continents..."[8]

Hydraulic Power

Darwin's rush to judgment leaves hanging a batch of questions!

Can giant-sized dinosaur fossils form if covered gradually, at a minuscule pace, when preservation requires prompt and complete burial with multiple tons of sediment? How could billions of barrels of petroleum and tons of coal form without sudden submersion of flora, inundated by sweeping water action? How can mass burials that created fossil cemeteries crammed with disarticulated bones from multiple species be explained apart from the churning force of unleashed hydraulic energy? What rationale other than hydraulic catastrophe better accounts for the preservation of Wyoming's giant palm leaf fossils—up to eight feet long and four feet wide—remnants of a long-ago temperate climate in an area now exposed to wind-blown winter snows?

There is pervasive evidence of past water intrusion on all worldwide land masses. An evolutionist expert cited by the defense in the *Scopes* trial avowed that "...practically all of the earth has at some time or other been covered by water."[9]

Since flood water can saturate any part of earth's surface at any time, why couldn't the entire land mass be inundated simultaneously?

If earth's entire land mass were level, there would be enough water to inundate the face of it to a depth of several hundred feet. Although the date may be suspect, it's been said that, "...the world got soaked seventy million years ago, as sea levels rose five hundred feet."[10]

A cataclysmic deluge rearranged the face of Planet Earth in the recent past, no more than 11,500 years before the present if Carbon-14 dating methodology is accurate.[11] Perhaps it's more than coincidental that the rings of bristlecone pines extend to 9,040 years before the present while Northern Hemisphere oak tree rings with overlapping dates reach back a projected 11,000+ years—then abruptly dead-end.

Does a cataclysmic deluge that devastated the entire planet account for these approximate time boundaries?

Ice Age

Observers of contrasting views agree that at one time or another, excessive water has swamped all earth's land masses. The Biblical account describes a non-stop torrent of rain for forty days and nights combined with an internal explosion of water from the "fountains of the deep" that buried the planet in water and left it uninhabitable for a year.

What happened to excess water left from the cataclysm that devoured the earth? Is this the source of ice-age water? If not, where did the water for the glacier that buried Manhattan Island 300 feet deep come from?

Antarctica, Greenland, and the Arctic bear immense burdens of frozen water. Snow masses still cap the poles and crown mountain ranges. Sea-bound glaciers inch their way down craggy mountain slopes feeding thirsty oceans that encroach on shorelines as warming trends continue.

The Antarctica ice cap towers two miles high in some locations. One estimate suggests the ice and snow saturating the surfaces of Greenland and Antarctica together contain 70% of the planet's fresh water. In the event this frozen water storage plant should feel the heat of global warming and melt entirely, ocean levels could rise eventually as high as 230 feet according to some extreme estimates!

The Greenland ice sheet, "roughly the size of Mexico," covers 80% of its surface. "...Researchers found that in 2005, the glaciers discharged more than twice as much ice as they did in 1996--- enough fresh water to supply Los Angeles for 220 years."[12]

Then what triggered the freeze that introduced vast sheets of ice and an ice age so bitterly frigid that thousands of years after the fact, parts of the planet are still clamped in its grip?

Dr. Larry Vardiman offers insight as to the havoc an over-heated ocean might wreak. "It has been shown that the ocean temperature at the end of the Genesis Flood was likely as warm as 100° F or more. Such a warm ocean would be an explanation for the Ice Age because of the excessive evaporation of water into the atmosphere and deposition of snow in the polar regions and on mountaintops that would have occurred.

"An ocean with a SST [sea surface temperature] equal to or greater than 100° F would also likely have produced large frequencies and intensities of hurricanes beyond anything experienced today. It has been shown that giant hurricanes called *hypercanes* would likely have occurred over major portions of the earth. They would have grown to hundreds of miles in diameter, produced horizontal winds of over 300 miles per hour, had vertical winds of 100 miles per hour, and precipitated rain at rates greater than 10 inches per hour.

"Large amounts of erosion of the unconsolidated sediments would have occurred on the continents following the Flood. In this context, today's increasing hurricane activity represents a minor oscillation in the steady-state condition at the end of about 5,000 years of cooling."[13]

And don't underestimate the impact of volcanoes on world climate!

"...Requirements for an ice age are a combination of much

cooler summers and greater snowfall than in today's climate... These requirements are very difficult to meet with uniformitarian theories...Volcanic dust and aerosols remaining in the atmosphere following the Flood would provide one such mechanism." And "...the abundant layers of lava and ash, mixed with sedimentary rocks around the world, attest to extensive volcanism during the flood."[14]

The 1980 St. Helens "nozzle" style eruption spewed "100 cubic kilometers of volcanic products" with sobering results. But when a "linear fissure" supervolcanoe exploded in the prehistoric past, it dwarfed St. Helens' awesome fireworks by depositing 300,000 cubic kilometers of material on the surface of what is now Mexico forming "'the largest ignimbrite field in the world.'"[15]

An estimated forty active and inactive supervolcanoe sites exist.

The cataclysmic consequences strain imaginations should these smoldering monsters erupt in unison. Even without the "super" title, the earth's mantle shakes and shivers when "nozzle" or "ring fissure" volcanoes blow their tops.

Krakatoa exploded August 23, 1883 snuffing out 36,000 human lives and lifting ocean waves fifty feet into the air. The twenty billion cubic meters of ash and debris blown more than 20 miles into the global stratosphere caused temperatures to drop radically during the next three years, impacting climates as far distant as Europe.[16]

The volcanic dust from Tambora's eruption in 1815 is believed to have upset climates 10,000 miles distant in New England, parts of Canada and Europe. The following year was dubbed "the year without a summer" when an "unprecedented series of cold snaps chilled the area. Heavy snow fell in June, and frost caused crop failures in July and August. Sea ice was extensive in Hudson Bay and Davis Strait..."[17]

Writing for a community newsletter, Tom Canby, a feature writer for *National Geographic*, reported on the event drawing from nineteenth century Maryland archives. "Frost and ice were common in every month of the year, and very little vegetation matured. The sun's rays seemed to be destitute of heat, all nature seemed to be clad in a sable hue, and men exhibited no little anxiety concerning the future of this life.

"So the *Annals* historian recalled 1816, the dreadful 'year without a summer.' In Sandy Spring and all across the northern hemisphere there was misery and despair. In Canada and northern Europe shriveled crops and dying livestock brought starvation to 80,000.

"What happened to bring on a cataclysm so widespread and abrupt?

"The answer smoldered 10,000 miles away, in today's Indonesia. There on April 15, 1815, the 13,000-foot volcano Tambora erupted on an island near Java. For a week thunderous explosions rocked the region and were heard a thousand miles away. Fiery ejections of rock, flame, gas, and steam shot into the stratosphere.

"Thirty-six cubic miles of earth blasted heavenward---the greatest release of energy ever known, dwarfing a nuclear explosion and even a nuclear war. At week's end 12,000 Javanese lay dead, tsunamis had killed thousands more on distant islands, and the volcano stood a mile shorter than before.

"The trillions of tons of material that Tambora shot into the atmosphere circled the earth with the winds. For more than a year they blocked sunlight from the northern hemisphere, dimming the planet with that 'sable hue.'

Quoting from *Annals* written at the time, Canby describes the rare summer climate.

"'June was the coldest ever known in this latitude; frost, ice and snow were common; almost every green thing was killed. Fruit was nearly all destroyed; snow fell to the depth of ten inches in Vermont, seven inches in Maine, and three in Central New York.

"'July was accompanied by frost and ice. On the 5th ice formed of the thickness of a window throughout New England, New York and parts of Pennsylvania; Indian corn was nearly all destroyed.

"'August was more cheerless if possible than the summer months already passed. Ice formed half an inch thick; Indian corn was so frozen that the greater part was cut and dried for fodder. Almost every green thing was destroyed, both in this country and in Europe. There was no summer in 1816, and seed-corn kept over from 1815 sold for four and five dollars a bushel.

"'Let us hope,' concluded the Annalist, 'our generation will not have a repetition of such an experience as this.'"[18]

Glaciers still exist.

Eight spanking new U.S. warplanes bound for Europe while World War II raged, never reached the battle front. Encountering an emergency, the flights were aborted and the aircraft landed safely on Greenland's white landscape. The U.S. Coast-guard rescued all the airmen but the eight snowbound airplanes were abandoned to nature's whims. With the site navigationally marked, this piece of rare history was not forgotten. Toward the end of the century, a band of enterprising Americans launched a rescue mission.

"The Greenland Society of Atlanta…excavated a 10-foot diameter shaft in the Greenland ice sheet in the late 1980's to remove two B-17 Flying Fortresses and six P-38 Lightning fighters trapped under an estimated 250 feet of ice for almost 50 years."[19]

The mission proved more time consuming, costly and technically challenging than conceived. Initially, the planes could not be located at the landing site. In the fifty year interval, nature did its thing, shifting the locale by a mile. Undeterred, the rescuers cut a vertical tunnel to one of the long-frozen P-38s. It was dismantled, lifted piece-by-piece to the surface, and returned triumphantly to the United States. Victoriously salvaged from its deep-freeze, the reassembled aircraft glistens on public display in pristine glory---a fighter plane that never fought a battle.

"Aside from the fascination with salvaging several vintage aircraft for parts and movie rights, the fact that these aircraft were buried so deeply in such a short time focuses attention on the time scales used to estimate the chronologies of ice core data.

"If the aircraft were buried under about 250 feet of ice and snow in about 50 years, this means the ice sheet has been accumulating at an average rate of five feet per year. The Greenland ice sheet averages almost 4000 feet thick. If we were to assume the ice sheet has been accumulating at this rate since its beginning, it would take less than 1000 years for it to form and the recent-creation model might seem to be vindicated.

"However, life is never as simple as implied...In making our calculations, we did not take into account the compaction of the snow into ice as it is weighted down by the snow above. Neither did we consider the thinning of ice layers as the tremendous weight above forces the ice at lower levels to squeeze out horizontally. More importantly, we did not consider the average precipitation rate and actual depths of ice for different locations on the Greenland ice sheet.

"When these factors are taken into account, the average annual thickness of ice at Camp Century located near the southern tip of Greenland is believed to vary from about fourteen inches near the surface to less than two inches near the bottom."[20]

"If, for simplicity, we assume the average annual thickness to be the mean between the annual thickness at the top and at the bottom (about eight inches), this still gives an age of less than 6000 years for the 4000-foot-thick ice sheet to form under uniformitarian conditions.

"Perhaps as much as 95% of the ice near the poles could have accumulated in the first 500 years or so after the Flood...The 'annual' layers deep in the Greenland ice sheet may be related to individual storms rather than seasonal accumulations...Calculations of the number of layers laid down assuming the ice sheet accumulated rapidly near the bottom show that as many as 100 storms may have swept the polar regions each year accompanied by frequent volcanic eruptions."[21]

Even without a precipitous temperature drop triggered by an atmosphere overloaded with volcanic ash, water residue from the deluge described in Genesis could not readily evaporate overnight. Such ingredients seem conducive for an ice age.

Clues in the Strata

Maryland's east/west bound Interstate #68 slices through a cross-section of striking geologic scenery. Not only does Rocky Gap strata harbor a rainbow of earth tone colors, it also presents graceful arches of multiple strata layers that could only have hardened after folding. Enormous pressure must have shifted giant chunks of still damp sediments producing arced designs when solidified.

"Simultaneous tight folding of different sediment layers is easier to explain if the sediments did not turn to rock before folding…if the sediments were deposited only months apart rather than millions of years apart."[22]

Footprints of cataclysmic intervention pervade dry land masses. Marine type relics of ancient history have been discovered strewn across land masses not directly adjacent to present day oceans. "Marine sedimentary rocks are far more common and widespread on land today than all other kinds of sedimentary rocks combined. This is one of those simple facts that fairly cry out for explanation and that lie at the heart of man's continuing effort to understand more fully the changing geography of the geologic past."[23]

The moon, pushes and pulls ocean tides, building multi-layers of sand and eroding sand banks. Overnight changes delivered by surging currents of seawater can be observed any day on a visit to Florida's Grayton Beach shoreline.

Since creation of the Scablands didn't involve the gradual erosion of a river through solidified rock, others reason that the Grand Canyon resulted from the impact of an immense surge of water churning through still soft sediments. "The evolutionists' view is that a little bit of water eroded the Canyon over a long period of time through hard rock. The creationists' view is that a whole lot of water over a relatively short amount of time cut the Canyon through the still 'soft' rock layers laid down by the Flood."[24]

Conventional theory posits that the most recent sediment layer fronting the Grand Canyon's rim took millions of year to accrue. If true, did sufficient time remain to carve the ditch? Was there no new sediment being added during erosion?

When Mt. St. Helens blew its top in 1980, it cut deep gashes in the land within hours while creating entirely new layers of strata. The Scablands water explosion did its thing overnight. Neither cut took millions or even thousands of years. Unlike Arizona's Grand Canyon where a river meanders through its valley, the core of the Scablands does not cradle a river basin.

Sudden cataclysm, a la the Scablands scenario, presents a persuasive alternative explanation.

The Bretz findings in the Scablands geology underscore the power of hydraulic action in carving canyons and laying multiple sediment layers in brief time frames. Even if today's rate of sedimentation is any measure of past natural action, it doesn't begin to consume the multi-millions of years conjectured by evolutionism's gradualism. "The average thickness of the sediments on all of the continents is approximately 1,500 meters...The average sedimentation rate measured over a period of one year is approximately 100 meters per thousand years."[25] Even authoritative estimates suggesting current average rates of erosion at 60 millimeters per 1000 years, put evolutionism's gradualism out-of-sync with conventional deep time scenarios. Either way, the Scablands hydraulic action turned traditional erosion/sedimentation ratios topsy-turvy, shattering the status quo in just a few hours.

The Scablands did it in a few hours!

Test results presented to the National Congress of Sedimentologists at Brest in 1991 "...contradict the idea of the slow build up of one layer [of sediment] followed by another. The time scale is reduced from hundreds of millions of years to one or more cataclysms producing almost instantaneous laminae. These innocent-sounding words are the death knell of...the idea that the existence of thousands of meters of sediments is by itself evidence for a great age for the Earth...Today, there are no known fossiliferous rocks forming anywhere in the world..."[26] other than coral reef fossils and others from landslides, volcanoes and tsunamis.

J. Harlan Bretz might agree!

Fossil Enigma

Not only can a strong argument be made that most geological features trace their origin to a global cataclysm, but also that a majority of the world's fossils resulted from rapid water burial.

Fossils typically result when hydraulic action engulfs a plant or animal suddenly with pressure exerting sediment. Even tiny fossil embryos discovered in China were "...most likely buried alive one day in a sudden catastrophic overflow of sediment."[27] Absent such a process, dead organic material, exposed to the surface, will naturally decay.

When ecological balance exists, earth's ecosystem recycles naturally. Marine invertebrates characterized the Cambrian period when oceans provided the water suitable for fossil creation. That changed when hydraulic cataclysms struck the land. Sudden inundation by water-borne sediment wiped out entire species creating jumbled masses of disarticulated fossil bones, jammed together in fossil graveyards.

"...Some kinds of catastrophic action is nearly always necessary for the burial and preservation of fossils. Nothing comparable to the tremendous fossiliferous beds of fish, mammals, reptiles, etc. that are found in many places around the world is being formed today."[28]

Mass species extinctions pervade the fossil record. One popular belief points to catastrophic life extinctions near the end of the Permian period alleged to be 250 million years before the present. Another postulate suggests a meteorite struck and erased dinosaurs 65 million years ago. Regardless of conjectured time frames, "dinosaur bones...had to fall into water and be buried to be preserved, and most dinosaurs spent most of their time on dry land." [29]

With or without the meteorite, sudden hydraulic action fossilized the Gobi dinos. At the time it was a wetter and greener Gobi and home to "...hundreds of dinosaurs and mammals... Avalanches of water-soaked sand buried the animals alive, creating one of the world's richest fossil sites. The fossils appear remarkably complete in that...all the bones are connected to form whole skeletons...suggesting...death was sudden, and the ill-fated creatures were quickly buried before scavenging animals could make off with the meaty bits."[30]

Thousands of fossil dinosaur eggs have been discovered strewn across a parched square mile of layered mudstone within the Argentine badlands at Auca Mahuevo. "Every evidence shows that the embryos may have perished in a flood that quickly buried the eggs in a layer of silt and mud. This made it possible for the soft tissues to fossilize before decaying, an extremely rare occurrence."[31]

"Fossilized dinosaur tracks scale sheer mountain cliffs, which are tilted topsy turvy by some unseen, latent power—trademark testimony to the magnitude of cataclysmic force. Seashells and fossilized marine life litter bone-dry hilltops and mountain slopes, far above today's sea level. Chains of today's high-altitude, rugged terrain lay submerged underwater in the past, until sea beds awash in the currents of a cataclysmic deluge or powered by some convulsive thrust inside the Earth's crust pushed mountains skyward from the ocean's floor.

"A fossil fish has been unearthed 17,000 feet up the slopes of the Andes and marine fossil limestone has been spotted in the Himalayas at an altitude of 20,000 feet! 'Marine fossils are found on top of glacial deposits as in the case of the whale skeletons… covering glacial deposits in Michigan…Whale fossils have also been found 440 feet above sea level north of Lake Ontario; more than 500 feet above sea level in Vermont; and some 600 feet above sea level in the Montreal area.'"[32]

Far above sea level, graveyards of disparate fossils, including remnants of marine life, are found stacked in jumbled piles—stark evidence of colossal deluge! The Siwaliks, foothills to the Himalayas, which run for several hundred miles and are 2,000 to 3,000 feet high "…contain extraordinarily rich beds crammed with fossils: hundreds of feet of sediment, packed with the jumbled bones of scores of extinct species…the remains of terrestrial animals, not marine creatures.'"[33]

The planet has endured violent land mass convulsions causing massive crustal displacement, collapse, subsidence, and upheavals. Combine turbulent water with a gargantuan cosmic discordance that smashes the earth with some celestial force, and the ingredients fall in place for the "perfect" cataclysm.

A long time ago, dry land succumbed to ancient hydraulic power that destroyed species and wreaked environmental havoc. Extinction of species and the ecological decline facing survivors are cataclysm's joint casualties. Residual fossils provide clues to original biodiversity. Fossils confirm extinctions.

Is it reasonable that this horrific loss of life occurred during the same year, a fall-out of a flood that devastated the entire earth?

Coal & Oil

Industry rides on wheels greased by non-renewable resources extracted from earth's recesses. Gasoline prices spike as demand increases and supply equivocates.

A few minutes wedged in the crush of Los Angeles traffic or the mish-mash of Interstate #95 bridges lacing Springfield, Virginia, confirms the horse and buggy era is long gone.   Voracious fuel consumption collides with sober reality: production of oil and natural gas liquids peaked in 1970.[34]

Nature's reservoir of carbon-based fuel is non renewable. So when did this prodigious wealth of lush vegetation and animal life become buried under ocean and land masses? How did it first get there? Is any answer more logical than a world-wide deluge?

A global-scale catastrophic deluge shouts for recognition as the most reasonable explanation.

The remains of plants or animals stranded on the earth's surface, exposed to nature's ravages, will decay. But that same organic matter can provide the raw material for fossil fuel if buried suddenly, pressured by tons of sediment, deprived of oxygen, and subjected to heat.[35]

Petroleum pools rest within continental shelves below ocean floors. Where flourishing forests once shaded the land, seas of sand drift and shift, sheltering a wealth of fossil fuels. Masses of compressed ferns and trees, a residue of another time, provide the raw material for rich veins of coal several hundred feet deep. Fossil fuels driving international economies are by-products of hydraulic action that buried and crushed a planet load of organic life forms while inundating then scouring the earth's face.

Despite conventional geologic time frames that postulate a lengthy process for building sedimentary strata, polystrate trees, poking through multiple veins of coal, add a quandary not readily resolved by millions-of-years scenarios. The polystrate phenomena argues for sudden and near-simultaneous burial of adjacent strata.

"Polystrate trees are fossil trees that extend through several layers of strata, often twenty feet or more in length. There is no doubt that this type of fossil was formed relatively quickly; otherwise it would have decomposed while waiting for strata to slowly accumulate around it."[36]

It would be no small feat for a twenty-foot tall tree to stand patiently for eons of time, waiting to be buried by multiple layers of accruing sediment, without rotting to nothingness in the process. Human imaginations may craft a variety of quaint, alternative scenarios, but the simplest and most likely explanation is that fossilized, polystrate trees resulted from multi-layered sediment delivered and deposited suddenly, by cataclysmic hydraulic action, within a short period of time.

Carbon-based energy resources critical to modern industry are available thanks to the sudden pressure of sediments piled high, crushing organic matter. Gradual decay won't do it. This subsurface resource is finite. Nowhere is nature manufacturing a replacement supply. Peat bogs can't do it.

Shifting Earth

Convulsive violence ripped the earth bordering the Mississippi River during the 1811-12 winter months. The quake unleashed ripples of land in rolling waves, five feet high. The violent shake created Tennessee's Reelfoot Lake basin and rang church bells in Boston.

The even more intense 1967 Alaska shock, strongest earthquake in North American recorded history, sloshed water in Texas swimming pools. When earth's crust rips, devastation reigns.

A balmy Sunday, December 26, 2004 started like every previous remembered morning-after-Christmas in Southeast Asia's favorite get-a-ways. Holiday celebrants basked beach side in the tropical breezes that bathed resorts lining the shores of the Indian Ocean. The "Tsunami" label lurked outside the vocabulary of most tourists. But nature, sometimes a cruel teacher, delivered a crash course in demonstrating the unimaginable havoc possible from an undersea earthquake carrying a force equal to hundreds of atomic explosions.

Without warning, the angry ocean, with mountainous waves surging at speeds estimated to reach 500 miles-per-hour, swept all in its path. The grim reaper's scythe rode those furious walls of water, overwhelming shores in Tanzania, Kenya, Somalia, Seychelles, Maldives, India, Bangladesh, Burma, Sri Lanka, Indonesia, Thailand, and Malaysia. An estimated 175,000+ lives were snuffed out by the vicious surge of a devouring ocean triggered by a Richter Scale 9.0 earthquake epicentered off the coast of Sumatra.

The impact shifted the geographic foundation of one Indonesian island. A piece of the ocean floor more than 700 miles long (distance between Denver and Chicago) and 10 miles wide jolted 100 feet upward unleashing a raging torrent of 135 cubic miles of water. The magnitude of the destruction removed entire towns and left battered human remains mixed with the debris of civilization strewn helter-skelter in grotesque heaps.

The ripple effect stretched ugly tentacles westward 3,750 miles to the east coast of Africa killing 298 Somalia residents in the coastal village of Foar. The initial surge of the crushing onslaught, ripped seashore lobster beds, depositing a harvest of death high up the side of nearby hills. [37]

The "Perfect" Cataclysm

Any single attack on the planet at any time and in any one place releases power that may be monitored but rarely controlled by human action. Imagine nature harnessing all its destructive forces, flexing its collective muscle in a simultaneous onslaught.

Suppose the Indian Ocean tsunami and quake was but one of many earthquakes, in the world's oceans, each with a Richter rating of 9.0 or better rippling landscapes and shifting land masses? Combine this with a shower of earth-bound meteorites, cutting 120-mile wide craters as in the seabed off the Yucatan Peninsula, while triggering multiple Indian Ocean style tsunamis. [38]

Add to this fearsome mix the fire, smoke, and molten lava from three or four dozen earth-shattering supervolcanoes, upsetting environments and climates. Nature's colossal rampage might also feature Katrina-style, mega-force hurricanes, tornadoes and wind-driven powers sculpting grotesque face-lifts on the planet's surface.

"Gullywashers" or "frog stranglers" shrivel to the size of pesky faucet drips when compared to the incessant forty days and nights of drenching rain described in Genesis. Merge the cascading water from the exploding sky with geysers bursting from underground fountains and the churning caldrons of angry currents could spill blankets of continent-wide sediment layers while gouging craggy swaths on the rebuilt face of a tormented earth.

Repeated bursts of tsunami triggered swells traveling at 500 miles per hour would dump layer-upon-successive-layer of sediments. Mega-tons of shifting layers of sediment would engulf and bury lush plant and animal life in haphazard stacks of instant death--an ultimate treasure trove of carbon-based fuels. Jagged mountain ranges, larded with fossil-bound remains of marine creatures, would be propelled skyward, towering above once undulating fields.

Earth's crust would be shredded like a bolt of sheer cloth creating gouged chasms slashing across the earth's face. Smashed tectonic plates might break land masses into continent-sized pieces of a ragged jig-saw puzzle, disrupting magnetic fields. Mushrooming clouds of climate-modifying volcanic ash could diminish the sun's warming rays isolating a blanket of water, stranded in the grip of an ice age.

Was it the gradual thawing of glaciers that raised sea levels around the world that accounted for the thunder of water that tore through a land mass at the Bosporus Valley inundating the Black Sea basin with a flood of Mediterranean sea water projected by some to have occurred 7600 BP?[39]

As well as at the Scablands? And the Grand Canyon?

Now the big question!

Suppose a full menu of natural destructive forces combined with hydraulic action to create a "perfect" cataclysm, etching its imprint on the face of the entire world?

Does that sound something like the Genesis account of the disastrous deluge of Noah's day?

12

Big! Bigger! **Biggest!**
Devolution

*"Natural selection only eliminates,
and its adoption as a mechanism of origin
is like explaining 'appearance' by 'disappearance'."*
Giuseppe Sermonti[1]

Red tile roofs frame the shores of Rio de Janeiro's Guanabura Bay. Eight hundred eighty-seven feet above the Bay's purple-blue water, expansive threads of taut steel cables swag the open space anchoring the span to the top of Päo de Azucar (Sugarloaf Mountain).

A North American visitor stood transfixed at sight of the swaying gondola riding the cables spanning the blue-jeweled bay. Gravity defying cable cars were not a common sight in the United States early in the twentieth century. Concealing casual concern, the visitor asked the operator in broken Portuguese, "Is it safe?"

The spontaneous question flowed in admiration of the engineering spectacle. The semi-assuring response came back in heavily accented English graced with a teasing smile.

"It hasn't broken yet!"

Since that 1926 day, thousands of tourists have flocked to experience the thrill of Rio's ride over water. Despite an impressive safety record, similar questions have been repeated hundreds of times by tourists aware that without meticulous maintenance, steel rusts over time.

San Francisco, another bejeweled bayside city, blessed with a shining beauty rivaling Rio de Janeiro's, is also crowned with an engineering masterpiece of its own: the suspension band of steel bridging the Golden Gate. And like Rio's cable car, San Fran's Golden Gate Bridge demands constant maintenance to defeat the relentless encroachments of the second law of thermodynamics in action. A team of daredevil artisans work year-round, scaling the network of cabled arches, applying the latest formula of weather resistant paint designed to deter the second law's onslaught.

Grandfather clocks, symbols of punctuality, regularly chime each quarter hour but eventually go silent if the gravity powered weights are not reloaded by a human hand.

When the burner on a range top shuts down, boiling water cools to room temperature. Wood rots, paint peels, metal rusts, ink fades, paper yellows, batteries give out, and grandfather clocks wind down. Century old Hollywood celluloid movies crack and crumble unless preserved in climate controlled safe havens. Bullet proof vests deteriorate when touched by light, heat and moisture. An orbiting space station is doomed to decay without regular maintenance.

Ocean waves erode shorelines; volcanoes build islands; tectonic plates shift land masses; desert sands engulf once verdant forests; and mountains rise and fall when pushed by forces inside the earth.

The second law of thermodynamics always has the last say! Sir Arthur Eddington credited it's pervasive presence as the "supreme" law of nature.[2]

Inevitably, devolution takes the stage.

The Second Law of Thermodynamics and Entropy

The label "evolution" has been high-jacked when used to connote upside progress while the term "devolution" more accurately reflects reality. Upside-down rhetoric infiltrates a culture intent on giving God a bum rap.

For example, purveyors of neo-Darwinism commit to a faith in materialism that credits an "act of nature" as the originator of life. But when natural forces demolish the landscape, knee-jerk semantics label the disaster an "act of God."

Let's see now, something is out-of-kilter here!

Seems as though Planet Earth, with its teeming biodiversity, should be rationally ascribed to an intelligent Creator, while the destructive forces of hurricanes, earthquakes, floods, and tornadoes should be attributed to acts of rampaging nature.

According to the first law of thermodynamics, energy can neither be created nor destroyed.

The second law of thermodynamics is qualitative. It confirms the tendency of energy to flow away, to disperse from concentration in a single, localized place. Entropy is the quantitative measure of the dispersion or spreading out of the qualitative. It represents a measure of change of energy distribution after some spontaneous event.[3]

Mathematician Granville Sewell, with a Purdue University Ph.D. in Numerical Analysis, describes the dilemma confronting evolutionism when scrutinized under the laws of physics, mathematical probability and the second law. "...The underlying principle behind the second law of thermodynamics is that natural forces do not do extremely improbable things...natural forces do not do macroscopically describable things which are extremely improbable from the microscopic point of view...

"...The second law predicts that, in a closed system where only natural forces are at work, every type of order is unstable and will eventually decrease, as everything tends toward more probable (more random) states---not only will carbon and temperature distributions become more random, but the performance of all electronic devices will deteriorate, not improve.

"Natural forces, such as corrosion, erosion, fire and explosions, do not create order, they destroy it. The second law is all about probability. The reason natural forces may turn a spaceship into a pile of rubble but not vice-versa is probability: of all the possible arrangements atoms could take, only a very small percentage could fly to the moon and back."[4]

The organic world can't escape the second law.

Any 75-year-old person understands the ravages of decline. Once robust and graceful twenty-year-old bodies tend to falter and bend; blotches mar once-radiant skin that dries and folds into wrinkles; eyesight and hearing require artificial boosts; hair thins into wisps of gray and mental marbles roll in slower motion as memories fade. Cosmetic surgery may camouflage, but an undeterred second law always delivers the last word.

Left alone, nature scoffs at Darwin's "progress towards perfection" prediction. Neither man nor matter escapes the ravages of decline administered by the second law of thermodynamics.

Sooner or later the all-powerful second law touches the lives of every one of the world's six billion humans. A combo of daily exercise, heavy doses of vitamins, and great genes won't prevent the most beautiful young woman or the most muscular young man from deteriorating, cell by cell.

Life slips into the slow lane as systems decay downhill.

Humans confronting signs of aging know the inevitable date with the grim reaper approaches, no longer deterred by a once formidable immune defense. Sooner or later the heart stops beating and black curtains shroud a cold-dust destiny.

The second law of thermodynamics, the "supreme" law of nature, erodes evolutionism's essence. Still, loyalists, refusing to recognize the emperor lacks clothes, fall back on a "yes, but" argument: "Yes, but the rule doesn't apply to an 'open' system."

Closed System v. Open System

Closed or open, a key obstacle to the adequacy of neo-Darwinian theory explaining origins on earth "...is that information cannot be defined in terms of physics and chemistry. The ideas of a book are not the same as the paper and ink which constitute the book...Meaning cannot spontaneously arise, since meaning presupposes intelligence and understanding..."[5]

In living systems, "...information...has been there from the beginning." Andrew McIntosh, with a doctorate in the Theory of Combustion, agrees with Professor Werner Gitt that "'No information can exist without an initial mental source. No information can exist in purely statistical processes.'...Information does not equal energy or matter....There is no mechanism in Darwinian evolution to add new information to a species at the macro level..."[5]

"...When there is any work done due to energy conversion, there is always some dissipation of useful energy...disorder increases, cars rust and machines wear out...sustained order can never be achieved, because no new information is available...the very existence of the DNA coded language stalls evolution at the first hurdle."[5]

Obviously, order decreases in a closed system.

Consequently, as Dr. Granville Sewell explains, "...It is often argued that any increase in order is allowed in an open system as long as the increase is 'compensated' somehow by a comparable or greater decrease outside the system...According to this logic, then, the second law does not prevent scrap metal from reorganizing itself into a computer in one room, as long as two computers in the next room are rusting into scrap metal---and the door is open.

"The spectacular increase in order seen here on Earth does not violate the second law because order is decreasing through-out the rest of this vast universe, so the total order in the universe is surely still decreasing."[6]

Dr. Sewell's logic notes that "...If an increase in order is ex-tremely improbable when a system is closed, it is still extremely improbable when the system is open, unless something is enter-ing which makes the increase not extremely improbable.

"The fact that order is disappearing in the next room does not make it any easier for computers to appear in our room---un-less this order is disappearing into our room...Importing thermal order will make the temperature distribution less random, and importing carbon order will make the carbon distribution less random, but neither makes the formation of computers more probable.

"...Order can increase in an open system, not because the laws of probability are suspended when the door is open, but simply because order may walk in through the door...If we found evidence that DNA, auto parts, computer chips, and books en-tered through the Earth's atmosphere at some time in the past, then perhaps the appearance of humans, cars, computers, and encyclopedias on a previously barren planet could be explained without postulating a violation of the second law here...But if all we see entering is radiation and meteorite fragments, it seems clear that what is entering through the boundary cannot explain the increase of order here."[6]

The issue becomes simply: are "macroscopically describable events extremely improbable from the microscopic point of view (extremely improbable after taking into account what is entering from outside the system naturally). The evolutionist therefore, cannot avoid the question of probability by saying that anything can happen in an open system...He is finally forced to argue that it only seems extremely improbable, but really isn't, that...the influx of stellar energy into a planet could cause atoms to rearrange themselves into computers and nuclear power plants and spaceships." [6]

Simply suggesting "Something had to happen" doesn't explain "...how the fundamental forces of Nature could rearrange the basic particles of Nature into libraries full of encyclopedias, science texts and novels, and computers, connected to laser printers, CRT's and keyboards...

"There is no other phenomenon anywhere that gives such an extreme impression of violating the second law; the development of life on Earth is completely unique." [6]

Random chance odds calculated as "extremely improbable" approach the "virtually impossible." Imagine six billion earthlings, each with a pair of dice, throwing constantly, night and day for their joint lifetimes. What are the odds of all six billion dice pairs coming up with the identical set of numbers at the precise nanosecond of time in 4.6 billion years---assuming each player could live so long?

Extremely improbable? Virtually impossible? How about absolute impossibility? Try the math: the odds stretch beyond plausibility!

An "open system" placebo serum can't immunize evolutionism from second law consequences. With or without an open system, evolutionism confronts the same underlying nemesis that corrodes its closed system credibility. It remains glaringly improbable (read virtually impossible) that influx of stellar energy delivers the order essential to convert atoms into automobiles and molecules to man without information input and active intelligent design.

Meanwhile decay continues with relentless abandon!

Is it then consistent to argue "open system" rather than "closed system" while simultaneously relying on decay rates of the elements to gauge deep time using radiometric dating technologies?

The second law of thermodynamics always has the last laugh!

Giants in the Land

Sewell dismisses gradualism by noting that "...new orders, classes and phyla consistently appear suddenly." Confirming this view, he cites a November, 1980 *New York Times News Service* report of a Chicago meeting of 150 scientists where evolutionist Niles Eldridge reminded the audience, in the words of the *Times*, that "Species simply appear at a given point in geologic time, persist largely unchanged for a few million years and then disappear." The report quotes Eldridge saying, "'The pattern that we were told to find for the last 120 years does not exist.'"[6]

Whether or not the system is open or closed, the second law's presence cuts a consistent swath. With less energy available for useful work coupled with dissipation of useful energy when any work is done, increased disorder and degeneration follows. Living organisms ultimately return to inert, inorganic elements.

Planet Earth's ecological balance has been upset. Desert sands, like the Sahara's, overwhelm previously lush green spaces. Erosion thins agricultural top soils diminishing crops. Plant and animal species disappear. DNA life sequences carry corrupting mutations.

Fickle climates rearrange environments.

"Drill cores from beneath the floor of the Arctic Ocean have revealed a startling find. Fossils from around the 430 meter mark indicate the seabed was once a balmy 23 degrees centigrade (74 degrees Fahrenheit). Today's temperatures beneath the Arctic vary within a few degrees of zero."[7]

A diminished genetic base can also set in motion a "...decline to oblivion for small populations...called the 'extinction vortex.'...Reduced genetic variation has been shown to reduce population growth and increase probability of extinction."[8]

Darwin friend and committed evolutionist, Alfred Russell Wallace, recognized "...we live in a zoologically impoverished world, from which all the hugest, and fiercest, and strangest forms have recently disappeared."[9]

Extinctions confirm shrinking biodiversity not evolutionism.

Darwinian doctrine infers "...not one living species will transmit its unaltered likeness to a distant futurity."[10] The fossil record brims with evidence contradicting this inference, confirming stasis instead---descendant life forms tend to mirror image their ancient ancestors.

The corollary prediction, that parent species will not transmit their "unaltered likeness to a distant futurity" because descendants will cause their "extermination," also fades under scrutiny. As to the promised "...improved and modified descendants,"[11] the second law of thermodynamics intrudes, tilting toward decline.

Tenacious species, bridging the gap of time rather than going extinct, proliferate. Stasis thumbs its nose at predictions living species disappear due to "improved" descendants. A host of surviving offspring live with us today, albeit many are radically downsized compared to fossil ancestors. Once again, the fossil record sabotages evolutionism's prediction. While descendants show "modifications," the changes don't correlate with "improvement" unless smaller is better!

"*Evolutionism*, or the 'theory of evolution'...is the erroneous idea that evolution is the source of progress and the cause of the cosmos structure---life and any other systems in the universe."[12] Reality shouts devolution, not "progress towards perfection."

No genealogical trail precedes the sudden appearance of giant ancestors in the fossil record. Genetically complete prototypes appear fully formed and in place from ground zero. For example, today's armor-plated armadillo missed Darwin's message that descendants must not only modify but also improve. Instead, armadillos are puny versions of their nine-foot-long ancestors. Since when does runt-of-the-litter mean "improved?"

The roster of these jumbo-sized ancestors features a crocodile with a seven-foot head and a cow-sized pig whose bones are housed in a Denver museum. Massive dinosaurs, some estimated to extend more than one-hundred feet from tip-to-tail, once roamed the earth. High foothills in the Himalayas reportedly "contain fossil beds rich with extinct terrestrial animals, a tortoise twenty feet long, a species of elephant with tusks fourteen feet long, and three feet in circumference."[13]

Twenty-foot-long great white sharks patrolling Pacific shores strike terror, but an ancestor shark found in the turf near Oildale, California, measured forty feet in length, weighed an estimated eight times as much as its modern counterpart, and sported a twelve-foot sized head. And speaking of fearsome, how about "...The monstrous *Carcharodon*...possessing distinctive triangular teeth up to 8" long, [that] may have had a 6-7 ft wide jaw gape, and a length of 80 ft."[14]

Washington, D.C.'s Smithsonian displays a sloth as large as a pickup truck...rhinoceros-sized marsupials and giant kangaroos once inhaled Australian air...foot-long trilobites occupied what is now Morocco...the Caribbean's Anguilla Island was home base to a three-hundred pound rat...oversized lemurs hung out in Madagascar...and colorful dragonflies with inch-thick bodies propelled by two-and-one-half foot gossamer wings hovered over pools of cool water in some ancient past.

The eye-catching list of giant-sized fossils includes a fourteen-inch tarantula...a two-foot scorpion...a millipede-like creature six feet long and a foot wide...a forty-foot crocodile twice the length of its living descendants...giant beavers...*eurypterids* (enormous crabs), ranked among the largest invertebrates ever...ammonites several feet in diameter...pterosaurs with wingspans stretching out as far as the wings on a small, private airplane...canary-size mayflies...and the enormous Australian bird, *Genyornis newtoni*, which makes the emu appear scrawny by comparison.

Imagine the pesky cockroach, equipped with an intimidating, oversized body...fossil clams spanning 12 feet across, weighing in at 650 pounds when living, discovered in the Andes 13,000 feet above sea level in the Huancavelica province of Peru[15]...or scorpions estimated to have been 2.5 meters in length based on their fossil tracks.[16] A jellyfish 28 inches in diameter that "...must have been buried extremely rapidly..." was discovered in a Wisconsin "fossilized beach."[17]

Mosses 2-3 feet high (compared to today's 1 to 3 inches) brightened the landscape; horsetail reeds grew up to 50 feet high (ten times today's 5 to 6 feet); and a hornless rhinoceros towered 18 feet tall and stretched 30 feet long.[18] For an up-close inspection of giant plant life, next time you explore the California coast, be sure to gaze up the trunk of a three-hundred-foot sequoia, with its offspring still stabbing at California skies.

Don't overlook the over five-foot long, coiled shellfish (compared to 8 inches today); the eight foot wide bison skull on display at the Mt. Blanco Fossil Museum, Crosbyton, Texas; the ten-foot tall ammonite shell on display in a German museum; turtles nearly four meters long;[19] the eight-foot long shell of the giant nautiloid (like a modern squid);[20] and finally the fossil footprints in Canadian sandstone believed to be those of a twenty inch long centipede, five times the length of its mini-sized descendant.[21]

The second law of thermodynamics impacts earth's ecosystem. Does the second law account for the downsizing of animal and plant life? Is it a matter of *res ipsa loquitor* (the thing speaks for itself) or do other factors contribute? One certainty emerges: there was a long ago time when giants roamed Planet Earth!

Ancient writers addressed nature's downside trend. Referencing the heavens and the foundations of the earth, the Psalmist predicted "...they will all wear out like a garment."[22] Nearly two millenniums in the past, Paul the Apostle wrote, "We know that the whole creation has been groaning as in the pains of childbirth right up to the present time."[23]

Rusty Chinks in Evolutionism's Armor

The second law of thermodynamics puts yet another chink in evolutionism's crumbling armor. The "flaws" and "holes" that perplexed Darwin continue to expand.

Prime examples to consider:

Life didn't originate by spontaneous generation---Evolutionism's foundation is built on a fabric of unproven assumptions---No evo evidence exists explaining the source of the information contained in the DNA of first life. Information requires an intelligent source---Each genome displays a design dictated by the information in its DNA---Fully formed, complex organic life appears suddenly and without evidence of fossil ancestry---Darwin's much touted transitional chain of organic life doesn't exist---Irreducibly complex living systems cannot function in some incomplete, intermediate stage of development---Mutations corrupt the genetic code without providing new information---Descendants Darwin defined as "improved and modified" species range somewhere between rare and non-existent.

So, regardless of personal reaction to the weight of evidence, the "supreme" law of nature kicks in—the second law of thermodynamics speaks the last word!

13

Cosmic Convergence
Environment for Life

The Big Bang is merely *"...a myth that attempts to say how the universe came into being...."*
Hannes Alfvén[1]

Earth-launched rockets routinely evade gravity's grip, favoring human eyes with never-before-seen glimpses of the universe. In 1969, astronauts left footprints on the moon's volcanic dust. Nosy, unmanned robotic devices crawl the surface of the red planet, exploring its geology. Space missions can be plotted, engineered and accomplished through calculations tied to precise formulas of physics and mathematics.

Big Bang or Big Bust

Cosmology wows us with grandiose words and phrases such as Doppler Effect, redshift, blueshift, and the Steady State Theory. And measuring the speed light travels in a single year to calculate distance at 5.88 trillion miles per year boggles minds. The ostentatious sounding "Big Bang Theory" inspires more boggle!

NASA's Robert Jastrow made it sound simple, suggesting a beginning time in which matter "was compressed into an infinitely dense and hot mass" that eventually exploded after which "the primordial cloud of the Universe expands and cools, stars are born and die, the sun and earth are formed, and life arises on earth."[2]

Is something missing here? Skeptics abound!

Evolutionist Don Page expressed his doubts six years after Dr. Jastrow spoke his mind. "There is no mechanism known as yet that would allow the Universe to begin in an arbitrary state and then evolve to its present highly ordered state"[3]

Seven years after Jastrow's statement, Fred Hoyle compared facts to theory. "...I have little hesitation in saying that a sickly pall now hangs over the big bang theory. When a pattern of facts becomes set against a theory, experience shows that the theory rarely recovers."[4]

John Gribbin considered the "standard theory" obsolete. "... Many cosmologists now feel that the shortcomings of the standard theory outweigh its usefulness..."[5]

Jeff Lindsay wrote the theory's obituary early in century twenty-one. "...While few people have seen the obituary...the reality is that the immensely popular Big Bang Theory is dead... The Big Bang cannot explain the nature of the universe as we know it."[6]

Tom Wolfe added his voice to the chorus of doubters, opining online with a dire prediction as to Darwinism's longevity. "That's a fairly recent theory, and it is already burning out. There are too many scientists who are saying this is rubbish. Just think about the theory of the Big Bang or this ridiculous theory about where the first cell came from...It is because of all this silly stuff that Darwinism is going to go down in flames."[7]

Intractable problems overwhelm Big Bang conjecture!

Imagine that prior to the conjectured "explosion," the universe to be existing compressed to the size of a pinhead, what laws of physics were suspended or modified enabling the explosive action? If energy and matter can neither be created nor destroyed, where did the energy come from prior to the moment of the big bang? If neither energy nor matter existed prior to the big bang's boom, how is it possible for an explosion to create something out of nothingness?

"If all the matter and energy in the Universe were packed into a point 'many billions of times smaller than a single proton,' why would that not constitute a black hole?"[8]

Response to these queries rides a wave of silence!

A missile from the skies, allegedly 65-million years before the present, hit earth off the Yucatan peninsula with a destructive force so powerful as to presumably exterminate, world-wide, all dinosaur species. Another explosive force, supposedly several billion years earlier, allegedly created billions of bits and pieces of original matter, producing orbiting spheres arranged in one grand format of universal order.

Can one explosion from space destroy while another creates?

How did a cosmic explosion create a balance of orbiting spheres, tracking individually in galaxy formations---from nothingness? Or is it intellectual flim-flam to argue order as the natural consequence of a "Big Bang?"

Explosions observed on earth rip matter apart, leaving fragments of rubble, strewn helter-skelter in disorganized trash heaps. Where is verifiable evidence that a single, cosmic explosion behaved diametrically the opposite, creating order? Is there an inconsistency here? Is it logical to argue in one breath that explosive power destroyed the dinosaurs while in the next, to claim that an even bigger bang created a universe of orderly matter in symmetric balance?

Each year, Washington D.C.'s celebratory July fourth fireworks shower the evening skies above the Washington Monument, silhouetting the skyline with rainbowed canopies of multi-hued embers. The next day, little remains of the showy explosives other than the blackened ashes strewn across the mall's green grass blanket.

Suggesting billions of orbiting spheres of matter originated from an unobserved explosion in space billions of years in deep time before the present doesn't correlate with observable explosions that shatter and destroy.

So what is right? Does an explosion create or destroy?

The Blue Planet brims with life forms that dazzle imaginations! A theoretical big bang is woefully inadequate to explain the origin of the environmental conditions essential for life's genesis on earth.

Cosmic conditions conducive to life must converge in an instant of time at a point within a fragment of space for life to even exist.   Plants and animals are inter-dependent. Mutual survival requires they appear simultaneously, fully formed and in place ecologically.

Cosmic Precision

While astronomers track stellar paths in the sky, finite intelligence can't explain space without an ending, time without a beginning, or nothingness. Could there even be absolutely nothing---no energy, no matter, no light, not even space? "Don't imagine outer space without matter in it. Imagine no space at all and no matter at all. Good luck."[9]

If nothing existed, what would there be? If nothing existed before a "Big Bang," just what was the something that exploded---other than an abstract idea? Can nothingness explode? The big bang theory "...represents the instantaneous suspension of physical laws, the sudden, abrupt flash of lawlessness that allowed something to come out of nothing. It represents a true miracle---transcending physical principles...."[10]

Given predictable order in space, mathematical measurements plot the time and place of cosmic orbits with uncanny precision, whether the time dimension dips millenniums into the past or extends outside the reach of an uncharted future.

Photographer Ansel Adams earned his spurs capturing graphic glimpses of nature in black and white. His view of an *August Moon*, as seen from atop Yosemite Park's Glacier Point, repeats every 19 years. By checking the position of the sun and moon relative to the surrounding mountains, an astronomer team from Texas State University calculated "that Adams snapped the shutter precisely at 7:03 p.m. on Sept. 15, 1948."[11]

"Until May 15, [2002], the five brightest planets---Mercury, Venus, Mars, Jupiter and Saturn---will cluster together in the western sky at dusk...The last widely visible five-planet array was in February 1940, and astronomers calculate that another one won't take place until Sept. 8, 2040."[12]

As scheduled, the parade of planets blazed across the evening sky in precise pattern---more punctual than Big Ben's sonorous chimes. Not mere chunks of matter strung out in space without visible foundation but individual orbits, cutting interrelated swaths at different speeds and angles. Routinely reliable mathematical calculations target the next comparable space show to the absolute year, month and day. Not just 38-years down the line, in 2040---but at subsequent intervals later into the future!

On Wednesday, August 27, 2003, the Red Planet, Mars, rotating clockwise, approached our Blue Planet, rotating counterclockwise, 34,646,418 miles distant, the closest proximity in living history.   The next year, Venus slipped directly between the earth and the sun, Tuesday, June 8, 2004.

Medieval superstition imagined a flat earth. But two-and-one-half millenniums before the big bang theory claimed currency, Isaiah not only pictured the scientifically enlightened "circle of the earth" but also identified the Designer who hung the round earth and the stars in space.

Leaving no doubt as to the inspiration behind his message, the Old Testament visionary asked rhetorically, "Who created all these?" Answering his own query he describes "...He who brings out the starry host one by one, and calls them each by name...The Lord is the everlasting God, the Creator of the ends of the earth."[13]

Isaiah made no reference to a cosmic explosion!

Suspended in space without cables or foundations, earth moves in three directions simultaneously: spinning on its axis; orbiting the sun; and floating in sync with the other components of the Solar System and the Milky Way galaxy.

Humans can't duplicate the cosmic balancing act. Keeping multiple, free-floating balls in perpetual motion without strings defies duplication.

Nothing random about this system of planets hanging about the sun; nothing chaotic; nothing the product of unpredictable chance!   The mind-boggling precision of cosmic convergence, establishing conditions favorable to life, characterizes the natural world.

Canada's Sudbury Observatory, operating 6,800 feet deep in the Creighton Nickel Mine, measures microscopic matter one ten-millionth the mass of an electron. Subatomic elementary particles (Electrons, Muons and Tau neutrinos) are believed to be the most miniscule form of matter presently known to man.

Equally invisible to the naked eye is the atom, with its positively charged nucleus encircled by an array of electrons, the smallest unit of the elements charted in the classic periodic table displayed in High School classrooms. Inorganic molecular matter can be built from a mix of these elements in carefully measured chemical recipes producing results capable of replication ad infinitum.

Middle school kids explain, matter-of-factly, that two atoms of hydrogen joined to a single atom of oxygen build a water molecule---it always has, and always will. They also understand that water, this elixir of life, will boil or freeze consistently when subjected to calibrated temperatures and altitudes. Nor are they unmindful of the role of "that lucky ol' sun" and its reliable rays, essential to life.

Mandatory Ingredients for Human Life

Viewed from space, the still-sterile surface of the moon, hostile to organic life, rotates in contrast to the marbled colors of our own blue-and-white planet where life flourishes. Why life on earth and not the moon?

Molecular bonding essential to life requires the presence of no less than 40 different elements with successful bonding contingent upon the functioning force of electromagnetism operating within a delicately balanced electron-to-proton mass ratio. Relying on a spontaneous universal explosion as the creative source of these finely tuned elements equates tooth fairy fantasy.

What's the probability of finding a free-floating space-station offering an environment capable of generating organic life by chance? Life as we know it has yet to be observed in space.

While odds favor life existing somewhere beyond earth's boundary, the likelihood of cosmic convergence delivering the key ingredients necessary to sustain life simultaneously, via some big bang, in one place, at one instant in time, and by chance without intelligent action, overwhelms logic.

Fragile human life hinges on access to air, water, sunshine and food. Explorers expecting to survive in space bring along their own supply. Air deprivation for a few minutes guarantees suffocation; too much water drowns its victims, but without water, death by dehydration awaits; starvation takes longer but is just as certain.

Consistent doses of sunlight, radiating beams of ultraviolet and infrared, sustain life. Instead of blistering heat or deadly radiation, energy from the sun comes calibrated in a range to maximize an environment friendly to all forms of life. Much closer, and the earth would be scorched; much farther and life would shrivel into deep freeze mode. If the sun's relationship to the electromagnetic spectrum shifted imperceptibly, the chance of life could vanish.

"That lucky ol' sun" refuses to burn up.

Sunlight provides a collateral bonus in the riot of colors that embellish the face of the earth. Restful sky-blues, backlighting forests of multi-hued greens, define the landscape. A rainbow of kaleidoscopic accents ranging from pastel shades of shimmering pinks and lavenders to crimson-golds, trace the arc of a daily rising and setting sun. Shifting combinations conspire to induce psychological peace.

Life-friendly parameters represent a broad spectrum of physical properties. The mass, color, location, and luminosity of stars; earth's orbit inclination and axis tilt; surface crust thickness; gravity that keeps feet planted securely; magnetic fields; balanced land/water ratios with a reliable supply of fresh water; and delicately balanced proportions of oxygen, carbon dioxide, ozone, and nitrogen in an atmospheric envelope.

And don't forget the ozone shield, wrapped conveniently around earth, protecting life from being overpowered by ultraviolet radiation. Too much, too little, too far, too near, too late, too soon—any factor out of kilter and life could never happen.

Atmosphere

The odds of a big bang generating an environment with an atmosphere friendly to the production of organic life, seems mathematically less likely than all of earth's six billion citizens solving the riddle of a Rubik cube---in a chorus of coordination, simultaneously, in less than a minute---then successfully repeating the exercise, without error, a million more consecutive times.

As per the Oparin-Haldane hypothesis, life demands a reducing atmosphere, where atoms and molecules bond with hydrogen rather than oxygen. Simply put, the amino acids essential to evolutionism's formula for generating organic life requires an oxygen-free, reducing environment—a condition missing when spontaneous generation was supposedly doing its thing on the Blue Planet!

To be viable, spontaneous generation must assume earth's atmosphere lacked oxygen when life formed. Evidence points to the fact that "Oxygen was likely present in the early earth's atmosphere."[14] "...Significant levels of oxygen would have been necessary to produce ozone which would shield the earth from levels of ultraviolet radiation lethal to biological life."[15]

The fully oxidizing nature characteristic of earth's prehistoric atmosphere is hostile to the assembly of new life, creating a chemical dilemma. Atoms and molecules tend to bond with oxygen atoms. Free oxygen inclines to oxidize organic compounds. "Oxygen destroys the chemical building blocks of life..." If the "early atmosphere was oxygen-free...then there would have been no protective ozone layer. Any DNA and RNA bonds would be destroyed by UV radiation...Either way, oxygen is a major problem."[16]

"...All experiments simulating the atmosphere of the early earth have eliminated molecular oxygen...Oxygen acts as a poison preventing the chemical reactions that produce organic compounds...If any chemical compounds did form, they would be quickly destroyed by oxygen reacting with them..."[17]

"Even if oxygen was not present in the early earth's atmosphere, the absence of oxygen would present obstacles to the formation of life. Oxygen is required for the ozone layer which protects the surface of the earth from deadly ultraviolet radiation. Without oxygen this radiation would break down organic compounds as soon as they formed."[18]

Dr. Michael Denton pinpoints the consequences of ultraviolet radiation! "In an oxygen-free scenario, the ultraviolet flux reaching the earth's surface might be more than sufficient to break down organic compounds as quickly as they were produced...In the presence of oxygen, any organic compounds formed on the early Earth would be rapidly oxidized and degraded...

"The level of ultraviolet radiation penetrating a primeval oxygen-free atmosphere would quite likely have been lethal to any proto-organism possessing a genetic apparatus remotely resembling that of modern organisms. What we have then is a 'Catch 22' situation. If we have oxygen, we have no organic compounds but if we don't have oxygen we have none either."[19]

Spontaneous generation can't coexist with an oxidizing atmosphere! Life could not evolve with oxygen; and once formed, life could not survive without it! The most persuasive explanation avoiding the doomsday scenario is that life, together with an atmosphere with oxygen, were created simultaneously, a mutually dependent "package deal."

Water

Water, a rare commodity in the Solar System, inundates 70 percent of Planet Earth's surface. A nagging problem looms: how could a cosmic big bang swamp earth in a wet blanket but leave the circling moon and planets as high and dry as the desert sands?

Its axiomatic: no water, no life!

Conventional science does not expect to find life flourishing on a dry planet. The creation story describes an originally empty and formless earth with darkness "...over the surface of the deep and the Spirit of God was hovering over the waters."[20]

Viewed from space, our own planet reflects bright blue swathed in streaks of white clouds. And no wonder---70% of the earth is covered with water. So much water, if the earth's land crust was flattened, water hundreds of feet deep would cover its surface.

Scholars have drawn startling conclusions about this natural water supply. For example, 96.5% of earth's water consists of ocean marine water and 0.97% brackish water (An incidental aside is the report suggesting that 95% of the total fossil record consists of marine life remnants). That leaves 2.53% of earth's water supply as fresh. This comparatively minuscule amount is allocated as: 69.6% glaciers and permanent snow; 30.1% ground water; 0.29% lakes, marshes, and swamps; 0.05% soil moisture; 0.04% atmosphere; 0.006% rivers; and 0.003% living organisms.[21]

Starting with a two-to-one mix of hydrogen and oxygen, the world thrives with plain old-fashioned water, a cornerstone to life's recipe. Next add a dash of carbon and a touch of sulfur. Finally, bolster the formula with some nitrogen and phosphorous. That constitutes a beginning inorganic base upon which to build life!

Ambidextrous Amino Acids

Even stretching the logic and making believe an explosion in space could by random chance provide a free floating planet blessed with the warming rays of the sun, not less than 40 inorganic elements, fountains of water, and an atmosphere, is that enough coincidental good fortune to foster the spontaneous generation of life from scratch?

It's not even a remote chance! Think impossible sounding odds!

Its no more than one chance in 10^{161} that a single useable protein might just happen "even if all the atoms on the earth's surface, including water, air, and the crust of the earth were made into conveniently available amino acids and four to five billions of years were involved."[22] The random chance "for producing the necessary molecules, amino acids, proteins...for a cell one-tenth the size of the smallest known to man is less than one in...10 with 340 million zeros after it."[23] Even if all conditions mandatory to sustain life existed in perfect calibration, "To get a cell by chance would require at least one hundred functional proteins to appear simultaneously in one place." [24]

Amino acids build cell proteins. Amino acids can't order themselves. When manufactured artificially from non-biological systems two forms result: a mirror image *left* and *right* in essentially equal amounts. Virtually all living systems require only the left-handed brand. For reasons unknown and perhaps unknowable, *amino acids never appear ambidextrous in living systems!* It's always either/or and never a mirror image containing both left and right!

This left/right conundrum is no incidental footnote relating to flawed theories of organic life's origin. It's landmark stuff!

"Amino acids are in one or two forms: L-amino acids (left-handed molecules) or D-amino acids (right-handed molecules), each a mirror image of the other. Only left-handed amino acids...are contained in biologically functional proteins. None of the acids produced in the experiment combined with each other in any way.

"For protein functions amino acids must combine in a sophisticated sequence. This sequence is not easy to obtain by random processes, because L-amino acids and D-amino acids bond without distinction, and D-amino acids and L-amino acids are equally present in the physical world.

"Forming a sequence of only L-amino acids is necessary for the formation of a protein with enzymatic functions necessary for life."[25]

"...Living things use only left-handed amino acids in their proteins. Right-handed ones don't 'fit' the metabolism of the cell any more than a right-handed glove would fit onto your left hand. If just one right-handed amino acid finds its way into a protein, the protein's ability to function is reduced, often completely."[26]

Walt Brown adds his voice confirming nature's persistent whim!

"Amino acid, when found in nonliving material...comes in two chemically equivalent forms. Half are right-handed and half are left-handed—mirror images of each other. However, the amino acids in life, including plants, animals, bacteria, molds, and even viruses, are essentially all left-handed. No known natural process can isolate either the left-handed or the right-handed variety. The mathematical probability that chance processes could produce merely one tiny protein molecule with only left-handed amino acids is virtually zero."[27]

Now here's a mind-blower: at death, amino acids revert to left/right mirror image forms.

Finite minds struggling to interpret issues touching edges of the infinite, hit walls of futility! The natural world overwhelms human comprehension. Cosmic mysteries confront science with intellectual hurdles yet to be scaled. Myth or miracle, the earth exhibits a life-friendly system in which the essential composites converged concurrently, at a precise time and place in space.

Put in size context, if the Milky Way galaxy were "...represented as the size of North America, our entire solar system would fit in a coffee cup somewhere in Idaho.

"Astronomers estimate that there are as many galaxies outside the Milky Way as there are stars in it. The Hubble Ultra Deep Field taken in 2004, imaged 10,000 galaxies in a cone of space so slim you could cover it with a grain of sand held at arm's length.

"Integrated over the entire sky, that would mean there are more than 100 billion galaxies in the visible universe, many with more than 100 billion stars each."[28]

Cosmic Enigmas

Could a big bang create infinite order able to hang billions of spinning spheres, orbiting in perfect balance?

Where is the foundation of the Blue Planet? Does anyone believe it rests on the shoulders of a mythical Atlas!

What accounts for the mutually predictable orbits balancing sun and earth, suspended in a spatial pattern so precise that the exact proximity can be pinpointed a thousand years past or future?

Why doesn't the sun exhaust its fuel and burn to a crisp? What placed the sun at the optimum distance from earth to sustain life: too near and life would suffocate; too far and the planet would slip into deep freeze mode.

What would there be if there was "nothing?" No matter, no energy, no space, no universe---how could there be empty nothingness in a never-was environment?

Does the Universe have a boundary? Is there an edge? What lies beyond the edge of space? Can space be infinite, without an edge?

Can you calculate time without a beginning? What, if anything, existed before the beginning of finite time? Can we comprehend or explain infinite time, without beginning or ending?

If matter, energy and space pre-existed, what intelligent process explains the creation of first life? What random chance source converted inorganic matter into a living organism imbued with the power to replicate "after its kind?"

How did energy and matter create information all by themselves, by accident, no less? Where did first life derive the genetic information built into its DNA independent of an intelligent source?

Science flounders when it limits consideration of origins to "inside the box" materialism, and then resorts to "outside the box" philosophical assumptions. Darwin's nonsense, garbed in ponderous phraseology and propped up by backtracking advocacy, remains dubious. Today's unproven conjecture touts repackaged myth.

Garbage in, garbage out!

Evolutionist Carl Sagan entertained the likelihood of the existence of intelligent life beyond earth's bounds. Belief in beings on other planets, is logical given the scope of space. If true, does that suggest another series of random chance accidents creating life from inanimate matter? Or does reason suggest intelligent design with a Master Designer at work? Panspermia, the postulate that life originated by chance in some remote spot in the universe, and managed to survive a hazardous cosmic voyage to plant the seed of life on earth, only begs the question.

Life on earth, courtesy of cosmic ancestry, doesn't cut it! That dog won't hunt!

Evolution's construct offers no scientific, testable answer. Instead it offers a litany of fancy-sounding rhetoric that worships at the shrine of an inanimate idol of "stone." *Homo sapiens* are urged to buy into the belief that intelligent life originated by chance, from nowhere in a deep time past, only to hitch a ride on a conveyor belt of time that eventually discards its passengers in a purposeless death.

Admitting wonderment while adrift in awe, humans concoct fantasized "religious" scenarios. Pagan rites seek to appease imaginary gods of fire, thunder, love, and war. Superstition worships at the feet of man-made idols of wood and stone while bowing to a disk representing the energizing rays of the sun.

In contrast, Elvis Pressley sang the message-loaded melody, acknowledging "Somebody Bigger Than You and I." Why not recognize and worship that "Somebody," the Creator of the cosmos, an all powerful Supreme Being who cares for His creation? Belief in the living God represents belief in life-giving power, all-wise intelligence, perfect justice and an infinite love for each human being.

Earth Does Revolve Around the Sun

When exploring beyond the edge of the observable into the realm of the unseen, human nature craves to be correct, assuaging personal ego. Minds debating an issue risk arrogant exclusivity's contagious infection. Despite Dr. Kerkut's assumption label pinned on evolutionism's unproven explanation of first life's origin and its subsequent series of transitions, devout apologists cling persistently to discredited myth.

Richard Dawkins, renowned for intemperate outbursts, resolutely declares evolution "theory is about as much in doubt as the earth goes round the sun."[29] Of course earth "goes round the sun," but the comparison smacks of hot-air posturing.

Dawkins took umbrage at Richard Milton's book, *Shattering the Myths of Darwinism,* labeling the contents 'loony,' 'stupid,' 'drivel,' and its author a 'harmless fruitcake' who needs 'psychiatric help.'"[30] Despite verbal sticks and stones, bootstrap science rooted in assumption still doesn't explain just how first life could have sprouted by accident in some "warm little pond" whether bubbling on earth or in a far corner of the cosmos.

Spontaneous generation trivializes life by reducing its origin to coincidence in nature's test tube. The "warm little pond" scenario bows at the feet of a trinity of the absurd, surrendering intellect to the illusion of the coincidental: (1) Nothingness exploding into a universe of precise balance put in place by chance; (2) residual matter from the big bang organizing itself into an information-loaded life format; and (3) that original cell riding oblivion's treadmill over millenniums of tortured trial and error to evolve the human thought process without input from an intelligent source. Cut through empty rhetoric and evolutionism surfaces high and dry---as bereft of life as a withered chip from a fossil bone

The conceptualized cosmic accident insults intelligence, demeans humanity, and prostitutes science. Forget the knee jerk mantra asserting life's random chance emergence from primordial soup followed by a mindless march from the sea---primitive single cell-to-fish-to-monkey-to- mankind---it didn't happen!

The core issue represents more than intellectual swashbuckling! Belief systems impact most all phases of human lives.

Is life nothing anything more than a capricious Mother Nature and a reckless Father Time randomly juggling inorganic elements like a kid with a toy chemistry set? Is life a cheap, chemical accident? Are humans alone in the universe or is there a Supreme Intelligence so awesome that His mere words created the cosmos?

Nobel Prize winning Francis Crick, biochemist and co-identifier of DNA's double helix structure, expressed personal awe. "An honest man, armed with all the knowledge available to us now, could only state that in some sense, the origin of life appears at the moment to be almost a miracle, so many are the conditions which would have had to have been satisfied to get it going."[31] While Crick was not about to surrender turf to creationists, any spokesperson committed to the miracle of creation could hardly have said it better.

In the beginning, fully-formed, original life was created, "unborrowed" from outer space and "underived" from some "warm little pond!" Far above and beyond the limits of science is any rational explanation for the flame-of-fire powering the human soul.

The hypothetical "big bang" contributes nothing to the equation!

14

Numbers Game
Dating Planet Earth

"Ultimately, the Darwinian theory of evolution is no more nor less
than the great cosmogenic myth of the twentieth century."
Michael Denton[1]

Geochronology turned topsy-turvy in 2004 when paleontologist Mary H. Schweitzer believed she may have discovered soft-tissue inside a piece of a dinosaur femur unearthed in Montana. If true, the implications could send waves of ripples across ancient time zones, real and imagined.[2]

No human being walking today's earth witnessed its beginning. The brightest minds, evolutionist or creationist, cannot pinpoint the exact date. The issue triggers vociferous discussions as to just when to celebrate the Blue Planet's birthday!

Time looms as a lynchpin to the comprehension of pre-history. It defines a cutting-edge issue. But given the stakes, it rises to the significance of an ideological touchstone!

Biblical creationists require a literal, seven-day creation week. While the Bible doesn't target an exact Genesis moment, the age of the earth is typically measured in thousands rather than millions of years before the present---and never less than 6,000 years BP. If the Genesis literal-day creation week account is deep-sixed, Christ's words corroborating the event might then be challenged, sending seismic shock waves rocking Christendom's roots.

Evolutionism requires multi-millions of years to work its gradual "tree of life" transition myth: from microbes to fish, to amphibians, to reptiles, to mammals. The theory dissolves in prebiotic soup unless earth counts its birthdays in mega-millions of years. Given probability mathematics, evolutionism's uncertain "iffiness" collapses in a cloud of cosmic dust without open-ended, deep time in play.

Time projected in millions-of-years since the origin of life on earth beckons refuge for Darwinian thought. Deep time pumps the life-blood of its thesis. A multi-million-year time stretch is imperative for Darwin's "natural selection" to "advance by short and sure, though slow, steps."

Nineteenth century evolutionists conjectured 25 million years as the time-frame necessary for random chance to work the wonders envisioned by *Origin of Species* conjectures. This number has been overwritten by today's popular 4.5 billion year conventional date---a magnitude of 180 times beyond 1859's conventional thought.

A key caveat in play requires attention! The numbers game is anything but slam dunk! Nor is it precise rocket science!

For example, a cadre of evolutionists insist dinosaurs died out 65 million years ago, allegedly before large mammals appeared on the scene. But if a discovery reported in the January 13, 2005 issue of *Nature* proves authentic, the reptile-to-mammal mantra is due for an overhaul---major-size mammals cohabited with dinos..

"Villagers digging in China's rich fossil beds have uncovered the preserved remains of a tiny dinosaur [a juvenile *Psittacosaurus*] in the belly of a mammal, a startling discovery for scientists who have long believed early mammals couldn't possibly attack and eat a dinosaur." *Nature* writer Ann Weil concluded that "Discoveries of large, carnivorous mammals from the Cretaceous challenge the long-held view that primitive mammals were small and uninteresting."[3]

Human nature craves knowledge. Teetering on the edge of infinity, numerical labels, measures, and scales are concocted to grasp a handle on the here and now. Tucked in a galaxy of precision, humans measure the time of day, relying on Earth's orbit around the Sun.

Curiosity propels finite minds to dig deeper in a quest to understand life's origin, purpose, and direction. Just how deep in time did the Blue Planet and its proliferation of life forms first début? Mega-millions-of-years or merely thousands-of-years BP?

Written records collaborate with archaeology and science to shape provocative glimpses of the immediate past four or five millennia. Animal and plant life flourished, a virtual mirror image of today's fauna and flora. (eg. Egyptian mummies represent four blood types, identical to their 21st century counterparts).

Archaeology reveals the geometric glory of Egypt's towering monuments of stone. The Chinese calendar boasts antiquity. The reign of Yu, the first emperor of the first Chinese dynasty (Xia), arose BC 2205.[1] "Methuselah", a scrawny bristlecone pine clinging to the rugged slopes of the Sierras, survives as a living contemporary, rooted in more than 4,000 years of our immediate past.

But attempts to measure unlimited stretches of uncharted past time,   can strain the most agile mental gymnastics. The enigma of pre-history challenges thought while inspiring a major modicum of faith. Time flows perpetually as a meaningless flatline unless the Creator-God, the Designer of all time clocks, provides cohesion to the equation.

The Biblical Account Confronts Deep Time

Genesis 1:2 describes the existence of a sterile sphere, hanging in space, at the beginning of creation week: "...formless and empty, darkness was over the surface of the deep, and the Spirit of God was hovering over the waters." Some scholars consider it plausible that such a blob of lifeless matter could have existed in deep time prior to the literal seven-day creation week.

Dr. Robert H. Brown, distinguished physicist committed to the literal, seven-day creation week, interprets the Bible account to mean what it says: an earth covered with water, cloaked in a blanket of darkness. Brown describes the possibility of "radioactive decay over hundreds of millions of years prior to Creation Week" as feasible if Genesis 1:2 is taken at face value.

"New Testament writers make it absolutely clear that all components of the physical universe were created by God, but do not specify a time frame. The only necessary basic time specifications are provided in the first 11 chapters of Genesis. And those specifications apply only to living organisms and the environment that supports them.

"Nothing is said in the Bible about time in connection with the creation of water or the creation of the inorganic material that was raised above surface water on the third day of Creation Week---these components are simply stated as being 'there' at the beginning of Creation Week."[5]

Another creationist perception accommodates deep time by suggesting earth and its life forms may have been created in a fully mature format, imbued with an appearance of age.

Adam did not arrive as a helpless infant, but walked the planet as a fully grown human, capable of caring for himself. He required food to sustain life---not just seeds to sow. Trees towered, fish swam, birds flew, flowers bloomed and animals roamed. Lush vegetation, loaded with abundant fruits and grains, spread a built-in banquet. Without plants and trees bursting with ready-to-eat fruits, grains and nuts, the first man could have starved as creation's first casualty!

The Bible identifies Christ as the Creator of the worlds.[6] The Bible also reports that Christ turned water into wine at the Cana of Galilee wedding feast. The same Creator who transformed water into an aged beverage by His spoken word could readily crown a new creation with the appearance of antiquity.

The late Frank Lewis Marsh, an avowed creationist with a University of Nebraska Ph.D. in biology (plant ecology) and a co-founder of the Creation Research Society, embraced this possibility. "Our earth was created, along with the living forms with which it was furnished, with an appearance of age."[7]

Its no stretch for a believer in the miracle of the literal, seven-day Creation Week to recognize that the planet itself, including its rock foundations, could have been created mature, and given the appearance of age. If mature life and matter can be brought into existence by the word of the Creator, without a prior age-history, would there be any reason nuclear decay rates could not be awarded any age---billions, millions or thousands of years?

Nature's ability to mimic the appearance of age astounds!

The volcanic island of Surtsey, just south of Iceland, first surfaced the Atlantic Ocean, November 14, 1963. A casual observer could mistake the landmark to be several thousand years old. Less than four years after its birth, a paleontologist flew in to inspect the pristine landscape.

The brand-new chunk of raw geography projected an aged, weatherworn appearance. Already, a relentless sea had ground out black sand beaches. Multi-layered cliffs composed of a series of lava flows, guarded the four-mile coastline, carved randomly by Atlantic tides. Foot-long stalactites hung from the ceilings of caves. Basalt blocks appeared as rounded boulders, chiseled by the elements. At this tender age, sea gulls, insects, and at least three species of plants called Surtsey home.[8]

God is not limited to a single creative event in the context of infinite time. The Creator possesses the power to create all of Planet Earth's life forms in real-time days by His command. Anything less and He would not be the all-knowing, all-powerful, all-loving God worthy of human worship.

Radiometric Dating

In a quest for comprehension, geochronology penetrates deep into the recesses of rocks, deciphering time in the context of atomic age clues. The lofty title, "Radiometric Dating," resonates authenticity, inspiring confidence. Isotopes of elements like uranium (U) and potassium (P) undergo radioactive decay to produce daughter elements. Radiometric isotope ratios between parent and daughter elements are analyzed to interpret the ages of rocks.

Since the inception of radiometric dating, competing scientific camps have split between "millions" and "thousands-of-years" interpretations. Without an extraordinary display of objectivity, the mind closes to innovative thought, galvanized in rigid subjectivity.

At first blush, radiometric dating appears to play into the hands of the "millions-of-years" dogma---a cosmetic "silver bullet" used to gloss over glaring weaknesses in neo-Darwinian philosophy. Mega chunks of deep-time, built into the core of evolutionism, carries a collateral bonus for Darwinian wishful thinking---immunity from testing for falsification. Without a deep time crutch, evolutionism fades away, conceptually DOA (dead on arrival) and intellectually irrelevant.

The nuclear decay rate formulas that fuel evolutionism's hopes pose an apparent conundrum for those convinced life began only "thousands-of-years" before the present.

The late Dr. Henry M. Morris, prolific writer and patron saint of the Genesis account of origins, saw no problem. He reasoned, "The evolution model does require a long time scale. The creation model is thus free to consider the evidence on its own merits, whereas the evolution model is forced to reject all evidence that favors a short time scale."[9]

Consideration of "evidence on its own merits" became the north star of a research team composed of scientists leaning to time measurements in the thousands rather than millions of years. The investigative group examined radiometric dating and published preliminary findings under the title, *Radioisotopes and the Age of the Earth*.[10] Conclusions of the eight year research project were released to the public in 2005.[11] These findings, together with the thinking of other academics, offer a range of arguments incongruous with mega-million-year thought.

Testing Time Trails

Just what are the foundation assumptions critical to an authentic reading of time clocks based upon nuclear decay rates in rocks?

Three assumptions are inherent to the radiometric dating process: (a) Have test samples been altered by atoms moving in or out over time? (b) Has the decay rate remained constant? and (c) What quantity of the test material existed when the clock began to run?

Trevor Major believes "...all radiometric results should be influenced adversely by the failure of these assumptions to work in normal circumstances."[12] Major articulates the closed-system problem. "This assumption is unrealistic when one considers normal, natural geological conditions...Water originating from the surface can permeate pores in mineral grains and in microcracks, or literally flow within joints and through highly porous rocks...The effect of geothermal water originating from or near magmatic sources…" offers even greater potential impact. "…Magmatic fluids are most likely to possess minerals which will affect the sort of isotopes used in radiometric dating schemes…" Considering "…the intimate association of magmatic activity with igneous rocks (and many metamorphic rocks), contamination should be considered the rule rather than the exception." Major discloses "…a serious stumbling block in the case of the potassium-argon method. Both leakage and contamination are possible due to the gaseous nature of the daughter component."[13]

Physicist Brown, endorses Major's reasoning. "The heat of an igneous process would expel both radioactive parents and their daughters that are in the gaseous state, modifying some radioisotope 'ages' of igneous formations in comparison with the source magma. Age determinations based on helium and argon as the daughter-product clearly demonstrate such daughter-product loss."[14] [Other nuclear dating methods such as U-Th-Pb, Rb-Sr and Sm-Nd, would not be so affected].

Given the impact of temperature, pressure, and cataclysmic events, has the decay rate remained constant? Earth's magnetic field has reversed multiple times and now points south to north. What event changed the direction? Could a hydraulic cataclysm have modified the decay rates or the ratios of the products used for radiometric dating?

Mineral radioisotope "dates" are characteristic features that may, or may not be transferred, in whole or in part, when material from one formation is transferred to another in a sedimentary or igneous process and may not be reliable if the radiometric time clock did not reset to zero when the transfer occurred. That zero moment can elude even the most sophisticated geochronologist.

Creationist-writer Richard Milton thinks "Radioactive decay… is badly compromised as a historical timekeeper because it is not the rate of decay that is being measured by the amount of decay products left. For this reason, all radioactive methods of geochronometry are deeply flawed….Accuracy in the measurement of elapsed time requires that the process does in fact remain constant...the starting value of the clock...and certainty...that some external factor cannot interfere with the process."[15]

What quantities of the test material existed in the sample when the clock began to run?

The candle industry brightens holiday seasons with an array of bright colored, deliciously scented candles shaped to create happy moods. Once lighted, its possible to measure the rate of burn and to project a time when the candle will burn itself out. But, to project burn out, it must be known "how tall the candle was when lighted?" and "when the candle was lighted?" [16]

Geochronology requires more than a conjectured beginning fashioned from unproven assumption.

Discordant Dating

A supposedly 425-million-year old crustacean, *Colymbosathon ecplecticos*, has amazed experts because it's soft tissue anatomy is "eerily similar" to its modern relatives. Koen Martens, University of Amsterdam zooligist, admitted to being "flabbergasted" by the discovery. The U.S. Geological Survey's, Tom Cronin, reacted with surprise at the "demonstration of unbelievable stability."[17]

The stunning 2003 report exemplifies findings that leave evolutionism's reliance on a radiometric dating crutch between a rock and a hard place: One or both conclusions jeopardize evolutionism's "big gun" issue. Either the creature didn't "evolve" in millions of years or else the projected date is grossly erroneous!

Discordant radiometric dating lurks as an open secret. It exists out-of-sync with dates of time-certain events. Uranium-Thorium-Lead, Rubidium-Strontium, and Potassium-Argon dating methods can even generate discordant dates from identical test samples.

Gunter Faure warned of such *discordance* in isotope geology. "Unquestionably, 'discordance' of mineral dates is more common than 'concordance'...the mineral dates generally are not reliable indicators of the age of the rock...Although examples of nearly concordant U, Th-Pb dates can be found in the literature...in most cases U-and Th-bearing significance is questionable."[18]

Shortly before Faure's assessment, the 1980 media reported that Washington State's Mt. St. Helens had blown its top. Torrents of hyper-heated ash engulfed and destroyed wholesale quantities of plant and animal life---including *Homo sapiens*. Graphic pictures documented the drama. The yawning chasm where the mountain peak once towered confirmed the reality of nature's catastrophic reach, exploding on an observable date.

The recorded time of the event stands undisputed. But the nagging truth exposes drastically out-of-kilter radiometric time measurements of the lava dome age, underscoring the discordant dating dilemma.

"...Rocks formed in and subsequent to the 1980 eruption... should date 'too young to measure.'" Irregardless, "According to radioisotope dating, certain minerals in the lava dome are up to 2.4 million years old. All of the minerals combined yield the date of 350,000 years by the potassium-argon technique." This, despite the fact, "...these minerals and the rocks that contain them cooled within lava between the years 1980 and 1986."[19] This stretch from 350,000 to 2.4 million years shouts discordance.[20]

Discordant dating plagues Hawaiian Island time measurements as well. Using the potassium-argon method, ages ranging from 160 million to 2.96 billion years have been obtained from lava flows that occurred in the years 1800-1801.[21]

A cross-section of lava specimens taken from New Zealand's Mt. Ngauruhoe volcanic eruptions in 1949, 1954, and 1975 show potassium-argon dates ranging from a more recent 270,000 years before the present to a distant 3,500,000 years BP.[22]

Richard Leakey discovered what he believed to be a human skull in Kenya below rock assumed to be securely dated at 2.6 million years BP. Radiometric dating of the KBS Tuff site ranged in extremes from 0.52 million BP to 17.5 million BP.[23]

"Since formations we study today inherit radioisotope features from previous formations (erosion processes forming sediments; volcanic process forming igneous deposits), there is uncertainty as to how much of the daughter-product concentration in the formations we study accumulated during the geologic lifetime of those formations, and how much of the current daughter-product concentration was inherited from their source material.

"The well-defined starting point for radioisotope age determination does not assure a relationship between the radioisotope 'age' and the geological age (true time of existence) of a specimen."[24]

Robert A. Kerr, hardly a young-earth apologist, issued "A Call for Telling Better Time Over the Eons" to the readers of the October 17, 2003 issue of *Science*. He urged that anomalous, conventional dating results be addressed by fine tuning the process. Kerr targeted "Long-recognized problems with standards, interlab-calibration, and sample processing have limited both the precision and the accuracy of uranium-lead and argon-argon radiometric dating."[25]

The merry-go-round effect, with its dizzying circular reasoning, permeates geochronology's effort to seize an accurate handle on time. A key challenge is to ascertain time zones that track with a paleontology tainted with a mega-million-year bias. While fossil sites exist where a portion of evolutionism's postulated succession can be observed, a complete succession eludes. "...Nowhere in the earth is the complete succession of fossils found as they are portrayed in the chart..."[26] although the general scheme is represented in several regions.

Attempts to correlate fossil remains with the date of surrounding inorganic material is hampered by anomalous and conflicting test results. Which leads to a thought-provoking question: Does the radioisotope age characteristic of the rock that enshrouds a fossil cemetery represent the actual date of the burial event?

Richard Leakey's 1973 fossil find demonstrates the circular reasoning dilemma. Was the burial site of Leakey's find correctly dated at 2.6 million years BP? Was the fossil assigned an age based upon the assumed age of the burial site, or was the site assigned a date tied to the conjectured age of the fossil?

The date of burial does not necessarily reconcile with the age of the surrounding turf anymore than the date of the surrounding turf provides the time of death of the organic life it embraces. Suppose a farmer buries a deceased family pet on the "back-forty" on a date certain such as November 24, 2006 (the 147th anniversary of *Origin's* publication). No rational observer would claim the date of the dog's burial matched the much older age of the field or that the age of the ancient field coincided   with the date of the dog's burial.

The circular impossibility of the logic makes no sense. Correlating the event of burial as a match for the age of the surrounding cemetery soil is patently illogical. Then can it be beyond a reasonable doubt that the time of the event marking the cataclysmic extinction of dinosaurs matched the theoretical age of the rocks that buried their bones?

Bottom line: Circular reasoning hangs one unproven assumption on another. Time-scale computation using circular reasoning projects boot-strap science---a conclusion based on predetermined conjecture. It looks good on paper, but it delivers nothing more than subjective dating derived from extrapolation founded on pre-determined assumption. It is useless to rely on one unproven assumption to document a subsequent assumption.

Leonard R. Brand touches the issue with a savvy observation. He points out that radiometric dating is used to date minerals in igneous rock. Conversely, "...Most fossil-bearing rocks cannot be dated with radiometric dating methods."

Dr. Brand reasons that "...the age of these Phanerozoic deposits is determined primarily by biostratigraphy...Fossils in the rock and in the formations above and below them are compared with the sequence of fossils in other locations to see where it fits in the sequence...Fossils found in rock can only be used for comparing the sequence of rocks in different locations and don't indicate the age in years of the rocks."[27]

Young Earth Indicia

Accelerated Nuclear Decay Rate: Andrew A. Snelling and Mark H. Armitage, both young-earth scientists, theorize a short period of time existed in which radiometric decay rates were many orders of magnitude greater than at present. They propose that the half-life rate of nuclear decay may not have been constant and could have been accelerated.

"We consider this to be evidence of accelerated nuclear decay during the catastrophic flood. Accordingly, conventional radio-isotopic dating of rocks based on the assumption of constancy of decay rates is grossly in error. Furthermore, the heat generated by this accelerated nuclear decay would have contributed to catastrophic tectonic and geologic processes during the flood."[28]

Committed to cataclysmic Flood geology, Dr. Snelling believes "...any granites formed at any time during earth history would have formed rapidly, in days rather than seconds." As to radiohalos he summarizes, "In a nutshell, both polonium and uranium radiohalos are found side-by-side in the same biotite grains in granites that can be shown to have formed during the Flood by the melting *in situ* of fossiliferous Flood-deposited sedimentary rocks, with the granites intruding into other fossiliferous Flood-deposited sedimentary strata as hot magmas."[29]

Sometime in the past, natural forces have collectively contributed resources to build mountains, raise and lower ocean levels, shift tectonic plates, reverse geomagnetism, and modify climate. The Snelling/Armitage argument adds nuclear decay rates to the roster of dramatic possibilities for change.

Radiohaloes: Creationist researcher, Robert Gentry, seeking to reconcile radiometric dating and nuclear decay rates with young-earth thought, theorizes that radiohalos in Precambrian granite formed at creation and imply the planet didn't take millennia to cool from a molten state.[30]

Snelling and Armitage agree that the earth didn't take millennia to cool, but diverge from Gentry's controversial argument. They believe that granites with polonium radiohalos were formed both at Creation Week as well as during mountain building events at the time of the Flood.

"...The presence of dark, mature U and Th radiohalos in the same biotites in these same granitic rocks may be considered physical evidence of at least 100 million years worth of radioactive decay at today's rates. We consider this to be evidence of accelerated nuclear decay during the catastrophic Flood...Furthermore, the heat generated by this accelerated nuclear decay would have contributed to catastrophic tectonic and geologic processes during the Flood."[31]

Lava: Referencing strata accumulation from lava, ash, and cinders, Ariel A. Roth, a respected scientist with a University of Michigan Ph.D., calculates: "At the current production rate extended over 2,500 million years, there should be 74 times as much volcanic material as we now find."[32]

The "…Cardenas Basalt lavas near the bottom of Grand Canyon strata sequence" show a conventional "rubidium-strontium isochron age of 1.111 ± 81 million years…" After the formation of the Grand Canyon, "…basalt lava flows cascaded like molten waterfalls over the Canyon rim, down the walls and into the Canyon…" While more recent than the Cardenas Basalt strata that rests below evidence of fossils, this lava cascade down Canyon walls shows a "rubidium-strontium isochron age of 1.43 ± 220 million years"---virtually identical to the Cardenas strata.

"The molten rock that produced the young basalt lava flows came from deep inside the earth, from…the earth's mantle; so these lavas have inherited the rubidium-strontium composition from their mantle source. That is, their rubidium-strontium composition has nothing to do with their age, but everything to do with their source!"[33]

Erosion: Dr. Roth points to geological changes occurring so rapidly "…that they challenge the idea that rock layers have existed for the eons of time postulated by the standard geologic timescale." He sees the rates of erosion, sedimentation, volcanic residues, and mountain building as prime evidence of the fossil bearing sediment measured in thousands rather than millions of years, concluding that "…current rates of geologic change can be fitted with the concept of a recent creation and a subsequent catastrophic flood."[34]

Mountain uplift: Imperceptible to the eye but not to measurement, mountain ranges generally rise "at a rate approaching 7.6 millimeters per year." Ariel Roth observes what he describes as "present rapid rates" and the momentous uplift potential if calculated in deep-time years.

"One cannot extend the present rapid rates of mountain uplift very far into the past without getting into difficulty. Using an average rate of five millimeters per year would result in mountains 500 kilometers high in 100 million years.

"...In order for erosion [that is faster in high mountains] to keep up with what is called a 'typical rate of mountain uplift' of 10 millimeters per year, a mountain would have to be 45 kilometers high. This is five times as high as the world's highest mountain, Mount Everest." As to the Himalayas (not Mount Everest itself), "fairly recent tropical plant and rhinoceros fossils...appear uplifted 5,000 meters..."[35]

Sedimentation: Excluding catastrophic events, the major rivers of the earth carry an aggregate average of 24,108 metric tons of sediment to the oceans each year. "At this rate, the average height of the world's continents (623 meters) above sea level would erode away in about 9.6 million years"[36] in a world in which standard geology postulates that the beginning of sedimentation started 2.5 billion years before the present. "In large areas of the ocean basins, the sediment thickness averages only a few hundred meters. Major river deltas are not nearly as large as they should be"[37] within the context of evolutionism's time scale.

Paraconformities: Abundant paraconformities in geologic structures reveal gaps that lack both the deposition and erosion required for evolutionism's long time stretches. "A paraconformity exists when a part of the geologic column is missing in the layers...Much geologic time is often inferred to be represented by the gap of missing layers...The lack of evidence of time at the surface of the underlying layer of a paraconformity, especially the lack of erosion, suggests that the long ages never occurred.

"The difficulty with the extended time proposed for these gaps is that one cannot have deposition, nor can one have erosion. With deposition over time there is no gap because sedimentation continues. With erosion over time one would expect abundant channeling, the formation of deep gullies, canyons and valleys, yet the contacts are nearly flat.

"Paraconformities suggest that little time was involved in the deposition of the sedimentary layers, and these are the layers that harbor the fossil record."[38]

Amino acid behavior: "When an organism dies, its amino acids slowly change (racemize) from all L amino acids to a 50/50 mixture of R and L forms...The rate 'constant' for calculating ages from amino acid data is not constant on the evolutionary time scale. This scale requires this rate to "...change [decrease] progressively with the age of the fossil by three orders of magnitude...If the rate 'constant' is kept constant [as required by a Biblical time scale] the method gives ages in the range of a few thousand years."[39]

Human population: Gaging historical population sizes must be measured in the context of factors such as diseases and wars as well as changes in cultures, technologies and environments. Still, there had to be a first-ever *Homo sapiens* couple---a beginning time whether thousands or millions of years before the present.

Human reproduction rates hardly match the lightning speed of bacteria—or rabbits. Quantitatively speaking, the species must have been comparatively limited at its beginning—a single couple!

Estimates of world population by mid-twenty-first century, run to 9.8 billion humans. A thousand years ago, earth accommodated 265 million inhabitants. In the year A.D. 1, humans totaled an estimated 170 million. These extrapolations suggest a two-millennia population burst fifty-six times over![40]

Reversing geometric progression by extrapolation, a time frame spanning back to the first-ever human couple, would run a few thousand years at most---far less time than that postulated moment when a *Homo sapiens* "...left footprints on the sandy shore of a South African lagoon after a violent rainstorm some 117,000 years ago."[41]

Helium diffusion: Helium diffusion based on analysis of helium in radioactive crystals points to an earth that could be as young as 6,000 years. If earth boasted a time clock measured in mega-millions-of-years, more helium should have diffused into the atmosphere.

Russ Humphreys, with a doctorate in physics from Louisiana State University and career roots in Sandia National Lab, calculates that "Up to 58% of the helium (that radioactivity would have generated during the alleged 1.5 billion year age of the granodiorite) was still in the zircons" limiting the Biblical Flood to 4,000-14,000 years BP. While disputed by some, according to Humphreys, most of the helium should have escaped from rocks supposed to be more than a billion years old. Instead, "...the crystals in granitic rock presently contain a very large amount of helium, and the new experiments support an age..." within the 4,000-14,000 year range. [42]

"If we take the measured amount of helium 4 in the atmosphere and apply the radioactive dating technique to it...we find that the calculation yields an age for the Earth of around 175,000 years...The only conclusion that can be safely drawn from the discordance between the uranium-lead and uranium-helium dates is that this form of radioactive dating is unreliable."[43]

[14]Carbon: The ratio of ^{14}C to ^{12}C dates organic life systems. Measuring isotope ratios with new technologies can produce startling results. Coal seams, fossil residue from trees and vegetation buried deep in the geologic column, may not be as ancient as conventional radiometric dating techniques once seemed to indicate. Coal samples, "millions-of-years" old by conventional dating methods, should be ^{14}C dead, but they are not.

As early as 1988, Dr. Robert H. Brown reported on the unexpected presence of ^{14}C in coal seams conventionally dated in multi-million-year time zones. "'Infinite age' samples such as anthracite coal from deep mines in Carboniferous geologic formations (270-350 million years conventional age assignment) have yielded AMS C-14 ages in the 40,000-year range at laboratories in Europe, Canada, and the U.S.A."[44]

In a similar vein, "Paleozoic and Mesozoic coal and oil dates with the Accelerator Mass Spectrometer (AMS) method...give maximum ages between 50,000 and 70,000 years. This indicates that they still have ^{14}C and seem to be younger than 70,000 years."[45] Physician Paul Giem cites comparable data, concluding

"There is measurable carbon-14 in material that should be 'dead' according to standard evolutionary theory."[46]

John R. Baumgardner, a Ph.D. in Geophysics and Space Physics, once affiliated with New Mexico's Los Alamos National Laboratory and currently a member of the auspicious RATE team, presented similar findings in 2003. Using the AMS method and calculating ^{14}C's half-life at 5730 years, he recognized the raw measurement of the ^{14}C/^{12}C ratio improved from about "...1% of the modern value to about 0.001%, extending the theoretical range of sensitivity from about 40,000 years to about 90,000 years."[47]

Baumgardner obtained ten test coal samples from the U.S. Department of Energy Coal Sample Bank: "...three coals from the Eocene part of the geological record, three from the Cretaceous, and four from the Pennsylvanian."[48] The ten samples represented a 200-million-year time spread in conventional geological time.

Given the AMS limits of the 90,000 year measurement for traces of ^{14}C, the coal should be ^{14}C dead. Instead of confirming absence of detectable levels of ^{14}C, the AMS tests disclosed "...remarkably similar values of 0.26 percent modern carbon (pmc) for Eocene, 0.21pmc for Cretaceous, and 0.23 pmc for Pennsylvanian...little difference in ^{14}C level as a function of position in the geological record."[49] While the issue of possible contamination during sample preparation has been raised, the question daunts imaginations as to just how readily coal seams buried deep underground would be otherwise exposed to contamination.

So! Just how old is Planet Earth?

There is at least one response likely shared by creationists and evolutionists! A literal, seven-day creation week requires a miracle!

Creationists take it another step, seeing the world and its life systems as designed and put in place at the command of an eternal God, so wise and powerful that no human mind can begin to understand, much less explain, the event!

Come to think of it, evolutionism requires blind faith in a miracle built on assumptions---independent of any act of intelligence, no less!

15

Stacking the Deck
The Fraud Factor

"As evidence for evolution,
the four-winged fruit fly is no better
than a two-headed calf in a circus sideshow."
Jonathan Wells [1]

Darwin bemoaned the paucity of fossil evidence supporting the grand scheme he presented in *Origin of Species*. Twelve years later he pushed the speculative envelope forward another notch. His 1871 *Descent of Man* wove family genealogy into the equation by claiming humans shared common ancestry with apes.

He offered no earth-shaking discovery bolstering this conjecture!

Darwin didn't live to witness "confirmatory" support that surfaced 41 years later. Charles Dawson, British lawyer and amateur fossil connoisseur, rose to the challenge in 1912, proclaiming to the world the "discovery" of the fossil remains of Piltdown Man, an alleged "missing link" ancestor tying apes to *Homo sapiens*.

News of the find sent shivers of satisfaction down the spines of Darwin aficionados. The darkened fossil skull and jaw bone shouted "transitional"---at last the fruition of Darwin's dream!

Establishment Darwinists embraced the hokum, hook line and sinker!!!

The ballyhooed "fossilized" remains were theoretically authenticated and awarded a place of honor in the British Museum. By the time attorney Clarence Darrow, took on the John Scopes defense in 1925's showcase "monkey trial," good-ol'-boy Piltdown's credentials enjoyed enshrinement in science's citadel of "fact."[2]

The passionate Darrow pitched an eloquent argument for academic freedom, defending the right of professor John Scopes to teach evolution to Dayton, Tennessee high school students. Mr.

Piltdown's bones surfaced in prime time to serve as an irresistible piece of evidence. In a written filing for the defense, University of Chicago Anthropologist, Dr. Fay Cooper-Cole, added his voice to the chorus preaching glowing admiration of the find.

Both Darrow and his expert witness had been hoodwinked, conned by the infectious ballyhoo touting egregious deceit. They bit on the phony discovery by cluttering the trial's record with written quotes classifying Piltdown Man as "...distinctly human...an approach toward man in very ancient strata...

"...The crushed skull of a woman and a jaw can scarcely be distinguished from that of a chimpanzee...The skull is exceedingly thick and its capacity much less than a modern man, but it is distinctly human, while, as indicated, the jaw approaches that of an anthropoid. Here again we seem to have an approach toward man in very ancient strata."[3]

The celebrated defense counsel further buttressed his case by introducing into the Scopes Trial record, citations from the 1914 edition of George W. Hunter's *Civic Biology*, the textbook approved for use in Dayton's 1925 science classrooms. The evolution dogma in the text embraced a racist, survival of the fittest mentality. Ugly, hopelessly out-of-tune words glare ominously from pages 195-6 of the now out-of-print volume.

"...there is a greater difference between the lowest type of monkey and the highest type of ape than there is between the highest type of ape and the lowest savage...Undoubtedly there once lived upon the earth races of men who were much lower in their mental organization than the present inhabitants...we find that at first he must have been little better than one of the lower animals...

"...At the present time there exist upon the earth five races or varieties of man, each different from the other in instincts, social customs, and, to an extent, in structure...Ethiopian or Negro type, originating in Africa; the Malay or brown race...the American Indian; the Mongolian or yellow race...and finally, the highest type of all, the Caucasians, represented by the civilized white inhabitants of Europe and America."

Unlike Piltdown Man who cheated "death" for a prolonged period, Hunter's obsolete *Civic Biology* is long since out-of-print. Thanks to stalwart backers like Arthur Smith Woodward, influential geologist with the British Museum's Natural History Branch and friend of alleged "discoverer," Charles Dawson, the Piltdown hoax fraud flummoxed evolutionists for nearly half the twentieth century.   The museum's geologist died before the "fossil" find was exposed for what it was---some say with a questioning dark cloud hanging over Woodward's own reputation.

The Piltdown fabricator had pieced together a modern human skull with the jaw of an ape, then stained the monstrosity to assure the appearance of antiquity. The faked "evidence" was then planted in an English gravel pit in prep for its orchestrated 1912 "discovery."

The much hyped patchwork of old bones thrived as scientific "gospel" for forty-one years. It took until November 21, 1953, for the bald-faced fraud to be exposed as a sham---the year DNA structure burst on the stage, revolutionizing genomic science. By then, even devout Darwinists recognized bright minds had been hornswagled by a cunning hoax.

Ironically, the downtime beginning with the flurry of initial publicity up to the embarrassing exposure equaled the forty-one year time span between publication of *Descent of Man* to the moment the cleverly calculated Piltdown deceit had been foisted on a trusting public. The scientific establishment that ran interference for the perpetrator should have known better! More than a half century after the infamous "Mr. Piltdown" was exposed as deliberate fraud, the story still draws national headlines.[4]

One paradox to the hype of the *Scopes* trial: not only was Defendant John Scopes an admirer of William Jennings Bryan, but also, according to one teenage student who sat in Scopes' biology class, he never actually taught evolution to his students much less promoted the racism that leaps from the pages of Hunter's *Civic Biology*.

By the time the "monkey trial" awakened the public to the growing evolutionism controversy, the United States had pushed its own candidate to the forefront of the "missing link" sweep-stakes. Three years prior to the trial, geologist Harold Cook un-earthed a fossil fragment in the Nebraska heartland (Of all places, William Jennings Bryan's home base).

"Nebraska Man" took its place competing for the pedestal status awarded "Mr. Piltdown" thanks to the lofty assessment of Henry Fairfield Osborn, a top gun at the American Museum of Natural History. Osborn honored the discoverer by dubbing the relic *Hesperopithicus harold cooki*, a fossil piece of a *Pithecanthropoid*.

"Mr. Nebraska's" credentials were further hyped when an artist's conception gratuitously awarded worldwide attention to the ancient guy and his favorite gal compliments of a two page spread in the June 24, 1922 edition of the *Illustrated London News*. With both "Nebraska" and "Piltdown" to flaunt, evolutionists had a field day filing written "evidence" in the Scopes trial record. But as the old saw says, "Anything too good to be true, usually isn't."

While Piltdown's doom was not sealed until the 1953 expo-sure, Nebraska's fate bit the dust in 1928. The now famous fossil find faded into obscurity when someone spilled the beans that the tooth that had been the "model" for the artist's sketch of hu-man ancestors belonged not to a "transitional" human but to a peccary or pig![5]

Sure, the artist may have flunked "Integrity Science 101," but what could a man's imagination do with only a pig's tooth to work with! Perhaps design a silk purse out of a sow's tooth? Had Oscars been available at the time, the depiction might have earned the artist an award for creative innovation in the tradition of Walt Disney's Mickey Mouse!

Fraud Invades Science

Football fans watching from deep in the end zone or high up on the 50-yard line have different perspectives of the same game. Built in bias for or against a team colors reaction to a called pen-alty: "We was robbed" may echo from one side of the green grass while a roaring "Great call" echoes from stands across the field.

Variant responses to identical action events, are shaped by

seat location, attention to detail, and home-town loyalty. Witnesses to an auto accident may offer conflicting accounts depending on the vehicle in which they were riding or what side of the street they were standing at the moment of collision.

Minds of unquestioned integrity examining identical scientific evidence may reach diametrically opposing views. Observations vary if from the end zone or the fifty-yard line. Honest differences are predictable. Sometimes home team bias shades the equation with slants and spins. But intentional fraud and deliberately concealed evidence sends truth into a tailspin, skewing perceptions.

Mining opinions for objectivity, law courts require witnesses to take an oath to "tell the truth, the whole truth and nothing but the truth." Despite deliberate perjury by a dishonest witness intending to muddy the evidence waters, legal due process does its best to protect the quest for facts through cross-examination and open discovery. Criminal justice requires evidence "beyond a reasonable doubt." A jury's opinion in a civil action is built upon the "weight of evidence." Even with rigid strictures, juries can split just as political partisans shout discordance and biased economists misinterpret market signals.

While the scientific method postures integrity by commitment to primary source material, objective research, and peer review, it lacks the equivalent to the legal system's adversarial exposure via pre-trial discovery under oath and cross examination. Arrogant egos woven into the human equation infect perceptions.

Science journal editors have the discretion to screen out, rejecting for publication non-establishment or unpopular views. Peer review limited to pre-approved dogma serves as a crutch bolstering majoritarian thought. This cloistered approach doesn't guarantee "whole truth." Despite best efforts to pursue and protect scientific fact, fraud can still confound prestigious institutions.

Fraud didn't go extinct with the interloper twins, Messers "Piltdown" and "Nebraska."

Paleontologist, Viswit Jit Gupta scrambled his 25-year reputation by salting Himalayan stratigraphy with fossils lifted from "teaching collections" and then reporting his alleged "finds" in "close to 300" published papers. "'...The database for the Palaeozoic and Mesozoic of the Himalayas has, as a consequence of these publications, become so marred by inconsistency as to throw grave doubts on the scientific validity of any conclusions that might be drawn from it.'"[6]

The thirty-year career of German anthropologist, Reiner Protsch von Zieten, came crashing to a close in February, 2005 when he was forced into premature retirement for falsifying "dates of human remains." Using carbon dating, "...a team of Oxford University scientists showed very different 'dates' than those obtained earlier by Protsch."[7]

Allegedly using radiocarbon dating, the "defrocked" professor inflated the Hahnöfersand Man's age at 36,000 years old, far older than the redated 7,500 year age. He did the same with the Binshof Woman by fudging her age at 21,300 years BP, nearly seven times the redated 3,300 years. As to the Paderborn Man, Protsch awarded the age of 27,400 years rather than the relatively recent 255 years obtained by the Oxford University team.

South Korean stem-cell researcher, Woo Suk Hwang pulled off "one of the boldest scientific frauds in memory" when he conned the establishment journal *Science* into publishing his "findings." The Hwang report passed muster with nine independent peer reviewers before *Science* went public with the bogus data in June, 2005. It all came crashing down December 29, 2005, when a red-faced Seoul National University announced "...they could find no evidence of any of the 11 stem cell lines claimed in the paper."[8]

The scandal had "only just begun." The "once famed, now disgraced cell pioneer" was far from escaping out of the woods. On May 12, 2006, he and five colleagues "were indicted...on charges of fraud, embezzlement, and violations of a bioethics law."

A Pantheon of Deceit

The enigma of the disputed identity, heritage and authenticity of fragmented chips and shards of ancient bones baffles reputable scholars. What is not in dispute is the reputation of Ernst Haeckel, a 19th century German biologist who ranks as a classic perpetrator of fraud, earning high marks in evolutionism's "hall of shame."

Embracing Darwin's conjecture as definitive gospel, he announced with a hint of grandiose glee "the end of the Deity" and touted evolutionism with evangelistic fervor. Assuming Teutonic certitude, this charlatan excluded God as explanation for "the mystery of the universe" proclaiming "the Deity annulled and a new era of infinite knowledge ushered in."[9]

The fertile mind of this big-time hustler trotted out a make-believe, pet idea in a tree of life format showing supposed inter-relationships of organic life forms echoing Darwinian thought. What Haeckel lacked in evidence, he supplied glibly with inno-vative imaginings.

Clueless as to how inorganic matter at the trunk of his "tree" managed to spontaneously generate organic life, he invented *"monera."* Without a scintilla of evidence that these alleged bits of protoplasm even existed (they did not), he supplied drawings of his own imaginings to cover the shortfall.

Thomas Huxley, Darwin friend and fiery spokesman of evolu-tionism, swallowed whole this Haeckel make-believe, confidently alleging the aptly named *Bathybius haeckelii* "...probably forms one continuous scum of living matter...on the sea bed...girding the whole surface of the earth..." It all sounded downright authori-tative and scientific until reality revealed the "scum" as nothing more than a mix of alcohol and seawater forming gypsum.[10]

An ever resourceful Haeckel earned notorious spurs as a manipulative artisan who intentionally doctored animal embryo drawings masquerading as evidence promoting Darwinian spec-ulations. Bereft of authentic data endorsing his faith, he shame-lessly thumbed his nose at any semblance of scientific method by manufacturing counterfeits of the real to prove the never was.

The bold shyster modified and then flaunted comparative em-bryonic drawings of different animals, displaying his concocted flim-flam as "evidence" ratifying evolutionism. Skeptics smelled something fishy and were on to the fraudulent scam by the mid 1870s. Though Haeckel was exposed, censored and professionally disgraced in 1874, his fictitious art survived as a mainstay of mega-evolutionary hype, irresponsibly haunting pages of biology textbooks for more than a century after the fact.

"Haeckel's drawings...are substantially fabricated...his oldest 'fish' image is made up of bits and pieces from different animals—some of them mythical...it is the discredited 1874 drawings that are used in so many British and American biology textbooks today."[11] The phony illustrations have plagued school textbooks since 1868, unabashedly posing as authentic science. The third edition of *Molecular Biology of the Cell* allegedly carried Haeckel's dishonest art work until relatively recently. (Reportedly the fakes have been junked for the fourth edition).

This arrogant deceit elicited little more than a shrug from those intent on promoting evolutionism under the guise of science. Then along came a gutsy, nineteen-year-old high school senior from Perkasie, Pennsylvania who questioned the status quo.

Joe Baker challenged the school board to pull back the rug and expose the frauds that have cluttered academic landscapes for more than a century, and attach warning labels to textbook errors at the very least. The high school scholar called it as he saw it. "I believed in evolution for a long time, eighth grade through ninth grade. And, as someone presented to me the facts of science, I began to question what I believed.

"This isn't about typos.

"These are the main icons that are used to teach evolutionary theory. Many of them are fraud.

"I think the remedy for all of this is having people like me stand up and say, you know, this is wrong, at least in their classes. And maybe, if they get really radical, go up and stand against the school board...These aren't small errors." [12]

Karen Sterling, a Pennridge School Board member, admitted, "There is misinformation in textbooks." Then she sidestepped, passing the buck with words less reassuring. "We do not have control of publishing companies."[13]

Paleontologist David Raup addressed science textbook fantasies in a 1981 letter to the editor of *Science*. "...After Darwin, his advocates hoped to find predictable progressions [in the fossil record]. In general, these have not been found---yet the optimist dies hard, and some pure fantasy has crept into textbooks."[14]

It's a Bird... It's a ....It's a...Dinosaur?

A cross-section of late, nineteenth century European scientists zealously endorsed Darwinian philosophy. When he confessed puzzlement in his 1859 *Origin* at the fossil record's lack of intermediate varieties, "a charter was provided for fossil forgers."[15] The race was on for fame and fortune in the quest for evidence corroborating his view.

The never was Piltdown Man didn't début until 1912. But as early as 1861, paleontologist Hermann von Meyer was ready to cash in with the pigeon-sized imprints of dinosaur bones unearthed in Southern Germany's Solnhoffen Quarry.

Twenty-eight years earlier, French paleontologist Geoffrey Saint-Hilaire, floated the unlikely concept that birds evolved from reptiles ignoring radical dissimilarities between the two animal types (eg. warm-blooded birds v. cold-blooded reptiles). Darwin loyalists, eager to bridge the fossil record's yawning gaps, seized upon the *Archaeoptyrx* remains, etched in the Solnoffen limestone slabs, as evidence suggesting this supposed transition. Despite being crowned the Rosetta Stone "providing irrefutable evidence that evolution of the species actually occurred," its hold on such a lofty pedestal has been tenuous.

At the time, Andreas Wagner, discoverer of a dino fossil he named *Compsognathus*, doubted the claim, warning that "Darwin and his adherents will probably employ the new discovery as an exceedingly welcome occurrence for the justification of their strange views upon the transformation of the animals. But they will be wrong."[16]

At best, *Archaeopteryx* is rare. Apart from the 1861 discovered specimen housed in Berlin and the 1877 specimen preserved in London, the four specimens that surfaced and joined the category between the years 1956 through 1988, include at least two with reassigned identities from their previous dino classifications.

Skeptics are aware of fossil forgeries that flourished near Solnhofen for the century immediately preceding the 1861 find.

Dr. Lee Spetner and Sir Fred Hoyle, were privileged to see and photograph the London specimen. The two investigators "…concluded the London Specimen was actually a genuine fossil of the *Compsognathus*, an extinct reptile, to which had been added the impressions of modern feathers. Hoyle suggested that the forgers had spread a mixture of finely ground limestone and gum arabic thinly across the wing and tail areas then pressed modern feathers into this mixture."[17] The forgery claim itself has been hotly disputed.

Citadels of science, brandishing broad discretion, control research purse strings as well as access to research data and specimens. London's British Museum, caretaker of a vast array of artifacts, is no exception. After Hoyle and Spetner's initial observations, their further access to the *Archaeopteryx* specimen was blocked for unspecified reasons.

Writing in 1990, Ian Taylor expressed his own belief that the London and Berlin specimens were both a "clever hoax." After reviewing Taylor's opinion, Dr. Spetner took a more cautious approach. While noting that his examination of "about a milligram of material from the feathered area in the fossil" suggested "evidence pointing to a forgery" he cautioned that "unequivocal substantiation…of a hoax can only be arrived at with a similar examination of several samples from different places on the fossil." He expressed frustration that the British Museum "refuses to grant us any more material and refuses to make any tests themselves."[18]

Whether or not a forged transitional, this textbook "pin up" generates controversy. Its characterization ranges from "forgery;" or a "transitional" linking reptiles to birds; or possibly just another chicken-sized dino; and perhaps nothing more than an extinct bird.

Much Ado About Something

As for the dinosaur-to-bird scenario, evolutionist Alan Feduccia doesn't buy it. "The theory that birds are the equivalent of living dinosaurs and that dinosaurs were feathered is so full of holes that the creationists have jumped all over it, using the evolutionary nonsense of 'dinosaurian science' as evidence against the theory of evolution...To say dinosaurs were the ancestors of the modern birds we see flying around outside today because we would like them to be is a big mistake."[19]

Evidence of bird fossils allegedly pre-dating *Archaeopteryx* substantiates Feduccia's view.

No sooner had the twenty-first century dawned than the bird-to-dino scenario took another hit from a fraudulent fossil. The victim was much more than a bit player in the quest for evidence supporting Darwinian theory. Splashed across the full-color pages of the November, 1999 issue of the prestigious *National Geographic* were photos of fossil remnants trumpeted as "...a missing link between terrestrial dinosaurs and birds that could actually fly...a true missing link in the complex chain that connects dinosaurs to birds."

The endorsement came loaded with monumental consequences given the journal's multi-million subscriber circulation and its proud tradition of editorial excellence!

Despite the pretty pictures and the exuberant tone implying authenticity, by January of the new millennium, the speculative dreams of the sponsor came crashing to the earth with the revelation that the costly find, imported from the Liaoning Province in China, amounted to nothing more than a carefully concocted hoax. In a game of "Pin the Tail," some enterprising huckster had hitched the tail of a long-deceased, unsuspecting dinosaur onto the fossil remains of an equally unsuspecting bird.

Some dogs won't hunt and that bird could hardly have flown with the attached encumbrance. The only thing the weird dino/bird fossil achieved was the egg it smeared on the faces of over-eager promoters.

Even a February 17 issue of the establishment journal *Nature* compounded the confusion by mixing up its own report of the hoax with a picture caption alleging "the tail of a primitive bird" appended "to the body of a dinosaur." Most other commentaries suggested the precise opposite.

Oh, well!

In the never-never land of mega-evolutionary make-believe, this was not the first, and not likely to be the last, of overreaching interpretations of life's origin gone awry.

Popular examples of overreach carried long-term are the light and dark samples of peppered moths, glued to white and dark tree-trunk backgrounds and photographed to illustrate evolutionism in action. Apart from the dubious technique to prove a point, the moths never evolve into some new and different animal but remain peppered moths, albeit of contrasting colors. Photos of light and dark moths still litter school textbooks although they prove nothing more than genetic adaptability inherent in every genome.

Truth, the Ultimate Bedrock

Science doesn't need to stack the deck to prove the law of gravity. Every step taken every day by every walking person confirms the law. Suspend gravity's inexorable pull and the world's population could suddenly become space travelers.

Tampered evidence suggests the weakness of the proposition and implies the credential shortfall of an artful proponent. Slick counterfeits can tempt biased "experts" vulnerable to a flabby theory when verifiable evidence is non-existent.

Evo "science" survives as both a victim and a perpetrator of insidious fraud. Dishonest scholars corrupt evidence to corroborate pet theories or to grab headlines. Our non-existent "ancestor," Piltdown Man, flummoxed hard-core evolutionists for a big chunk of the twentieth century. Ernst Haeckel's deliberately misleading embryonic drawings along with peppered moth photos persisted in haunting the pages of science textbooks until recently.

Attorney Phillip E. Johnson, Intelligent Design champion, warns "The scientific method can be counterfeited, and the counterfeit may be certified as genuine by the most prestigious authorities in our culture."[20]

Scholars cherishing competing worldviews may reach radically different conclusions drawn from identical facts when shaded by bias. Those acting conscientiously, manage to skirt the minefield of hype and hokum that taints objectivity. It takes a giant mind to avoid the pitfall of preconception and entrenched bias that generates rigid calcification.

Stephen Schneider, a Stanford University climatologist, recognized for his studies relating to global warming, pinpoints the moral burden vested in objective research. His analysis resonates with North Star clarity, warranting the attention of creationists and evolutionists alike. "Science is a self-correcting institution. The data changes, so of course you change your position. Otherwise, you would be dishonest."[21]

No matter how you slice it, unverified Darwinian spin relies on a fabricated blanket of assumptions tied to wishful thinking. Søren Løvtrup warned "...that one day the Darwinian myth will be ranked the greatest deceit in the history of science"[22]

16

Teaching the Controversy
Academic Freedom

"Scientists who go about teaching that evolution is a fact of life are great con-men,
and the story they are telling may be the greatest hoax ever...
It is a tangled mishmash of guessing games and figure jaggling..."
T. N. Tahmisian[1]

"Nashville, Tenn., May 25---John T. Scopes, young Dayton (Tenn.) high school teacher, tonight stands indicted for having taught the theory of evolution to students attending his science classes in violation of a law passed by the Tennessee Legislature and signed by the Governor on March 21, 1925."[2]

Not bad for a rural southern town to seize the moment and make the front page of the *New York Times*! The imaginative savvy of hometown promoters, working from a drugstore table, not only created a media stir in the midst of the "roarin' twenties" but also unleashed a seismic dispute that resonates today!

Teaching the controversy moved front and center when local leaders teamed with an ACLU itching to challenge the state's newly enacted prohibition against teaching anything but creation in public schools.   The carefully contrived extravaganza, affectionately dubbed the "monkey trial," catapulted the origin of life issue to the international stage, capturing the fancy of a curious world.

Rigged to boost the flagging fortunes of a rural southern city coping with a lagging economy, town fathers tagged the affable John Scopes as the ideal poster-boy designate as the defendant party in interest. Powers-that-be scripted John as potential star attraction. Forget the fact that the youthful and popular high school phys ed teacher, temporarily filling in as biology instructor, never spent a moment teaching evolution.[3]

The contrived specatcle basked in the luster of its staging, perched strategically atop the buckle of the Bible-belt south.

A nationally-known, stellar cast assured media attention! William Jennings Bryan---lawyer, orator, and three-time presidential candidate, joined the state as co-prosecutor. Shrewd trial lawyer, Clarence Darrow, signed on as primary defense counsel, welcoming the chance to go toe-to-toe with Bible-belt hero, Bryan.

Those were the days when a defendant faced an all male jury and the trial Judge, John T. Raulston, catered to religiosity by inviting a local clergyman to use the courtroom as a pulpit to invoke God's blessing on the trial. To assure impartiality, four-year old Thomas J. Brewer, too young to read, was recruited to reach into a hat to draw names for the all-male jury.

Traditionally formal legal proceedings soon escalated to celebratory festival status. The media bit the bait and flocked to rural Tennessee. Emerging radio introduced live coverage, static and all. Bevies of reporters included *Baltimore Sun's* acerbic-tongued H.L. Mencken who didn't care much for religion and didn't hesitate to express his contempt for country folk.

When the July spectacle overloaded the second floor courtroom with several hundred onlookers, the proceedings moved outside to the courthouse lawn to accommodate as many as 5,000. Despite July's stifling southern sun, fresh air beat the stuffy interior of a Victorian building that had yet to lavish spectators with air-conditioned luxury.

Buoyed by overconfidence, crowd favorite Bryan voluntarily took the stand as a woefully under-prepared witness. A sitting duck, he faced the stiletto-like verbal thrusts of Darrow whose courtroom skills overmatched the aging orator's bluster. Regardless, the Dayton citizens and the jury remained loyal to Bryan and his views.

Scopes spoke to the newspapers, advocating academic freedom. "Education, you know, means broadening, advancing; and, if you limit size to only one side of anything, the whole country will eventually have only one thought, be one individual. I believe in teaching every aspect of every problem or theory."[4]

Bryan sounded philosophically close to Darrow. "The majority is not trying to establish a religion or to teach it -- it is trying to protect itself from the effort of an insolent minority to force irreligion upon the children under the guise of teaching science."[5]

The canny Darrow, ACLU prime spokesman in Scopes, argued against a Tennessee law mandating teaching creation in the Public Schools to the exclusion of evolutionism. His pitch for academic freedom, in the cause of equal time for evolutionism, rings true today.

Darrow's wisdom advances provocative guidelines for teaching the controversy. This suspender-snapping barrister railed eloquently against "...a law to inhibit learning...If men are not tolerant, if men cannot respect each other's opinions...then no man's life is safe...Bigotry and ignorance are ever active. Here, we find today, as brazen and as bold an attempt to destroy learning as was ever made in the middle ages..."[6]

"...Along comes somebody who says we have got to believe it as I believe it. It is a crime to know more than I know. And they publish a law to inhibit learning....If men are not tolerant, if men cannot respect each other's opinions, if men cannot live and let live, then no man's life is safe..."[7]

Darrow's astute advocacy left no room for the book-burning trauma and sieg-heil mentality surfacing in Europe in the early 1930's. Democracy's open forum approach to cultural equality, dissent and independent thought beckoned the Albert Einstein's of the world to find intellectual refuge in a multi-cultured republic flourishing with a government "of the people, by the people, and for the people."

The tough lawyer's call for teaching the controversy survives as positive fallout from the *Scopes* trial. Still, some scraps of defense written exhibits intended to bolster Darwinian thought, such Dr. Fay-Cooper Cole's touting of Piltdown Man as a missing link allegedly connecting humans to ape-like ancestors, proved less than enlightening.. The only thing Piltdown proved was that credentialed "experts" can be conned by deliberate fraud.

Despite Clarence Darrow's passion for academic freedom, the jury found Scopes guilty and levied a $100 fine. The ACLU appealed the verdict which was overturned on a technicality and remanded for further proceedings---which never happened. The legal clash faded from front page news while the cultural ripple effects reverberate in courtroom clashes long after the fact.

Its axiomatic: competition of ideas anchors academic freedom!

Evo's Evolution

Tennessee v. Scopes fueled the fires of public debate triggering all the action as with a referee's whistle signaling a football game's kick-off. Evo's revisionists rushed to salvage a faltering idea by plugging its more obvious "holes" while skeptics rallied to unleash verbalized volleys of deep dissent.

Barely eight years after *Scopes*, Albert Fleischmann issued his stinging indictment, charging that Darwin "...ransacked other spheres of practical research work for ideas..."[8] Even after Darwinian theory survived its mid-life face-lift, dubious creationists hung tough, with Randy Wysong penning his analysis that "...evolution is not a formulation of the true scientific method..."[9] given its reliance on a series of "unknowns." Later, Wolfgang Smith, a UCLA and MIT teacher, added his voice to the doubting chorus, challenging "extravagant claims" and characterizing the doctrine as "...totally bereft of scientific sanction"[10]

Within fifty-years after Scopes, evolutionists were no less vehement than the most devout creationists despite having to work through a daunting litany of disconcerting realities!

Mutations replaced gemmules as the critical component to be paired with natural selection; the paucity of organic chains of transitional life forms in the fossil record is admitted; fictional never-beens, Piltdown and Nebraska, vanished as much ballyhood links tying humans and apes to a common ancestor; molecular biology reveals the primacy of the cell's complexity; and the origin of information directing DNA stymies.

Shifting perceptions rallied loyalists to ride to evo's rescue with audacious, sometimes ingenious, adaptations of the theory's cardinal claims.   Undeterred, they addressed the spectacle of evo's slips and slides, by reinventing the splintered trunk of its "tree of life," and crowning the updated approach with the high-sounding title: *neo-Darwinism*.

The new approach didn't satisfy all evolutionists. Superficial cosmetic touch-up was not enough for Stephen Jay Gould, a Harvard scientist who committed his life to spreading the gospel of life without a Creator. Gould wrote with elegant-phrased passion, articulating prolific opinions, wielding an almost poetic pen.

He and colleague Niles Eldridge proposed yet another appendage to evo's lexicon. Aware of the sudden appearance of fully formed organisms in the fossil record without a trace of prior ancestry, the two scientists saw stasis and rejected gradualism in favor of change by sudden leaps. Graced with its own high-sounding title, *punctuated equilibrium* put an agravating burr under the saddle of traditional evolutionists.

"...Most species exhibit no directional change during their tenure on earth. They appear in the fossil record looking much the same as when they disappear."[11] "...The fossil record with its abrupt transitions offers no support for gradual change...macro-evolution proceeds by the rare success of these hopeful monsters, not by continuous small changes within populations."[12] "In any local area, a species does not arise gradually by the steady transformation of its ancestors, it appears all at once and 'fully formed.'"[13] Not surprisingly, this anti-gradualism heresy ruffled feathers in the ranks of evo's loyal traditionalists.

But Gould's innovative mind took on yet another icon of the repackaged *Modern Synthetic Theory*. He rejected mutations as a contributing cause of evolutionary change, powering his thinking through the heart of neo-Darwinism like a George Patton tank smashing through Europe. "You don't make new species by mutating the species...That's a common idea people have, that evolution is due to random mutations. A mutation is not the cause of evolutionary change."[14]

While Gould offered ideas that crept dangerously close to those of a creationist, he maintained a fervent evolutionist's creed repeatedly pronouncing evolutionism to be a "fact." Clinging to his faith, he candidly acknowledged causative factors triggering across-the-board changes were anything but proven.

So what evidence anchored his belief?

This illustrious man of independent thought, proved vulnerable to thin rationale. Hornswoggled and hoodwinked, he clung to changes routinely demonstrated by Intra-Genomic Adaptability inherent in each life kind as evidence confirming his faith. Gould rested his case for evolutionism on extrapolation from the real to prove the never was. "We have direct evidence of small-scale changes in controlled laboratory experiments of the past hundred years (on bacteria, on almost every measurable property of the fruit fly *Drosophila*), or observed in nature (color changes in moth wings, development of metal tolerance in plants growing near industrial waste heaps) or produced during a few thousand years of human breeding and agriculture."[15]

"Punk Ek" ignited reverberating controversy within evo's domain. Interpretations of the theory bristle with conflicting views evolving from Darwin's non-existent gemmules, to neo-Darwinism's gradual accumulation of mutations, and on to Gould's "hopeful monster" style idea.

Sooner or later, humans die! Gould couldn't escape the inevitable. However upbeat his attitude, death cut short his career prematurely at the age of 60, a victim of the cancer scourge. His premature death deprived the world of his insight. Make no mistake: despite moving away from Charles Darwin's gradualism to his punctuated equilibrium, Gould authored a legacy of non-belief in any future beyond the grave. In the name of evolutionism, he committed his considerable talents to "nothingness."

Exploration of life's origin will be woefully short-changed if exempted from the scrutiny guaranteed by teaching the controversy. Progress in science demands placing all issues on the table for discussion and debate.

The First Amendment Impact

Earlier, during the 1925 Scopes trial year, Benjamin Gitlow, an avowed anarchist, took his case to the United States Supreme Court, opening the door to vigorous legal disputes testing the U.S. Constitution's First Amendment guarantees. Not remotely a religious activist, Gitlow had spewed inflammatory rhetoric pushing the limits of free speech under New York state law. The court responded with a ruling that extended First Amendment guarantees to individual states, courtesy of the 14th Amendment.[16] Religious establishment and free exercise guarantees rode the coattails of Gitlow, bringing state and local law under the First Amendment's purview.

When John Scopes went to trial in Dayton, the full impact of *Gitlow* had not filtered through to the Rhea County judiciary and First Amendment clauses from the Federal Constitution had yet to be seriously tested in state courts. The Tennessee *Scopes* trial presented a spectacle of what existed up to that threshold year, while providing a hint of things to come.

Scopes stepped into the legal hot-seat for allegedly teaching evolution. Today, tables have turned. Students and teachers risk facing retribution for questioning assumptions constructed with the tools of conjecture and the architecture of the never-was!

Classroom Autocracy

Darwin at least talked a good game, giving boost to "a fair result." "I am well aware that scarcely a single point is discussed in this volume on which fact cannot be adduced often apparently leading to conclusions directly opposite to those at which I have arrived. A fair result can be obtained only by fully stating and balancing the facts and arguments on both sides of each question..."[17] His message sounds in tune with Darrow's plea for open search for truth in the public classroom.

Still, words are not enough! Fair results are not necessarily automatic.

A Colorado high school teacher faced suspension in 2006 for suggesting to students that President George Bush reflected some of Hitler's authoritarian characteristics. The issue inspired classroom discussion that spread to community conservatives and liberals, opening doors to hot exchanges of verbal fire.

Political science thrives on open discussions. Competing interpretations liven history class exchanges. Views of the causes, events and results of the American Civil War vary by region and political persuasion.

Controversial science perceptions also deserve open discussion! Craving access to power, human nature sometimes blocks access to "fair results."

Political and corporate interests underwrite financial support which drives pressures to conform. Personal opinion can be pushed to the back burner to access research funding loaded with a hook baited with bias. Scientists are no more objective and free from pressures to fudge results than any other professional group. Human egos don't relish admitting error.

When a totalitarian mindset grips public education, study of life's origin can be engulfed in controversy. Academic casualties litter the landscape of dissenters who dared to expose chinks in evolutionism's armor. Caught in the intellectual cross fire, scholars sometimes pay lip service to neo-Darwinism to earn a degree, to gain tenure, to be published, or to be rewarded with research grants.

"At Ohio State University, a graduate student's dissertation is in limbo because he was openly critical of Darwin's theory. At George Mason University, a biology professor lost her job after she mentioned intelligent design in class."[18]

Burlington, Washington high school biology teacher, Roger DeHart, ran afoul of censorship during the 2000-2001 school year. When he showed students articles critical of Ernst Haeckel's faked embryo drawings and the peppered moth's white-to-gray color changes, the administration removed him from teaching biology and forbade him to further address the evolution issue.

Rod LeVake, devout creationist, taught biology at Minnesota's Faribault High, a public school. He never taught creation, nor highlighted evo's flaws, but this didn't spare his being reassigned (without pay loss) to teach Introduction to Physical Science to freshmen---a class that doesn't deal with the evolution issue. His after-the-fact comments clarify his position.

"I have never felt led to teach aspects of creation science to my public school students. I did not, and still do not, feel that imposing my beliefs about origins on my students was in their collective best interest. If I were to teach creation science correctly, after all, I would need to use a Bible, which is something I was not hired to do. A student's education about God and His creation are best handled by his or her family along with their place of worship. Instead, in Biology class, I concentrated on highlighting the extraordinary complexity of life to my students.

"Once my peers discovered I had serious reservations about *macro*evolution (molecules evolving into man), however, I was reassigned to 9th grade science. Because of my personal convictions, I was not able to stand in front of my students and teach them about evolution without also pointing out the theory's many flaws and inconsistencies. As I found out, the school administration wanted evolution taught without mentioning the concerns I had. The ironic thing about this whole situation was that I was reassigned, not for what I had actually said in class, but for what I thought about evolution."[19]

LeVake understands and discounts evo's proof by extrapolation.

"Those committed to evolution use a technique called 'bait and switch' to confuse and convince the public. More specifically, they illustrate one type of evolution (the bait) and then convince them that a second type of evolution logically follows. They do this without informing them of the differences between the two types (the switch).

"...Microevolution occurs when one kind of creature passes on various traits to their offspring. There is abundant evidence for this type of evolution. The key idea to understanding microevolution is both the parent and the offspring are still the same kind of creature...Macroevolution is when one kind of creature changes into a completely different kind of creature. No evidence exists for this type of evolution."[20]

College professor, Dr. Nancy Bryson, felt the sting of academic intolerance. With an undergraduate degree in biology and a Ph.D. in Chemistry, this career science teacher headed the Division of Science and Mathematics at Mississippi University for Women, a publicly financed institution. Impeccable credentials didn't spare her the fallout pain erupting from a February 20, 2003 Honors Forum speech she titled, "Critical Thinking on Evolution."

Addressing an audience of around fifty, she offered some "contrarian" thinking. She recounts the event in her own words. "I discussed the non-existence of evidence for chemical (prebiotic) evolution, the 'Haeckel's embryos fraud,' from developmental biology, evolution disconfirming evidence from paleontology (the Cambrian explosion), and the subjectivity of paleoanthropology in its interpretation of the place of human-like fossil skulls in 'human evolution.'"[21]

A heated reaction rode hard on the coattails of her lecture.

"At the conclusion of the talk, senior professor of biology, Dr. William Parker, asked to speak. I said 'sure'. He rose and read a 4-to-5 minute prepared diatribe against me and my talk. He said I was unqualified to speak on the subject of evolution [She notes that none of the life sciences faculty, including Parker, had credentials as evolutionary biologists at the time.] and said the presentation was 'religion masquerading as science'. When I asked him to identify even one incorrect statement I had made, he could not...In the written evaluation of my talk given me by the Honors Forum director, all responding students (low 20's) said they enjoyed my talk, and expressed disapproval of Parker's behavior."

The day following the Forum appearance, the university's Vice-President for Academic Affairs appeared in Bryson's office, requesting her resignation. He refused to give a reason for the demand and she refused to resign. She recalls that "The Administration...steadfastly denied that the talk and the non-renewal decision were in any way related. This denial just compounds the error. No one doubts that the talk precipitated the decision."

This thoughtful lady wants "...the world to know how much it can cost an academic person to challenge evolution...I was the victim of the usual sort of politics that goes on in academia. But I strongly feel that my Christian stance hurt me, the final straw being the evolution talk."[22]

So much for Clarence Darrow's idealistic plea for academic freedom!

Totalitarianism, minted under any label, flying any ism's banner, and exploiting whatever power pedestal it confiscates, by its nature destroys whatever it touches, snuffing out the essence of the human spirit. All that is right and true risks being trampled by the insecure greed of the tyrant's heel.

Freedom stands tall, always barring the path of totalitarian triumph, but not without casualties.

The whisper of totalitarianism conjures up visions of an arena where a merciless political power, contemptuous of human rights, intimidates citizens, imposing coercive shackles. But totalitarianism also raises its ugly head in corporate board rooms and academic circles. Even churches, mosques, and synagogues are not immune to the intrusion of intolerance to missions intended to honor God.

Dissenters beware!

William A. Dembski, a senior fellow at Seattle's Discovery Institute's Center for the Renewal of Science and Culture, served with distinction as a member of Baylor University's faculty. He also walks point for Intelligent Design, writing prolifically with graphic insight. ID theory pioneer and onetime director of Baylor university's Polyani Center, he circulated an on-campus email raising hackles of academic peers.

His "crime?"

He reported "...the triumph of intelligent design as a legitimate form of academic inquiry...Dogmatic opponents of design who demanded the Center be shut down have met their Waterloo. Baylor University is to be commended for remaining strong in the face of intolerant assaults on freedom of thought and expression."

These comments incensed evolutionist colleagues who reacted by pushing political buttons intended to curtail his on-campus influence.

Dembski owns Ph.D.s in math from the University of Chicago and in philosophy from the University of Illinois. He has authored several books including: *Intelligent Design: The Bridge Between Science and Theology*; *The Design Inference: Eliminating Chance Through Small Probabilities*; and *Mere Creation*.

Auspicious credentials did not spare him the ire of faculty members at war with his views. Baylor's faculty senate responded on April 18, 2000, with a 26-2 vote calling for the center's dissolution.

Later, eight Baylor science teachers contacted Indiana Congressman Mark Souter, voicing vigorous objections to a May 10 Capital Hill intelligent design conference. The objectors branded ID theory "an old philosophical argument that has been dressed up as science."

The gutsy Congressman struck a blow for academic freedom in the Darrow tradition, publishing a pointed inquiry in the Congressional Record. "I am appalled that any university seeking to discover truth, yet alone a university that is a Baptist Christian school, could make the kinds of statements that are contained in this letter. Is their position on teaching about materialistic science so weak that it cannot withstand scrutiny and debate?"

When the fire and smoke cleared, Dr. Dembski lost his post as director of Baylor's Michael Polanyi Center for Complexity, Information and Design. Eventually, he left the campus for affiliation with another organization.[23]

Synthetic Science on Trial

The science definition can be so narrowly drawn that it cripples learning. Exceptions to such s restrictive definition of science eat up the rule. Encased within the limits of inside the box thinking, evo becomes an abstract religion built on metaphysical philosophy.

"Our present system of undergraduate education in the sciences is futile---it is too authoritarian…and too impersonal. What is urgently needed is an educational program in which the students become interested in actively knowing, rather than passively believing…"[24]

A spokesperson for an organization committed to barring challenges to evo in public schools, argues extravagantly that Darwinian theory is every bit as factual as the law of gravity![25]

Not so fast!

Comparing evo theory to the law of gravity makes less sense than introducing a raging bull to the inventory of a china shop! Is evolution so fragile that it needs a palace guard to bolt shut the academic door to prevent teaching the controversy?

Gravity needs no national mouthpiece to prop up and promote its presentation as fact. Gravity is an established law of physics, tested and consistently verified. Inorganic chemistry thrives on the absolute validity of the atomic numbers of the elements depicted in the Periodic Table. Mendel's law of heredity anchors the science of genetics with reliable precision.

In contrast, evolutionism can't be tested, predicted, or proven. It never happened! Ritualistic extrapolations citing the Intragenomic Adaptations offer obsolete clichés that prove nothing about evo. Despite subtle semantics, no amount of synthetic "science," derived by extrapolation, can effectively redefine "assumption" as fact. An assumption lacks factual legs and stands out as an interloper in the pantheon of life sciences. Neo-Darwinism takes the blue ribbon for random chance chutzpah by anointing itself as scientific fact on a par with gravity's predictable precision.

Brainwashing doesn't track with academic freedom. The state's money is not well spent if establishment dogma is force fed as the exclusive diet in the public school learning process. One teacher acknowledged he used "...trust to effectively brainwash them [students]...our teaching methods are primarily those of propaganda. We only introduce arguments and evidence that supports the currently accepted theories and omit or gloss over any evidence to the contrary."[26]

Newsweek feature writer Sharon Begley raised the censorship issue in 1992. "Despite its objective face, science is as shot through with ideology as any political campaign, and now that dirty secret is coming out. The party line is that papers submitted to journals are rejected for reasons of substance...But lately scientists have been privately fuming over rejections they blame on censorship."[27]

Nobel Prize winner, James Watson, rejected pedestal status for scientists in a no-holds-barred observation. "In contrast to the popular conception supported by newspapers and mothers of scientists, a goodly number of scientists are not only narrow-minded and dull, but also just stupid."[28]

A onetime editor of *Science* charged bigotry in scientists' ranks. "One of the most astonishing characteristics of scientists is that some of them are plain, old-fashioned bigots. Their zeal has a fanatical, egocentric quality characterized by disdain and intolerance for anyone or any value not associated with a special area of intellectual activity."[29] In fairness, no profession can claim immunity from such frank assessments.

Academic intolerance cuts wide swaths impeding or derailing careers. Independent-minded students fall before the blade swung at the whim of an autocratic professor. Bias drips from the words of one university teacher who threatened students with failing grades if they referenced creationist and ID themes. "…You will be penalized for citing anti-evolutionary material. It is not science…If the thesis of your paper is anti-evolutionary (akin to arguing against the germ theory of disease or against the atomic theory of matter) you will receive a failing grade. Scientific journals do not publish papers with creationist and ID themes. I will certainly not accept them."[30]

Medical school aspirants, seeking letters of recommendation from a university teacher, were warned to tow the line, or else… "I will ask you: `How do you think the human species originated?' If you cannot truthfully and forthrightly affirm a scientific answer to this question, then you should not seek my recommendation for admittance to further education in the biomedical sciences …"

Trying to rationalize this threat, outrageous arrogance reached lamely beyond reason, suggesting a physician that rejects Darwinism could be prone to "bad clinical decisions" and "malpractice regarding the method of science…It is easy to imagine how physicians who ignore or neglect the Darwinian aspects of medicine or the evolutionary origin of humans can make bad clinical decisions…So much physical evidence supports the evolution of humans from non-human ancestors that one can validly refer to the 'fact' of human evolution, even if all of the details are not yet known….How can someone who denies the theory of evolution---the very pinnacle of modern biological science---ask to be recommended into a scientific profession by a professional scientist?"[31]

Perhaps this professional bigot never read Clarence Darrow's plea for academic freedom!

Inside-The-Box Syndrome

Investigative science boldly confronts and regularly conquers untested frontiers. Thinking "outside the box" enjoys premium status. The revolutionary discoveries of independent thinkers, Newton, Mendel, and Pasteur, changed history. But when it comes to evolutionism, its advocates close ranks, conspiring to narrow the box's dimensions, creating an intellectual prison for all but the most adventurous. Evo imposes a cultural throttle, strangling dissent.

"Belief in God has also been sidelined at research universities and in the courts, neutering one key argument of all creationism. As the campus saying goes, 'Every department can preach except religious studies.'...Evolutionists alone receive federal dollars... control the accrediting agencies, research centers, and nearly all the universities. The news media and the courts, mavens of the old 'knowledge class,' are required by definition to rule negatively on creationists and their agenda."[32]

Jonathan Wells, articulate front rank ID spokesman, sums up one bottom-line reason to teach the controversy. "...When the false 'evidence' is taken away, the case for Darwinian evolution, in the textbooks at least, is so thin it's almost invisible."[33]

Scholarly research has been dismissed summarily under cover of the convenient rationale that the work "has not been published in peer reviewed journals." This ignores the reality that the authority to publish or reject is typically vested in an establishment, evo-oriented board of editors. In the quest for academic freedom's pursuit of truth, this makes no more sense than presenting a course evoking the history of the electric light bulb by deliberately excluding the role of Thomas Edison.

Suppression of innovative thought reaches beyond publication. Research funding can be threatened or denied. Mary H. Schweitzer, the paleontologist who spotted what looked like tissue inside the femur of a *T. rex* fossil femur, doubts she could have been awarded research funding without first publishing a journal article. "Without the papers in *Science*, I didn't stand a chance...That's the saddest part about doing science in America: you are totally driven by what gets you funding."[34]

GPA's may suffer; advance degrees can be derailed for non-conventional thought; teaching positions may be withheld, tenure postponed or in an extreme case, a teacher might risk dismissal.

Pouring the gasoline of intolerance on the fire of ideas only increases the heat. Arbitrary academic discrimination ultimately boomerangs. Just as, at one time, the best publicity for a book was to have it "banned in Boston," independent minded journals and books, flourish in the flames intended to suppress dissent.

More than one felon has avoided time in the slammer by skillfully hiding behind a presumption of innocence. Science provides no such refuge. In the grand jury of world opinion, as-sumptions don't cut it. Remember Phillip E. Johnson's warning that a "...counterfeit may be certified as genuine by the most prestigious authorities in our culture."[35] T.H. Tahmisian, who served the U.S. Atomic Energy Commission, accused the teachers of evo to be the perpetrators of a hoax. "Scientists who go about teaching that evolution is a fact of life are great con-men, and the story they are telling may be the greatest hoax ever. In explaining evolution, we do not have one iota of fact."[36]

So then, anchored in assumptions, neo-Darwinism clearly lacks scientific credentials and must be cast on the discard heap of obsolete myth by serious scientists, right?

The short answer is "no." The long answer is another "no," with an exclamation mark!

Has anyone observed evolution in action? Not yet!

Can the theory be scientifically tested, falsified in the lab? No!

Then is the hypothesis factual, a proven science? Big time, no!!!

Sounds suspiciously like a faith-based secular religion!

While it hardly resembles an objective learning process, John Dunphy urged public school teachers of evolutionism to "...cor-rectly perceive their role as the proselyters of a new faith, a religion of humanity...they will be ministers of another sort, utilizing a classroom instead of a pulpit to convey humanist values in whatever subject they teach, regardless of the educational level..."[37]

Originally a committed evolutionist, Dr. Jonas Spock, author of, *Baby and Child Care*, took another look and reevaluated his thinking. "...Man has lost his belief in himself and his sense of direction because the concepts of evolution, of psychology, and of sociology have undermined the authority of religion and man's identification with God. They have induced man to belittle himself as merely an animal divisible into a number of mechanical parts and drives..."[38]

The Bible's blunt candor projects a hard-to-swallow assessment, rejected *ab initio* by any atheist who perceives *Homo sapiens* alone atop life's universal batting order. In upfront language, the Psalmist charges, "The fool says in his heart 'There is no God.'"[39]

Myths plague our culture, encroaching on religion and polluting science. Evolutionism is not now and never has represented true science. To deliberately exclude even the possibility of a Supreme Being with intelligence superior to man is akin to a geography class prohibiting study of continents outside North America.

Until absolute fact is established beyond a reasonable doubt, science shifts, bobs, and weaves in a progressive quest for truth. Incremental discoveries encourage and excite but the final answer beckons beyond forever because the quest passes the limits of the finite mind. Science and religion can both be victimized by superstitious ritualism that activates mind paralysis, tyrannizing the spirit. Entrenched bias in either discipline builds barriers impervious to change. If science and religion appear contradictory, either one or both misunderstands or misapplies truth.

Religion without true science does injustice to the Author of science. Science without the truth about God fosters circular fantasy. Neither stands alone.

Science builds towers of achievement deserving respect, enhancing human life. Objective research driven by intelligent creativity finds reward in discovery. Studying evidence believed to offer a glimpse of life's origin reaches to the heavens, beyond laboratory confines.

Limiting the study of life's origin "inside the box" without considering the creative role of the Author of science makes no more sense than a student of astronomy refusing to look up at the stars! "If there is a God, He must by definition be the God of science, as well as the God of theology...any seeming contradictions between science and theology are no doubt due to man's incomplete knowledge of one or both..."[40]

Little has changed since Sir William Dawson's nineteenth-century prescience challenged objective thought. "This evolutionist doctrine is itself one of the strangest phenomena of humanity...a system destitute of any shadow of proof, and supported merely by vague analogies and figures of speech....Now no one pretends that they rest on facts actually observed, for no one has ever observed the production of even one species...Let the reader take up either of Darwin's great books, or Spencer's *Biology*, and merely ask himself as he reads each paragraph, 'What is assumed here and what is proved?' and he will find the whole fabric melt away like a vision...We thus see that evolution as an hypothesis has no basis in experience or in scientific fact, and that its imagined series of transmutations has breaks which cannot be filled."[41]

Evolutionism carries earmarks of medieval superstition masquerading as science. It bows at the feet of the god of blind chance and embraces dogma that exalts power while demeaning the disadvantaged. Its talisman consists of a fossil bone fragment dangling from a non-existent chain of transitionals. It is nothing more nor less than a pagan religion, perpetuated by coercion and in the last analysis, guaranteeing ultimate death for its congregants.

17

The Unconstitutional Sneeze
Evo Meets the First Amendment

*"...Teaching a variety of scientific theories
about the origin of humankind to school children
might be validly done with the clear secular intent
of enhancing the effectiveness of science instruction."*
William J. Brennan[1]

Internet anecdotes, however apocryphal, occasionally deserve retelling! Call this "The Unconstitutional Sneeze," or whatever, its worth a smile.

"They walked in tandem, each of the ninety-three students filing into the already crowded auditorium. With rich maroon gowns flowing and the traditional caps, they looked almost as grown up as they felt.

"Dads swallowed hard behind broad smiles, and moms freely brushed away tears. This class would not pray during the commencements-not by choice but because of a recent court ruling prohibiting it. The principal and several students were careful to stay within the guidelines allowed by the   ruling. They gave inspirational and challenging speeches, but no one mentioned divine guidance and no one asked for blessings on the graduates or their families.

Ritual speeches drew polite applause "...until the final speech received a standing ovation. A solitary student walked proudly to the microphone. He stood still and silent for just a moment, and then he delivered his speech."

No words. Just a resounding--sneeze!

"The rest of the students rose immediately to their feet, and in unison they said, 'God Bless You.' The audience exploded into applause. The graduating class...invoke[d] God's blessing on their future with or without the court's approval."[2]

Far out? Perhaps! In sync with majority thought that leans to "teaching the controversy" in public schools?   Quite likely. Americans believe, by an overwhelming margin of 77% to 19%, that "when Darwin's theory of evolution is taught in school, students should also be able to learn about scientific evidence that points to an intelligent design of life."[3]

The Classroom: A Marketplace of Ideas

Respected judicial opinions traditionally stand tall, immune to the push and pull of public opinion. Blind justice demands objectivity. Just how blind can provide fodder for debatable hindsight.

Pennsylvania's Dover Area Public School District voted 6-3 requiring ninth-grade biology students to listen to a statement that "Intelligent Design" differs from Darwin's view of origins. It   recommended students read *Of Pandas and People* for additional perspective. Eight families objected and filed a complaint claiming First Amendment infringement. Federal District Court Judge John E. Jones heard the case September 26, 2005.[4]

So what's the big deal?

The school board's words advised that "...Darwin's theory is a theory...not a fact;" that "...Intelligent design is an explanation of the origin of life that differed from Darwin's...;" and that "...With respect to any theory, students are encouraged to keep an open mind."[5] Clarence Darrow might have seen the phrases as responsive to his 1925 plea for academic freedom rather than some dangerous state-sponsored religious establishment.

Of Pandas and People has never been viewed as a theological book. Authored by Dean H. Kenyon and Percival Davis with academic editing by Charles B. Thaxton, the book's most grievous "sin" may be its failure to exalt "spontaneous generation" as the source of original life. Asking a federal court to prevent reference to such a book is not exactly book burning censorship, but depriving prior access to independent viewpoints contributes little positive to a high schooler's education.

In a plethora of words, reminiscent of the legendary clergyman raising his voice and pounding the pulpit when dishing out thin substance, the judge penned a 139-page opinion concluding that reference to Intelligent Design in a ninth-grade public school biology classroom violated the U.S. Constitution's ban on religious establishment.[6]

The judge bought into the arguments of the protesting parents and interpreted the school board's nod to academic freedom as religious establishment. Lack of credentials as scientist or theologian didn't deter the judge outlawing Intelligent Design as "...an interesting theological argument, but...not science," and eventually finding it "...unconstitutional to teach ID as an alternative to evolution."[7]

In a burst of judicial exuberance, the Pennsylvania judge branded the school board's venture into the issue as "breathtaking inanity" and the resulting dispute an "utter waste of monetary and personal resources." He elevated his views as worthy of legal precedent, suggesting "...no other tribunal in the United States is in a better position to traipse into this controversial area..."[8]

The brash "traipse" lacked legs of logic by insisting that ID, despite absence of any worship protocol, is an impermissible front for religion.

Intelligent Design involves no liturgy; has no clergy or churches; outlines no profession of faith; is not listed in telephone directories as a religious organization; and offers no prayers. Nor does the theory make any direct reference to any deity. Given this reality, the court's view of ID as violating the First Amendment's Establishment Clause coupled with allusion to "an interesting theological argument," conjures up visions of judicial overreach.

Almost before the ink dried on the *Dover* opinion, a subtle incongruity haunted the result. Charles Darwin's own words, just beyond the judicial "traipse," arguably turns the court's rationale upside down. The guru's writings confessed to his readers that "science...throws no light on...the essence or origin of life." Then, in the final paragraph on the last page of *Origin of Species*, he capped his treatise acknowledging "life" had been "...originally breathed by the Creator into a few forms or into one...," identifying the "Creator" with a capital "C."

So Darwin's vague reference to an Intelligent Designer is ok for public school classrooms while study of ID theory is verboten? If ID doesn't pass constitutional muster because of religious implications, then how can the assumptions permeating Darwinism with its explicit reference to life being "originally breathed by the Creator" make the grade?

Imagine presenting a jury with the notion that the mass-produced Model "T" Ford rolled off the assembly line without input from a designer? Or that an Egyptian pyramid lacked an engineered plan? Or that a photo-quality, high-definition television screen appeared in homes independent of scientific thought?

Yet, the intelligent judicial mind, that cobbled the court's opinion, implicitly directs school kids to believe human brains derived from some unintelligent source. So how can it be anathema for a public school classroom to even reference, much less discuss, the possibility that the human brain is the product of an intelligent act?

A public school's science package implies intelligence and design in physics, mathematics, and chemistry, while biology is mandated to languish at the mercy of the judicially imposed, hodge-podge explanation of life's origin. John Q. Student is shoehorned into a lock-step, cosmic dice throw, taught to embrace "a blind, uncaring process." By court order, John Q. Student's biology text, discards reference to Intelligent Design while embracing *The Origin of Species* despite Darwin's nod to a "Creator."

Judicial authority has sentenced 9th grade kids studying biology to a state-funded diet of unproven assumptions. Rather than inheriting human brains from an intelligent source, they are to be fed unproven nonsense that their own family is descended from some ancient, ancestor fish!

The *Dover* opinion resorted to the tired canard chastising ID for "...the complete absence of peer-reviewed publications supporting the theory."[9] It is as likely for the editor of a fundamentalist publication to welcome an atheist's submission arguing "there is no God," as to expect a devout evolutionist editor to embrace an article authored by an ID proponent. It can happen, but when it does, emotional fallout can soon follow. "At the Smithsonian, an evolutionary biologist was harassed and vilified for permitting an article favoring intelligent design to be published in a peer-reviewed biology journal."[10]

John G. West, ID proponent and associate director of Discovery Institute's Center for Science and Culture, called the decision "...a real overreach by an activist judge who thinks he can stop the spread of a scientific idea through government-imposed censorship."[11]

"No legal decree can remove the digitally coded information DNA...Efforts to mandate intelligent design are misguided, but efforts to shut down a scientific idea through harassment and judicial decrees hurt democratic pluralism. The more Darwinists resort to censorship and persecution, the clearer it will become that they are championing dogmatism, not science."[12]

West cut the Pennsylvania judge no slack! He questioned the jurist's activist bent rather than the judicial restraint expected of a Federal judge.

"It is a standard principle in good constitutional jurisprudence that a judge should only go as far as necessary to answer the issue before him. So if a judge can decide a case on narrow grounds, that's what he ought to do. He shouldn't try to use his opinion to answer all possible questions.

"In the present case, Judge Jones found that the Dover board did not act for a legitimate secular purpose. Instead, he determined that board members acted for clearly religious reasons. Having made this determination, the specific policy adopted by the Dover board was plainly unconstitutional under existing Supreme Court precedents. End of story.

"There was no need for the Judge to launch an expansive discussion of whether intelligent design is science, whether there is scientific evidence for the concept, whether it is inherently religious, whether Darwinism has flaws, or whether Darwinian evolution is compatible with faith. A judge who actually adheres to the idea of judicial restraint would not have ventured into these other areas, because they were completely unnecessary for the disposition of the case.

"Why, then, did Judge Jones venture so far afield from what was necessary to determine the case? From the comments he made to the news media, it seems that he wanted his place in judicial history. He relished the idea that he could be the first judge to give a definitive pronouncement on ID, and he didn't want to let go of that opportunity just because good judicial craftsmanship wouldn't allow it. Judge Jones also had no small estimate of his own importance in the scheme of things."[13]

Richard Thompson, attorney for the *Dover* case defendants and President and Chief Counsel for the Thomas More Law Center, warns that "The Supreme Court's modern Establishment Clause jurisprudence is in hopeless disarray.

"Despite giving lip service to the concept that the Establishment Clause prohibits both the promotion of and hostility towards religion, this and several other recent decisions by federal judges have demonstrated that there is a double standard.

"The Ten Commandments and the Nativity scene are out and public schools can't mention intelligent design, but an overtly, anti-Catholic display is permissible because it allegedly enhances aesthetics. Apparently, the Establishment Clause protects atheists and secular humanists, but affords no comparable protection for Christians..."[14]

What at first blush seemed to be a judicial "Christmas gift," buoying the spirits of Darwinian loyalists, may eventually prove a Pyrrhic victory. Those rejoicing at the suppression of dissent by one judge "permanently enjoining" mention of ID in science classes have won a temporary battle of technical definitions. But the nearby Liberty Bell in Philadelphia is not ringing celebratory chimes. In the much bigger war of ideas, academic freedom is the bottom-line loser.

Let's get this straight!

No thinking citizen wants an atheist teaching religion to kids in a tax-funded classroom. The First Amendment blocks such a dismal result. But there's nothing in the U.S. Constitution demanding government hostility toward religion, rather than neutrality. The controversial *Dover* decision pushes the envelope in the direction of hostility--- hardly the last word on the issue!

Is it consistent for a courtroom witness to take the oath reciting the words, "So Help Me God?" How about "In God We Trust" engraved on the currency of the judge's tax-funded salary, while the same judicial authority forbids kids to hear the words "intelligent design" because it evokes thoughts of God?

Does it make sense that while an activist judge dubs the reference to ID a prohibited "establishment of religion" while evo's "secular religion" slips by with an "out of jail free" constitutional pass?

Buried in its judicial salute to unintelligent cause as the original parent of human reason, the court offered a one-sentence rhetorical sop to academic freedom. "We do not controvert that ID should continue to be studied, debated and discussed."[15]

Wait just a minute! Let's pause for station identification!

If it please the court, a question remains! If the study, discussion and debate of Intelligent Design is constitutionally barred from the classroom by judicial decree, just where should the academic process take place?

Would an after-school-hours, voluntary seminar on the school lawn pass muster? Or discussion in some corner of a tax supported city library? Does a publicly funded street corner qualify for a debate? Would the Dover ruling bless the use of a church building that enjoys indirect government financial support by its tax exemption? As for discussing ID in the family home, isn't tax largess lavished on private residences through a cornucopia of politically popular services and programs a potential constitutional bar?

So is it necessary to book a cruise ship to seek a safe haven twelve miles out to sea where ID and the evo's "flaws" and "holes" can be "studied, debated, and discussed" without running afoul of the restrictions leveled by Judge Jones?

Galileo Galilei (1564-1642), an advocate of Nicholaus Copernicus' *earth rotates around the sun* idea, faced an Inquisition for heresy. Coerced to recant his belief, and sentenced to house arrest, tradition credits his muttering to himself, something like, "The earth still circles the sun." Committed to factual science and protesting authoritarian mandates defining truth, Galileo's logic still shines like a beacon. "I do not feel obliged to believe that the same God who endowed us with sense, reason and intellect has intended us to forgo their use."[16]

Political science partisanship that confines classroom discussion to one party while excluding all others, contributes zip to a well-rounded education. Twentieth century fascist totalitarianism imposed the twisted ramifications of one party rule with cataclysmic results.

Studying biology by rigid rote methodology while ignoring the exploration of alternatives as to life's origin and development, glorifies a "one-note Charlie" science education that hides behind an arguably tortured interpretation of First Amendment guarantees.

Some of the same special interests promoting evo in public schools also invoke the constitution in attempts to ban religious symbolism in government ceremonies and on government property. Prior to *Dover*, opponents of religious symbolism met with success when a Federal court ordered the removal of a Mojave Desert cross memorializing WWI dead.[17]

No question about it, the First Amendment to the United States Constitution requires that "Congress shall make no law respecting an establishment of religion." But in the case of the offending cross, no government action created the monument. Tax dollars did not fund the memorial. Visitors look in vain for any verbalized message or government action invoking or establishing religion at the site.

Does the judicial overreach in the Mojave Desert case mean that the government-funded cemetery crosses overlooking Normandy's Omaha Beach landing of June 6, 1944 will be a future target of the overzealous in the name of religious freedom? Is that what Thomas Jefferson, George Mason and James Madison intended?

Evo Meets the First Amendment

It wasn't until 1925 that the U.S. Supreme Court looked to Fourteenth Amendment mandates as a legal conduit to rule First

Amendment guarantees are binding on state and local governments. Coincidentally, this landmark ruling emerged as the law of the land the year Tennessee's *Scopes* trial attracted international attention. Since the First Amendment guards against religious totalitarianism, the court's *Gitlow*[18] reasoning crafted the framework for a century of religious liberty tests: flag salutes, prayers, religious symbols on public property, and Sunday blue law restraints.

After *Gitlow*, the Supreme Court has held the First Amendment's Establishment and Free Exercise Clauses prevent the teaching of sectarian religion in public schools. The position makes sense constitutionally and practically. The most fervent believer in God would object to a committed atheist putting a biased spin on the Genesis account of Creation Week. The imposition would prove counterproductive in substance and in spirit.

Once the First Amendment came into play at local government levels, the legal door swung full circle. Teaching evolutionism as "science" to the exclusion of alternate views has inspired an authoritarian voice in which students, teachers, school boards, parents and the public have been swept into a whirlpool of confrontation.

In 1982, Federal Judge William Overton ruled the teaching of "creation science" in public schools violated the First Amendment's Establishment Clause since its purpose was to advance religion and would result in an entanglement with religion.[19] The *McLean* case adopted evolutionist Michael Ruse's qualifying five-part evaluation test for science. Applying the Ruse test, the court concluded that creation science more closely approximated religion than science. It sounded like evo had been awarded carte blanche exclusivity.

In *Edwards v. Aguillard*, five years after *McLean*, the nation's highest court struck down Louisiana's balanced treatment statute that would have allowed tax-funded schools to teach a package of both evolutionism and "creation science." Justice William J. Brennan spoke for the majority but penned dicta signaling the court's endorsement of academic freedom. "…Teaching a variety of scientific theories about the origin of humankind to school children might be validly done with the clear secular intent of enhancing the effectiveness of science instruction."[20]

Justice Lewis F. Powell agreed, elaborating that "a decision respecting the subject matter to be taught in public schools does not violate the Establishment Clause simply because the material to be taught 'happens to coincide or harmonize with the tenets of some or all religions'"[21]

Justice Anton Scalia, joined by Chief Justice William H. Rehnquist, disagreed with the majority's narrow holding but not with the dicta of Brennan and Powell. In a blistering dissent, Justice Scalia recounted the reasoning placed in evidence before the trial court by State Senator Keith, a sponsor of the Louisiana law.

"The censorship of creation science has at least two harmful effects. First, it deprives students of knowledge of one of the two scientific explanations for the origin of life and leads them to believe that evolution is proven fact; thus, their education suffers and they are wrongly taught that science has proved their religious beliefs false. Second, it violates the Establishment Clause. The United States Supreme Court has held that secular humanism is a religion. Belief in evolution is a central tenet of that religion."[22]

Taken together, the 1987 words of Justices Brennan, Powell and Scalia suggest secular guidelines for the use of citizens challenging evo's right to usurp a pedestal position, immune to constitutional challenge.

Government Neutrality, Not Hostility

Union of church and state offers not a whit of refuge to religious liberty. It cripples all it touches---both religion and government. Citizens are denied a clear picture of the truth about God. A legal environment preserving an individual's freedom to openly study, search and share rather than to be force-fed gross error, promises the best of all worlds.

Tyranny flows from a totalitarian state controlled by a majoritarian faith, naturalistic or faith-based, that suppresses dissent--shades of the excesses of medieval Europe. Where religious practice exists at the state's whim, spirituality is compromised, if not persecuted---witness the surreptitiously scribbled symbols of a cross or a fish on walls sheltered in the hide-a-way haunts of Roman catacombs.

History overflows with pages dripping the blood of intolerance where majoritarian religion denies the right to dissent. The First Amendment to the United States constitution prevents horrific injustice both by protecting Free Exercise and by preventing Establishment of preferential sectarianism.

Imposition of coercive legislation to enforce religious practice is counterproductive. It represents the antithesis of a God committed to free moral agency. Belief in God is best fostered by a legal environment that assures free choice and allows a heart to respond to the "still, small voice" voluntarily. Rigid conformity ordered by authoritarian fiat does nothing to promote religion of the heart. The theme itself smacks of anti-religion, alienating all who conscientiously resist unconscionable mandates. When God is mischaracterized as an unfair tyrant, arbitrary and vengeful, truth vanishes.

Tax supported school teachers lack the credentials and the legal authority to teach religion. Unbelieving educators would be less than persuasive in presenting any curriculum based on a unique theology.

Government protection of individual religious practice doesn't remotely imply that citizens can be coerced to worship any shrine, bow down to any deity, or swear allegiance to any sectarian dogma. The United States stands as a neutral protector of a citizen's Free Exercise of faith whether creationist, secular evolutionist, atheist, agnostic, Jew, Muslim, or Christian.

Has Establishment concern dominated legal perceptions since *Gitlow* leaving Free Exercise with the short stick? To avoid state-sponsored religion, has the pendulum swung so far as to subordinate Free Exercise? Is there a clear and present danger that an over-emphasis on concern for Establishment will impose a secular humanism by a government overtly hostile to a religion that worships a living God?

Establishment and Free Exercise Clauses present a twin protection package. Interpretation of either one with a blind eye to the other throws the equation out of balance. A "one note Charlie" case that fights Establishment while trampling Free Exercise, risks jeopardizing the delicate balance between the two mandates.

American Civil War infantryman, Frank Haskell, kept a diary of the grizzly, hour-by-hour details of the epic, three-day Battle of Gettysburg. Strip out Haskell's account of the last day of the battle, and his gripping, eye-witness portrait of the watershed event paints an incomplete picture.

In a similar way, evaluating the Establishment Clause out-of-context, without balancing the protective guidlines required by the Free Exercise Clause, risks an inadequate legal result! Government action that projects *hostility* toward religious practice is out-of-kilter with the First Amendment's two-part package guaranteeing *neutrality*.[23]

The United States Constitution requires government to "...be neutral in matters of religious theory, doctrine, and practice. It may not be hostile to any religion or to the advocacy of no-religion; and it may not aid, or foster or promote one religion or religious theory against another or even against the militant opposite."[24]

Retired Supreme Court Justice Sandra Day O'Connor is credited with understanding that "The [First] Amendment's Establishment Clause is not a sword, driving private religious expression from the marketplace of ideas; rather, it is a shield that constrains government precisely to protect religiously motivated speech and action." In case after case, O'Connor has vindicated this understanding

"...In the 1994 *Kiryas Joel* case, she insisted that 'government impartiality, not animosity, toward religion' is the constitutional touchstone, and that the First Amendment neither requires nor permits 'hostility to religion, religious ideas, religious people, or religious schools.'"[25]

Evolutionism Is A Secular Religion

If the 2005 *Dover* decision characterizing Intelligent Design as religious establishment is correct, then, to be consistent, shouldn't the religion of secular humanism also fail the establishment test? If teaching evo in the classroom imposes a secular religion of atheism, its establishment should be prohibited. Government action neutrality required by the First Amendment cuts both ways.

Religion wears many faces.

Some believers render obeisance to the infinite Creator of the universe while others are content to worship the mirror image of their own intellect. Tradition and fear build a religious mythology that generates false faith. Evo's caretakers point accusing fingers at Intelligent Design theory as a front for religion. But neo-Darwinism can't dodge scrutiny of its own suspect credentials.

Evolutionists embrace a postulated dogma that masquerades as "science" loaded with the trappings of a humanistic religion. "Heretics" refusing to bend intellectual knees risk punishment imposed by zealous congregants who embrace a faith-based academic ritual anchored in occult orthodoxy.

Evo lingers as a faith-based religious cult, a counterfeit faith scam! The fiction of spontaneous generation, medieval alchemy and superstition mix the foundation for its mythology.

Neo-Darwinism flunks at least three of Michael Ruse's five qualifying criteria for determining science as cited in the 1982, *McLean v. Arkansas* case: it is not falsifiable; it is not readily explainable under natural law; and it cannot be adequately testable. Unlike mathematics, chemistry or the undisputed law of gravity, belief in evolutionism arrives laced with secular religious overtones. It postulates a hodgepodge of obsolete, imprecise, undirected randomness without plan, purpose, or design

Ruse, promulgator of the science determinants adopted in *McLean*, acknowledged evo "...depends upon certain unprovable metaphysical assumptions."[26]

The articulate Ruse admits that "Evolution is promulgated as an ideology, a secular religion—a full fledged alternative to Christianity, with meaning and morality...Evolution is a religion. This was true of evolution in the beginning, and it is true of evolution still today."[27] Confirming his perception of two conflicting religions, Ruse fortifies his view by referencing his personal resume. "My area of expertise is the clash between evolutionists and creationists, and my analysis is that we have no simple clash between science and religion but rather between two religions."[28]

Others share Michael Ruse's characterization of evo as religion.

"1 think evolution is as much a religion as creationism...I think we should add an ism to the end of evolution because 1 think they both require a certain amount of faith."[29] "In fact, evolution became in a sense a scientific religion; almost all scientists have accepted it and many are prepared to 'bend' their observations to fit in with it."[30]

Justice Anton Scalia's bold logic in *Edwards v. Aguillard* contending evolution is the religion of secular humanism, endorsed this view. "The United States Supreme Court has held that secular humanism is a religion. Belief in evolution is a central tenet of that religion. Thus, by censoring creation science and instructing students that evolution is fact, public school teachers are now advancing religion in violation of the Establishment Clause."[31]

To the dismay of science colleagues, life-long evolutionist Colin Patterson publicly questioned whether evolution should be taught in high schools. His 1981 words shocked an audience of peers assembled to hear the words of an esteemed colleague.

He described "evolution as faith" admitting "...evolution does not convey any knowledge, or if so, I haven't yet heard it...if you had thought about it at all, you've experienced a shift from evolution as knowledge to evolution as faith...I've tried putting a simple question to various people and groups of people: 'Can you tell me anything you know about evolution, any one thing, any one thing you think is true?'

"...I tried it on the members of the Evolutionary Morphology Seminar in the University of Chicago, a very prestigious body of evolutionists, and all I got there was silence for a long time, and then eventually one person said: 'Yes, I do know one thing. It ought not to be taught in high school.'"[32]

Evolutionism panders to a religion without God.

"As the creationists claim, belief in modern evolution makes atheists of people. One can have a religious view that is compatible with evolution only if the religious view is indistinguishable from atheism."[33] Paul Lemoine, one-time president of the Geological Society of France and director of the Natural History Museum in Paris, characterized evolution theory as "...impossible ...a kind of dogma which the priests no longer believe, but which they maintain for their people."[34]

Evo functions as a pseudo-intellectual religion that worships at the feet of random chance and unobserved events. It's a metaphysical philosophy masquerading as science; a secular religion requiring absolute devotion, preaching a futile doctrine beginning nowhere and ending in oblivion. Because it requires constant, unpredictable, gradual change it exists inherently out-of-step with true sciences physics, chemistry, mathematics, and molecular biology.

Classroom Strategies

Conscientious teachers deal with the daily reality of inspiring students, communicating effectively with parents, and satisfying the political and contractual demands imposed by the school board. A teacher faces the slings and arrows of parents reacting to subjective grading and discipline. Under the gun, teachers risk becoming political canon fodder, links in a chain of trickle-down intimidation, jeopardizing promotion and tenure.

Students become the ultimate victims when coerced to conform to what is presented as fact or suffer the displeasure of a teacher. Nowhere is the intimidation curse more acutely obvious than in the presentation of neo-Darwinism's fact-free science. False science spreads like a virus, infecting the intellectual atmosphere of a culture. Litigation proliferates trapping boards, teachers and students in the cross-hairs of the debate.

Seeds sown by trickle-down intimidation that presents assumption as fact in the classroom, reap whirlwinds of negative reaction---and for cause. "Scientists who go about teaching that evolution is a fact of life are great con-men, and the story they are telling may be the greatest hoax ever."[35]

Academic freedom implies investigative science by which postulates are scrutinized through free and open examination. Anything short of comprehensive exposure to intellectual sunshine short-changes students, trapping young minds in a quagmire of pretend science propped up by speculative tradition.

"...Evolution is not a formulation of the true scientific method...(it is) the initial formation of unknown organisms from unknown chemicals produced in an unknown atmosphere...of unknown composition under unknown conditions, which organisms have then climbed an unknown evolutionary ladder by an unknown process leaving unknown evidence."[36]

"Evolution is today, as it was 140 years ago, a clever speculation and a weak hypothesis, unsupported by the scientific evidence."[37] Boards of public education exist duty bound to assure an open, comprehensive system of learning that doesn't knee-jerk surrender to the shrill voices of closed-end parochialism.

So what's a citizen to do to contend with pseudo-science that contaminates public school curricula, stifling dissent? No need to batter down the wall separating church and state (actually the U.S. Constitution makes no reference to a "wall" of separation). Instead, those committed to teaching the controversy can take their cue from green-light guidelines outlined by Supreme Court justices.

In the name of Free Exercise of religion and academic freedom, a legal door opened in 1987, inviting classrooms to focus on the "marketplace of ideas." Existing law beckons mature school kids to raise their voices in discussion and debate.

"The Court explicitly stated in *Edwards* that it is constitutionally lawful for teachers and school boards to expose students to the scientific problems with current Darwinian theory as well as to any scientific alternatives...'teaching a variety of scientific theories about the origin of humankind to school children might be validly done with the clear secular intent of enhancing the effectiveness of science instruction.'"[38]

Testing Science Theory

Suppression of challenges to majoritarian assumptions as to life's origin codifies a crippled curricula. While the First Amendment prohibits teaching religion in public schools, it does not bar classes in "Genomic Science," "Testing Science Theory," or a constitutional law agenda, "Exploring the Limits of Free Speech."

Such subjects open the door for students to invite teachers to explain the "flaws" and "holes" burdening neo-Darwinism. Assertive challenges deserve analysis and debate. It doesn't take a court order or curricula adjustment for gutsy students to initiate classroom queries that expose evo's tattered fabric. No need to allude to ID, religion, or creation. Certainly no occasion to harass teachers or to annoy classmates. Pursuit of scientific truth can be pressed openly and constitutionally, without arrogance or apology!

Sample classroom questions testing science theory include---

Could a cosmic explosion create matter and hang the moon? How, when and where did first life originate spontaneously from inorganic   matter? What was the source of the first ever gene and its DNA information code?

What happened to Kerkut's seven assumptions? Why do the thousands of predicted fossil chains of transitionals continue missing in the fossil record? Without adding new genetic information, can mutations, allied with natural selection, provide the raw material to power evolution? Doesn't devolution, the exact opposite of evolution, dominate the fossil record?

What mutation ever delivered entirely new genetic information? What new and different organism has been produced by mutations? Does extrapolating from finch beak adaptations really prove evolutionism? Have Intra-Genomic Adaptations in bacteria and fruit flies ever produced organisms other than bacteria and fruit flies?

Just how did a human brain, intelligent enough to conjecture origin of life without a designer, manage to design and create itself? What evidence connects humans to fish or ape-like ancestry? How did human male and female genders evolve from Darwin's conjectured hermaphrodite ancestor? And by the way, just how did the law of gravity originate?

Evo's narrative continues incompetent to respond with persuasive answers. No matter how you cut the deck, one truth card trumps a full hand of myths!

Dr. Howard Glicksman's succinct perspective provokes thought. "Ideas have consequences. We all are human and have philosophical and ideological models that we follow in life…Scientists who continue to expound dogmatically on the truth of macroevolution, without at least admitting to the weaknesses of their claims, while showing no appreciation for its effect on our culture, at best, are ignorant of the human heart and mind, and at worst, are being disingenuous and intellectually dishonest."[39]

Free and open discussion rests in the hearts and minds of a fired-up grass roots demanding truth in science. Eventually, the neo-Darwinian charade, spoon-fed to public school students, will be exposed as frivolous sham.

18

A Cultural Virus
Evo's Dark Side

*"Evolution is today, as it was...,
a clever speculation and a weak hypothesis,
unsupported by the scientific evidence."*
Duane Arthur Schmidt[1]

The nine-year-old "big" sister and the six-year-old "little" brother were close. She looked out for his care and keeping in the tradition of most big sisters. While they shared many similar characteristics she usually picked her luncheon from the restaurant salad bar while little brother always chose grilled cheese sandwiches.

She knew little brother loved watermelon, but it was available only as a salad bar side. Without prompting or request, she always returned to the table with a couple of choice watermelon slices for little brother to compliment his grilled cheese. No one asked or requested her to do it. She acted automatically; sibling love in action! Survival of the fittest had nothing to do with it.

Self-centered "me first" conduct creates radically different consequences, even between siblings. Out-of-control, ego-driven pride filled Cain's heart with hatred for his brother. In a fit of violence, Cain murdered Abel, hid his body in the ground, pretending ignorance. His "Am I my brother's keeper?" alibi resonates millenniums after the fact.

Love enhances life; hate hastens death. That first murder took place long before Darwin's 1809 birth and the publication of his strong-over-the-weak philosophy.

Survival of the Fittest Fallout

Darwin showed a tone-deaf esteem toward women. He didn't hesitate to publicize his elitist bent. He penned biting appraisals of the feminine gender at a time when women lacked political muscle--they had yet to gain the power to vote. He didn't mince words.

"The chief distinction in the intellectual powers of the two sexes is shewn [shown] by man attaining to a higher eminence in whatever he takes up, than woman can attain—whether requiring deep thought, reason, or imagination, or merely the use of the senses and hands...

"If two lists were made of the most eminent men and women in poetry, painting, sculpture, music—comprising composition and performance, history, science, and philosophy, with half-a-dozen names under each subject, the two lists would not bear comparison.

"We may also infer...that if men are capable of decided eminence over women in many subjects, the average standard of mental power in man must be above that of a woman...Thus, man has ultimately become superior to woman."[2]

Darwin didn't rail against the pitifully meager wages paid to labor or the demeaning conditions foisted on children in the work place. Nor did he raise his voice in protest against the exploitation of the human and material resources expropriated from British colonies. Born to wealth, he gazed down on society from the perspective of a privileged perch, justifying the power and material advantages of presumed social class.

"...Without the accumulation of capital the arts could not progress...The presence of...well-instructed men, who have not to labour [labor] for their daily bread, is important to a degree which cannot be overestimated; as all high intellectual work is carried on by them, and on such work material progress of all kinds mainly depends."[3]

Those empowered with wealth, relished the thought while strolling through symbolic fields of "tall cotton."

Industrialist Andrew Carnegie, remembered for his ruthless suppression of his employees' quest for economic justice at the Homestead steel plant in 1892, built a fortune riding working men's backs. Taking his cue from Charles D., Carnegie bragged about his wealth and explained his trek to atheism. After coming "fortunately upon Darwin's and Spencer's works...I remember that light came as in a flood, and all was clear. Not only had

I got rid of theology and the supernatural, but I had found the truth of evolution."[4]

Saturated with the arrogant psyche of imperial empire, Darwin contributed an influential voice to the seduction of science. Cultural Darwinism reared its ugly head. The tenor of his words ring suspiciously racist.

Blanket judgments derived from inflammatory labels subvert personal relationships and obscure the unique qualities inherent in each individual. Humanity deserves better. Darwin's ivory-towered blandishments contribute nothing to bridging gaping chasms of diverse cultures much less to blazing a pathway to peace on earth. European racial stock ranked at the pinnacle of his cultural portfolio.

"The western nations of Europe…immeasurably surpass their former savage progenitors and stand at the summit of civilization…"[5] Built-in biases led him to stray from the reality of authentic human physiology. "Various races differ much from each other…the capacity of the lungs, the form and capacity of the skull…in their intellectual, faculties…mental characteristics are… very distinct."[6]

"…It is chiefly through their power that the civilized races have extended, and are now everywhere extending, their range, so as to take the place of the lower races."[7]

A cold-blooded prediction left no doubt as to his extremist assessment. "At some future period, not very far distant, as measured by centuries, the civilised [civilized] races of man will almost certainly exterminate and replace throughout the world the savage races."[8]

Looking down his patrician nose while demeaning "bestial Fuegians,"[9] the Britisher's imperial mind-set spoke from a self-appointed pedestal of gross subjectivity. Serious academics subsequently refuted his harsh, "passing tourist" appraisals. His blatantly biased views "…were completely demolished by the findings of two missionary priests, both highly qualified scientists…Darwin had no scientific qualifications at all."[10]

Charles' younger cousin, Francis Galton, enamored by survival of the fittest mentality, introduced "eugenics" in 1883. Since evo didn't bow to the Creator as the source of a moral code or ethical guidelines, it was every man for himself. Galton's raw racism offered no quarter, posturing as science while theoretically "...improving the stock...to give the more suitable races or strains of blood a better chance of prevailing speedily over the less suitable."[11]

Thanks to vaccination developed by Jonas Salk, the insidious polio scourge no longer looms as a child crippler. Incredibly, such life-saving serum likely would have raised Darwin's hackles. The guru wrung his hands verbally, branding this style of preventive medicine "injurious to the race."

"...Vaccination has preserved thousands, who from a weak constitution would formerly have succumbed to small-pox. Thus the weak members of civilized societies propagate their kind... this must be highly injurious to the race of man. It is surprising how soon a want of care, or care wrongly directed, leads to the degeneration of a domestic race...we must bear without complaining the undoubtedly bad effects of the weak surviving and propagating their kind..."[12]

Charles' heart broke at the death of Annie, his ten-year-old daughter. If vaccination could have saved her life, would he have welcomed the reprieve? Would he have rationalized that his dire warning of the "...bad effects of the weak surviving and propagating their kind" didn't apply to the clan Darwin?

George Bernard Shaw's blunt take on British cultural conditions cuts no slack for the Victorian era. "Never in history...had there been such a determined, richly subsidized, politically organized attempt to persuade the human race that all progress, all prosperity, all salvation, individual and social, depend on an unrestrained conflict for food and money, on the suppression and elimination of the weak by the strong...in short, on 'doing the other fellow down' with impunity."[13]

Murderous wars unleashing brutal killings ravaged humanity long before Darwin published his thoughts. But his ideas have risen as guiding stars for evil hearts seeking justification for schemes of imperial conquest. It would be unfair to charge "survival of the fittest" theory as the exclusive factor inspiring tyrant war-mongers. But the idea emerged as an enticing tool to justify crimes inflicted against humanity. After Darwin's "survival of the fittest" mentality took root and spread like a virus, twentieth century mass killings destroyed human life on an unprecedented scale.

Darwinian thought evolved as the predecessor of more than one vile "ism." His cruel doctrine served as guiding scripture, painting the social landscape with brush strokes exalting the profane. Hearts seared by infernos of hate, stoke the raging wildfires of war.

Seven years after *Origin of Species* went public, Germany's Otto von Bismarck invaded Austria. Oscar Peschel, a German supremacist supporting the invasion, rationalized war as a function of evolutionism. "Even we in Germany should view the most recent events as a lawful evolutionary process...With such magnificent events it is no longer a matter of right or blame, but rather it is a Darwinian struggle for existence, where the modern triumphs and the obsolete descends into the paleontological graves."[14]

The 1871 publication of *The Descent of Man* provided an appropriate vehicle for Darwin to disavow this horrific connection and to disparage Peschel's exaltation of war as a "magnificent event." He failed to repudiate.

Shortly before the First World War exploded, Wilhelm Shallmayer argued preposterously that wars elevated the human race, because they resulted in the annihilation of 'lower' races and as "...between races that are unequal---such as between Europeans and black Africans---are beneficial, especially if they lead to the extermination of the 'lower' races."[15]

Ernst Haeckel, best known for his fictitious embryo drawings in his corrupt effort to prop up Darwinian doctrine, exposed overt arrogance when he unabashedly played the race card. Ten years before WW I, he described "...Lower races...psychologically nearer to the mammals (apes or dogs) than to civilized

Europeans..." rationalizing "we must therefore, assign a totally different value to their lives."[16]

Long before Adolph Hitler's monstrous reign, German philosopher Freidrich Nietzsche sowed seeds of hate, setting the stage for the horrors of the blitzkrieg and the Holocaust that engulfed a continent. On fire with the superman mentality, he blazed a path for Hitler's maniacal scourge. He "advanced the idea of the 'superman' and the master race," calling "Darwin one of the three greatest men of his century."

The Science of Power, published the year WW I ended, warned of Germany's "superman" doctrine. "Within half a century *The Origin of Species* had become the bible of the doctrine of the omnipotence of force...Nietzsche's teaching represented the interpretation of the popular Darwinism delivered with a fury and intensity of genius." Nietzsche "gave Germany the doctrine of Darwin's efficient animal in the voice of his superman...military textbooks in due time gave Germany the doctrine of the superman translated into the national policy of the super state aiming at world power."[17]

Joseph Stalin read Darwin's writings and became an atheist murderer of multi-millions who blocked his path. And surprise, surprise...Karl Marx cited "Darwin's book" as "very important and serves me as a basis in natural science for the class struggle in history."[18] An impressed Marx went so far as to send galley proofs of *Das Kapital* to Darwin, offering to "dedicate it to him."

The surging currents of Darwin's racist opinions offered fertile soil for the terrors of war inundating Europe. Most wars testify to spiritual shortfall---even when perpetrator's brandish the claim of "God's will" to pacify subjects. Arrogant pride collaborates with greed to mobilize killer machines. Evolutionism doesn't necessarily instigate war, but the theory's "survival of the fittest" mentality has been seized upon as justification.

"During the Holocaust, every institution established to uphold civilized values failed---the academy, the media, the judiciary, law enforcement, the churches, the government, and yes, the medical and scientific disciplines as well.' So much for the virtues of civil society, and so much for the hallowed purity of science."[19]

The perverted passion of Hitler harnessed "survival of the fittest" thought to his visions of Aryan supremacy and managed to fine-tune a government into an efficient, death-dispensing machine. This essence of egocentric evil convinced subjects of their inherent superiority, inspiring a maniacal fury. When trumped by the sacrifice of brave hearts, the warped dictator seized the coward's way out, opting for a self-inflicted death in a pile of rubble, but not before snatching away the lives of millions. .

The precise opposite of the life-taking curse unleashed on humans by Hitler is memorialized in the saga of John Weidner and his Dutch-Paris Underground. Gallant hearts sacrificed their own lives to save humans they had never met previously. Valorous souls, working with Weidner, spared more than 1,000 lives of downed Allied airmen and Jews at risk by whisking them away to safety in Switzerland.

John himself kept on the run; was arrested and escaped several times; and managed to survive by repeatedly assuming fake identities. Unable to capture the mastermind of a courageous underground, calloused Gestapo agents burst into a Paris church during a worship service and arrested John's sister. Gabrielle vanished from the scene, forever.

When the war ended, Weidner was awarded The *French Legion of Honor*, the *French Medaille de la Resistance* and the *American Medal of Freedom with Gold Palm*.[20] John Weidner, a devout Christian who believed in the Creator, is remembered for his gutsy commitment to the sanctity of life. Risking your own life to save another represents the antithesis of "survival of the fittest."

Darwin, presumably a sensitive soul, would likely have abhorred the senseless slaughter unleashed by the Holocaust. But patently racist advocacy blighted the social fabric, inadvertently providing the Nazi leader a philosophic hook upon which to hang demonically perverted aspirations.

War's devastation left a brutal footprint on the twentieth century. Ten million deaths wiped out the cream of a European generation in World War I. World War II agonies and atrocities snuffed out another 60-million lives.

The Iron Empire

Military power pervades history. Armies unleash death as the ultimate weapon. Survival of the fittest feeds fuel to the fires of war, contributing nothing to platitudes of peace.

Conquest and coercive control by force of arms corrupted the human condition long before the terms "evolution" and "survival of the fittest" crept into common usage. Imperial Rome worshiped at the feet of power, dominating and degrading human kind, empowering a culture of death run amok. Pride, amplified by military power, trampled, confiscated and subjugated at will.

During an era when the pagan Iron Empire ruled at its zenith, the culture that placed a premium on life and the dignity of the individual in the context of the golden rule, took front-and-center stage. Paradoxically, and seemingly against all odds, two millennia after-the-fact, the fledgling faith built on God's love, swept the earth while Rome's legions have vanished.

Long before Darwin added his voice to the power game, the malignant survival of the fittest theme spurred Caesar's legions to cut swaths across the landscape reaping bitter harvests of hate, as unstoppable as the roaring waves pounding ocean beach sands.

Contaminated by conquest's contagious epidemic, Julius Gaius Caesar's empire epitomized the reach of unleashed physical power.   By any name, it presented a culture of death running rampant.

Remote geography offered no immunity. The heel of the empire's boot planted prints of avarice from the Middle East, North Africa and north through Europe and Britain. Gold's siren song enticed legions to distant Wales where they excavated square-hewn tunnels deep in the soil of Carmarthenshire's Dolau Cothi mine. The mouth of the long abandoned venture still yawns skyward, a testament to unquenched greed.

Pity the army unit that caved and retreated during the battle. Survivors of the disgraced unit faced retribution. Theoretically a motivator, decimation couldn't have done much for an army's morale. Imagine a line-up of 1,000 men ordered to count-off 1 to 10. After an officer picked a number arbitrarily, the unlucky victims were required to step forward. Punishment came promptly. The fortunate nine, whose numbers were not called, had to summarily execute erstwhile comrades whose "numbers were up." Life was cheap---the decimated could be replaced.

Battles raged relentlessly. Cunning tactics, intensive military training, iron-clad discipline, mixed with implementation of avant-garde weaponry combined to cast Romans as odds-on favorites for battlefield victories. Still, a tradition lingers that on at least one occasion its army was overwhelmed and as many as 50,000 legionnaires were slaughtered in a single battle.

Every triumph brought spoils. Prized booty included confiscated material wealth and humans not killed in the defense of their homes. The threat of rape confronted women; the most skilled fighters survived as gladiators; and the young and strong could expect a future as slaves.

Slaves survived as property, lacking the faintest whiff of civil rights. An owner chose the food they ate, clothes they wore, and tasks assigned. Typically, death broke the bonds, becoming the ultimate emancipator.

Blood sport entertained citizens desensitized to the miracle of life. As many as 5,000 animals might be slaughtered in a single day in the public arenas. The public's taste for blood seemed insatiable.

Gladiators, armed with the "gladius," a 22" sword, earned the chance to live by killing other gladiators in arenas designed for entertainment. The City of Capua provided basic training. Conscripted war prisoners were not the only members of the gladiator fraternity. Citizens desperate to raise money to pay taxes voluntarily signed into the ranks of the kill-or-be-killed.

There came a time when the blood sport menu was upset by Sparticus, a gladiator with character forged tough as the steel in his gladius. He successfully led the escape of a band of brother gladiators determined to at least die as free men rather than drench arena sands with their blood. To the chagrin and embarrassment of the iron empire, the escape blossomed into a mini-rebellion that repeatedly escaped the long arm of the tyrant---for a time.

Eventually, Sparticus and his stalwarts surrendered to the inevitable. While Roman engineers built superb highways, the road linking Capua to Rome is best remembered for the crosses lining its route, bearing the crucified remains of 6,000 escapees who dared to follow Sparticus. Crucifixion meant pinning a victim to a cross using spikes driven through the wrist between the radius and ulna of each arm, sending a victim into a paroxysm of writhing agony until death came to call 72 hours later.

Betrayal, murder and assassination were common in the pagan environment that degraded human values at all cultural levels. The turnover of emperors assassinated by poison or by the knife became endemic to the office. Without a moral compass, debauchery and iniquity prevailed. Emperor worship became more than a test of national loyalty but a life and death matter for those daring to dissent. Wild animals tore out the hearts and devoured the bodies of Christians who refused to worship the emperor.

City of Rome streets served as killing fields for lurking criminals with voracious appetites for evil. Only the wealthiest dared to venture into darkened corridors after sunset under the protective swords of a hired band of torch-bearing courtiers. Come daylight, carts combed the byways, picking up unidentified corpses to dump unceremoniously on slag heaps outside the city. Fresh mantles of lime erased the residue of what had been spirited human beings walking the city the day before.

Ultimately, the legions could not salvage a corrupt empire. An exhausted Rome decayed from within, declined and ultimately fell as documented eloquently by Edward Gibbon.[21]

"Survival of the fittest" fosters a cultural virus that inflames animosities engendering violence. It generates a philosophical excuse justifying war. Charles Darwin didn't contribute to the bloody history of Rome. Nor did he invent elitism. But some of his takes on life reflected what he absorbed from Britain's colonial era, which in turn was likely tainted by the inauspicious example of previous empires.

Winner-take-all motivation contrasts with the caring big sister delivering watermelon slices for a little brother. Another big sister story depicts a little girl voluntarily giving her own rare type blood to save the life of a dying brother. After the transfusion she asked, "Is my brother going to live?" Once assured he would recover, she responded with a tear, "Is now when I'm supposed to die?" She had been willing to sacrifice her life to save his.

Ever since Cain killed Abel, the extremes between give and take stand in bold relief. Givers and takers co-exist in every culture. In Roman times, just as today, big sisters, big brothers and John Weidner hero-types lived unselfish lives powered by love and respect.

Building a destiny by trampling the necks of the conquered may deliver temporary material advantage. A person or a nation that adopts a self-serving mantra built on physical and military power can beguile with transient benefit but in the long run delivers disillusionment. The Roman Empire and Hitler's Third Reich exist only in bitter chronicles.

Percy Bysshe Shelley's *Ozymandius*, exemplifies evolutionism. The siren song of illusion paraphrases the boast of an arrogant ruler, underscoring the limits of human power while delivering a theology of death. Shelley visualizes broken remnants of a sculpted statute, strewn in disarray across the landscape of an "antique land," symbols of vanished glory and a long forgotten ruler, anonymous to history.

> I met a traveler from an antique land
> Who said: Two vast and trunkless legs of stone
> Stand in the desert. Near them, on the sand,
> Half sunk, a shattered visage lies, whose frown,
> And wrinkled lip, and sneer of cold command,
> Tell that its sculptor well those passions read
> Which yet survive, stamped on these lifeless things,

The hand that mocked them and the heart that fed;

And on the pedestal these words appear:
"My name is Ozymandius, king of kings:
Look on my words, ye Mighty, and despair!"
Nothing beside remains. Round the decay
Of that colossal wreck, boundless and bare
The lone and level sands stretch far away.

19

Empowering Reason
A Fresh Look at Old Ideas

*"I find it as difficult to understand a scientist
who does not acknowledge the presence
of a superior rationality behind the existence of the universe
as it is to comprehend a theologian who would deny the advances of science."*
Wernher von Braun[1]

Thomas A. Edison's (1847-1931) incandescent light brightens the world 24/7. A tungsten filament built into a vacuum tube made it happen. Building on the earlier findings of Henry Woodward, Mathew Evans, and Sir Joseph Wilson Swan, Edison's plodding patience eventually paid off. His trial-and-error genius opened the door to the longer-lasting, glowing magic of incandescent lighting.

The determination of a brilliant mind to look outside-the-box for scientific answers turned the switch on an electric powered glow that converted night into day at the flick of a switch. Hot on the trail of a successful formula, he kept his options open. Had Edison confined his research to a materials list that excluded tungsten and a design that ruled out vacuum tubes, his discovery might have been limited to illumination by candle power and the smoky flame of a kerosene lamp.

No one doubts human intelligence designed the incandescent light! No living human remembers meeting Thomas Edison in person. We can't see his face but the glow of light bulbs and history book references identify his inventive genius. Reason dictates faith in the electric light bulb's intelligent design and confirms the existence of the designer. No one contends the electric light bulb designed itself.

Edison's intellect employed reason to design and discover. He put information to work to figure out the formula that delivered light to the world economically in 1879 by merging matter with electrical energy. Without information, reason could not function and without reason, all the matter and energy in the world could not, by itself, create a functional light bulb. "...Information...cannot be a property of matter, and its origin cannot be explained in terms of material processes."[2]

Human-designed systems originate by processing information through reasoning. "A creative source of information is always linked to the volitional intent of a person; this fact demonstrates the nonmaterial nature of information...All technological systems as well as all constructed objects, from pins to works of art, have been produced by means of information. None of these artifacts came into existence by the self-organization of matter, but all of them were preceded by establishing the required information."[3]

Knee-jerk religion and knee-jerk science can both shut down thought in favor of brain-washed behavior. In-the-box mind sets misunderstand either the truth about God, the truth about science, or the truth about both. Science cannot be incompatible with faith in the Author of science.

Some mindsets ascribe belief in God as patently unscientific. The precise opposite is true! The essence of the unscientific is to stifle rational thought outside the box, rejecting even the possibility of God's existence. To place arbitrary limits on investigative science is less logical than investigating the history of the incandescent light by ruling out Edison's role.

Can you think of any human-created invention or device designed and built independent of an information-powered process? Does anyone seriously believe the computer being used to compose these words crafted itself without information assessed by an intelligent, reasoning designer?

Of course not!

The discovery of a formula for a powerful, new adhesive may not be as newsworthy as the electric lighting system invention, but when it can handle "...two to three times more force than the best retail glues..." the event deserves more than footnote status.[4] Unlike man-made material, this intelligently designed brand of "super glue" is produced by a single-celled bacterium, *Caulobacter crescentus*.

All scientists agree, Edison designed the incandescent light bulb! Is it consistent to suggest a human-designed invention results from an intelligent act but that a more complex system delivered through nature appears accidentally, independent of intelligent input?

Information + Reason = Truth

In a quest for truth, reason can't fully function without information in play. To substitute assumption for informative evidence and to replace reason with coercion generates superstition and propagates tradition.

Evolutionism can neither explain nor replicate the origin of life from non-living matter. Evo starts with unproven assumptions and ends with inevitable death the out-of-tune theme song of the theory. Is it worth betting your life on evolution, a "metaphysical research program"? Evo exists as a composite mix of hoped-for assumptions. Assumptive theories represent faith-based opinions. Assumptions flunk scientific methodologies. Abstract assumptions can't be successfully reprogrammed and disguised as synonyms for science.

Observable phenomena that defy provable explanation are dubbed miracles. Reliance on unintelligent, random process to explain life's origin is a faith-based assumption that spells "miracle." Belief in life created by an Intelligent Designer also requires faith. Either view reaches outside the box of traditional science. One opinion builds on fortuitous accident; the other suggests an intelligent act.

As to rationality, intelligence trumps chance every time.

No one disputes the presence of genetic information contained in the first ever living cell. Information technology requires an intelligent source to create, organize, store and deliver its data. If life originated accidentally, could a "warm little pond" have been the source of its non-material information?

Reason insists information doesn't create itself. So is it rational to claim spontaneous generation of the simplest living system is compatible with reason? Is it consistent to acknowledge every known man-made, non-living system requires information input from an intelligent source while alleging infinitely more complex living systems came into existence independent of an identifiable information source?

How does reason fit this formula?

Is it within reason to suggest the stars, planets and moons floating in space hung themselves by means of an explosion? Has there ever been an explosion on earth that organized matter and created order?

A phony myth gathers superficial credibility when foisted on the public in repetitive doses. Picturing science as allied with reason in support of evo while implying religion thumbs its nose at science mischaracterizes both science and religion..

Nothing could be further from the truth.

Rational religious faith requires evidence-based reason at its core. So what about faith in the idea that the universe and all life on earth happened by accident? Where's the reasoning if the source of the original genetic information continues missing?

Let's see now!

With reason in play, truth needs no defender. But delete reason from the equation in favor of authoritarianism and truth is cut adrift. Consider the perils in a classroom dictating the absolute, where inside-the-box thinking is exalted and reason is put on hold!

"'You should be ashamed of yourself...what you're doing is criminal!' That was the response student Josh Dill received from a biology professor at Highline Community College in Washington State when he booked a room at the college to show the videos *Unlocking the Mystery of Life* and *Icons of Evolution*.

"Later the professor met with Josh privately to insist that he was a dishonest person and should have at least offered a preamble to the videos telling students not to bring these questions into the classroom."[5]

Hostile rhetoric polarizes. Coercion is incompatible with reason. Academic freedom is routinely put to the test. The classroom is the last place you'd expect reason to be subverted. The injunction to "come now, let us reason together..."[6] promises the surest path to knowledge and understanding.

Bottom line: Reasoning that evaluates evidence trumps chance!!!

The Author of Science

God created science. Nature is the imprimatur of the Creator. Its not God or science, the two are inextricable. To investigate natural science while banning reference to its Author makes no more sense than refusing to recognize the role of Edison in the origin of the incandescent light bulb.

St. Patrick admired nature as the "Book of God" the "Creator of Creation." Darwin turned the obvious upside down, expropriating nature, the "Book of God," to deny the Creator's existence. The roots to this deceitful illusion were planted by the cunning Adversary who lied to Adam and Eve.

Is human vision so miniscule and its arrogance so gargantuan as to rule out, ab initio, even the possibility that intelligence and power above and beyond finite comprehension exists in the universe?

By itself, science operates inside a three-dimensional box confined by time, space and finite comprehension. Far from isolated abstraction, comprehensive study of science requires reaching out to its Author. The Creator of all things built the universe's balanced order, energy and matter. Complex information, existing from the beginning secreted in the DNA molecule, could no more appear by accident than a roll of a standard dice pair can produce a number higher than twelve.

Infinity contains knowledge outside human mental capacity because it supercedes humankind's power to comprehend. No human understands fully all science disciplines. Nor does a fallible finite mind comprehend all truth about God. Events beyond our experience are conveniently labeled "miracles." Life doesn't make sense until we accept we were God made. And in God's image, no less, vested with domain over all other life on earth.

Doors of discovery redefine the icons of science as knowledge is assembled. Subjected to the test of time, much of today's science can slip into tomorrow's obsolete quaint notion.

Faced with deteriorating health, George Washington experienced the misfortune of being served by physicians who pre-scribed blood letting as therapy. After siphoning blood from one arm, they took an equal amount from the other to "balance" his system. This primitive medical care was based on assumption. Understandably, the cure didn't work and the nation lost its first president.

There was a time when the pleas of flu patients, burning with fever, were denied a glass of water on the twisted rationale that the cold water would hinder recovery. This fiasco science repre-sented tradition built on erroneous assumption.

As recently as the 1930's, the fluoroscope's penetrating eye proved a popular sales tool in shoe stores. Kids could examine the bones of their own feet and shoes could be fitted comfort-ably. But the fluoroscope fell into disrepute when it became known that one zap of the machine exposed a child's extremity to as much as twenty-times the radioactivity delivered by a single X-ray.

Another fiasco science trivia, built on assumptive gross er-ror.

The mantra alleging "evolution is fact" is theoretically cor-roborated by spinmeisters, glibly citing "the fact we are here" and the process needs only fine tuning for validation. At its best, evo attempts to perpetuate an inside-the-box assumption. "The fact we are here" could more rationally confirm intelligent design.

With the glaring exception of evolutionism, science embraces reason by artfully discovering, scrutinizing and authenticating evidence. But when it comes to explaining how life on earth got here and where it came from, all bets are off. Science draws a blank.

Rational faith, examining the weight of evidence, sees order, in-telligence and a Supreme Designer. The Scriptures present a blunt assessment: "The fool has said in his heart, there is no God."

The jungle of data studied in natural science to the exclusion of intelligence beyond human knowledge leads nowhere. Im-posing arbitrary limits on scientific inquiry smacks of intellectual totalitarianism.

Operations science is observable and enjoys the respect of creationists and evolutionists alike.[7] But neither evolutionism nor creation represent observable operations science. As to evo, a faith-based theory laced with unproven assumptions, Mark Twain's "wholesale conjecture" phrase kicks in. At the juncture of unobservable history, the divergent paths of evolutionism and creation split like the waters of the Red Sea.

Destructive natural forces wreaking havoc by flood, fire, and earthquake are routinely labeled "acts of God" while life's elegant beauty is dubbed an "act of nature." This mischaracterization paints a painful paradox: destructive natural force is attributed to the God of order, while nature alone is credited with accidentally salvaging order from chaos.

Empowered reason suggests otherwise.

20

Glory Forever
The Big Picture

*"If you want to know why you were placed on this planet,
you must begin with God. You were born by His purpose and for His purpose."*
Rick Warren[1]

Every known formula combining matter with energy cannot create genetic information. Miller/Urey's attempt to formulate life in a test tube didn't come close to producing a living cell or its genetic information.

Evolutionism insists *Homo sapiens* was a late arrival to join in life's parade thereby eliminating human action as even a remote source of the genetic information pre-loaded into the simplest cell. So what intelligence delivered the information essential to first-ever life on Planet Earth?

Rocket scientist Wernher von Braun acknowledged the "presence of a superior rationality" behind the complexities of the universe.

The so-called evolution/creation debate is considerably more than an intellectual song and dance or an interplay between matter and energy. The issue reaches beyond the physical body, into the soul, touching every fabric of the person.

Humans are bit players in a universal, "Big Picture" drama involving more than material mechanics of life and death. We are pitted in a struggle between good and evil with consequences beyond the moment. Character, relationships, goals, and peace of mind are up for grabs.

Pivot Player in the Universal Drama

Any manufactured device testifies to the creative genius of its designer. Machines don't design themselves. Neither do complex living systems. Identification of the Designer of life propels a thinking person to the threshold of faith. But finite minds lack the intuitive resources to even begin to comprehend infinite power.

To bridge this gap of understanding, God took on human form in the person of Jesus Christ, to humanize the Big Picture and to translate direction and inspire purpose to human lives through His perfect example.

Occasionally, the voice of a single human like Saul of Tarsus, grasping the Big Picture, sends ripples effects beyond the immediacy of time and place. This magnificent human being eventually put his life on the line in order to articulate the good news route to enriched living.

The passionate Saul met his Creator unexpectedly in dramatic fashion while traveling a dusty roadway en route to Damascus. A Roman citizen, he marched in the vanguard of those intent on wiping out Christian heresy. His was a mission of suppression! Holding the cloaks of angry zealots heaving stones at a heroic Stephen, Saul stood by, approving the death of an early Christian martyr.

Committed to the extermination of dissent, he faced an unexpected epiphany on the Damascus road. Temporarily blinded by Divinity's radiating light, his spiritual eyes were opened and his heart changed forever in a hearbeat. The relentless persecutor, emerged as Paul, the Apostle, now despised and persecuted himself for his new found faith. In a letter to Christians in Ephesus, he confirmed this seismic heart revolution by declaring his unequivocal allegiance to the "...God who created all things through Jesus Christ."[2]

Boldly, he accepted the turn-about mission and stepped into the teeth of contemptuous intolerance. Paul traveled throughout empire energized by his conscientious commitment to "the call." Paying expenses by making tents, he circled the Mediterranean three times---preaching, teaching and writing spiritually insightful letters of instruction and encouragement that eventually were selected as text for New Testament Scripture.

First century Athenians relished discussing innovative ideas.

An articulate Paul aroused interest by identifying a Creator who promised life after death. Visiting the marketplace, he confronted Epicurean and Stoic listeners who branded him a "babbler," and escorted him to a "meeting of the Areopagus" to explain his words.

"Paul then stood up in the meeting...and said: 'Men of Athens! I see that in every way you are very religious...I even found an altar with this inscription: *To An Unknown God.* Now what you worship as something unknown I am going to proclaim to you.

"'The God who made the world and everything in it is the Lord of heaven and earth and does not live in temples built by hands...He himself gives all men life and breath...From one man he made every nation of men.

"'...Since we are God's offspring, we should not think that the divine being is like gold or silver or stone---an image made by man's design and skill. In the past God overlooked such ignorance, but now he commands all people everywhere to repent.

"'...For he has set a day when he will judge the world with justice by the man he has appointed. He has given proof of this to all men by raising him from the dead."[3]

Paul astounded listeners by referencing the resurrection of the dead. Some sneered. Others believed, fervently embracing the good-news message. Acknowledging the creative intelligence guiding the designs woven into all life forms takes a giant leap of faith for any mind tainted with the ideology that life is a random chance crap shoot.

Paul did not buy into evo's fish-to-man, cunningly-devised fables. He advised residents in Corinth that "All flesh is not the same: Men have one kind of flesh, animals have another, birds another and fish another."[4]

He also endorsed the historicity of the deluge by ranking Noah within a roster of faith-driven lives. "By faith Noah, when warned about things not yet seen, in holy fear built an ark to save his family. By his faith he condemned the world and became heir of the righteousness that comes by faith."[5]

Recognizing the hand of the Master Designer through the miracle of original life signals the beginning of wisdom. When Paul experienced the radical redirection of his life powered by

the Creator of all living things, he unfolded the roadmap directing believers to an enriched life on Planet Earth topped with the
assurance of life eternal.

Writing to friends in Rome, Paul pointed to the natural world
as evidence of God's creative power while defining risks to all
who ignore the obvious. "The wrath of God is being revealed
from heaven against all the godlessness and wickedness of men
who suppress the truth by their wickedness...For since the creation of the world God's invisible qualities---his eternal power
and divine nature---have been clearly seen, being understood
from what has been made, so that men are without excuse."[6]

He reminded his readers that God spoke to them through His
Son, "through whom he made the universe."[7] Optimistically he predicted "creation itself will be liberated from its bondage to decay..."[8]

Articulate spokesman for the fledgling faith, and in language
touching the poetic, he reminded a band of truth seekers in
Corinth that "The weapons we fight with are not the weapons of
the world. On the contrary, they have divine power to demolish
strongholds. We demolish arguments and every pretension that
sets itself up against the knowledge of God, and we take captive
every thought to make it obedient to Christ."[9]

Eventually, and perhaps inevitably, Paul himself suffered the
fate of a Christian martyr---beheaded in a Roman dungeon for
the crime of teaching the truth about God and the miracle of His
creative and recreative power.

A citadel of stalwart strength while fully aware that "the time
has come for my departure," Paul summoned the energy to compose a classic memo of encouragement to his younger friend,
Timothy. "I have fought the good fight, I have finished the race,
I have kept the faith. Now there is in store for me the crown of
righteousness, which the Lord, the righteous Judge, will award
to me on that day---and not only to me, but also to all who have
longed for his appearing."[10]

Paul anticipated God's gift of "glory forever," and beyond.
The epitome of self-sacrificing service to his Creator, the Apostle's
name is memorialized in lofty church cathedrals and city identi-

ties. His memory is preserved in his words of counsel enshrined in Scripture as well as in the thousands of lives who follow his example and by faith, worship the God of the universe.

Roman persecution threw gasoline on the spiritual fire, further igniting and spreading the pristine faith. Eventually, depravity eroded Rome's national character until the iron power rusted, melting away in the caldron of its dissipation. The merciless empire is long gone, a victim of its own voracious appetite for evil.

The truth about God thrives, blazing a future path beyond forever.

The Big Picture

Life's origin is critical to the essence of being and life with a purpose.

"It all starts with God...It's not about you. The purpose of your life is far greater than your own personal fulfillment, your peace of mind, or even your happiness. It's far greater than your family, your career, or even your wildest dreams and ambitions. If you want to know why you were placed on this planet, you must begin with God. You were born *by* his purpose and *for* his purpose."[11]

Perfection graced the original creation. God-given life existed in peaceful harmony. Today's world is out of sync with God's order. Civilization is dazzled and side-tracked by the forces of deceit, the "secesh" spiritual rebellion against God. Consequently, pernicious hate saturates the world with war, disease and a culture of death.

The Big Picture offers a culture of vibrant life.

Imagine if evolutionism represented fact? And God didn't exist? Here and now, by random chance accident, and gone tomorrow, without trace or future? Suppose nothingness triumphed, the forever reward of evil?

Evolutionism explains zip; it offers no verifiable alternative; it draws a blank! In contrast, the Creator of the universe promises life in full dimension. Paraphrased rhetoric loaded with logic is attributed to Wernher von Braun: "Do we need to light a candle to see the sun?"

Think about it!

Six billion human miracles represent God's masterpiece, breathing the air and drinking the water He provides. The all-time best selling library, the Bible of sixty-six books, comes loaded with the wisdom of the ages, publishing words relevant to a purposeful life. The story of the miraculous birth of Christ, God's Son, His flawless life, cruel death and predicted resurrection binds the books with a common thread. God's character of love and power over life and death is exemplified in the person of His Son.

The truth about God is revealed in the miracle of His Creation; the life, words and ministry of Christ; the transforming influence of His Spirit on human hearts; and the insightful testimony of the Bible. It paints a picture of a once perfect creation, marred by a "War in Heaven," a raging spiritual conflict between good and evil, ultimately spilling across space, infecting Planet Earth.

Lucifer (the "Light Bearer"), vested with the power of free choice, allowed malignant pride to fester in his thoughts, feeding a jealousy that inspired his challenge to God's authority. This father of evil, deceived other angels who fell for his selfish lies and joined his grab for power. He and his rebel band were expelled from God's presence.

If the Creator was all-powerful and loving, why couldn't He have prevented this torrent of suffering by creating humans without the power to sin?

Logical question, rational answer!

"Stepford Wives," the cookie-cutter women pictured in the movie, were programmed to react to a pre-determined format. God could have created a race of automated Charlie McCarthy's guaranteed to respond with CD-ROM-like conversation, pre-loaded with make-believe passion and a pre-wired loyalty to God. But it would have been meaningless without free volition and individual choice to love and serve the Creator voluntarily. The string-pulled "love" of a wooden robot is far from a parent's dream come true.

The Creator made humans in His own image, vested with the

authority to be individually creative, to make free moral choices in order to respond to the Creator with the love he showered on them. Just as human parents desire their children to respond to them with the same kind of love and respect showered on them by their parents, God wants those created "in His image" to love and honor Him by choice, and not from coercion or fear of punishment.

Adam and Eve were created as free moral agents. The test of love for their Creator was reduced to ultimate simplicity---avoiding the fruit of a single tree in their lush garden home.   Their curiosity fired by gross deceptions pitched to them by the sworn adversary of God, seduced their minds. The Biblical Satan lied outright promising "you will not die" if you taste the fruit from the single forbidden tree. He accused God of being a duplicitous tyrant, deliberately denying humans access to universal wisdom.

Dazzled and deceived, the first human parents bought the lie, disobeyed God and flunked the test. And they didn't die---at the moment. But kicked out of the garden and access to the source of life, Adam and Eve, along with all the natural world, began to deteriorate and eventually die. Once the contagious virus of evil blackened human hearts, it inflicted a debilitating degradation, an inexorable consequence visible to the entire universe.

But since evil is incompatible with a perfect universe, why didn't the all-powerful, all-wise God simply destroy Satan and his followers immediately and spare the suffering that has followed?

One likely explanation could be that Satan's fraudulent allegation that God was an unfair tyrant might then have seemed credible to other created beings whose worship thereafter would be motivated by fear for their own survival rather than the reciprocal love inspired by free choice!

To instantly terminate the rebellion by destroying Satan and his followers might have lent credence to Satan's unfair charge that God was a tyrant. Loyalty would have been inspired by fear rather than love-inspired free choice. But by allowing evil to run its self-destructive course, all created beings are given opportunity to understand that Satan's charges are patently false and that God is not a vengeful tyrant.

Degeneration and death kicked-in when original sin marred perfection. Death's curse is the dividend of deceptive evil that masquerades as light and fronts false knowledge and fake wisdom.

Christ, the Hero of the Controversy

A just Creator could not arbitrarily destroy the miracle of His creation. Instead, He offered a "Plan B" second chance, available by faith to all generations and peoples, leading to the restoration of perfection and life eternal. "For God so loved the world that He gave His one and only Son, that whoever believes in Him shall not perish but have eternal life."[12]

All created beings are vested with the power of choice to believe or not to believe God's "Plan B" promises. Given the finite limits of human lives and minds, perhaps that's why the forever life reward for faith is awesome and the test for belief simple!

At the height of Rome's pagan era of squandered lives and cruel deaths, Christ appeared on the scene to change history. Avoiding even a hint of supernatural advantage, He was born in a country suffering military oppression where poverty knocked at the door. Rather than arriving in a palace with the privileges of a king, he appeared, peasant born, in a barn.

He grew up in an environment, notorious for its wicked ways, where wagging tongues questioned his parentage,. He walked the countryside under the oppressor's heel, challenging tyranny with spiritual weaponry. He acquired no property other than the clothes he wore.

His immaculate incarnation pointed to Divine power to create original life; His life on earth exemplified God's character of love, justice and forgiveness; His death and resurrection showed victory over death, not only for Himself but also for all believers.

Christ's own words confirmed the miracle of creation and the planet-wide destruction wreaked by cataclysmic deluge. If you believe in the reality of Christ's ministry, you must also believe in the authority of His creation testimony! It's a package deal wrapped in faith!

"...At the beginning of creation 'God made them male and female'."[13] He authenticated the flood of Noah's day. "As it was in the days of Noah, so it will be at the coming of the Son of Man. For in the days before the flood, people were eating and drinking, marrying and giving in marriage, up to the day Noah entered the ark; and they knew nothing about what would happen until the flood came and took them all away."[14]

He lived a life of perfection confronting critical circumstances. He preached a revolution of the spirit, a message of hope with a premium on life. Guiltless of any moral lapse or legal crime, adversaries of good railroaded His death.

Miracle One: Original Life

Evolutionists, like creationists, build their doctrine on miracles---faith-based opinions. Explanations for the origin of the universe; earth's life friendly environment; and the origin of first life defy explanation by scientific method. No matter how the letters are rearranged, "assumption" never spells "science."

So, what's a miracle? The term exceeds the vocabulary of science!

Phenomena beyond human capacity to understand, much less duplicate, touches the miraculous! An oak from an acorn that can be seen but can't be duplicated in the science lab, is an every day, taken-for-granted miracle. The birth of a human baby is another. Unless an ego-centered human prefers to contend *Homo sapiens* represents the highest order of life in the universe, it's reasonable to believe in the presence of a "superior rationality" that creates miracles.

Creation of the universe by an Intelligent Designer is miraculous!

No doubt about the miracle status of original human life. Evolutionism can't explain spontaneous generation with a speculative theory resting on faith-based assumptions! Scripture describes humans as miraculously fashioned in the image of the Creator by the spoken Word of the Lord.

Christ lives as eyewitness to the miracle of Planet Earth's creation. The sixty-six book Biblical library consistently confirms this message. "Through Him all things were made; without Him nothing was made that has been made."[15] "You alone are the Lord. You made the heavens, even the highest heavens, and all their starry hosts, the earth and all that is on it, the seas and all that is in them. You give life to everything, and the multitudes of heaven worship you."[16]

Creation Week is topped with a birthday celebration every seventh day to commemorate the event and to honor the Creator. Human rights are elevated to the pinnacle of a philosophical pedestal. The weekly rest day builds a bulwark against slavery and the 24/7 exploitation of human labor. The celebration also enshrines a triple meaning marking the beginning of original life; the miracle of a recreated human character that builds a quality life style; and the bonus of a future forever life.

Miracle Two: A Reprogrammed Life

Undeterred by death threats from venomous mobs, the gutsy Apostle Paul put his life on the line as a gladiator for souls. He anchored his mission on the miracle working power of God to recreate a corrupt heart enabling any human "...to put on the new self, created to be like God in true righteousness and holiness."[17] The apostle spoke with the authority of personal experience.

Beneficiaries of miracle one are free to opt for miracle two, an enhanced life on earth with a radical change of direction, a rejection of evil with growth toward a purpose-filled life awarded as a no-strings gift of God. The same force that created original life "by the word of the Lord," recreates the hearts of all who believe.

This "born again" life is above and beyond mere intellectual concession. It requires an intentional, inner desire to submit to the will of God. This is more than lip service to the Lord's prayer, "Thy will be done." It represents a conscious response to the Creator of the universe's invitation to accept the power of His Spirit in the reshaping of your person and putting you on the pathway to a redirected, purpose-driven life.

As with Paul, an inner life-style revolution occurs. Personal goals will be forever altered. Happiness, crowned with peace-of-mind comfort, floods the "born again" soul.

The miracle of radical spiritual change happens any time, anywhere, to anyone. Lives overwhelmed by evil and selfish purpose reverse course abruptly, a direct result of God's power to recreate through the miracle of the Holy Spirit's working inside-the-heart.

This spiritual empowerment opens doors to abundant living and a "peace that passes understanding." Inhaling the exhilaration of a clear conscience is the inevitable dividend of the "born again" lifestyle that worships the Creator, instinctively practicing the golden rule.

No alternative route to happiness exists!

When someone asked Christ which of the ten commandments was the greatest, he responded there were only two. "Love the Lord your God with all your heart and with all your soul and with all your mind. This is the first and greatest commandment. And the second is like it: Love your neighbor as yourself."[18]

Talk about the key to peace on earth! Without it, repetitious cries of "peace, peace" ring hollow!

A contrite David, acutely aware of serious shortfall in his personal behavior, found himself awash in guilt. The charismatic king longed for change, expressing his personal need in the prayer of a song. "Create in me a pure heart O God, and renew a steadfast spirit within me."[19]

This dramatic reversal of character requires much more than a look good cosmetic job on the public persona. As with the Apostle Paul, its an about-face, a directional change where the heart's motivations are reoriented. It's a miracle for a guy like Saul of Tarsus, responding to the blinding light on the Damascus Road, to switch directions radically.

From that Damascus road moment, the newly-minted Apostle devoted his God empowered life to telling the story of the Creator, his death, burial and resurrection and the new life possible for all who choose to accept the promises. Like Paul, individuals are justified by faith, with assurance that any shortfall is covered by Christ's perfect life.

Time-to-time stumbles don't count!

It's not the occasional good or bad deed that determines destiny but the direction you're going. Character building requires patience, the work of a lifetime. Paul wrote of his frustration at those moments when he did what he didn't want to do while failing to do what his heart told him he should do.

A spontaneous, unselfish act of a clergyman once carried a message more eloquent than words delivered from the pulpit. A few days after purchasing a cottage from a woman eager to sell, he met her on the street and asked how she liked her new home. When she admitted regret at the sale, without hesitation he took her to the bank immediately, and executed a deed restoring title to her name.

Behavior validates religious faith, not intellectual pontificating!

Wake Forest football captain, Brian Piccolo, of *Brian's Song* fame, stared down intolerance by putting his arm around the shoulders of Maryland's Darryl Hill, the first ever black player in the ACC, escorting him to the middle of the field, hushing the boo-birds with his act of human warmth. Soldiers throw their bodies on live grenades to take the murderous hit to save the lives of their "brothers." Admiral Marc Mischer, defies the wartime blackout cloaking his flagship carrier, turns on the landing lights to the cheers of the crew, to guide a lost pilot in a battle-torn plane to the safety of the ship's deck.

Evolutionism exalts the power of physical force. Believers open their hearts to a spiritual power that revolutionizes lives and redirects destinies.

Miracle Three: Forever Life

Egyptian pharaohs, engulfed in polytheistic superstition, appeased their gods to assure transit to a secure afterlife. Drowning deaths were seen as uniquely tragic in that the lost bodies could not be properly prepared for the trip. Investigation of the sumptuously equipped tombs and burial sites of the rich and famous of the time reveal designs and artifacts focused on enabling a successful journey to eternity.

Unlike religions that pursue human devised means to find life after death, Christians rely on an authentic historical narrative in which eyewitnesses memorialize a gripping account of a week-end event in which Christ died a cruel death, rested in a tomb and rose resurrected, victorious over death. Faith in the miracle of forever life after death is grounded on this written evidence.

The Bible's "Big Picture" account depicts the beginning of life and promises eventual victory over evil and death. As the drama plays to completion, the Creator promises to recreate the earth to perfection and to award life eternal to all who accept His promises.

Miracle three bridges the chasm between evolutionism's ticket to nowhere and the Creator's promise of eternal life: "...I am the way, the truth and the life."

Christ revealed his mission as bringing life so that people "might have it more abundantly."[20] He demonstrated His power over death by restoring life to his friend Lazarus. Prior to the miracle, he comforted Lazarus' sister Martha with the words: "I am the resurrection and the life. He who believes in me will live, even though he dies; and whoever lives and believes in me will never die."[21]

Christ was crucified on the sixth day of the week---the same day Adam was created. He rested in the tomb on the seventh day of the week, the moment of the weekly rest ordained for the welfare of mankind. He conquered death and was resurrected to a new life on the first day of the week symbolic of the beginning day of earth's original creation week.

The historic reality of Christ's death and resurrection is the clincher in the origins debate. Christ's conquest of the tomb attests to the reality of life beyond the grave. Many at-the-scene observers, reporting what they saw, suffered for telling the truth.

Why would they lie? What did they have to gain?

Here's what their testimony brought them!

Fierce agonies of unnamed martyrs, torn apart by ravenous

lions, titillated coliseum crowds. Some survived seeking sanctuary in the twisting, underground tunnels of the catacombs.

Not one derived the slightest political advantage from sharing the good news. None received a farthing of financial gain. Many were banished from family roots and shunned by cultural communities. All bet their lives on the truth about God preached by Paul.

John the Baptist lost his head to the executioner. John, the Beloved disciple, spent his last days isolated in social quarantine on the Island of Patmos. Stephen died under a volley of stones thrown by an angry establishment disdaining dissent. Tradition suggests the impetuous Peter suffered death by an upside-down crucifixion. The martyred Paul was beheaded by the ruthless blade of a Roman ax. For the next three centuries, Christians survived as hunted fugitives, meeting surreptitiously in private homes.

Hardly motivation to fabricate!

An international family of believers from all eras and cultures share the common bond of faith in God, the Creator. This fellowship of believers, described by Paul as a "great cloud of witnesses,"[22] resonates historically with stand-out names like Abraham, Joseph, and Moses.

Following Christ's death, resurrection and ascension into the sky, "Two men dressed in white" appeared to awe struck disciples promising, "This same Jesus, who has been taken from you into heaven, will come back in the same way you have seen Him go into heaven."[23] Earlier He had predicted a future time of "…great distress, unequaled from the beginning of the world…"[24] as a sign of His soon return and the gift of life eternal.

Paul passionately taught the truth about God without fear or favor. The day came when he stood falsely accused, a prisoner, before Governor Felix. In ringing defense of his cause, Paul courageously presented the good news about Christ's righteousness, the resurrection and the judgment to come. The words jolted the governor who responded with trepidation. "Go thy way for this time; when I have a convenient season, I will call for thee."[25]

The "convenient season" to embrace Paul's resurrection message never arrived. Instead, Felix settled for "...a way that seems right to a man, but in the end it leads to death."[26] The Governor kept Paul in prison to appease the apostle's accusers. Two years later, Felix disappeared from history's pages.

All too soon, Paul was shipped to Rome to suffer a martyr's death.

God Speaking

St. Patrick's "book of nature" confirms God's life-giving power; the life, death, and resurrection of His Son, exemplifies His love; the Scripture's 66-book library provides Big Picture perspective; and God speaks to hearts through the quiet influence of His Spirit. Unparalleled inner-peace pervades hearts that listen to God speaking and join the fellowship of believers that encompasses all nationalities and cultures. There is no other route to the much bally-hoed quest for "peace on earth."

A mortal author can't do justice attempting to describe the "Big Picture" and the relevance of the Creator to life's origin and purposeful living. The "mystery of Godliness" is out-of-reach of finite comprehension, surpassing the limits of human vocabulary. Every person is a player, endowed with the reasoning power to discover the truth about God and the miracle of His **creation**. All are individually accountable for choices made.

God, the Creator of all things, lives!

Life's world stage is the setting for the end-time act in the spiritual war's "Big Picture" drama. "God's gavel will someday slam down and pronounce this case closed."[27]

From this pinnacle moment, deep time stretches in all directions---out of sight into the misty past and beyond forever into the future.

Acknowledgements

The Bible, the sixty-six book library of inspired thought, proved to be the ultimate resource for this book. Insightful truth offers rich perspective as to the miraculous origin of life on earth, egregious human error with the tragic fallout, and a glimpse of the Big Picture guaranteeing hope and life eternal for all who believe.

More than a picture of Christian theology, the Scriptures provide profound glimpses of science, law, history, and human drama complimenting evidence observed looking through a microscope, shaking a test tube, and deciphering ancient parchments.

Bible writers like the courageous Apostle Paul and heroic translators such as William Tyndale, graphically demonstrate the human dimension in the great spiritual controversy pitting good versus evil.

Beyond Forever might never have been written but for the influence of the writings of two brilliant gentlemen I've communicated with but never met: the late Dr. Henry M. Morris and Attorney Phillip E. Johnson, champions of truth. A wealth of other titles exploring the origin of life have captured the fancy of serious scholars in the last half century Brilliant minds contributed foundations of thought. My favorites read like a modern "Whose Who" of reason, science and faith.

Attorney Norman Macbeth's, *Darwin Retried: An Appeal to Reason,* 1971; *Scientific Creationism*, Henry M. Morris, 1974; *Evolution: A Theory in Crisis*, Michael Denton, 1985; *Of Pandas and People*, Dean Kenyon, Percival Davis, and Charles Thaxton, 1989; *Darwin on Trial*, Phillip E. Johnson, Esq., 1991; *The Evolution of a Creationist*, Jobe Martin, 1994; *Evolution: The Fossils Still Say No*, Duane Gish, 1995; *Darwin's Black Box*, Michele Behe, 1996; *Intelligent Design*, William Dembski, 1999; and *Icons of Evolution*, Jonathon Wells, 2000.

The 2004 DVD entitled, *The Incorrigible Dr. Berlinski*, offers insightful rationale exposing the paltriness of the Darwinian hypothesis. Research papers written jointly by Brad Harrub and Bert Thompson and released by Apologetic Press in 2002, are loaded with keen thinking and reliable source material: "15 Answers to John Rennie and *Scientific American's* Nonsense;" and "Creationists Fight Back: A Review of *U.S. News & World Report's* Cover Story On Evolution."

The composite scholarship of Ariel Roth, Duane Arthur Schmidt, Harold G. Coffin, Donald R. Moeller, Joseph Mastropaolo and Karl C. Priest delivered insightful editorial input. I'm indebted to James Gibson for an unsparing and meticulous line-by-line analysis. And not only did Wayne Frair contribute editorial ideas but also wrote a supportive review of the MSS. All recommendations were evaluated and most were implemented.

This cross-section of scholars, together with the authors of the books noted, should not be saddled with the implication that they either endorse or disagree with the interpretations presented in *Beyond Forever*. As to core theological concepts endnoted by Scriptural reference, the compilation represents my personal, faith-based beliefs.

The journals *Science, Nature, National Geographic* and *Discover* provided glimpses of neo-Darwinian thought typically at odds with the theme of this book, while nevertheless enriching my research of controversial issues.

I'm appreciative of Nancy Page's sprinkling of down-home phrases that added expressive change-of-pace to the book's "magazine style" language. There couldn't have been a premium book layout without the technical skills of Allen D'Angelo and Kim Leonard of Archer Ellison, Inc.

Writing for publication requires heavy doses of determination. While I like to think I harnessed nose-to-the-grindstone persistence, it was my wife, Ruth Page Johns, whose exemplary Christian life contributed a consistent source of love-inspired patience, personal loyalty, and unquestioning support above-and-beyond the call of duty.

My daughter Lynn; my son Rick and his wife Rissa; along with my stepdaughter Judy and her husband, Tommy; together with my grandkids Tiffany, Cassie, Bru, Chandler & Jackson, were constantly in mind when this book was written---all are living symbols of God's love and the miracle of His creation. I like to think that *Beyond Forever* passes the "best evidence rule" with flying colors and will contribute positively to their life choices.

Warren L. Johns, Esq.

Cover Design
By
Cheryl Adams Palmer

The art gracing the front cover is an original composite
featuring some of
the most revered and beautiful places on earth,
created exclusively for *Beyond Forever's* premier edition..

The background waterfall represents the North American
continent, and can be found at Yellowstone National Park. The
craggy, snow-capped peaks are from the Patagonia region of
Argentina, symbolizing the
majesty of the South American Continent.

The river valley and left foreground vegetation depicts
the historical Hoz del Duratón in Segovia, Spain
where ancient monks sought solitude and inspiration.

The expansive tree, central to the artwork, is the boabab tree
of Tanzania. Some call it the "tree of life" as it can live for
hundreds of years.
The exotic ferns in the foreground
can be found in lush forests near Victoria, Australia.

Blended together, these diverse and beautiful locations present
a surprisingly cohesive and alluring scene.

**Cheryl Adams Palmer is a free lance artist known for her jewelry
and fashion designs as well as her computer skills.
She resides in Houston, Texas:
palmer_house_designs@yahoo.com.**

Resources

Authoritative sources articulating
perspectives that challenge neo-Darwinism.

Creation Research Society
www.creationresearch.org

Answers in Genesis
www.answersingenesis.org

Institute for Creation Research
www.ICR.org

The Discovery Institute
www.discovery.org/csc/

Access Research Network
www.arn.org

Intelligent Design Network
www.intelligentdesignnetwork.org

Creation Studies Institute
www.creationstudies.org

Creation Science Association of Mid-America
www.csama.org

Geoscience Research Institute
www.grisda.org

Creation Digest
www.creationdigest.com

Genesis File
www.GenesisFile.com

Endnotes

Chapter 1

1---G A. Kerkut, *The Implications of Evolution* (London: Pergamon, 1960) 157.

2---Charles Darwin, *Origin of Species and Natural Selection* (First Edition, 1859) 184, as quoted by Norman Macbeth, *Darwin Retried*, 30, 1971.

3---Charles Darwin, *Descent of Man*, Vol. I, 206.

4---Joseph Mastropaolo, *The Rise and Fall of Evolution, A Scientific Examination*, (Huntington Beach, California: a manuscript in revision, 2003) 115-123.

5---See endnote #4.

6---Gilbert Chin, "Ecology/Evolution," *Science*, 9 January 2004, 146.

7--- Hans Ellegren, "Genomics: The Dog Has Its Day," *Nature*, 8 December 2005, 745, referenced in "Scientists Put Dogs on Genome Map," *USA Today* (Thursday, December 8, 2005) 8D.

8---Elizabeth Culotta and Elizabeth Pennisi, "Evolution in Action," *Science*, 23 December 2005, Vol. 310, 1878-79.

9---Lane P. Lester & Raymond G. Bohlin, *The Natural Limits to Biological Change*, Probe Books, 1989, 73.

10---Thomas Hayden, "A Theory Evolves," *U.S. News & World Report*, July 29, 2002, 42-44.

11---Jonathan Wells, *Icons of Evolution* (Washington, D.C.: Regnery Publishing, Inc., 2000) 182, 245. Dr. Wells holds Ph.D.s from both Yale University and theUniversity of California at Berkeley.

12---David Brown, "Limits to Genetic Evolution," *The Washington Post*, July 7, 2003, A7.

13---Reported in *Science*, Vol. 295, 25, 11 Jan 2002.

14---Maynard M. Metcalf in Adams, Leslie B., Jr., Editor/Publisher, *The Scopes Trial*. Birmingham, Alabama: The Legal Classics Library, 1984; a reprint of *The World's Most Famous Trial*, Third Edition (Cincinnati: National Book Company, 1925) 253.

15---See endnote #10, 253, 258.

16---Anthony Brown, Environment Editor, *The Times* (London, UK) 20 February 2003, reported by *info@creationresearch.net*, February 27, 2003.

17---Alan Feduccia, as quoted by Kathy A. Svitil, "Discover Dialogue," *Discover*, February, 2002, 16.

18---Carl Zimmer, "Testing Darwin," *Discover*, February, 2005, 29-35.

19---Kerkut, *Implications of Evolution*, 154.

20---Phillip E. Johnson, *Darwin On Trial* (Washington, D.C., Regnery Gateway,1991) 10, referencing Irving Krisol's, "Room for Darwin and the Bible," *New York Times*, op-ed page, September 30, 1986.

21---Randy L. Wysong, *The Creation-Evolution Controversy: Implications, Methodology and Survey of Evidence Toward a Rational Solution* (East Lansing, Michigan: Inquiry Press, 1976) 434; as cited by Duane Arthur Schmidt, *And God Created Darwin* (Fairfax, Virginia: Allegiance Press, 2001) 84, quoting from John Ankerberg and John Weldon's, *Darwin's Leap of Faith.*

22---Michael Denton, *Evolution: A Theory in Crises* (Bethesda, Maryland: Adler & Adler, 1986) 62, 358.

23---Harold Coffin, John Hergenrather, Dennis Bokovoy and Michael Oard, "Road Guide to Yellowstone National Park," (Chino Valley, Arizona: Creation Research
Society, 2005) 5.

24---Giuseppe Sermonti, *Why Is A Fly Not A Horse?* (Seattle: Discovery Institute Press, 2005) 12.

Chapter 2

1---Mark Twain, *Life on the Mississippi* (Boston: J.R. Osgood, 1883) 156 as quoted by Brad Harrub, *Reason and Revelation*, May, 2001, 21(5):38.

2---Adrian Desmond & James Moore, *Darwin*, (New York: W.W. Norton and Company, 1991) 477.

3---Charles Darwin to T. Huxley, June 2, 1859, Desmond & Moore, *Darwin*, 475.

4---Charles Darwin, *The Origin of Species*, (New York: Random House, 1993) 637.

5---Darwin, *Origin*, 648.

6---Charles Darwin letter to Asa Gray, cited by Desmond and Moore, *Darwin*, 456.

7---"'Intelligent Design' smacks of Creation by Another Name," *USA Today*, Editorial Page, August 9, 2005.

8---G. A. Kerkut, *Implications of Evolution* (London: Pergamon, 1960) 6, 7.

9---See endnote #8.

10---Sir Fred Hoyle, "The Big Bang in Astronomy," *New Scientist* (November 19, 1981) 92:527, cited by Harrub and Thompson, "Creationists Fight Back."

11---See endnote #8.

12---Kerkut, *Implications of Evolution*, 157.

13---See Colin Patterson, lecture, "Can You Tell be Anything About Evolution," as transcribed by Wayne Frair and reported in "Bridge to Nowhere," *CreationDigest. com*, Autumn 2004 Edition.

14---Stanley Salthe, as cited by *Access Research Network*, "2003 Annual Report," and referenced online by *Creation Equation*, January 19, 2004.

15---Michael Denton, *Evolution: A Theory in Crisis* (Bethesda, Maryland: Adler & Adler, 1986) 77.

16---Jerry Adler, "Evolution of a Scientist," *Newsweek* (November 28, 2005) 56

17---Desmond and Moore, *Darwin*, 396.

18---Pat Shipman, *Taking Wing* (New York: Simon & Schuster, 1998) 27. See also Desmond & Moore, *Darwin*, 461; and Ian T. Taylor, *In the Minds of Men* (Minneapolis: TFE Publishing, 1996) 133. Estimates of Darwin's annual income range from 2,000 to 8,000 pounds sterling with an estate valued at 250,000 British pounds at death. Dr. Charlie Kramer computes Darwin's 1861 annual income of 8,000 British pounds sterling to be the equivalent of $526,928 U.S. 1996 dollars—or $43,910 per month.

19---Darwin, *Descent*, Vol. 1, 169.

20---Desmond & Moore, 47.

21---Desmond & Moore, 623.

22---Rev. 14:11 and Rev. 19:21, *Bible*, New International Version.

23---Desmond & Moore, 634-636.

24---Darwin, *Descent.*, Vol. II, 386.

25---Duane Arthur Schmidt, *And God Created Darwin* (Fairfax, Virginia: Alliance Press, 2001) 181.

26---Darwin, *Descent*, Vol. II, 328.

27---Darwin, *Descent*, Vol. II, 327.

28---Darwin, *Descent*, Vol. II, 327.

29---Darwin, *Descent*, Vol. I, 168, 169.

30---Rappuoli, Rino, Henry L. Miller, and Stanley Falkow, "The Intangible Value of Vaccination," *Science* Vol. 297, 9 August 2002, 937.

31---Darwin, *Origin*, 261.

32---Darwin, *Origin*, 247.

33---Darwin, *Origin*, 648.

34---Darwin, *Origin*, 232.

35---Darwin, *Origin*, 247.

36---Darwin, *Origin*, 232.

38---Darwin, *Origin*, 175.

39---Charles Darwin., *The Descent of Man and Selection in Relation to Sex*, Vol. I (Princeton, N.J.: Princeton University Press, 1981) 38.

40---Darwin, *Origin*, 277, 279.

41---Darwin, *Origin*, 246.

42---Darwin, *Origin*, 221.

43---Darwin, *Origin*, 219-220.

44---Charles Darwin, (1881) from F. Darwin, *The Life and Letters of Charles Darwin*, Vol. 3, 309.

45---Darwin, *Origin*, 617, 618.

46---Darwin, *Origin*, 406.

47---Darwin, *Origin*, 212.

48---Darwin, *Origin*, 643.

49---Darwin, *Origin*, 642.

50---Darwin, *Descent*, Vol. I, 203.

51---Darwin, *Descent*, Vol. I, 207.

52---Darwin, *Descent* , Vol. II, 389, 390.

53---Darwin, *Descent* , Vol. II, 389.

54---Darwin, *Descent* , Vol. II, 385-386.

55---Darwin, *Descent* , Vol. II, 389.

56---Darwin, *Descent* , Vol. I, 201.

57---Louis Bounoure (former director of the Strasbourg Zoological Museum, and later director of research at the French National Center of Scientific Research). *The Advocate*, 8 March 1984, 17, cited in *The Revised Quote Book*, 5.

58---Michael Denton, *Evolution: A Theory in Crises* (Bethesda, Maryland: Adler & Adler, 1986) 62, 358.

59---Michael Denton, "An Interview with Michael Denton," Access Research Network, Origins Research Archives, Vol. 15, Number 2, July 20, 1995.

60---Geoffrey Simmons, M.D., *What Darwin Didn't Know* (Eugene, Oregon: Harvest House Publishers, 2004) 309.

61---Søren Løvtrup, *Darwinism: The Refutation of a Myth* (New York: Croom Helm, 1987) 422.

Chapter 3

1---Chandra Wickramasinghe "Threats on Life of Controversial Astronomer," *New Scientist*, January 21, 1982, p. 140, as quoted by Overman, 60.

2---Charles Siebert, "Unintelligent Design," *Discover*, Vol. 27, No. 3, March, 2006, 31.

3---Siebert, See endnote #2.

4---Siebert, 34.

5---Richard Hutton, "Evolution: The Series," *Washington Post.com, Live Online*, Wednesday, September 28, 2001.

6---Darwin, *Origin of Species*, 637.

7---Darwin, *Origin*, 649.

8---Percival Davis, Dean H. Kenyon, and Charles B. Thaxton, Academic Editor, *Of Pandas and People* (Dallas: Haughton Publishing Company, 1993) 2.

9---Percival Davis, Dean H. Kenyon, and Charles B. Thaxton, 2, 3.

10---Percival Davis, Dean H. Kenyon, and Charles B. Thaxton, See endnote # 6.

11---Ashby L. Camp, *The Myth of Natural Origins* (Tempe, Arizona: Ktisisa Publishing, 1994) 31, 32.

12---Dean L. Overman, *A Case Against Accident and Self-Organization*, 40, 41.

13---Dean L. Overman, *A Case Against Accident and Self-Organization*, 45, 46.

14---Percival Davis, Dean H. Kenyon, and Charles B. Thaxton, Academic Editor, *Of Pandas and People* (Dallas: Haughton Publishing Company, 1993) 3.

15---Kirk R. Johnson and Richard K. Stucky, *Prehistoric Journey* (Boulder, Colorado: Roberts Rinehart Publishers, 1995) 16.

16---Hubert P. Yockey, *Information Theory and Molecular Biology* (Cambridge: Cambridge University Press, 1992), pp. 235, 236, 238, and 335 as quoted by Overman, 48.

17---Mark Twain, *Life on the Mississippi* (Boston: J.R. Osgood, 1883), 156 as quoted by Brad Harrub, *Reason and Revelation*, May, 2001, 21(5):38.

18---Bert Thompson, *The Scientific Case for Creation* (Montgomery, Alabama: Apologetics Press, 2002) 83.

19---G.A. Kerkut, *Implications of Evolution* (New York: Pergamon Press, 1965) 6, 7.

20---Brad Harrub and Bert Thompson, "Creationists Fight Back." (Montgomery, Alabama: Apologetics Press, 2002) p. 3, referencing Sir Fred Hoyle, "The Big Bang in Astronomy," *New Scientist* (November 19, 1981) 92:527.

21---Sir Francis Crick, *Life Itself: Its Origin and Nature* (New York, Simon & Schuster, 1981) 88, cited by Brad Harrub and Bert Thompson, "Creationists Fight Back," (Montgomery, Alabama: Apologetics Press, 2002) 2.

22---Ian T. Taylor, *In the Minds of Men* (Minneapolis: TFE Publishing, 1996), 161 and 182, quoting Pasteur as cited by Rene J. Dubos, *Louis Pasteur: Freelance of Science* (New York: Charles Scribner's Sons, 1976) 395.

23---George Wald, "The Origin of Life," *Sci. Am.*, August, 1954, 191(2):44-53, cited by Coffin, 376, 377.

24---Byron C. Nelson, *After Its Kind* (Minneapolis: Augsburg Publishing House,1927)

27, quoting *History of Creation*, 348.

25---Michael Denton, *Evolution: A Theory in Crisis*, (Bethesda, Md.: Adler & Adler, 1986) 264.

26---Phillip E. Johnson, *Darwin on Trial* (Washington, D.C.: Regnery Gateway, 1991) 103.

27---Robert Jastrow, *Until the Sun Dies* (New York, W.W. Norton, 1977) 62, 63, as quoted by Bert Thompson, *The Scientific Case for Creation*, 76.

28---Dean L. Overman, *A Case Against Accident and Self-Organization* (New York: Rowman & Littlefield Publishers, Inc., 1997) 38. See Aleksander I. Oparin, *The Origin of Life* (New York: Dover Publications, Inc., 1938).

29---Charles B. Thaxton, Walter L. Bradley and Roger L. Olsen, *The Mystery of Life's Origin* (New York: Philosophical Library, 1984) 182, 183, 185, quoted by Bert Thompson, 80.

30---Denton, 261.

31---Hubert P. Yockey, *Information Theory and Molecular Biology* (Cambridge: Cambridge University Press, 1992), 257, quoted by Overman, 61, 62.

32---Gunter Wachtershauser, Letter to Editor, *Science*, 25 October 2002, vol. 298.

33---Larry A. Witham, *Where Darwin Meets the Bible* (New York: Oxford University Press, 2002) 129.

34---Denton, 328, 329.

35---Geoffrey Simmons, M.D., *What Darwin Didn't Know* (Eugene, Oregon: Harvest House Publishers, 2004) 43, 53.

36---I.L. Cohen, *Darwin Was Wrong* (Greenvale, New York: New Research Publications, Inc., 1984) 38, 39, referencing H.G. Wells, Julian S. Huxley, and G.P. Wells, *The Science of Life* (New York: The Literary Guild) 41-43.

37---Duane Arthur Schmidt, *And God Created Darwin* (Fairfax, Virginia: Allegiance Press, 2001) 24, 25.

38---Denton, 250.

39---Denton, 328, 329.

40---Thomas Woodward, *Doubts About Darwin* (Grand Rapids: Baker Books, 2003)

44. Woodward referenced Sydney Fox in his review of *Mystery of Life's Origins* in *Quarterly Review of Biology*, June, 1985.

41---Joshua Lederberg, "A View of Genetics," *Science* 131 (3396) 1960: pp. 269-280 cited by Harold Coffin, *Origin by Design*, 377, 378.

42---Harold Coffin, *Origin by Design* (Hagerstown, Maryland: Review and Herald Publishing Association, 1983) p. 379.

43---Denton, 315.

44---Denton, 323.

45---Dean L. Overman, 59, citing Hoyle and Wickramasinge, 148, 24, 150, 30, and 31 as quoted in Thaxton, Bradley, and Olsen, 196.

46---Bert Thompson & Brad Harrub, "15 Answers to John Rennie and *Scientific American's* Nonsense," (Montgomery, Alabama: Apologetics Press, 2002) 31.

47---Harold J. Morowitz, *Energy Flow in Biology* (New York: Academic Press, 1968); cited by Coffin, 376.

48---Dean L. Overman, *A Case Against Accident and Self-Organization*, 63, 64.

49---John Keosian, In Haruhiko Nada, ed., *Origin of Life* (Tokyo: Center for Academic Publications, Japan Scientific Publications Press, 1978) 573, 574, quoted by Coffin, 377.

50---Walter L. Bradley and Charles B. Thaxton, "Information and the Origin of Life," in *The Creation Hypothesis*, ed. J.P. Moreland (Downers Grove, Illinois: Inter-Varsity Press, 1994) 190 as quoted by Overman, 62.

51---Overman, 58, 59.

52---Denton, 249, 250.

53---Denton, 290.

54---Denton, 290, 291.

Chapter 4

1---Søren Løvtrup (Swedish biologist), Darwinism: The Refutation of a Myth (New York: Croom Helm, 1987), p. 422.

2---Michael Denton, *Evolution: A Theory in Crisis* (Bethesda, Md.: Adler & Adler, 1986) 345.

3---Jonathan Sarfati, "The Second Law of Thermodynamics: Answers to Critics," www.answersingenesis.org/docs/370.asp#crystals (2002b), as cited by Burt Thompson and Brad Harrub, "15 Answers to John Rennie and *Scientific American's Nonsense*" (Montgomery, Alabama: Apologetics Press, Inc., 2002) 44.

4---See Charles Siebert, "Unintelligent Design," *Discover*, Vol. 27, No. 3, March, 2006.

5---Denton, 250.

6---Denton, 306.

7---Dean L. Overman, *A Case Against Accident and Self Organization* (New York: Rowman & Littlefield Publishers Inc., 1997) 59, citing Hoyle and Wickramasinge, *Evolution from* Space, (London: J.M. Dent & Sons, 1981)148, 24, 150, 30, and 31 as quoted in Charles B. Thaxton,Walter L. Bradley, and Roger Olsen, *The Mystery of Life's Origin: Reassuring Current Theories* (New York: Philosophical Library, 1984) 196.

8---See William A. Dembski, *Intelligent Design* (Downer's Grove, Illinois: InterVarsity Press, 1999.

9---Lee M. Spetner, *Not by Chance* (Brooklyn, New York: The Judaica Press, Inc., 1997) 30.

10---See *Unlocking the Mystery of Life*, an Illustra Video production, 2002.

11---Spetner, 31.

12---Denton, 329.

13---Denton, 320, 321.

14---Walt Brown, *In the Beginning: Compelling Evidence for Creation and the Flood* (Phoenix, Ariz.: Center for Scientific Creation, 1996) 11, 12.

15---Brown, 11, 12.

16---Spetner, 32.

17---Denton, 331.

18---Denton, 331.

19---I. L. Cohen, *Darwin Was Wrong*. (Greenvale, New York: New Research Publications, Inc., 1984) 40-42.

20---Cohen, 209.

21---George Javor, "5,000 Years of Stasis," ("Genomic Science: 21st Century Threat to 19th Century Superstition," www.*CreationDigest.com*, Summer Edition, 2002).

22---Cohen, 35, 54.

23---Denton, 334

24---Bill Gates, *The Road Ahead* (Boulder: Blue Penguin, 1996) 228; from "ID in PS Curricula," 1999.

25---George Javor, *CreationDigest.com*, Summer Edition, 2002.

26---Joel Achenbach, "The Origin of Life Through Chemistry," *National Geographic*, March, 2006, 31.

27---Spetner, 30.

28---Cohen, 208.

29---Denton, 338.

30---Javor, *CreationDigest.com*, Summer Edition, 2002.

31---Cohen, 40-42.

32---Javor, *CreationDigest.com*, Summer Edition, 2002.

33---Javor, *CreationDigest.com*, Summer Edition, 2002.

34---Richard Willing, "DNA Tests Offer Clues to Suspect's Race," *USA Today*, August 17, 2005, 2A.

35---Denton, 342.

36---Denton, 296, 323.

37---Cohen, 205.

38---Alan Hayward, *Creation and Evolution.* (Minneapolis: Bethany House Publishers, 1995) 35; referencing F. Hoyle, *The Universe: Past and Present Reflections* (University College, Cardiff, 1981).

39---Denton, 348, 357.

40---G.A. Kerkut, *Implications of Evolution* (New York: Pergamon Press, 1965). 6.

41---Richard Milton, *Shattering the Myths of Darwinism* (Rochester, Vt.: Park Street Press, 1997) 184; referencing Denton, *Evolution: A Theory in Crises.*

42---Denton, 324.

43---See *A Scientific Dissent From Darwinism*, www.dissentfromdarwin.org.

Chapter 5

1---Lee Spetner, *Not by Chance: Shattering the Modern Theory of Evolution* (Brooklyn: Judaica Press, 1997) 160.

2---Ian Taylor, *In the Minds of Men*, 160, 161.

3---Byron C. Nelson, *After Its Kind* (Minneapolis, Augsburg Publishing House, 1927) 98, 99.

4---Nelson, 101, referencing Alfred Russel Wallace, *Letters and Reminiscences*, 340.

5--Jonathan Wells, *Icons of Evolution* (Washington, D.C.: Regnery Publishing, Inc., 2000) 180.

6---Nelson, 101, quoting Wallace from *Letters and Reminiscences*, 95.

7---Alfred Russel Wallace, "The Present Position of Darwinism," *Contemporary Review*, August, 1908.

8---Nelson, 101, citing *Theory of Evolution*, 163.

9---Nelson, 99,101 citing *Smithsonian Institute Report*, 1916, 343.

10---Nelson, *After Its Kind*, 101, 102, citing *Science Progress*, January, 1925.

11---Albert Fleischmann, "The Doctrine of Organic Evolution in the Light of Modern Research," *Journal of the Transactions of the Victoria Institute* 65 (1933): 194-95, 205-6, 208-9.

12---Wells, 181.

13---Michael Denton, *Evolution: A Theory in Crisis* (Bethesda, Maryland: Adler & Adler, Publishers, inc., 1986) 75 citing Julian Huxley, *Evolution After Darwin* ed. Sol Tax, vol. 3 (Chicago: University of Chicago Press, 1960) pp. 1-21, see 1.

14---Albert Fleischmann, University of Erlangen Zoologist. See John Fred Meldau, ed., *Witnesses Against Evolution* (Denver: Christian Victory Publishing, 1968), 13.

15---Henry M. Morris, "The Microwave of Evolution," *Back to Genesis*, August, 2001, a.

16---Pierre-Paul Grassé, *The Evolution of Living Organisms*, (New York: Academic Press, 1977) 88, 103.

17---Henry M. Morris, "What They Say," *Back to Genesis* (March 1999) a.

18---Morris, b.

19--Bert Thompson, *The Scientific Case for Creation* (Montgomery, Alabama: Apologetic Press, Inc., 2002) 124.

20---Noble, et. al, *Parasitology*, sixth edition, "Evolution of Parasitism," Lea and Febiger, 1989, 516, as cited by Frank Sherwin, *Origins Issues*, "Natural Selection's Role in the Real World."

21---Colin Patterson, "Cladistics," *The Listener* (1982) 106:390.

22---Søren Løvtrup, *Darwinism: The Refutation of a Myth* (London: Croom Helm,1987) 352.

23---Charles Siebert, "Unintelligent Design," *Discover*, Vol. 27, No. 3, March, 2006, 35.

24--- Siebert, 34.

25---Richard Milton, *Shattering the Myths of Darwinism* (Rochester, Vt.: Park Street Press, 1997) 169, 170.

26---See Tim Friend, "Gene Defect is Linked to Parkinson's," *USA Today* (June 27, 1997) and *USA Today*, January 17 (180, 2005.

27---Josie Glausiusz, "The Genes of 1996," *Discover* (January 1997) 36.

28--David A. Demick, "The Blind Gunman," *Impact* (El Cajon, Calif.: Institute for Creation Research, February, 1999) iv.

29---*The Star*, Ventura, California, June 24, 1997.

30---*The Star*, June 24, 1997.

31---Elizabeth Pennsi, "New Gene Found for Inherited Macular Degeneration," *Science* 281 (July 3, 1998) 31.

32---Marcia Barinaga, "Tracking Down Mutations That Can Stop the Heart," *Science* 281 (July 3, 1998) 32.

33---Reuters, "Genetic Error Causes Rapid-Aging Syndrome," *The Washington Post*, Thursday, April 17, 2003, A6.

34---Rick Weiss, "Defect Tied to Doubling of Risk for Colon Cancer," *The Washington Post*, August 26, 1997.

35---Daniel C. Weaver, "The River of Life," *Discover* (November 1997) 55.

36---Karen P. Steel and Steve D. M. Brown, "More Deafness Genes." *Science* 280 (May 29, 1998) 1403.

37---Rob Stein, "Sex May Rid Us of DNA Flaws," *The Washington Post* (February 1, 1999) A9.

38---Morris, c, citing Richard Lewontin, *The Triple Helix* (Cambridge, Massachusetts: Harvard University Press, 2000) 91.

39---Spetner, 97-103.

40---Spetner, 139, 141.

41---Kevin Anderson, "Radio Interview with Dr. Kevin Anderson," *Creation Matters*, No. 4 July/August 2004, 1.

42---Spetner, 131, 141, 143.

43---Spetner, 181, 198.

44---See Jobe Martin, *The Evolution of a Creationist* (Rockwall, Texas: Biblical Discipleship Publishers, 2002) 131, 132.

45---Denton, 322.

46---Anderson, 1.

47---Anderson, "Definition of Evolution," Anderson@nsric.ars.usda.gov, 9-4-2002.

48---David Berlinski, *The Incorrigible Dr. Berlinski*, DVD, ColdWater Media, 2004.

49---Lane P. Lester and Raymond G. Bohlin, *The Natural Limits to Biological Change* (Dallas: Probe Books, 1989) 85, citing Fred Hoyle and N. A. Wickramasinghe, *Evolution From Space* (London: Dent, 1981).

50---Denton, 91.

51---Norman Macbeth, *Darwin Retried*, 36, citing Wilbur Hall, *Partner of Nature* (Appleton-Century, 1939).

52---Lane P. Lester & Raymond G. Bohlin, *The Natural Limits to Biological Change* (Dallas: Probe books, 1989) 95.

53---Adrian Higgins, "Why the Red Delicious No Longer Is," *The Washington Post National Weekly Edition*, August 15-21, 2005, 19.

54---Louis Bounoure *The Advocate*, 8 March 1984 , 17, quoted in *The Revised Quote Book*, 5. Bounoure has served as director of the Strasbourg Zoological Museum, and research director at the French National Center of Scientific Research.

55---Stephen J. Gould, Speech at Hobart College, February 14, 1980, cited by Luther Sunderland, *Darwin's Enigma* (El Cajon, California: Master Books, 1984), 106 (emphasis in original) cited by Bert Thompson and Brad Harrub,"*National Geographic* Shoots Itself in the Foot Again," (ApologeticsPress.Org online report, 2004) 36.

Chapter 6

1---Ernst Mayr, *The Growth of Biological Thought: Diversity, Evolution and Inheritance* (Cambridge, Massachusetts: The Belknap Press of HarvardUniversity Press, 1982) 524.

2---Charles Darwin, *The Origin of Species*, 647.

3---Darwin, *Origin*, 247.

4---Darwin, *Origin*, 637.

5---Darwin, *Descent of Man*, Vol. II, 389.

6---Darwin, *Origin*, 219.

7---Darwin, *Origin*, 6th Edition (1872), (New York: New York University Press, 1988) 154.

8---Darwin, *Origin*, 617, 618.

9---Darwin, *Origin*, 406.

10---Darwin, *Origin*, 406.

11---The Associated Press, "'Jurassic Beaver' Turns Theory on Its Tail," *CNN.com/2006/TECH/science/02/23/jurassic.beaver.ap/index*; See also Thomas Martin, "Early Mammalian Evolutionary Experiments," *Science*, Vol. 311, 24 February 2006, 1109.

12--- Kathy Sawyer, "New Light on a Mysterious Epoch," *The Washington Post* (February 5, 1998); Copyright 1998, The *Washington Post*.

13---James Gibson, letter to Warren L. Johns (August 28, 1997); citing David Raup, *Zoologic Record* published in *Paleobiology* 2 (1976) 279-288.

14---A. G. Fisher, *Grolier Multimedia Encyclopedia*, 1998, fossil section.

15---Francisco J. Ayala and James W. Valentine, *Evolving, The Theory and Processes of Organic Evolution*, 1979, 266.

16---Peter Ward & Donald Brownlee, *Rare Earth*, Feb 2000, 150.

17---Darwin, *Origin*, 647, 453.

18---Henry Gee, *In Search of Deep Time* (London: Comstock Publishing Associates, 1999) 108, 110.

19---Erik Stokstad, *Science*, 5 December 2003 1645.

20---Steven A. Austin, ed., *Grand Canyon: Monument to Catastrophe* (Santee, Calif.: Institute for Creation Research, 1994) 149.

21---Michael Denton, *Evolution: A Theory in Crisis.* (Bethesda, Md.: Adler & Adler, 1986) 298, 302.

22---Peter D. Ward, "Coils of Time," *Discover* (March 1998) 106.

23---Henry Gee, *In Search of Deep Time*, pp. 177 & 155.

24---Gee, *In Search of Deep Time* (New York: The Free Press, 1999) 133.

25---Gee, *In Search of Deep Time*, 108.

26---Gee, *In Search of Deep Time*, 127.

27---Gee, *In Search of Deep Time*, 32.

28---R.L. Wysong, *The Creation-Evolution Controversy.* (Midland, Michigan: Inquiry Press, 1978) 348, 352-354.

29---See *Creation ex Nihlo*, December, 2000, 6.

30---Oliver & Boyd, *Contemporary Botanical Thought*, 1971, 97.

31---Darwin, C. (1881) in Darwin, F., *The Life and Letters of Charles Darwin,* (London: John Murray, 1888) vol. 3, 248; cited by Michael Denton, *Evolution: A Theory in* Crisis, 163.

32---Phillip E. Johnson, *Darwin on Trial* (Washington, D.C.: Regnery Publishing, 1995) 179; citing Charles Darwin 1879 letter to Joseph Hooker as quoted by Kenneth Sporne's 1971 monograph, "The Mysterious Origin of Flower Plants."

33---T.S. Kemp (Curator of Zoological Collections), *Fossils and Evolution*, (Oxford University, Oxford University Press, 1999) 253.

34---Byron C. Nelson, *After Its Kind*, (Minneapolis: Augsburg Publishing House, 1927) 120, quoting from the *New York Times*, December 27, 1925.

35--- See P.L. Forey, *Neontological Analysis Versus Palaeontological Stories*, 1982, 120-121.

36---David G. Kitts, "Paleontology and Evolutionary Theory," *Evolution* (September, 1974), 28:466.

37---Francisco J. Ayala and James W. Valentine, *Evolving, The Theory and Processes of Organic Evolution*, 1979, 266.

38---George Gaylord Simpson, *The Meaning of Evolution* (New Haven, Connecticut: Yale University Press, 1949) 231.

39---George Gaylord Simpson, *The Sudden Appearance of Higher Categories, in Evolution of Life* 149 (S. Tax ed. 1960) as quoted by W.R. Bird, *The Origin of Species Revisited*, Volume I: Science (Nashville: Regency, 1991) 57.

40---Elizabeth Pennisi, "Fossil Shows an Early Fish (Almost) out of Water," *Science*, Vol. 312, April 7, 2006, 33.

41---Ian Taylor, "The Ultimate Hoax: Archaeopteryx Lithographica," *ICC Symposium Sessions*, Vol. II (Pittsburgh: Creation Science Fellowship, Inc., 1990) 279-291.

42---R. A. Thulborn, "The Avian Relationships of *Archaeopteryx* and the Origin of Birds," *Zoological Journal of the Linnean Society* 82 (1984) 119, as cited by Walt Brown, *In the Beginning: Compelling Evidence for Creation and the Flood* (Phoenix: Center for Scientific Creationism, 1996).

43---Virginia Morell, "A Cold, Hard Look at Dinosaurs," *Discover* (December 1996) 102.

44---John Schwartz, "Paleontology: Another Aspect in the Bird Debate," *The Washington Post* (November 17, 1997); from a report in *Science*, November 14, 1997.

45---Bernice Wuethrich, "Stunning Fossil Shows Breath of a Dinosaur," *Science* 283 (January 22, 1999) 468.

46---Duane Gish, *Evolution: The Fossils Still Say No!*, p. 137; referencing Tim Beardsley, *Nature* 322 (1986) 677; see Richard Monastersky, *Science News* 140 (1991) 104, 105; and Alan Anderson, *Science* 253 (1991) 35.

47---S.M. Stanley, *The New Evolutionary Timetable: Fossils, Genes, and the Origin of Species*, 1981, 3.

48---Mark Ridley, "Who Doubts Evolution?" *New Scientist*, 25 June 1981, 90: 831.

49---Stephen Jay Gould, "Is a New and General Theory of Evolution Emerging?" *Paleobiology*, (Winter, 1980) 6[1]:127.

50---Stephen Jay Gould, "The Return of Hopeful Monsters," *Natural History*, 86[4]:22-30, June-July, 1977.

51---Stephen Jay Gould, "Cordelia's Dilemma", *Natural History*, Feb 1993, 15.

52---Stephen Jay Gould, *The Panda's Thumb* (New York: W.W. Norton, 1980) 182.

53---Stephen Jay Gould, *The Panda's Thumb* (New York: W.W. Norton, 1985) as quoted by Woodward, *Doubts About Darwin*, 40, 41.

54---Stephen Jay Gould, "The Episodic Nature of Evolutionary Change," in *The Panda's Thumb* (New York: W.W. Norton, 1985) 182ff as cited by Woodward, *Doubts About Darwin*, 41.

55---Eldredge & Tattersall, *The Myths of Human Evolution*, 1982, 45-46 .

56---Colin Patterson letter to Luther D. Sunderland, 10 April 1879, quoted by Luther D. Sunderland, *Darwin's Enigma: Fossils and Other Problems* (San Diego: Master Books, 1988) 89, cited by James Perloff, *The Case Against Darwin* (Burlington, Massachusetts: Refuge Books, 2002) 40.

57---David G. Kitts, "Paleontology and Evolutionary Theory," *Evolution* (September, 1974) 28:466.

58---David Raup, "Letter to the Editor," *Science*, 213 July 17, 1981, 289.

59---Michael Denton, *Evolution: A Theory in Crisis* (Bethesda, Md.: Adler & Adler, 1986) 160-162.

60---Denton, 249, 250, 278.

61---Michael Denton, 139, 140 citing Patterson, C. (1980) "Cladistics", *Biologist*, 27: 238, and Halstead, B., (1981) "Halstead's Defence Against Irrelevancy", *Nature*, 292: 403.

62---Jeremy Rifkin , *Algeny* (New York: Viking, 1983) 125.

Chapter 7

1---Michael J. Behe, *Darwin's Black Box*. New York: The Free Press, 1996) 39.

2---Albert Fleischmann, "The Doctrine of Organic Evolution in the Light of Modern Research," *Journal of the Transactions of the Victoria Institute 65* (1933) 194-95, 205-6, 208-9.

3---Sir William Dawson, *The Story of Earth and Man* (New York: Harper and Brothers, 1887) 317, 322, 330, 339.

4---Søren Løvtrup (Swedish biologist), Darwinism: The Refutation of a Myth (New York: Croom Helm, 1987) 422.

5---Darwin, *Origin*, 232.

6---Michael Denton, "An Interview with Michael Denton," Access Research Network, *Origins Research Archives*, Vol. 15, Number 2, July 20, 1995.

7---Michael Denton, *Evolution: A Theory in Crisis*. (Bethesda, Md.: Adler & Adler, 1986) 117, citing Darwin, C. (1858) in a letter to Asa Gray, 5 September, 1857, *Zoologist*, 16: 6297-99, see 6299.

8---Michael J. Behe, *Darwin's Black Box* (New York: The Free Press, 1996) 15.

9---Michael J. Behe, *Darwin's Black Box*, 69-73.

10---Michael J. Behe, *Darwin's Black Box*, 31-36.

11---Michael J. Behe, *Darwin's Black Box*, 73.

12---Michael J. Behe, *Darwin's Black Box*, 79.

13---Michael J. Behe, *Darwin's Black Box*, 74-97.

14---Michael J. Behe, *Darwin's Black Box*, 86, 87.

15---Michael J. Behe, *Darwin's Black Box*, 90.

16---Michael J. Behe, *Darwin's Black Box*, 93, 94.

17---Michael J. Behe, *Darwin's Black Box*, 96, 97.

18--Donald R. Moeller, "Does a Smile Need 500 Million Years to Evolve?", *CreationDigest.com*, Spring Edition, 2002. Dr. Moeller is both a Fellow, American Board of Oral and Maxillofacial Surgeons and a Diplomate, American Board, Oral and Maxillofacial Surgery.

19---Steve Austin, *Grand Canyon: Monument to Catastrophe* (El Cajon, California: Institute for Creation Research, 1994) 145 as cited by Frank Sherwin, "Un-Bee-lievable Vision," *Acts & Facts* (El Cajon, California: ICR, Vol. 35, No. 2, February, 2006) 5.

20---Graham E. Budd & Maximilian J. Telford, "Evolution: Along Came a Sea Spider," *Nature*, Vol. 437, Oct. 20, 2005, 1099, as cited by Frank Sherwin, "Un-Bee-lievable Vision," *Acts & Facts* (El Cajon, California: ICR, Vol. 35, No. 2, February, 2006) 5.

21---Frank Sherwin, "Un-Bee-lievable Vision," *Acts & Facts* (El Cajon, California: Institute for Creation Research, Vol. 35, No. 2, February, 2006) 5.

Chapter 8

1---Jonathan Wells, *Icons of Evolution* (Washington DC: Regnery Publishing, Inc., 2000) 188.

2---See Dennis Normile, "Gene Expression Differs in Human and Chimp Brains," *Science*, 6 April 2001, 44, 45, presented at "Genes and Minds Initiative Workshop on Ape Genomics" in Tokyo, March 14-15, 2001.

3---See Duane T. Gish, *Evolution: The Fossils Still Say No!* (El Cajon, Calif.: Institute for Creation Research, 1995), 19, 20; Michael Denton, *Evolution: A Theory in Crisis* (Bethesda, Md.: Adler & Adler, 1986) 330, 331; and Harold Coffin with Robert H. Brown, *Origin by Design* (Hagerstown, Md.: Review and Herald Publishing Assn., 1983) 382.

4---Michael Denton, *Evolution: A Theory in Crisis* (Bethesda, Md.: Adler & Adler, 1986) 330.

5---C.P. Yu, "The Human Brain Testifies Against Evolution: Confessions of a Neurosurgeon," (Internet Website: www.hkam.org.hk/temp/counterevolution, as noted 1-10-2005).

6---Harold Coffin, *Origin by Design* (Hagerstown, Md.: Review and Herald Publishing Association, 1983) 383.

7---Ian T. Taylor, "The Idea of Progress," *The Fifth International Conference on Creationism*, (Pittsburgh: Creation Science Fellowship, Inc., 2003) 578.

Chapter 9

1---Phillip E. Johnson, *Darwin on Trial*, p. 22.

2---Charles R. Darwin, *Origin of Species*, 637

3---Darwin, *Origin*, 219.

4---Henry Gee, *In Search of Deep Time: Beyond the Fossil Record to a New History of Life* (New York: The Free Press, 1999) 116-117.

5---Charles R. Darwin, *The Descent of Man*, Vol. II, 389.

6---Darwin, *Descent*, Vol. II, 389, 390.

7---Darwin, *Descent*, Vol. I, 203.

8---Darwin, *Descent*, Vol. II, 389.

9---Darwin, *Descent*, Vol. I, 207.

10---Darwin, *Descent*, Vol. II, 386.

11---Darwin, *Descent*, Vol. I, 206.

12---Darwin, *Descent*, Vol. II, 389.

13---Darwin, *Descent*, Vol. I, 201.

14---Darwin, *Descent*, Vol. I, 213.

15---Ernst Mayr, "Interview," *Omni* (March/April 1988) 46.

16---Darwin, *Descent*, Vol. I, 173.

17---Darwin, *Descent*, Vol. I, 216.

18---Darwin, *Descent*, Vol. I, 178.

19---Darwin, *Descent*, Vol. I, 201.

20---Darwin, *Descent*, Vol. II, 389, 390.

21---Howard Glicksman, M.D., "Sex and the Single Gene: Becoming a Man is not as Easy as X+Y," *Exercise Your Wonder* (Access Research Network, September 1, 2005).

Chapter 10

1---Henry Gee, *In Search of Deep Time* ((New York: The Free Press, 1999) 116, 117.

2---Richard Leakey and Roger Lewin, *People of the Lake* (New York: E.P. Dutton, 1978 19, as cited by Brad Harrub, "The 'Glorious Mess" of Human Origins," *Apologetics Press.org/articles/2831*, August 31, 2005.

3---David Raup, "Letter to the Editor," *Science*, 213 July 17, 1981, 289.

4---Gee, 202.

5---Gee, 210, 211.

6---Gee, 204, 205.

7---Mary Leakey, *Disclosing the Past* (Garden City, New York: Doubleday and Company, 1984) 214.

8---J.S. Jones and S. Rouhani, "How Small Was the Bottleneck?" *Nature* 319 (6 February 1986) 449.

9---Robert Martin, "Man is Not an Onion," *New Scientist* 4 (August 1977) p. 285 as cited by Marvin L. Lubenow, *Bones of Contention* (Grand Rapids, Baker Books: 1992 edition) 182.

10---G.A. Clark and C.M. Willermet, eds., "Conceptual Issues in Modern Human Origins Research," Aldine de Gruyter, 1997.

11---David Pilbeam, *The Evolution of Man* (New York: Funk & Wagnalls, 1970) 151.

12---Henry M. McHenry, "Fossils and the Mosaic Nature of Human Evolution," *Science* 190 (31 October 1975) 428.

13---Marvin L. Lubenow, *Bones of Contention* (Grand Rapids, Baker Books: 2004 edition) 70.

14---David Pilbeam, "Rearranging Our Family Tree," *Human Nature* (June, 1978) 44 as quoted by Marvin L. Lubenow, 182.

15---Marvin L. Lubenow, 180, 181.

16---Ann Gibbons, "Java Skull Offers New View of *Homo erectus*," *Science*, vol. 299, 28 February 2003, 1293.

17---Marvin L. Lubenow, 301, with quote from Charles Oxnard, "The Place of the Australopithecines in Human Evolution: Grounds for Doubt?" *Nature* 258 (4 December 1975), 389.

18---Marvin L. Lubenow, 301, with quote from Matt Cartmill, David Pilbeam, and Glynn Isaac, "One Hundred Years of Paleoanthropology," *American Scientist* 74 (July-August 1986) 419.

19---Darwin, *Descent of Man*, 404, 405.

20---See Harun Yahya, *Evolution Deceit* (London: Ta-Ha Publishers, Ltd., third edition, 2000) 135.

21---Frank Salisbury, "Doubts About the Modern Synthetic Theory of Evolution," *American Biology Teacher* (September, 1971) 338 as quoted by Harun Yahya, *Evolution Deceit*, 135.

22---Gee, 202.

23---Gee, 32.

24---Joel Achenbach, "Who Knew?", *National Geographic*, September, 2005, 1.

25---See Brad Harrub, "Evolutionary Chain Resolved or Chain of Confusion," *Apologetics Press.org/articles/2910*, May, 2006; citing Seth Borenstein (2006), "Fossil Discovery Fills Gap in Human Evolution," *msnbc.msn.com/id/12286206/*; and Rex Dalton (2006), "Feel It In Your Bones," *Nature*, 440:1100-1101, April 13.

26---*Science*, 6 April 2001, 44, 45.

27---David DeWitt, "Greater than 98% Chimp/human DNA Similarity? Not Any More", *Technical Journal* 17(1):8-10, April 2003, referencing Marks, J., 2000, "98% alike? What Our Similarity to Apes Tells Us About Our Understanding of Genetics," *Chronicle of Higher Education* May 12, 2000, B7.

28---David DeWitt, referencing Gibbons, A., "Which of Our Genes Make Us Human?" *Science* 281:1432-1434.

29---David DeWitt, referencing Archidiacono, N., Storlazzi, C.T., Spalluto, C., Ricco, A.S., Marzella, R., Rocchi, M. 1998, "Evolution of Chromosome Y in Primates," *Chromosoma* 107:241-246.

30---David DeWitt, referencing Kakuo, S., Asaoka, K. and Ide, T. 1999, "Human is a Unique Species Among Primates in Terms of Telomere Length," *Biochem Biophys Res Commun* 263:308-314.

31---Steve Sternberg, "Humans, Chimps Almost a Match," *USA Today*, September 1, 2005, 1A.

32---Rick Weiss and David Brown, "New Analyses Bolster the Theory of Evolution," *The Washington Post National Weekly Edition*, October 3-9, 2005, 29, 30.

33---Joseph A. Mastropaolo, *The Rise and Fall of Evolution* (Huntington Beach, California, a manuscript in revision, 2003) 49.

34---David DeWitt, "Greater than 98% Chimp/human DNA Similarity? Not Any More", (*Technical Journal* 17(1):8-10, April 2003.

35---*The Washington Post*, Monday, September 30, 2002, A7.

36---Don Batten, "Human/chimp DNA similarity," *Creation* 19 (1) 21-22, December 1996.

37---Walter James ReMine, *The Biotic Message* (Saint Paul: St. Paul Science, 1993) 208, 215-217.

38---J.E. O'Rourke, "Pragmatism vs. Materialism in Stratigraphy," *American Journal of Science* (January 1976) 53.

39---Gee, 210, 211.

40---Rick Warren, "Starbucks Stirs Things Up with a God Quote on Cups," *USA Today*, October 19, 2005, 8D.

Chapter 11

1---Joseph Mastropaolo, "The Maximum-Power Stimulus Theory for Muscle," *Creation Research Society Quarterly* (St. Joseph, Missouri: Creation Research Society) Vol. 37, Number 4, March 2001, 213-219.

2---"Mystery of the Megaflood," Nova, 2005, pbs.org/previews/Nova_ Megaflood.

3--- Genesis 7:11,19, 20, New International Version of the Holy Bible.

4---Genesis 8:1

5---Charles Darwin, *Origin of Species*, 648.

6---John Mackay, "Evidence News Update No. 4, *Creation Research*, April 2, 2003.

7---Matthew 24:38, 39, Bible, New International Version.

8---Alfred Russel Wallace, *Darwinism* (London and New York, Macmillan and Co., 1890) 379, 380.

9---Wilbur A. Nelson, *The Scopes Trial* (Birmingham, Ala.: The Legal Classics Library, 1984) 239; a reprint of *The World's Most Famous Trial* (Cincinnati: National Book Co., 1925) 238-241.

10---Gretel Schueller, "Australia's Ups and Downs," Earth (August 1998) 16.

11---See D.S. Allan and J. B. Delair. *Cataclysm.* (Santa Fe, N.M.: Bear & Company, 1997).

12---Dan Vergano, "Greenland Glacier Runoff Doubles Over Past Decade," *USA Today*, February 17, 2006, 24.

13---Larry Vardiman, "Are Hurricanes Getting More Destructive?", *Impact #390* (El Cajon, California: Institute for Creation Research, December, 2005) iv, referencing his previous research, L. Vardiman, 1996, *Sea-Floor Sediment and the Age of the Earth*, ICRTechnical Monograph, Institute for Creation Research, El Cajon, CA, 94 pp. and L. Vardiman., 2001, *Climates before and after theGenesis Flood: Numerical Models and Their Implications,* ICR Technical Monograph, Institute for Creation Research, El Cajon, CA, 110 pp.

14---Michael J. Oard, *An Ice Age Caused by the Genesis Flood* (El Cajon, California: Institute for Creation Research, 1990) 33.

15--- Steven A. Austin & William A. Hoesch, "Do Volcanoes Come in Super Size?", *Impact*, Institute for Creation Research, August, 2006.

16---See Michael Guillen, *Five Equations that Changed the World*, 210.

17---Michael J. Oard, *An Ice Age Caused by the Genesis Flood* (El Cajon, California: Institute for Creation Research, 1990) 34.

18---Tom Canby, "The Year Without a Summer," *Legacy* (Sandy Spring, Maryland: Sandy Spring Museum, 2002) Winter Edition.

19--- R. Bloomberg, "WW II Planes to be Deiced." *Engineering Report*, March 9, 1989.

20---See Hammer, C.U., H.B. Clausen, W. Dansgaard, N. Gundestrup, S.J. Johnsen, and N. Reeh, 1978. "Dating of Greenland Ice Cores by Flow Models, Isotopes, Volcanic Debris, and Continental Dust." *Journal of Glaciology*, 20:3.

21---Larry Vardiman, "Greenland Ice Cores," *CreationDigest.com.*, Winter, 2002; an updated version of "Impact Article #226" published by *The Institute for Creation Research* , April, 1992.

22---Kurt P. Wise, *Faith, Form and Time* (Nashville: Broadman & Holman, Publishers, 2002) 200, referencing the bending of Cambrian tapeats sandstone along a Cretaceous fault in the Grand Canyon (Steven A. Austin, "Geologic Structure of Grand Canyon," in Austin, Grand Canyon, 1994, 9-19), and the bending of rocks in the desert of southeastern California (Austin and Morris, "Tight Folds and Clostic Dikes," in Walsh, 1987).

23---Ariel A. Roth, *Origins* (Hagerstown, Md.: Review and Herald Publ. Assn., 1998), p. 216; citing J. S. Shelton, *Geology Illustrated* (San Francisco and London: W. H. Freeman and Co.) 28.

24---Tom Vail, *The Grand Canyon: A Different View* (Green Forest, Arkansas: Master Books, 2003) 9.

25---Leonard Brand, *Faith, Reason, and Earth History.* Berrien Springs, Mich.: Andrews University Press, 1997) 213, 217.

26---Richard Milton, *Shattering the Myths of Darwinism* (Rochester, Vermont.: Park Street Press, 1997) 77, 78.

27---Kathy Sawyer, "New Light on a Mysterious Epoch," *The Washington Post* (February 5, 1998).

28---John C. Whitcomb and Henry M. Morris, *The Genesis Flood* (Phillipsburg, New Jersey: Presbyterian and Reformed Publishing Company, 1995) 203.

29---Ida Thompson, *National Audubon Society Field Guide to North American Fossils* (New York: Alfred A. Knopf, Inc., 1994) 765.

30---Gretel Schueller, "Earth News: Death in the Dunes," *Earth* (June 1998) 11.

31---Luis Chiappe, "Dinosaur Embryos," *National Geographic* (December 1998) 38.

32---Milton, 92.

33---Milton, 93.

34---See *The Washington Post Weekly Edition*, June 13-19, 2005, 10.

35---See Trevor Major, *Genesis & the Origin of Coal* (Montgomery, Alabama: Apologetics Press, 1996).

36--- Scott M. Huse, *The Collapse of Evolution* (Grand Rapids, Michigan: Baker, 1997) 96. A 1910 Geological Survey of Canada pictured a polystrate tree protruding vertically through multiple layers of sedimentary rock. (See photo, Ian T. Taylor, *In the Minds of Men* (Minneapolis: TFE Publishing, 1996) 114.

37---Rob Crilly, "Remote Somali Village Reels from Latest Hardship," *USA Today*, January 7, 2005, 5A.

38---See Chris Hawley, 'Researchers Explore Mysteries Surrounding 65-million-year-old Crater," *USA Today*, March 2, 2005, 9D.

39---See William Ryan and Walter Pitman, *Noah's Flood* (New York: Simon & Schuster, 1998).

Chapter 12

1---Giuseppe Sermonti, *Why is a Fly not a Horse?* (Seattle: Discovery Institute Press, 2005) 13.

2---Arthur Eddington, *The Nature of the Physical World* (McMillan, 1929) as cited by Granville Sewell, "Evolution and the Second Law of Thermodynamics," www.isic.org, January, 2004.

3---For a detailed discussion see www.secondlaw.com/two.

4---Granville Sewell, "Evolution and the Second Law of Thermodynamics," www.isic.org/boards/ubb-get_topic-f-10-t-000038, January, 2004. Dr. Sewell serves in the Mathematics Department of Texas A&M University. Serious scholars deserve a look at Dr. Sewell's examination of evolution theory in the context of the second law of thermodynamics.

5---Andrew McIntosh, writing on the laws of thermodynamics and entropy, John F. Ashton, Ed., *In Six Days* (Sydney: New Holland Publishers, Ltd., 1999) 143-146.

6---Granville Sewell, "Evolution and the Second Law of Thermodynamics," (International Society for Complexity and Design) www.iscid.org, January, 2004.

7---William A. Hoesch, "Arctic Heat Wave," *Back to Genesis*, August, 2006, c.

8---Michael E. Soule and L. Scott Mills, "No Need to Isolate Genetics," *Science* (November 27, 1998) 1659; citing M. E. Gilpin and M. E. Soule, in *The Science of Scarcity and Diversity* (Sunderland, Mass.: A, Sinauer, 1986) 35-56; P. L. Leberg, *J. Fish Biol.* 37 (1990) 193; D. Newman and D. Pilson, *Evolution* 51 (1997) 354; and L. Saccheri, et al., *Nature* 392 (1998) 491. See *Science* (November 27, 1998).

9---Timothy F. Flannery, "Debating Extinction," *Science* 283 (January 8, 1999) 182; quoting from Alfred Russell Wallace, *The Geographical Distribution of Animals, With a Study of the Relations of Living and Extinct Faunas as Elucidating Past Changes of the Earth's Surface* (New York: Harper, 1876) 150.

10---Darwin, *Origin*, 647.

11---Darwin, *Origin*, 453.

12---Yuri N. Ivanov, "Laws of Fertility, Role of Natural Selection, and Destructiveness of Mutations." *Creation Research Society Quarterly*, Vol. 17, December, 2000, 157.

13---Duane Arthur Schmidt, *And God Created Darwin* (Fairfax, Virginia: Allegiance Press, 2001) 131.

14---D. S. Allen and J. B. Delair, *Cataclysm* (Santa Fe, N. M.: Bear & Co., 1997) 107.

15---*Creation*, 24(2):54, March-May, 2002.

16---John Yeld, "Fossil Tracks of Giant Scorpion a World First," *Independent Online 2002*, August 29, 2002.

17---See Ronald Pickering, *Nature Science Update*, 30 January 2002, online report Info@CreationResearch.net, February 14, 2002,

18---Dennis R. Peterson, *Unlocking the Mysteries of Creation* (El Dorado, California: Creation Resource Publications, 2002) 28.

19---Ariel A. Roth, *Origins*. (Hagerstown, Md.: Review and Herald Publishing Association, 1998) 182.

20---William Jacobs, "Goliath Squid by the Side of the Road," *Discover*, May, 2003, 16.

21---*Nature Science Update*, April 30, 2002.

22--- Psalms 106:25, 26, *Bible*, New International Version.

23---Romans 8:22, *Bible*, New International Version.

Chapter 13

1---Hannes Alfvén, Nobel Prize winning physicist, as quoted by Eric J. Lerner, "The Big Bang Never Happened," *Discover* 9 (June 1988), 78.

2---Robert Jastrow, *Until the Sun Dies* (New York, W.W. Norton, 1977) 2-3, as cited by Bert Thompson, "The Big Bang Theory---A Scientific Critique," *Reason and Revelation*, May, 2003) 23(5):32-47.

3---Don Page, "Inflation Does Not Explain Time Assymetry," *Nature* July 7, 1983, 304:40.

4---Fred Hoyle, "The Big Bang Under Attack," *Science Digest*, May, 1984, 92:[5]:84.

5---John Gribbin, "Thumbs Up for An Older Universe," *New Scientist* (1986, 110[1511]:30).

6---Jeff Lindsay, *The Bursting of the Big Bang* (Website jefflindsay.com/BigBang, 2001).

7---Tom Wolfe, *American Spectator Online*, Monday, January 10, 2005.

8---Bert Thompson, "The Big Bang Theory---A Scientific Critique," *Reason and Revelation*, May, 2003) 23(5):32-47.

9---Brad Lemley, "Guth's Grand Guess," *Discover* (Vol. 23, April 2002) 35.

10---Paul Davies, *The Edge of Infinity* (New York: Simon and Schuster, 1981) 161.

11---"Celestial Settings Realign for Famous Photo," *USA Today*, September 14, 2005, 5D.

12---*The Washington Post*, Tuesday, April 23, 2002.

13---Isaiah 40: 22, 26, 28, NIV.

14---Dean L. Overman, *A Case Against Accident and Self-Organization*, 40, 41.

15---Percival Davis, Dean H. Kenyon, and Charles B. Thaxton, Academic Editor, *Of Pandas and People* (Dallas: Haughton Publishing Company, 1993) 3, 4.

16---Ralph O. Muncaster, *Creation Versus Evolution* (Mission Viejo, Calif.: Strong Basis to Believe, 1997) 17.

17---Percival Davis, Dean H. Kenyon, and Charles B. Thaxton, Academic Editor, *Of Pandas and People*, 3.

18---Overman, 42.

19---Michael Denton, *Evolution: A Theory in Crisis* (Bethesda, Md.: Adler & Adler, 1986) 261, 262.

20---Genesis 1:2, *The Holy Bible, New International Version* (Grand Rapids: Zondervan Bible Publishers, 1983).

21---Rick Weiss, "Water Scarcity Prompts Scientists to Look Down," *Washington Post*, March 10, 2003, A-11.

22---Harold Coffin with Robert H. Brown, *Origin by Design*, 1983 edition, 376, citing James F. Coppedge, *Evolution: Possible or Impossible?* (Grand Rapids, Mich.: Zondervan Publishing House, 1973) 109.

23---Harold Coffin with Robert H. Brown, *Origin by Design*, 376, citing Harold T. Morowitz, *Energy Flow in Biology* (New York: Academic Press, 1968).

24---Denton, 323.

25---Overman, 44.

26---Davis, Kenyon, and Thaxton, 5.

27---Walt Brown, *In the Beginning: Compelling Evidence for Creation and the Flood* (Phoenix, Ariz.: Center for Scientific Creation, 1996) 11, 12.

28---David F. Coppedge, "How Big is God?", *Back to Genesis*, No. 210, (El Cajon, California: Institute for Creation Research, June, 2006) d.

29---Richard Dawkins, *The Selfish Gene* (London: Oxford University Press, 1976) 1, as cited by Michael Denton, 75.

30---Richard Milton, *Shattering the Myths of Darwinism* (Rochester, Vermont: Park Street Press, 1997) ix, citing *New Statesman*, 8.28, 1992.

31---Francis Crick, *Life Itself* (New York: Simon & Schuster, 1981) 88, as quoted by Denton, 268, and Thomas Woodward, *Doubts About Darwin*, (Grand Rapids: Baker Books, 2003) 45.

Chapter 14

1---Michael Denton, *Evolution: A Theory in Crises* (Bethesda, Maryland: Adler & Adler, 1986) 358.

2---Barry Yeoman, "Sweitzer's Dangerous Discovery," *Discover*, Vol. 27, No. 4, April, 2006, 37.

3---See Anne Weil, "Living Large in the Cretaceous," (*Nature*, 433, January 13, 2005) 116; Joseph Verrengia, "Fossils Show a Mammal Turned Tables, Devoured Dinosaur for Last Meal," (*Nature*, January 13, 2005) 433; cited by Bert Thompson, and Eric Lyons, "Dinosaurs and Humans---Together," (*Reason and Revelation*, 25 (3), 2005) 17-23.

4---Samuel Wang and Ethel R. Nelson, *God and the Ancient Chinese* (Dunlap, Tennessee: Read Books, 1998) 31.

5---Robert H. Brown letter to Warren L. Johns, 26 November 2003.

6--- Hebrews 1:1, 2, New International Version of the Bible.

7---Frank Lewis Marsh, "On Creation with an Appearance of Age," *Creation Research Society Quarterly*, 1978, 14[4] 187, 188 as cited by Bert Thompson, *Creation Compromises* (Montgomery, Alabama: Apologetics Press, 2000) 270. Dr. Marsh, a visionary scientist, articulated his views at the fulcrum of a growing interest in origins, late in the 20th century.

8---This summary is based upon the eyewitness account of Dr. Harold G. Coffin, paleontologist, who walked Surtsey July, 1967.

9---Henry M. Morris, *Scientific Creationism* (Green Forest, Ark: Master Books, 2001) 121. The late Dr. Morris, founder of the Institute for Creation Research, held a University of Minnesota doctorate in Geology, Mathematics, and Hydraulics.

10---Representatives of this blue ribbon panel presented updated findings to the Fifth International Creation Conference meeting near Pittsburgh in August, 2003. Presenters included Dr. Larry Vardiman, Dr. Steven Austin, Dr. Andrew A. Snelling, Dr. John R. Baumgardner, and Dr. D. Russell Humphreys.

11---See Don DeYoung, *Thousands...Not Billions* (Green Forest, Arkansas: 2005) summarizing *Radioisotopes and the Age of the Earth*, Vol. 1, 2000 and Vol. II, 2005, edited by Larry Vardiman, Andrew A. Snelling and Eugene F. Chaffin(published jointly by Institute for Creation Research, El Cajon, California and Creation Research Society, Chino Valley, Arizona).

12---Trevor Major, *Problems in Radiometric Dating* (Montgomery, Alabama: Apologetics Press, Inc.: undated publication from the "Research Article Series") 23.

13---Major, 10.

14---Robert H. Brown letter to Warren L. Johns, 26 November 2003.

15---Richard Milton, *Shattering the Myths of Darwinism* (Rochester, Vermont: Park Street Press, 1997) 38, 39.

16---Richard Milton, see endnote 14.

17---Erik Stokstad, "Gutsy Fossil Sets Record for Staying the Course," *Science*, Vol. 302, 5 December 2003, 1645.

18---Gunter Faure, *Principles of Isotope Geology* (Somerset, N.J.: John Wiley and Sons, Inc., 1986), 120, 121, 291; Copyright 1986, John Wiley & Sons, Inc. Reprinted by permission of John Wiley & Sons, Inc. as cited in Robert H. Brown letter to Warren L. Johns, October 22, 1995.

19---John Morris & Steven A. Austin, *Footprints in the Ash*, (Green Forest, Arkansas: Master Books, 2003) 67.

20---See Steven A. Austin, "Excess Argon with Mineral Concentrations From the New Dacite Lava Dome at Mount St. Helens Volcano," *Creation Ex Nihilo Technical Journal*10 (1996), part 3; cited by *Acts and Facts*, Institute for Creation Research (May,1997) 26:5.

21---Michael A. Cremo and Richard L. Thompson, *Forbidden Archeology* (Los Angeles: Bhaktivedanta Book Publishing, Inc., 1996) 694.

22---Andrew A. Snelling, "The Cause of Anomalous Potassium-Argon 'Ages' for Recent Andesite Flows at Mt. Ngauruhoe, New Zealand, and the Implications for Potassium-Argon Dating," *ICC Symposium Sessions* (Pittsburgh: Creation Science Fellowship, Inc., 1998) 510; *The Fifth International Conference on Creationism* (Pittsburgh: Creation Science Fellowship, Inc., 2003) 285-303.

23---Milton, 53-55.

24---Robert H. Brown letter to Warren L. Johns, 26 November 2003.

25---Robert A. Kerr, "A Call for Telling Better Time Over the Eons," *Science,* Vol. 302, 17 October 2003, 375.

26---R.L. Wysong, *The Creation-Evolution Controversy.* (East Lansing, Michigan: Inquiry Press, 1976) 348.

27---Leonard Brand, *Faith, Reason and Earth History,* (Berrien Springs, Michigan: Andrews University Press, 1997) 252.

28---Andrew A. Snelling, Ph.D., and Mark H. Armitage, "Radiohalos---A Tale of Three Granitic Plutons," *The Fifth International Conference on Creationism,* Robert L.. Ivey, Jr., Editor (Pittsburgh: Creation Science Fellowship, 2003) 260.

29--- Andrew Snelling letter to Warren L. Johns, December 5, 2003.

30---See Robert V. Gentry, *Creation's Tiny Mystery* (Knoxville: Earth Science Associates, 1992).

31---See Snelling & Armitage, endnotes 27 & 28.

32---Ariel A. Roth, *Origins* (Hagerstown, Maryland: Review & Herald Publishing Association, 1998) 268.

33---Andrew A. Snelling, "The Fallacies of Radioactive Dating of Rocks: Basalt Lave Flows in Grand Canyon," *Answers*, Vol. 1, No. 1, July/Sept., 2006, 67, 68.

34---Roth, 262, 271.

35---Roth, 268, 269.

36---Roth, 262, 272.

37---Brand, 253.

38---Roth, "Implications of Paraconformities," *Geoscience Reports*, No. 36, Fall 2003, 1-4.

39---Brand, 260; see also Robert H. Brown, *Origins*, Volume 12, 1985, 8-25; Brown and Webster, 1991.

40---See Dita Smith and Laura Stanton, "Population Momentum," *The Washington Post* (1996); citing Population Reference Bureau, World Bank, "World Population Projections." Copyright 1996, *The Washington Post*. See also, Joel E. Cohen, "Human Population: the Next Half Century," *Science*, Vol. 302, 14 November 2003) 1172-1175.

41---Kathy Sawyer, "Ancient Footprints Discovered," *The Washington Post* (August 15, 1997).

42---D. Russell Humphreys, Ph.D. with John R. Baumgardner, Ph.D., Steven A. Austin, Ph.D., and Andrew A. Snelling, Ph.D., "Helium Diffusion Rates Support Accelerated Nuclear Decay," *The Fifth International Conference on Creationism* Robert L. Ivey, Jr., Editor (Pittsburgh: Creation Science Fellowship, 2003) 175-195. See also, D. Russell Humphreys, "New Rate Data Support a Young Earth," *Impact* #366, Institute for Creation Research, December, 2003. It should be noted that Dr. Humphreys pinpointed "an age of *only* 6,000 years" in his original quote.

43---Milton, 46.

44---Brown, "The Upper Limit of C-14 Age," *Origins*, Volume 15, 1988, 39.

45---Brand, 262, referencing P.A.L. Giem, *Scientific Theology*, (Riverside, California: La Sierra University Press, 1997) 134-137.

46---Paul Giem, "Carbon-14 Content of Fossil Carbon," *Origins*, Number 51, 2001, 6.

47---John Baumgardner, Ph.D., with D. Russell Humphreys, Ph.D.., Ph.D., Steven A. Austin, Ph.D., and Andrew A. Snelling, Ph.D., "Measurable ^{14}C in Fossilized Organic Materials," *The Fifth International Conference on Creationism 2003*, 127; and reported in *Acts & Facts*, Vol. 32, No. 10, October 2003.

48---See Baumgardner, endnote 47.

49---See Baumgardner, endnote 47.

Chapter 15

1---Jonathan Wells, *Icons of Evolution* (Washington, DC: Regnery Publishing. Inc., 2000), p. 188.

2---See Dr. Richard M. Cornelius's definitive summary of the trial , "Scopes Trial: The Trial Gavel Heard Round the World," (*www.CreationDigest.com*, Winter, 2006) as excerpted from *Impact* (Dayton, Tennessee: Bryan College, 2000) v-xiii.

3---Fay Cooper-Cole, *The Scopes Trial* (Birmingham, Ala.: The Legal Classics Library, 1984) 237; a reprint of *The World's Most Famous Trial* [Cincinnati: National Book Co., 1925]), pp. 238-241.

4---See *The Washington Post*, 11-3-2003.

5---Ian T. Taylor, *In the Minds of Men* (Minneapolis, Minn.: TFE Publishing, 1991) 231-233.

6---Jerry Bergman, "Controversy in Paleoanthropology," *Creation Matters*, Vol. 11, Number 1, January/February, 2006, 1, 3-5, and quoting from J. Talent, "The Case of the Peripatetic Fossils," *Nature*, 338:613-615.

7---Peter Line, "Upper Paleolithic Blues: Consequences of Recent Dating Fiasco on Human Evolutionary Prehistory," *Technical Journal*, 19(2) 2005.

8---Sei Chong and Dennis Normile, "How Young Korean Researchers Helped Unearth a Scandal," *Science*, Vol. 311, 6 January 2006, 22, 25; and Jennifer Couzin, "And How the Problems Eluded Peer Reviewers and Editors," *Science*, 23, 24; and, D. Yvette Wohn and Dennis Normile, "Prosecutors Allege Elaborate Deception and Missing Funds," *Science*, Vol. 312, 19 May 2006, 980.

9---Ernst Haeckel, *The Wonders of Life*, translation, J. McCabe (London: Watts, 1905) 11.

10---Ian T. Taylor, *In the Minds of Men.*

11---Michael K. Richardson, "Haeckel's Embryos, Continued," *Science* 281 (August 28, 1998) 1289.

12---The words of Joe Baker and Karen Sterling are excerpted from the *CNN.com* transcript of *CNN Newsroom*, May 3, 2001. See also Phillip Johnson's "Icons of Evolution Exposed on CNN," *Weekly Wedge Update*, May 7, 2001, which referenced the CNN transcript.

13---See endnote 12.

14---David Raup, "Letter to the Editor," *Science*, 213 July 17, 1981, 289.

15---Ian T. Taylor, "The Ultimate Hoax: Archaeopteryx Lithographica," *Proceedings of the Second International Conference on Creationism, Vol II* (Pittsburgh: Creation Science Fellowship, Inc., 1990) 279-291. Taylor's opinions deserve reading in full.

16---Ian T. Taylor, see endnote 15.

17---Ian T. Taylor, "The Ultimate Hoax: Archaeopteryx Lithographica," 281-282.

18---Ian T. Taylor, see endnote 15.

19---Alan Feduccia, T. Lingham-Soliar and J.R. Hinchliffe, *Journal of Morphology* (2005) 266(2): 125-166 as reported by David Coppedge, "Have We Been Sold a Bill of Goods About Dinosaurs and Bird Evolution?", *Creation Matters* (St. Joseph, Missouri: Creation Research Society, September/October, 2005) 6, 7.

20---Phillip E. Johnson, *The Wedge of Truth* (Downers Grove, Illinois: InterVarsity Press, 2000) 37.

21--- Susan Kruglinski, "Whatever Happened to Global Cooling?" *Discover*, February, 2006, 10.

22---Søren Løvtrup (Swedish biologist), Darwinism: The Refutation of a Myth (New York: Croom Helm, 1987) 422.

Chapter 16

1---See N. J. Mitchell, *Evolution and the Emperor's New Clothes* (United Kingdom: Roydon Publications, 1983), title page, quoted in *The Revised Quote Book* (Acacia Ridge, Queensland, Australia: Creation Science Foundation, 1990), 5. See also The *Fresno Bee*, August 20, 1959. Theodore N. Tahmisian served the U.S. Atomic Energy Commission.

2---*The New York Times*, May 26, 1925, 1.

3---Wilma Humphreys, a student in John Scopes biology class, shared this information with the author in a recorded interview.

4---John Thomas Scopes, statement to the press at the Scopes Trial, quoted in P. Davis and E. Solomon, *The World of Biology* (1974) 414.

5---William Jennings Bryan, as quoted in *Science & Religion*, 1988, 46.

6---Adams, Leslie B., Jr., Editor/Publisher, *The Scopes Trial* (Birmingham, Alabama: The Legal Classics Library, 1984; a reprint of *The World's Most Famous Trial* (Third Edition) Cincinnati: National Book Company, 1925, 84. 75.

7---Adams, Leslie B. Jr., 75 & 84.

8---Albert Fleischmann, "The Doctrine of Organic Evolution in the Light of Modern Research," *Journal of the Transactions of the Victoria Institute* 65 (1933): 194-95, 205-6, 208-9.

9---Randy L. Wysong, *The Creation-Evolution Controversy: Implications, Methodology and Survey of Evidence-Toward a Rational Solution* (East Lansing, Michigan: Inquiry Press, 1976) 434; as cited by Duane Arthur Schmidt, *And God Created Darwin* (Fairfax, Virginia: Allegiance Press, 2001) 84, quoting from John Ankerberg and John Weldon's, *Darwin's Leap of Faith.*

10---Wolfgang Smith, *Teilhardism and the New Religion* (Rockford., Ill.: Tan Books, 1988) 5-6.

11---Stephen Jay Gould, "Evolution's Erratic Pace," *Natural History,* May 1977, 13, 14, cited by Thompson and Harrub, "Creationists Fight Back: A Review of *U.S. News & World Report's* Cover Story on Evolution," (Montgomery, Alabama: Apologetics Press, 2002) 12.

12---Stephen Jay Gould, "The Return of Hopeful Monsters," *Natural History,* June/July 1977, 86[6]:22-30, cited by Brad Harrub, "Creationists Fight Back," 2002, 11.

13---Stephen Jay Gould, *The Panda's Thumb* (New York: W.W. Norton, 1980) 182, cited by Harrub, "Creationists Fight Back," 2002, 12.

14---Stephen Jay Gould, in a speech delivered at Hobart College, February 14, 1980, cited by Luther Sunderland, *Darwin's Enigma* (El Cajon, California: Master Books, 1984) 106, and referenced by Thompson & Harrub.

15---Stephen Jay Gould, "Darwinism Defined: The Difference Between Fact and Theory," *Discover,* January, 1987, 8[1]:64-65, 68-70, as cited by Thompson and Harrub, "15 Answers to John Rennie and *Scientific American's* Nonsense" (Montgomery, Alabama: Apologetics Press, 2002) 10.

16---*Gitlow v. New York*, 268 U.S. 652 (1925).

17---Charles Darwin, Introduction, *The Origin of Species* (London: J.M. Dent & Sons, 1956 edition) 19.

18---John G. West, "Censorship of Intelligent Design Will Generate More Interest In It," *USA Today,* Thursday, December 22, 2005.

19---Rod LeVake "Interview," *www.CreationDigest.com,* Autumn Edition, 2003.

20---Rod LeVake "Interview", *www.CreationDigest.com,* Autumn Edition, 2003.

21---Nancy Bryson, "Interview," *www.CreationDigest.com,* Summer Edition, 2003.

22---Nancy Bryson, "Interview," *www.CreationDigest.com,* Summer Edition, 2003.

23---Art Toalston, "Intelligent Design Festers," *Baptist Press,* Tuesday, October 24, 2000.

24---Peter E. Volpe, *Science as a Way of Knowing,* 1984, 439.

25---The "National Center for Science Education," boasts its purpose is to defend "...the teaching of evolution in public schools" and "...to keep evolution in the science classroom…[while claiming to be] the only national organization to   specialize in this issue."

26---Mark Singham, "Teaching and Propaganda," *Physics Today*, (vol. 53, June 2000) 54; as quoted by Henry B. Morris, *Impact*, February, 2001.

27---Sharon Begley, "Is Science Censored?" Newsweek, September 14, 1992, 63, cited by Bert Thompson and Brad Harrub, "15 Answers to John Rennie and *Scientific* American's Nonsense," (Montgomery, Alabama: Apologetics Press, 2002) 22.

28---James Watson, *The Double Helix* (New York: Antheneum, 1968) 14, cited by Bert Thompson and Brad Harrub, "15 Answers to John Rennie and *Scientific American's* Nonsense," (Montgomery, Alabama: Apologetics Press, 2002) 22.

29---Phillip Abelson (former *Science* editor), "Bigotry in Science," *Science*, April 24,1964, 144:373, cited by Bert Thompson and Brad Harrub, "15 Answers to John Rennie and *Scientific American's* Nonsense," (Montgomery, Alabama: Apologetics Press, 2002) 22.

30---Homer Montgomery, University of Texas, Dallas, as reported by Ken Ham, *Answers in Genesis* newsletter, March, 2003.

31---Michael Dini, Texas Tech University, outline of pre-conditions for letters of recommendation for students to enter medical school as reported by Ken Ham, *Answers in Genesis* newsletter, March, 2003.

32---Larry A. Witham, *Where Darwin Meets the Bible* (New York: Oxford University Press, 2002) 270.

33---Jonathan Wells, "Survival of the Fittest," *The American Spectator*, December 2000/January 2001,19, 20, as cited by Jobe Martin, *The Evolution of a Creationist* (Rockwall, Texas: Biblical Discipleship Publishers, 1994) 251.

34--- Barry Yeoman, "Schweitzer's Dangerous Discovery," *Discover*, April, 2006, 40.

35---Phillip E. Johnson, *The Wedge*, (Downers Grove, Illinois: InterVarsity Press, 2000) 37.

36---T.N. Tahmisian, served the U.S. Atomic Energy Commission. See N.J. Mitchell, *Evolution and the Emperor's New Clothes* (United Kingdom: Roydon Publications, 1983) title page, referenced in *The Revised Quote Book* (Acacia Ridge, Queensland, Australia: Creation Science Foundation, 1990) 5.

37---John Dunphy, *The Humanist*, Jan/Feb. 1983, 26.

38---Lynn Z. Bloom, *Doctor Spock: Biography of a Conservative Radical* (Indianapolis/ New York: The Bobbs-Merrill Company, Inc., 1972) 213, referencing Benjamin Spock (M.D.), *Decent and Indecent. Our Personal and Political Behavior*,as cited by Jerry

Bergman, "The 'Baby Doctor,' Benjamin Spock, on Darwin and Morality," *Impact*. February 2003.

39---Psalms 14:1, *Bible, New International Version* (Grand Rapids: Zondervan Bible Publishers, 1978).

40---John Clover Monsma, *Behind the Dim Unknown* (New York: G.P. Putnam's Sons, 1966) 49.

41---Sir William Dawson, *The Story of Earth and Man* (New York: Harper and Brothers, 1887), pp. 317, 322, 330, 339. Dawson, pioneered Canadian geology and served as president of McGill University as well as the British Association for the Advancement of Science.

Chapter 17

1---Justice William J. Brennan, *Edwards v. Aguillard*, 482 U.S. 578-594 (1987)

2---Ellen Dutton, ellenc2c@msn.com.

3---"Results from Nationwide Pole" (February 27 to March 2, 2006) Zogby International, http://www.discovery.org. See also Brad Harrub, "Survey Says---Teach the Controversy," www.ApologeticsPress.org.

4---Associated Press, "'Intelligent Design' Debate Moves Into Federal Courtroom," *USA Today*, September 27, 2005.

5---Jill Lawrence, "Intelligent Design Is Religious, Judge Says," *USA Today*, Wednesday, December 21, 2005, 1, 3A. The US District Court for the MiddleDistrict of Pennsylvania, ruled on December 20, 2005 in the case of *Tammy Kitzmiller, et.al. v. Dover Area School District, et.al.* The 139 page opinion was rendered by republican Judge John E. Jones, a George Bush appointee.

6---Jill Lawrence, See endnote #5.

7---Jill Lawrence, See endnote #5.

8---Jill Lawrence, See endnote #5.

9---*The Washington Post*, Sunday, December 25, 2995, B5.

10---John G. West, "Censorship of Intelligent Design Will Generate More Interest In It," *USA Today*, Thursday, December 22, 2005.

11---Jill Lawrence, See endnote #5.

12---John G. West, See endnote #10.

13---John G. West, "Dover in Review," *Discovery Institute News*, January 6, 2006.

14---"Law Center Asks U.S. Supreme Court to Take Up Hostility to Religion Case,"*Thomas More Law Center News Alert*, Tuesday, Jan 24, 2006.

15---*The Washington Post*, Sunday, December 25, 2005, B5.

16---Internet, www.lucidcafe.com/library/96feb/galileo.html.

17---*Buono v. Norton*, 371 F. 3rd 543, 545, (9th Cir. 2004).

18---*Gitlow v. New York*, 268 U.S. 652, 666 (1925).

19---*McLean v. Arkansas*, 529 F. Supp. 1255 (E.D. Ark. 1982).

20---Justice William J. Brennan, writing for the majority, *Edwards v. Aguillard*, 482 U.S. 578-594 (1987).

21---Justice Lewis F. Powell's concurring opinion, citing *McGowan v. Maryland*, 366 U.S. 420, 422 (1961), *Edwards v. Aguillard*, 482 U.S. 605 (1987).

22---Justice Anton Scalia's Dissent, *Edwards v. Aguillard*, 482 U.S. 578-594 (1987).

23---See Warren L. Johns, "First Amendment Religious Liberty Guarantees: Neutrality Not Hostility," *Liberty*, July/August, 2005.

24---*Epperson v. Arkansas*, 393 U.S. 97 (1968), as cited by John H. Calvert, Esq. before the Standards Committee of the Ohio State Board of Education, January 13, 2001.

25---Richard W. Garnett, "Two Justices Who 'Get' Religion," *USA Today*, January 23, 2006, 11A.

26---Michael Ruse, "The New Anti-Evolutionism," Speech to the Symposium, Annual Meeting of the AAAS, February 13, 1993 as reported by David K. DeWolf, Stephen C. Meyer, Mark E. DeForrest, "Intelligent Design in Public School Science Curricula: A Legal Guidebook," *Foundation for Thought and Ethics*, 1999, 12.

27---Michael Ruse, "How Evolution Became a Religion." *National Post Online*, May 13, 2000. (www.nationalpost.com). See Glen W. Wolfrom, PhD, "Gish Was Right!" Creation Matters, May-June 2000, 8, 9. See also, Michael Ruse, "Saving Darwinism from the Darwinians," *National Post* (May 13, 2000) B-3; as cited by Henry B. Morris, "Evolution is Religion---not Science," *Impact*, February, 2001.

28---Michael Ruse, *The Evolution-Creation Struggle* (Cambridge: Harvard University Press, 2005) 287.

29---Claire Moore, "1925 Monkey Trial Still With Us," www.*ABCNEWS*.com, July 23, 2000.

30---H.S. Lipson, "A Physicist Looks at Evolution," *Physics Bulletin* 31 (May 1980), 138.

31---Justice Anton Scalia's Dissent, *Edwards v. Aguillard*, 482 U.S. 578-594 (1987).

32---See Wayne Frair's, "Can You Tell Me Anything about Evolution?" as published online, www.*CreationDigest*, Autumn Edition, 2001.

33---Will Provine, "No Free Will," *Catching Up with the Vision*, Ed. By Margaret W. Rossiter (Chicago: University of Chicago Press, 1999) S123; as quoted by Henry B. Morris.

34---Paul Lemoine abandoned evolution and as chief editor of the *Encyclopedie Francaise* wrote his views in the 1937 edition as cited by Henry M. Morris, *Men of Science-Men of God* (El Cajon, Calif: Master Books, 1988) 84.

35---T. N. Tahmisian referenced by N. J. Mitchell, *Evolution and the Emperor's New Clothes* (United Kingdom: Roydon Publications, 1983) title page, as quoted in *The Revised Quote Book* (Acacia Ridge, Queensland, Australia: Creation Science Foundation, 1990) 5.

36---Randy L. Wysong, *The Creation-Evolution Controversy: Implications, Methodology and Survey of Evidence-Toward a Rational Solution* (East Lansing, Michigan: Inquiry Press, 1976) 434; as cited by Duane Arthur Schmidt, *And God Created Darwin* (Fairfax, Virginia: Allegiance Press, 2001) 84, quoting from John Ankerberg and John Weldon's, *Darwin's Leap of Faith*.

37---Duane Arthur Schmidt, *And God Created Darwin* (Fairfax, Virginia: Allegiance Press, 2001) Introduction, xi.

38---David K. DeWolf, Stephen C. Meyer and Mark E. DeForrest, *Intelligent Design in Public School Science Curricula: A Legal Guidebook Foundation for Thought and Ethics*, 1999, 16 & 3..

39---Howard Glicksman, "Sex and the Single Gene: Becoming a Man is not as Easyas X+Y," internet, www.ARN.org, *Exercise Your Wonder*, September 1, 2005.

Chapter 18

1---Duane Arthur Schmidt, *And God Created Darwin* (Fairfax, Virginia: Allegiance Press, 2001) Introduction, p. xi.

2---Charles Darwin, *The Descent of Man and Selection in Relation to Sex,* Vol. II, 327, 328.

3---Darwin, *Descent*, Vol. 1, 169.

4---Andrew Carnegie, *Autobiography of Andrew Carnegie*, ed. John C. Van Dyke (reprint, Boston: Northeastern U. Press, 1986) 327 as cited by James Perloff, *The Case Against Darwin* (Burlington Massachusetts: Refuge Books, 2002) 10, 11.

5---Darwin, *Descent*, Vol. I, 178.

6---Darwin, *Descent*, Vol. I, 216

7---Darwin, *Descent*, Vol. I, 169.

8---Darwin, *Descent*, Vol. I, 201.

9---Darwin, *The Origin of Species*, 468.

10---Paul Kildare, "Monkey Business," *Christian Order*, Vol. 23 (December 1982) 591as cited by Henry M. Morris, *Their Words Against Them* (San Diego: Institute for Creation Research, 1997) 231.

11---Ruth Hubbard and Elijah Wald, *Exploding the Gene Myth* (Boston: Beacon Press, 1997) 14; citing Francis Galton, *Inquiries Into Human Faculty* (London: Macmillan, 1883) 24, 25.

12---Darwin, *Descent*, Vol. I, 168, 169.

13---Norman Macbeth, *Darwin Retried*, 57; citing George Bernard Shaw, "Preface,"*Back to Methuselah* (Penguin paperback, 1921).

14---Richard Weikart, *From Darwin to Hitler*, (New York: Palgrave Macmillan, 2004) 166, quoting Oscar Peschel, "Ein Ruckblick auf die jüngste Vergangenheit," *Das Ausland* 39, 36 (September 1866): 874.

15--Richard Weikart, *From Darwin to Hitler* (New York: Palgrave Macmillan, 2004) 177, citing Wilhelm Schallmayer, "Die Auslesewirkungen des Krieges,"*Menschheitsziele 2* (1908): 381-5. Reference to "lower" races represents Schallmayer's words.

16---Perloff, *The Case Against Darwin*, 13, 14 citing Ernst Haeckel, *The Wonders of Life* (New York: Harper, 1904) 56, 57.

17---Adams, *The Scopes Trial*, 336, 337; citing Benjamin Kidd, *The Science of Power* (1918) 46, 47 and 67 as referenced by William Jennings Bryan in a draft summary intended for presentation at the 1925 Scopes Trial.

18---Conway Zirkle, *Evolution, Marxian Biology, and the Social Scene* (Philadelphia:U. of Philadelphia Press, 1959) 86 cited by Perloff, *The Case Against Darwin*, 10.

19---Phillip Kennicott, "The Seduction of Science to Perfect and Imperfect Race," *The Washington Post*, April 22, 2004, C 1 & 5, quoting Sara J. Bloomfield.

20---See Herb Ford's, *Flee the Captor* (Nashville: Southern Publishing Assn., 1966).

21---See Edward Gibbon, The History of the Decline and Fall of the Roman Empire.

Chapter 19

1--- Wernher von Braun, as quoted by James Perloff, *Tornado in a Junkyard* (Arlington, Massachusetts: Refuge Books, 1999) 253.

2---Werner Gitt, *In the Beginning Was Information* (Green Forest, Arkansas: Master Books, 2006) 52.

3---Gitt, 53, 54.

4---Kyle Butt, "Stuck on Design," (2006), www.ApologeticsPress.org/articles/2898 referencing Corey Binns, (2006), "World's Strongest Glue! Available Only From Nature," www.livescience.com/animalworld/060410_nature_glue.

5---Dennis Wagner, "2005 Year-end Report" (Internet Website, Access Research Network, Number Fifty, December 1, 2005).

6---Isaiah 1:18, *The Holy Bible, King James Version,* 1611 (New York: Oxford University Press).

7---See John D. Morris, "From Dayton to Dover," *Acts & Facts* (El Cajon, California: Institute for Creation Research, Vol. 35, No. 2, February, 2006) 2, 3.

Chapter 20

1---Rick Warren, *The Purpose Driven Life* (Grand Rapids, Michigan: Zondervan, 2002) 17.

2---Ephesians 3:9, *King James Version of the Bible.*

3---Acts 17:16-32, *New International Version of the Holy Bible,* (Grand Rapids: Zondervan Bible Publishers, 1978).

4---1 Corinthians 15:39, *NIV.*

5---Hebrews 11:7, *NIV.*

6---Romans 1:18-20, *NIV.*

7---Hebrews 1:2, *NIV.*

8---Romans 8:21, *NIV.*

9---2 Corinthians 10:4, 5, *NIV.*

10---2 Timothy 4:6-8, *NIV.*

11---Rick Warren, 17.

12---John 3:16, *NIV.*

13---Mark 10:6, *NIV* (Paraphrasing Gen 1:27). See also Mark 13:19.

14---Mathew 24: 37-39, *NIV.* See also Luke 17:26, 27

15---John 1:3, *NIV.*

16---Nehemiah 9:6, *NIV.*

17---Ephesians 4;24., *NIV.*

18---Mathew 22:37, *NIV.*

19---Psalms 51:10, *NIV.*

20---John 10:10, *The Holy Bible, King James Version,* 1611 (New York: Oxford University Press).

21---John 11:25, 26, *NIV.*

22---Hebrews 12:1, *NIV.*

23--- John 3:16, *NIV.*

24---Matthew 24:21, *The Thompson Chain Reference Bible* (Grand Rapids: Michigan, 1983).

25---Acts24:25, *KJV.*

26---Proverbs 14:12, *NIV*.

27---A thoughtful end line suggested by Christian creationist, Karl C. Priest.

Bibliography

Adams, Leslie B., Jr., Editor/Publisher, *The Scopes Trial* Birmingham, Alabama: The Legal Classics Library, 1984; a reprint of *The World's Most Famous Trial* (Third Edition) Cincinnati: National Book Company, 1925.

Allan, D. S., and J. B. Delair. *Cataclysm.* Santa Fe, N.M.: Bea & Company, 1997.

Appenzeller, Tim. "The Genes of 1996." *Discover,* January, 1997.

_____. "Test Tube Evolution Catches Time in a Bottle, "*Science* 284, June 25, 1999.

Ashton, John F., Editor *In Six Days.* Sydney, Australia: New Holland Publishers, Ltd., 1999, with Andrew McIntosh, writing on the laws of thermodynamics and entropy.

Austin, Steven A. "Excess Argon With Mineral Concentrates From the New Dacite Lava Dome at Mount St. Helens Volcano." *Creation Ex Nihilo Technical Journal,* vol. 10, part 3, 1996; as reported in "Acts and Facts," *Institute for Creation Research,* May, 1997.

_____, Editor. *Grand Canyon: Monument to Catastrophe.*Santee, Calif.: Institute for Creation Research, 1994.

_____, "Interpreting Strata of Grand Canyon," in *Austin,Grand Canyon: Monument to Catastrophe,* Santee, California: Institute for Creation Research. 1994.

_____, "Nautiloid Mass Kill and Burial Event, Redwell Limestone, Grand Canyon Region," Pittsburgh: International Conference on Creationism, 2003.

Austin, Steven A. & William A. Hoesch, "Do Volcanoes Come in Super Size?", *Impact,* Institute for Creation Research, August, 2006.

Behe, Michael J. *Darwin's Black Box,* New York: The Free Press, 1996.

Berlinski, David, *The Incorrigible Dr. Berlinski,* DVD, ColdWater Media, 2004.

Bird, W.R., *The Origin of Species Revisited, Vol. I ,* Nashville: Regency, 1991.

Bounoure, Louis, *The Advocate,* 8 March 1984, quoted in *The Revised Quote Book.*

Bradley, Walter L. and Charles B. Thaxton, "Information and the Origin of Life," in *The Creation Hypothesis,* ed. J.P. Moreland, Downers Grove, Illinois: InterVarsity Press, 1994.

Brand, Leonard. *Faith, Reason, and Earth History.* Berrien Springs, Mich.: Andrews University Press, 1997.

Brinkley, Douglas, "Tour of Duty: John Kerry and the Vietnam War," *Atlantic Monthly,* December, 2003.

Brown, David, "Limits to Genetic Evolution," *The Washington Post,* July 7, 2003, p. A7

Brown, Robert H., "Amino Acid Dating," *Origins,*1985, 12-8-25.

_____, *Letter to Warren L. Johns,* 26 November, 2003.

Brown, Robert H, and C.L. Webster, "Interpretation of Radiocarbon and Amino Acid Data," Origins, 1991.

_____, "The Upper Limit of C-14 Dating?", *Origins,* Volume 15, 1988.

Brown, Walt, *In the Beginning: Compelling Evidence for Creation and the Flood* (Phoenix, Ariz.: Center for Scientific Creation, 1996).

Budd, Graham E. & Maximilian J. Telford, "Evolution: Along Came a Sea Spider," *Nature,* Vol. 437, Oct. 20, 2005, 1099.

Camp, Ashby L., *The Myth of Natural Origins* (Tempe, Arizona: Ktisis Publishing, 1994).

Coffin, Harold, John Hergenrather, Dennis Bokovoy and **Michael Oard,** "Road Guide to Yellowstone National Park," Chino Valley, AZ: Creation Research Society, 2005.

Coffin, Harold, with Robert H. Brown and James Gibson, *Origin By Design*, Hagerstown, Md.: Review and Herald Publishing Association, 1983 and 2005.

Cohen, I. L., *Darwin Was Wrong.* Greenvale, New York: New Research Publications, Inc., 1984.

Coppedge, David F., "How Big is God?", *Back to Genesis,* No. 210. El Cajon, California: Institute for Creation Research, June, 2006.

Cremo, Michael A., and Richard L. Thompson. *Forbidden Archaeology.* Los Angeles: Bhaktivedanta Book Publishing, Inc., 1996.

Crick, Sir Francis, *Life Itself,* New York: Simon Schuster, 1981.

Darwin, Charles, *The Origin of Species* (Sixth Edition), New York: Random House, Inc., 1993.

_____, *The Descent of Man, and Selection in Relation to Sex.* (Princeton, N.J.: Princeton University Press, 1981.

_____, Letter to Asa Gray, cited by Adrian Desmond and James Moore, *Darwin,* New York: W.W. Norton and Company, 1991.

Davies, Paul, *The Cosmic Blueprint: New Discoveries in Nature's Creative Ability to Order the Universe*, New York: Simon and Schuster, 1988.

Davis, Percival & Dean H. Kenyon, Charles B. Thaxton, Academic Editor, *Of Pandas and People*, Dallas: Haughton Publishing Company, 1993.

Dembski, William A., Editor, *Mere Creation*, Downers Grove, Illinois, 1998.

_____, *Intelligent Design*, Downers Grove, Illinois: InterVarsity Press, 1999.

_____, *Uncommon Dissent*, Wilmington, Delaware: ISI Books, 2004.

_____, Editor, *Darwin Nemesis*, Downers Grove, Illinois: InterVarsity Press Academic, 2006.

Denton, Michael, *Evolution: A Theory in Crisis*. Bethesda, Md.: Adler & Adler, 1986.

DeYoung, Don, *Thousands…Not Billions*, Green Forest, Arkansas, 2005.

Dubos, Rene J. ,*Louis Pasteur: Freelance of Science,* New York: Charles Scribner's Sons, 1976.

Eldredge, Niles & Tattersall, *The Myths of Human Evolution*, 1982.

Faure, Gunter, *Principles of Isotope Geology*. Somerset, N.J.: John Wiley and Sons, Inc., 1986.

Fleischman, Albert, "The Doctrine of Organic Evolution in the Light of Modern Research," *Journal of the Transactions of the Victoria Institute* 65, 1933.

Gee, Henry, *In Search of Deep Time: Beyond the Fossil Record to a New History of Life*, New York: The Free Press, 1999.

Gentry, Robert V., *Creation's Tiny Mystery*, Knoxville: Earth Science Associates, 1992.

Gibson, James, Letter to Warren L. Johns. August 28, 1997.

Gish, Duane T., *Evolution: The Fossils Still Say No!* El Cajon, Calif.: Institute for Creation Research, 1995.

_____, *Creation Scientists Answer Their Critics*. El Cajon, Calif.: Institute for Creation Research, 1993.

Gitt, Werner, *In the Beginning was Information*, Green Forest, Arkansas: Master Books, 2006.

_____, "Carbon-14 Content of Fossil Carbon," *Origins*, Number 51, 2001.

Glausiusz, Josie. "Fast Forward Aging." Discover, November 1996.

_____,"The Genes of 1996." *Discover*, January 1997.

Gould, Stephen Jay, *The Panda's Thumb*, New York: W.W. Norton, 1980.

_____, "Cordelia's Dilemma", *Natural History*, Feb 1993.

_____, "The Return of Hopeful Monsters, "*Natural History*, 86[4]:22-30, June-July, 1977.

_____, Speech at Hobart College, February 14, 1980, cited by Luther Sunderland, *Darwin's Enigma*, El Cajon, California: Master Books, 1984 cited by Bert Thompson and Brad Harrub, "*National Geographic* Shoots Itself in the Foot Again," Apologetics Press.Org online report, 2004.

Guillen, Michael, *Five Equations that Changed the World*, New York: Hyperion, 1995.

Hancock, Graham, ***Fingerprints of the Gods***, New York: Crown Publisher, 1995.

Hansen, Kent, *Grace at 30,000 Feet,* Hagerstown, Maryland: Review & Herald Publishing Association, 2002.

Harrub, Brad and Bert Thompson, "Creationists Fight Back: A Review of *U.S. News & World Report's* Cover Story On Evolution," Montgomery, Alabama: Apologetics Press, 2002.

Hayward, Alan. *Creation and Evolution.* Minneapolis: Bethany House Publishers, 1995.

Hoesch, William A., "Arctic Heat Wave," *Back to Genesis,* August, 2006.

Hoyle, Sir Fred, "The Big Bang in Astronomy," *New Scientist,* November 19, 1981, 92:527.

_____, *The Universe: Past and Present Reflections.* Cardiff: University College, 1981.

Hoyle, Sir Fred and Chandra Wickramasinghe, *Evolution from Space,* London: J.M. Dent & Sons, 1981.

Hubbard, Ruth and Elijah Wald, *Exploding the Gene Myth,* Boston: Beacon Press 1997, citing Francis Galton, *Inquiries Into Human Faculty,* London: Macmillan, 1883.

Humphreys, D. Russell Ph.D. with **John R. Baumgardner, Ph.D., Steven A. Austin, Ph.D.,** and **Andrew A. Snelling, Ph.D.,** "Helium Diffusion Rates Support Accelerated Nuclear Decay," *The Fifth International Conference on Creationism,* Robert L. Ivey, Jr., Editor, Pittsburgh: Creation Science Fellowship, 2003.

Hunter, Cornelius G., *Darwin's Proof,* Grand Rapids, Michigan: Brazos Press, 2003.

Hutton, Richard, "Evolution: The Series," *Washington Post.com, Live Online,* Wednesday, September 28, 2001.

Huxley, Sir Julian, *Evolution After Darwin* ed. Sol Tax, vol. 3, Chicago: University of Chicago Press, 1960, the Centennial Celebration of the *Origin of Species.*

_____, "The Emergence of Darwinism," *Evolution of Life,* ed. Sol Tax, Chicago: University of Chicago Press, 1960.

Javor, George, *Evidence for Creation,* Hagerstown, Maryland: Review & Herald Publishing Association, 2005.

Johns, Warren LeRoi. *Ride to Glory,* Brookeville, Maryland: General Title, Inc., 1999.

Johnson, Kirk R. and **Richard K. Stucky** *Prehistoric Journey,* Boulder, Colorado: Roberts Rinehart Publishers, 1995.

Johnson, Phillip E., *Darwin On Trial,* Washington, D.C., Regnery Gateway, 1991.

_____, *Objections Sustained.* Downers Grove, Illinois: InterVarsity Press, 1998.

_____, *The Wedge*, Downers Grove, Illinois: InterVarsity Press, 2000.

Kennicott, Phillip, "The Seduction of Science to Perfect and Imperfect Race," *The Washington* Post, April 22, 2004.

Keosian, John, In Haruhiko Nada, ed., *Origin of Life*, Tokyo: Center for Academic Publications, Japan Scientific Publications Press, 1978.

Kerkut, G.A., *Implications of Evolution*, New York: Pergamon Press, 1965.

Kildare, Paul, "Monkey Business," *Christian Order*, vol. 23, December 1982.

King, Colbert L., "Empty Words for the War Torn," *The Washington Post*. January 24, 2004.

Kruglinski, Susan, "Whatever Happened to Global Cooling?" *Discover*, February, 2006.

Kunzig, Robert. "The Face of an Ancestral Child." *Discovery*, December 1997.

Leakey, Mary D. "Footprints in the Ashes of Time." *National Geographic*, April 1979.

Lerner, Eric J. "The Big Bang Never Happened," *Discover*, 9 June 1988.

Lester, Lane P., and **Raymond G. Bohlin.** *The Natural Limits to Biological Change* Dallas, Texas: Probe Books, 1989.

Løvtrup, Søren. *The Refutation of a Myth*, New York: Croom Helm, 1987.

Lubenow, Marvin L. *Bones of Contention.* Grand Rapids, Michigan: Baker Books, 1992, 2004.

MacArthur, John, *The Battle for the Beginning.* Nashville: W. Publishing Group, 2001.

Macbeth, Norman. *Darwin Retried: An Appeal to Reason.* Boston: The Harvard Common Press, 1978.

Major, Trevor, *Problems in Radiometric Dating*, Research Article Series, Montgomery, Alabama: Apologetics Press, Inc., undated publication.

Marsh, Frank Lewis. "On Creation with an Appearance of Age," *Creation Research Society Quarterly*, 1978, 14[4].

Martin, Jobe, *The Evolution of a Creationist* (Rockwall, Texas: Biblical Discipleship Publishers, 1994.

Mastropaolo, Joseph A., *The Rise and Fall of Evolution*, Huntington Beach, California, a manuscript in revision, 2003.

Maxwell, Graham. *Servants or Friends: Another Look at God*, Redlands, California: Pine Knoll Publications, 1992.

_____, Graham Maxwell, *Can God Be Trusted?*, Redlands, California: Pineknoll Publications, 2002.

Mayr, Ernst. *Systematics and the Origin of Species.* New York: Columbia University Press, 1942; Dover Publications paperback, 1964.

McElheny, Victor K. *Watson and DNA*, Cambridge, Massachusetts: Perseus Publishing, 2003.

Meldau, John Fred, ed., *Witnesses Against Evolution* (Denver: Christian Victory Publishing, 1968.

Milton, Richard. *Shattering the Myths of Darwinism*. Rochester, Vermont.: Park Street Press, 1997.

Monsma, John Clover, *Behind the Dim Unknown*, New York: G.P. Putnam's Sons, 1966.

Morris, Henry M, *Scientific Creationism*, Green Forest, Arkansas: Master Books, 1974.

_____, *Their Words Against Them*, San Diego: Institute for Creation Research, 1997.

_____. "What They Say." *Back to Genesis*. N. Santee, Calif.: Institute for Creation Research, 1999.

Morris, John D., "From Dayton to Dover," *Acts & Facts*, El Cajon, California: Institute for Creation Research, Vol. 35, No. 2, February, 2006.

_____, "From Dayton to Dover," *Acts & Facts*, ElCajon, California: Institute for Creation Research, Vol. 35, No. 2, February, 2006) 2, 3.

Morris, John & Steven A. Austin, *Footprints in the Ash*, Green Forest, Arkansas: Master Books, 2003.

Morowitz, Harold J., *Energy Flow in Biology*, New York: Academic Press, 1968.

Nelson, Byron C. *After Its Kind*. Minneapolis: Augsburg Publishing House, 1927.

New International Version of the Holy Bible, Grand Rapids: Zondervan Bible Publishers, 1978.

Oard, Michael J., *An Ice Age Caused by the Genesis Flood* El Cajon, California: Institute for Creation Research, 1990.

Oliver & Boyd, *Contemporary Botanical Thought*, 1971.

Oparin, Aleksander I.., *The Origin of Life* (New York: Dover Publications, Inc., 1938.

Overman, Dean L., *A Case Against Accident and Self-Organization*. New York: Rowman & Littlefield Publisher, Inc., 1997.

Patterson, Colin, "Can You Tell be Anything About Evolution," lecture as transcribed by Dr. Wayne Frair and reported in "Bridge to Nowhere?", *CreationDigest.com*, Autumn 2004 Edition.

Pennisi, Elizabeth. "Genome Data Shakes Tree of Life." *Science* 280 (May 1, 1998.

_____, "New Gene Found for Inherited Macular Degeneration." *Science* 281 (July 3, 1998).

_____,. "Genetic Study Shakes Up Out-of-Africa Theory." *Science* 283, March 19, 1999.

Perloff, James. *Tornado in a Junkyard*, Arlington, Mass.: Refuge Books, 1999.

_____, *The Case Against Darwin*, Arlington, Mass: Refuge Books, 2002.

Pilbeam, David, "Rearranging Our Family Tree," *Human Nature*, June, 1978.

Raup, David. *Zoologic Record.* Published in *Paleobiology* 2, 1976.

Rappuoli, Rino, Henry L. Miller, and **Stanley Falkow,** "The Intangible Value of Vaccination," *Science* Vol. 297, 9 August 2002.

Rees, Martin and **Priyamvada Natarajan,** "Invisible Universe," *Discover*, December, 2003.

ReMine, Walter James, *The Biotic Message.* Saint Paul: St. Paul Science, 1993.

Rifkin, Jeremy. *Algeny.* New York: Viking, 1983.

Roth, Ariel A. *Origins.* Hagerstown, Md.: Review and Herald Publishing Assn., 1998.

Ruse, Michael, *The Evolution-Creation Struggle,* Cambridge: Harvard University Press, 2005.

Ryan, William and **Walter Pitman,** *Noah's Flood.* New York: Simon & Schuster, 1998.

Salthe, Stanley, as cited by Access Research Network, *2003 Annual Report,* and referenced online by *Creation Equation,* January 19, 2004.

Sarfati, Jonathan, *Refuting Evolution.* Green Forest, Arkansas: Master Books, 1999.

Sawyer, Kathy. "New Light on a Mysterious Epoch," *The Washington Post,* February 5, 1998.

Schmidt, Duane Arthur, *And God Created Darwin* (Fairfax,Virginia: Alliance Press, 2001.

Schueller, Gretel. "Australia's Ups and Downs." *Earth,* August, 1998.

Sermonti, Giuseppe, *Why is a Fly Not a Horse?,* Seattle: Discovery Institute Press, 2005.

Sewell, Granville, "Evolution and the Second Law of Thermodynamics," www. isic.org, January, 2004.

Shaw, George Bernard. *Back to Methuselah.* New York City: Penguin, 1921.

Sherwin, Frank, "Un-Bee-lievable Vision," *Acts & Facts,* El Cajon, California: Institute for Creation Research, Vol. 35, No. 2, February, 2006.

Shipman, Pat. *Taking Wing.* New York: Simon & Schuster, 1998.

Siebert, Charles, "Unintelligent Design," *Discover,* March, 2006.

Simmons, Geoffrey, M.D., *What Darwin Didn't Know*, Eugene, Oregon: Harvest House Publishers, 2004.

Simpson, George Gaylord. *The Meaning of Evolution*. New Haven, Connecticut: Yale University Press, 1949.

_____, *The Sudden Appearance of Higher Categories in Evolution of Life*, S. Tax, ed. 1960.

Smith, Dita, and **Laura Stanton.** "Population Momentum." *The Washington Post,* 1996.

Smith, John Maynard, "Life at the Edge of Chaos?" *New York Review.* March 2, 1995.

Smith, Wolfgang, *Teilhardism and the New Religion*. Rockford, Ill.: Tan Books, 1988.

Snelling, Andrew A., "The Cause of Anomalous Potassium-Argon 'Ages' for Recent Andesite Flows at Mt. Ngauruhoe, New Zealand, and the Implications for Potassium-Argon Dating." *ICC Technical Symposium Sessions*, Robert E.Walsh, Editor. Pittsburgh: Creation Science Fellowship, Inc. 1998.

_____, "The Fallacies of Radioactive Dating of Rocks: Basalt Lava Flows in Grand Canyon," *Answers*, Vol. 1, No. 1, July-Sept. 2006.

Sodera, Vij, *One Small Speck to Man*, Vija Sodera Productions, West Sussex, United Kingdom, 2003.

Spetner, Lee M. *Not by Chance*. Brooklyn, New York: The Judaica Press, Inc., 1997.

Stanley, S.M., *The New Evolutionary Timetable: Fossils, Genes and the Origin of Species*, 1981.

Stokstad, Erik, "Gutsy Fossil Record for Staying the Course," *Science*, Vol 302, 5 December 2003.

Strobel, Lee, *The Case for a Creator*. Grand Rapids, Michigan: Zondervan, 2004.

Sunderland, Luther, *Darwin's Enigma: Fossils and Other Problems*, San Diego: Master Books, 1988.

Svoboda, Elizabeth, "Quadrillions and Quadrillions of Stars," *Discover*, December, 2003.

Taylor, Ian T. *In the Minds of Men*. Minneapolis, Minn.: TFE Publishing, 1991.

Thaxton, Charles B., Walter L. Bradley and **Roger L. Olsen,** *The Mystery of Life's Origin*, New York: Philosophical Library, 1984.

Thompson, Bert, *Creation Compromises*. Montgomery, Alabama: Apologetics Press, Inc., 2000.

Thompson, Bert and **Brad Harrub,** "15 Answers to John Rennie and *Scientific American's* Nonsense." Montgomery, Alabama: Apologetics Press, 2002.

_____, "*National Geographic* Shoots Itself in the Foot Again," Apologetics Press.Org online report, 2004.

Thompson, Bert and Eric Lyons, "Dinosaurs and Humans---Together," *Reason and Revelation*, 25 (3): 17-23, 2005.

Thompson, Ida. *National Audubon Society Field Guide to North American Fossils.* New York: Alfred A. Knopf, Inc., 1982.

Yu, C.P., "The Human Brain Tesitifes Against Evolution: Confessions of a Neurosurgeon," Internet Website: www.hkam.org.hk/temp/counterevolution, as reported 1-10-2005.

Vail, Tom, *Grand Canyon: A Different View.* Green Forest, Arkansas: Master Books, 2003.

Vardiman, Larry, Andrew A. Snelling and **Eugene F. Chaffin,** Editors, *Radioisotopes and the Age of the Earth,* Vol. 1, 2000 and Vol. II, 2005, published jointly by Institute for Creation Research, El Cajon, California and Creation Research Society, Chino Valley, Arizona.

Verrengia, Joseph, "Fossils Show a Mammal Turned Tables, Devoured Dinosaur for Last Meal, "*Nature,* 433, January 13, 2005.

Wagner, Dennis, "2005 Year-end Report," Access Research Network, Internet Website, Number Fifty, December 1, 2005.

Wald, George, "The Origin of Life," *Sci. Am.,* August, 1954, 191(2).

Wallace, Alfred Russell. *The Geographical Distribution of Animals, With a Study of the Relations of the Living and Extinct Faunas as Elucidating Past Changes of the Earth's Surface.* New York: Harper, 1876.

Walsh, R.E., C.L. Brooks, and **R.S. Crowell** (eds.). *Proceedings of the First International Conference on Creationism,* Pittsburgh: Creation Science Fellowship, 1987.

Wang, Samuel and **Ethel R. Nelson** *God and the Ancient Chinese.* Dunlap, Tennessee: Read Books Publisher, 1998.

Ward, Peter D., "Coils of Time," *Discover,* March 1998.

Warren, Rick, *The Purpose Driven Life,* Grand Rapids, Michigan: Zondervan, 2002.

Weikart, Richard, *From Darwin to Hitler,* New York: Palgrave Macmillan, 2004.

Weil, Anne, "Living Large in the Cretaceous," *Nature,* 433:116, January 13, 2005.

Weiss, Rick. "Defect Tied to Doubling of Risk for Colon Cancer." *The Washington Post,* August 26, 1997.

Wells, Jonathan, *Icons of Evolution.* Washington, D.C.: Regnery Publishing, Inc., 2000.

_____, "Survival of the Fittest," *The American Spectator,* December 2000/ January 2001.

Whitcomb, John C. and **Henry M. Morris,** *The Genesis Flood,* Phillipsburg, New Jersey: Presbyterian and Reformed Publishing Company, 1995.

Wickramasinghe, Chandra, "Threats on Life of Controversial Astronomer," *New Scientist,* January 21, 1982.

Will, George F. "The Gospel of Science." *Newsweek,* November 9, 1998.

Wise, Kurt P., *Faith, Form and Time,* Nashville: Broadman & Holman, Pubs., 2002.

Witham, Larry A., *Where Darwin Meets the Bible.* New York: Oxford University Press, 2002.

Woodward, Thomas, *Doubts About Darwin.* Grand Rapids: Baker Books, 2003.

Wuethrich, Bernice. "Stunning Fossil Shows Breath of a Dinosaur." *Science* 283, January 22, 1999.

Wysong, Randy L., *The Creation-Evolution Controversy* East Lansing, Michigan: Inquiry Press, 1976.

Yahya, Harun, *Evolution Deceit,* London: Ta-Ha Publishers, Ltd., third edition, 2000.

Yeoman, Barry, "Schweitzer's Dangerous Discovery," *Discover,* April, 2006.

Yockey, Hubert P., *Information Theory and Molecular Biology.* Cambridge: Cambridge University Press, 1992.

Zimmer, Carl, "Testing Darwin," *Discover,* February, 2005.

ISBN-13: 978-0-9790958-0-1
ISBN-10: 0-9790958-0-8

52495

9 780979 095801

LaVergne, TN USA
30 October 2009

162539LV00001B/4/P